P9-ARS-679

THE COLLECTED POETRY OF ROBINSON JEFFERS

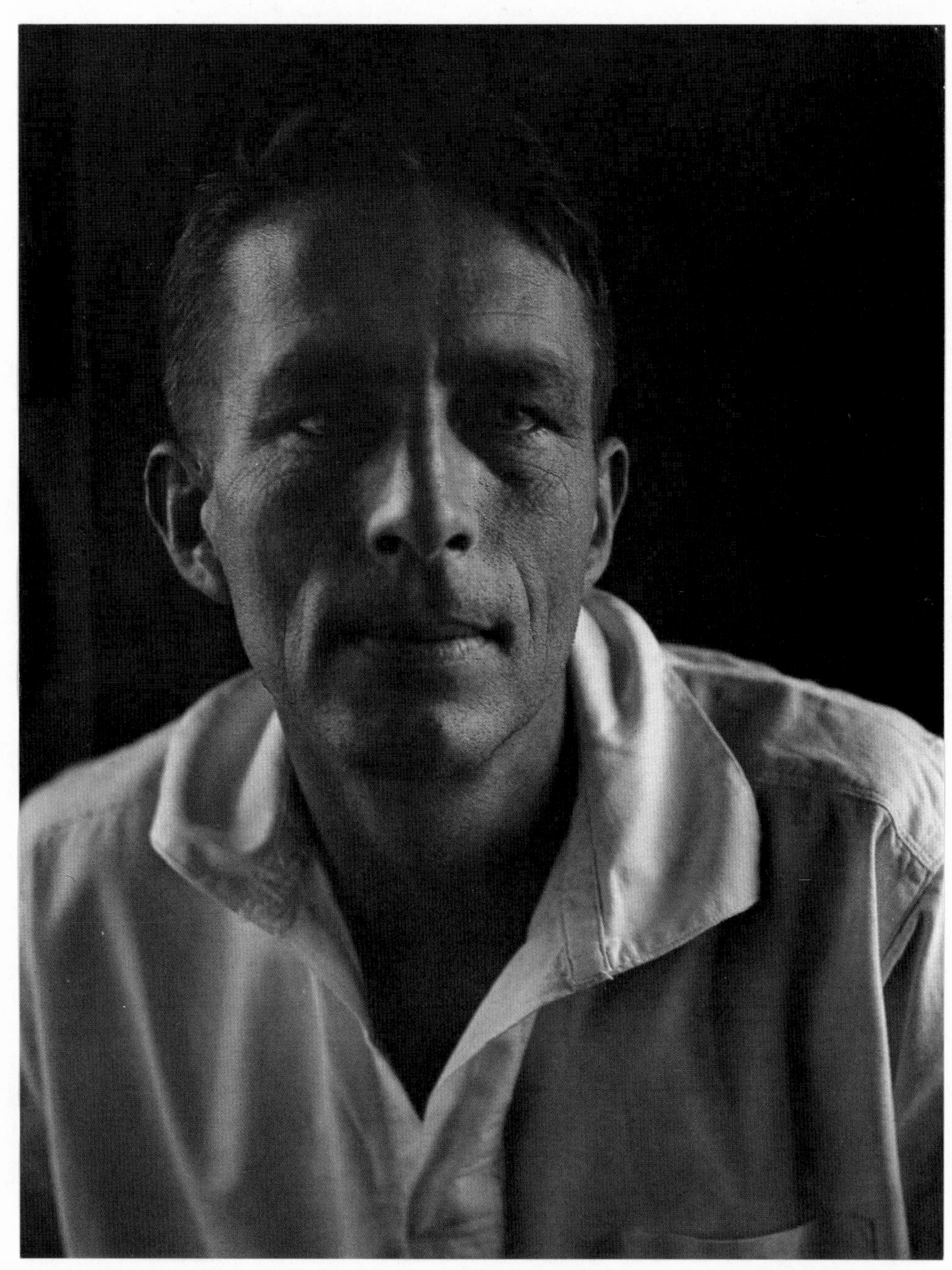

Robinson Jeffers, Carmel, California c. 1927
Photograph by Ansel Adams

THE COLLECTED POETRY OF
Robinson Jeffers

Edited by Tim Hunt

VOLUME ONE

1920-1928

STANFORD UNIVERSITY PRESS 1988
Stanford, California

Stanford University Press, Stanford, California

Published with the assistance of the National Endowment for the Humanities; and of H. A. Klein, in memory of Mina Cooper Klein

Printed in the United States of America
CIP data appear at the end of the volume

CONTENTS

I

TAMAR
1920-1923

II

ROAN STALLION
1924-1925

III

THE WOMEN AT POINT SUR

1925-1926

IV

CAWDOR
1926-1928

EDITORIAL NOTE

SELECTION AND ARRANGEMENT

The Collected Poetry of Robinson Jeffers includes all of Jeffers' published poems from *Flagons and Apples* (1912) through *The Beginning and the End* (1963) and those manuscript poems Jeffers considered publishing. It excludes the poems from his undergraduate years at Occidental College and incomplete poems, even when, as with "The Alpine Christ" and the versions of "Point Alma Venus," these are of considerable length and of some critical interest.

The edition presents Jeffers' work chronologically. The length of the narrative poems and other commercial factors often meant poems planned for one volume were set aside for a later one. Several poems in *Dear Judas*, for instance, were to have appeared two volumes earlier in *The Women at Point Sur*; several of the longer pieces in *Give Your Heart to the Hawks* actually precede work from the previous collection, *Thurso's Landing*. Reproducing the accidents of the original publication sequence would be of little use to a contemporary reader, while a chronological arrangement helps clarify the actual shape of Jeffers' career.

Arranging Jeffers' work chronologically, however, raises the problem of where to begin. The earliest published work, the privately printed *Flagons and Apples*, is quite different from his mature work, which began to develop, as Jeffers himself noted, during the First World War and to coalesce about 1920 in such lyrics as "To the Stone-Cutters" and the narrative *Tamar*. A primary aim of this edition is to clarify what might be termed the "Jeffers canon," and, therefore, Volume One begins with the poems of 1920, postponing apprentice work until Volume Four. Volumes One to Three thus present a complete, chronological edition of the work on which Jeffers' reputation rests and will continue to rest—the work of 1920 to 1962. Volume Four includes the work of 1912–19, poems left in manuscript, documents such as Jeffers' "Foreword" to *The Selected Poetry of Robinson Jeffers*, and the edition's editorial apparatus.

TEXTS

The primary textual issue with Jeffers' poems is punctuation. Particularly in his narratives, Jeffers let rhythmic and dramatic considerations, rather than grammatical ones, determine punctuation. His statements in various letters and the patterns of revision in his manuscripts show he did so knowingly. His publishers, though, at times adjusted his punctuation, typically by adding commas, presumably to bring it into accord with grammatical convention. As much as possible, the texts for this edition revert to Jeffers' own punctuation. In all cases the various published forms of the poems have been compared against each other and against all manuscript forms that can be located.

Unfortunately, in most cases Jeffers' final typescripts, used to set type for the original editions, were apparently discarded once the poems were published. The manuscripts used to prepare the final typescripts have typically survived but do not appear to include his final adjustments to punctuation, while the published forms typically show evidence of house styling. Study of the surviving galley and page proofs, the few surviving typescripts, and other textual evidence indicates that in most cases Jeffers' own manuscripts are closer to the missing typescripts than are the original published settings of the poems. In most cases, then, the manuscripts have been adopted as copy-text, and variant readings adopted from the published forms of the poems where the patterns suggested by the existing evidence indicate the published form likely follows the missing typescript. A full report of the edition's procedures, textual evidence, and adopted readings is included in Volume Four. In general, though, texts have been prepared following the guidelines developed by the Center for Editions of American Authors and its successor, the Committee on Scholarly Editions.

PRESENTATION

Jeffers' verse lines are often too long to be printed as a single line of type. In this edition, such lines are broken as close to the right margin as possible without breaking words (including Jeffers' hyphenated compounds); the remainder of the line is then indented and continued as a second line of type. Such lines should, though, be considered a single metrical unit.

Jeffers seldom utilized regular stanzas. However, he often divided his poems, both long and short, into a series of verse paragraphs. Jeffers used the traditional blank line to indicate a verse paragraph when the division occurs between two complete verse lines. At times, though, the sentence that begins the new verse paragraph occurs in the middle of a verse line rather than at the beginning. In such cases, Jeffers began the new verse paragraph on a separate line, indenting its first sentence to align with the end of the sentence concluding the preceding paragraph. The original settings of Jeffers' poems sometimes insert blank lines between such verse paragraphs and sometimes do not; this has given the impression that there may be a structural distinction between these two forms. Analysis of the manuscripts and typescripts suggest Jeffers intended no such distinction and that, as a general rule, either all verse paragraphs beginning mid-line should be preceded by a blank line or none should. The evidence further suggests that verse paragraphs occurring between completed verse lines and those beginning mid-line are also structurally equivalent. In this edition verse paragraphs are separated by a single blank line, unless unusual textual circumstances dictate otherwise. In Volume One, two poems are treated as exceptions, the dramatic poem *The Tower Beyond Tragedy*, where this procedure would unnecessarily introduce blank lines between many of the speeches, and "Prelude," where two blank lines are used at one point, since the manuscript evidence suggests Jeffers may have wished to indicate a greater structural break at the point where he joined what were originally two separate poems. These two exceptions, along with the evidence for Jeffers' approach to verse paragraphing and structural divisions, are discussed more fully in the textual commentary in Volume Four.

For clarity's sake, in this edition no verse paragraphs occurring between completed lines have been allowed to coincide with page breaks. In some instances paragraphs that begin in the middle of a verse line do coincide with a page break; these instances are readily apparent. Those poems utilizing regular stanzas have been arranged on the page without regard to page breaks, since the set number of lines for each stanza allows the reader to judge easily when a page break coincides with a stanza break and when not.

Finally, one adjustment has been made to Jeffers' punctuation. Jeffers typically placed colons and semicolons inside concluding quotation marks. His publishers sometimes followed his texts on this point and sometimes moved the colons and semicolons outside the concluding mark. In this edition, semicolons and colons follow the concluding quotation mark.

ACKNOWLEDGMENTS

Critical editions are often corporate activities involving the resources of one or more research departments, their faculty, and graduate students. This one has been more a cottage industry. It began when I was between academic affiliations, was continued at a small branch campus of a state university, and is being completed in the mountains of California at a school of 24 with no department at all. Fortunately, those who care about Jeffers' work often care deeply, and a number of colleagues have volunteered the guidance an inexperienced artisan could in no way presume to command.

Much of the credit for this edition goes to the Tor House Foundation of Carmel. Formed originally to preserve Robinson Jeffers' home and promote recognition of his work, the foundation instigated the project, helped fund its early expenses and provide release time from teaching duties, and supplied crucial encouragement. Without George White, Tor House president, there would be no edition; and without Nancy Miller, executive director, my work would have been much slower and more difficult. Other members of the foundation were also generous with resources and advice, especially Marlan Beilke, Richard Hayman, and Mel Smith.

Equally crucial have been the foresight and good offices of Mrs. Donnan Jeffers and Mr. Garth Jeffers. Their insistence that the work be presented in as comprehensive and attractive a manner as possible was instrumental in securing the necessary permissions from the different publishers controlling copyrights. They contributed as well invaluable insights into the poet's working habits, their own wonderful letters, and welcome hospitality. Few "literary estates" have been so willing to put the interests and needs of readers first and its own interests second.

I would also like to thank the edition's editorial board. William Everson's passion for Jeffers' vision was a continual warning to remember the limits of scholarship, and Robert Brophy, long a dean of Jeffers scholars, shared selflessly his own work. Albert Gelpi and James Miller both supported the project in its earliest stages, when such support was needed most, and were, in addition, the sympathetic but shrewd readers such projects always need. Two scholars not on the board also offered important advice: William Streitberger directed my early reading in the methods of textual scholarship, and David Nordloh offered telling critiques of my early work on Volume One. In addition, several long-time students of Jeffers were kind enough to contribute time, resources, and advice. Covington Rodgers prepared a collation of the published forms of many of the poems in Volume One and shared his sense of the textual issues raised by the evidence. And I owe a great debt to Commander Allen Mears, who also provided a collation of the same material and put in many hours of proofreading. Robb Kafka offered the results of his work with Jeffers' papers at the University of Texas. These gentlemen saved me many steps and many errors. James Karman and Robert Ian Scott were also kind enough to respond to my early commentaries, and Helen Tartar, Humanities Editor at Stanford University Press, has been as concerned and supportive as a scholar could wish and more patient of quirks and lapses than one could have any right to expect.

I have been equally fortunate in receiving support of a more technical kind. Alan Federman, Director of Academic Computing at Indiana-Purdue at Fort Wayne (IPFW), Rick Jackson of Bloomington Academic Computing Services, and Steven Hollander of IPFW's English Department all contributed to the edition's use of computers. The secretarial staff of IPFW's English Department, especially Gladys Thiele, logged too many hours at the copy machine. Finally, I would like to thank Norm Newell, IPFW director of sponsored research, for helping find resources to continue the project: two grants for research expenses from IPFW, another from the Indiana University President's Council for the Humanities, a grant-in-aid from the American Council of Learned Societies, an NEH Travel to Collections grant, an NEH Summer Stipend, and a research grant from the Texts Program of the NEH's Division of Research Programs. These programs have been exceedingly generous, and their support is greatly appreciated, as is the cooperation of Robert Otten and Julius Smulkstys, Chair of English and Dean of Arts and Letters respectively at IPFW, who made it possible to use these resources efficiently.

Editions of this kind would, of course, be impossible without libraries. Tyrus Harmsen of the Occidental College Library has been especially generous with his time and expertise. I would also like to thank Steven Corey of the University of San Francisco's Gleeson Library for his good humor and patience, and John Kirkpatrick and the staff at the Harry Ransome Humanities Research Center at the University of Texas for their exemplary efficiency and courtesy. My time at the Beinecke Library at Yale was made more productive by a number of the staff, but especially Steve Jones, and Robert Shatkin of the Brooklyn Public Library twice took time from a busy schedule to befriend a stymied scholar. In addition, the following libraries were kind enough to provide material bearing on the texts for Volume One: the Berg Collection of the New York Public Library; the Bancroft Library of the University of California, Berkeley; the Brooklyn Public Library; the California Historical Society; the Butler Library of Columbia University; the Houghton Library of Harvard University; the University of Houston Library; the Long Beach State University Library; Mills College Library; the Davis Library of the University of North Carolina, Chapel Hill; the Stanford University Library; the Alderman Library of the University of Virginia; and the William Jewell College Library. I would especially like to thank Andreas Brown of the Gotham

Book Mart for taking time away from pressing business matters to aid my search for several important manuscripts.

In closing I would like to note the patience of my wife and son. Projects like this always seem to take too many hours—and to take too many hours away from what are, in the end, the important things. The "fellowship" they have given me during this project is finally the most important of all that I've received and the one I can least merit or repay.

INTRODUCTION

By 1914 modernism was already transforming American poetry. Ezra Pound and Imagism were unavoidable presences; "Prufrock," as yet unpublished, was four years old; and Wallace Stevens was about to write "Peter Quince" and "Sunday Morning." In 1914, though, Robinson Jeffers was still poetically adrift. Two years younger than Pound, a year older than Eliot, he was still imitating his Romantic and Victorian predecessors. His mature idiom was a full six years in the future, and *Tamar*, which would make his reputation, would not be completed until 1923. Even so, by 1914 Jeffers had (by his own report) already made his "final decision not to become a 'modern.' "*

Even if the modernist work Jeffers would have been reading in *Poetry* and other magazines was not yet *The Waste Land* or *The Cantos*, it already offered the one decisive alternative to nineteenth-century attitudes and techniques, and Jeffers' rejection of it is in some ways surprising. Why should he have chosen to write long narratives when the mode seemed hopelessly old fashioned? Why, in his shorter poems, to blend painstaking naturalistic detail with direct statement and forego the sophisticated formal experiments and indirection of his most talented contemporaries? Why, most simply, should he turn his back on the dynamic world of modern British and European art to concentrate instead on the isolated landscape of California's Big Sur coast and the simple, though intense, people of the foothill ranches that surrounded his home in Carmel? Some have wanted to assume he was a California original, a primitive, looking west from the "continent's end" without realizing, or caring, what was behind him in New York or London or Paris. But Jeffers was not a primitive. Rather, the Calvinist faith of his minister father and his own im-

*Robinson Jeffers, "Introduction," *Roan Stallion, Tamar and Other Poems* (New York, 1935), p. x.

mersion in the world of modern science helped direct his sophistication in a radically different direction from his modernist contemporaries.

Jeffers' early years were dominated by his father, a professor of Old Testament literature and biblical history at Western Theological Seminary, a Presbyterian school on the outskirts of Pittsburgh. Dr. William Hamilton Jeffers was a 46-year-old widower when he married Annie Robinson Tuttle, a church organist 22 years his junior. John Robinson Jeffers was born a year and a half later on January 10, 1887. Jeffers' only sibling, Hamilton, a prominent research astronomer, was born in 1894. Jeffers' father was a reserved man impatient of childish play. He introduced his first son to Latin, Greek, and the tenets of Presbyterianism early on, and Jeffers' first ten years were a succession of houses and schools as the elder Jeffers looked for the right combination of seclusion for himself and intellectual rigor for his son. In 1898 Jeffers entered the first of five Swiss boarding schools, and four years later, when he entered what is now the University of Pittsburgh, Jeffers already had a mastery of French, German, Greek, and Latin to go with his newest enthusiasm — Dante Gabriel Rossetti and poetry. After his first year of college, the family moved to Los Angeles for Dr. Jeffers' health. Jeffers enrolled at Occidental College, where he graduated two years later with coursework in astronomy and geology to supplement biblical literature and Greek. Then came a year and a half of graduate study, first at the University of Southern California and then the University of Zurich. Jeffers' courses included Old English, Dante, Goethe, Spanish Romantic poetry, and late nineteenth-century French literature.

When Jeffers returned from Zurich in September 1906, he was not yet twenty and already had what even Pound would have seen as a promising start for a modernist-to-be. Had Jeffers encountered a Santayana at this point, as did Stevens and Eliot at Harvard, or even an energetic and opinionated peer such as Pound, as did H. D. and Williams at Pennsylvania, his work might well have developed differently, but Jeffers spent the next six months translating German medical papers and then in 1907 enrolled in the USC medical school, where he excelled in physiology and earned an assistantship in his second and third years. He left in 1910 without completing his training and entered the University of Washington to study forestry. A year later he returned to Los Angeles, again, without completing his studies.

How seriously Jeffers considered either profession is not clear. Certainly he was already developing his interest in poetry. By 1911 he had already written a number of the imitative, dandyish poems of *Flagons and Apples*, which he issued privately in 1912 after receiving a small inheritance. Whatever his sense of vocation, though, medicine and forestry would have been a sharp contrast to his literary studies. Both emphasized direct and close observation of the actual world and involved alternative views of time and tradition. Moreover Jeffers' medical studies would have introduced him to modern biology in a more than casual manner, while his study of forestry would have strengthened his interest in a specifically Western landscape and offered a view of nature unmediated by poetic conventions.

Jeffers' early and mid-twenties were also years of personal turmoil. However much he may have resented the strict round of study imposed by his father, Jeffers was, through his boarding school years, a properly shy and studious minister's son who presumably acted from his sense of doctrine and belief, rather than mere obedience. But by the time Jeffers entered medical school at twenty his allegiance had begun to shift to the religion of art and the wine, women, and song appropriate to a turn of the century poet-to-be. This drift might have simply replaced his earlier views (it did for many of his generation) had he not become increasingly involved with a married woman, a situation which neither his father's values nor the priorities of his bohemianism seemed able to resolve. Jeffers met Una Call Kuster when both were literature students at USC. She was three years older, and their relationship apparently started innocently and probably continued that way for a time. By 1910 the matter was a serious concern to both and likely a factor in Jeffers' decision to leave for Washington to study forestry. However, when he returned to Los Angeles at the end of that year, the affair began again and became known to Una's husband, a young Los Angeles attorney. Scandal and divorce followed.

On August 2, 1913, Robinson Jeffers and Una Call Kuster were married. Witty, vibrant, and ambitious, Una Jeffers became a prime force in her husband's life. She had faith in his talent as a writer and the will to discipline him to that faith. The crisis of courtship might have confirmed Jeffers' bohemianism. Instead it was the beginning of a renewed moral seriousness. This is not to suggest his affair left him guilty for his actions nor that he came to accept society's norms or his father's. Rather, the crisis seems to have combined with the deaths of his father and infant daughter and the discovery of the West as a subject for his writing to commit him to struggle with the question of whether actions have moral consequences in a world where the methods and discoveries of science had already undercut the pieties of the past.

It may seem odd to suggest Jeffers needed to discover the West when he had already spent a number of years in Los Angeles and Seattle. But Los Angeles took its cue from other centers of fashion. It was, that is, provincial. Los Angeles tyros read *The Smart Set* right along with their Chicago and New York counterparts, and their fantasies were of Europe. Jeffers, judging from his letters, even toyed with becoming a sort of Los Angeles F. Scott Fitzgerald. Certainly at the time of his marriage the West meant relatively little to him in terms of his writing. He and Una planned to settle in Europe and presumably would have done so had she not become pregnant. Their daughter, born in May 1914, survived only a day, and by the time the couple was ready to consider the move again, the war in Europe persuaded them to look closer to home.

In September of 1914, they traveled north to Carmel, probably because it was something of an artists' colony, a rustic and inexpensive spot of culture. The decisive factor that led them to settle there, though, and the decisive factor for Jeffers' work, was the landscape itself and the people of the isolated ranches and farms about it. These demanded to be viewed on their own terms, not through any European lens or lens of literary convention. As Jeffers wrote in the "Foreword" to *The Selected Poetry of Robinson Jeffers*, "for the first time in my life I could see people living—amid magnificent unspoiled scenery—essentially as they did in the Idyls or the Sagas, or in Homer's Ithaca. Here was life purged of its ephemeral accretions. . . . Here was contemporary life that was also permanent life; and not shut from the modern world but conscious of it and related to it" (pp. xv–xvi). The intensity of this new landscape coming on top of his scientific training, courtship and marriage, the death of a child, and the first signs of Europe's political and cultural collapse led Jeffers, apparently within months, to his aesthetic declaration of independence. Whatever he would be as a poet, he would not be "a 'modern.'"

For Jeffers (reacting against the modernist work found in the little magazines of the time) the moderns were writing a poetry of form, not content, a poetry that indulged technique for its own sake. And if this work celebrated the imagination's power to remake the materials of the tradition, to him it did so, finally, by celebrating the aesthetic object's superiority over the ordinary and actual. His training in science, however, meant he could only be satisfied with an art that used the imagination to attend to the actual, not escape it. To Jeffers, that is, the work of the early Pound and others seemed a poetry of fashion, and the world he had discovered in Carmel was anything but fashionable. It was, though, in Jeffers' view, fundamental, authentic, and relevant to the larger world. It offered the freedom to be regional without being provincial, which Los Angeles did not, and just as importantly, Carmel suited the energetic severity of his temperament at a time when his training in the sciences had freed him to respond to it. Just as importantly, this new, yet archaic, world seemed to require a poetry of moral seriousness at a time when his own personal experience and the reality of world conflict seemed to make such seriousness imperative. It's little wonder that Jeffers—in his own way and for different reasons than Pound—decided "Mauberly" was finally an inappropriate guide.

The first phase of Jeffers' independence appeared in *Californians*, published by Macmillan in 1916. Like his later volumes, *Californians* featured several narratives of the rural West. Narrative gave Jeffers scope to portray this new landscape and even more importantly allowed him to explore the connection between the land itself and the people who inhabited it (or as he would later think of the matter, the people who expressed it). But these early narratives, though a decisive turn from his contemporaries and his own earlier work, are largely unsuccessful. Their traditional meters, rhyme, and diction fail to match the expansiveness of the material, and they read as if Jeffers, freed from the need to be technically fashionable, simply assumed he could borrow his form from tradition and allow the subject to make its own way. More importantly, the narratives of *Californians*, and those recently recovered from the few years following it, show Jeffers vacillating between a sentimental and a superficially nihilistic treatment of nature. In some of the poems nature offers a simplistic, if reassuring, moral norm to the human world. In others the world of nature moves with one logic while a seemingly disconnected human world moves with quite another; characters violate norms only to find that nature has no interest in their affairs and that society is unlikely to discover what they have done. In these poems Jeffers' sense of science freed him to look intensely and without preconception, but it also effectively divorced the human world from the natural. If his mood demanded a poetry of moral seriousness, the lesson of modern science seemed to deny that possibility. The perspective of science undercut any sense of a moral outcome to what he observed, even as it gave him access to his material and freed him from his contemporaries.

In the years immediately following *Californians*, Jeffers struggled with his work and the problem of the war. He temporarily abandoned narrative, trying his hand at an epic drama modeled on Hardy's *The Dynasts*, and then turning to sonnets. Both directions provided elegant, but stiff and mannered, comments on the moral and political crisis of Europe. Meanwhile Jeffers worried whether or not to enlist. Twin sons born in 1916, a wife, and a less than ample income argued no, but his application to serve was pending when the war ended. The war years, though, did confirm his desire to stay in Carmel. Shortly after the Armistice, he and Una purchased a headland on the south edge of Carmel and hired a local mason to build a low stone cottage from the granite about the site. Working with the masons, Jeffers discovered his other life's work—building with stone. After the house was completed, he began a six-year project, the construction of a two-and-a-half story stone tower, and he fell into the routine of his mature years—writing in the morning, stone work or planting and caring for his forest of trees in the afternoon.

Whether it was the war, the increased pattern and discipline of his life, or simply the trial and error of poem after poem, Jeffers' work began to coalesce shortly after the move into Tor House when he returned to writing narrative and working with local material. The first narratives after the war were written as ballads, the one after that in long-line couplets. None are fully successful, but they show Jeffers worrying again the problem of violence and nature, as he had in *Californians*, and pressing toward a resolution that came first in several short poems sometime in the early 1920's. The key was a minor, but telling, shift in emphasis in his sense of nature. In lyrics such as "Natural Music" he began to focus on nature itself and view it as a living organism, with man simply one of its elements, one of its expressions.

This shift in emphasis, from the life of individuals to the life of nature, enabled Jeffers to synthesize his sense of science with his Calvinist heritage, even as he discarded the latter's specific forms and justifications. Both Calvinism and science taught that man was not the measure of the world, and both, in different ways, taught that the world itself might be inherently beautiful and worthy of worship. Once Jeffers came to see the observation of nature and the observation of human actions, even perverse and violent ones, as inherently the same act of witness and to see the expression of them as a further witness to the inscrutable dynamism of nature, he began to overcome the dichotomy that had marred much of his earlier work. Poetry could not resolve, nor need it, the conflicts of nature or human experience. Poetry's task was to confront, reveal, and praise the grandeur of a universe in flux.

Jeffers apparently thought of this new mode at first primarily as one that allowed him to write lyrics that praised the beauty of nature in a new, more direct way. The lyrics that followed "Natural Music" show him quickly mastering the long, unrhymed accentual line that would be the basis of the rest of his writing. But sometime in 1922, perhaps quite early 1923, he seems to have realized his new sense of nature could be the basis of narrative as well. His reading of Freud and Jung likely played a role in this, along with his reading of the Cambridge anthropologists and their studies of ancient myth and ritual. Whatever the impetus, the return to narrative fulfilled the promise of his first sense of his Carmel material and resulted in the poem that would gain him recognition as a major poet.

Like his earlier narratives (and later ones) *Tamar* portrays a perverse, violent human world: Tamar's incest with her brother and her father, her father's earlier incest with his sister, the conflagration Tamar brings about to destroy herself, her brother, her father, and her lover. But in *Tamar*, unlike the earlier narratives, Jeffers came to view nature itself as fundamentally in conflict—a cycle of destruction and renewal—and this recognition allowed him, finally, to write poems that combined his sense of modern science and high moral seriousness, even though the lessons of *Tamar* were neither specifically scientific nor moral in the usual sense of those words. In Jeffers' scheme, human conflict is an analogue of the larger rhythms of conflict in the natural world. The human world, though, is often blind to its own status and thus dooms itself to play out the cycles in an unnecessarily perverse, violent, and empty manner. In the narratives, Jeffers' characters are largely unable to recognize or accept themselves as elements of nature, and this dooms them to suffer nature's power without experiencing the compensatory vision of its beauty (even if that beauty is itself of the painful motion of stars consuming in flame, of rock eroding, of hawk dropping to feed). The characters can become more or less aware of their cycle and can even, as Tamar does, hurry on destruction, but finally the real salvation in these poems is the one available to reader and poet and comes from recognizing our place in nature, which frees us to witness the transcendent beauty of destruction and renewal and to accept its liberating beauty, even if the cycle of renewal takes place on a scale that never renews (only destroys) the individual ego.

Initially, Jeffers seems not to have known what to do with *Tamar*. He first considered grouping it with a series of poems written in response to the First World War, as if that violent episode would best explain the violence of this new work. He then, apparently, came to see this new direction in his narrative work as of a piece with his more recent lyrics, restructured the collection, and after some months of hesitation chose to issue the volume privately, even though the printer he'd hired was so impressed with the collection that he offered to act as publisher. When *Tamar and Other Poems* did finally appear in April 1924, it made no more impression initially than *Californians*. After nearly a year, though, chance brought it to the attention of several major reviewers, and Jeffers suddenly found himself compared to the Greek tragedians, Shakespeare, Whitman, and a few others for good measure. Whatever the reviews left undone, *Tamar*'s scandalous plot finished, and when Boni & Liveright reissued it in November 1925 in an expanded edition as *Roan Stallion, Tamar and Other Poems*, Jeffers became a popular, as well as critical, success. Ten major trade collections followed between 1927 and 1954, first with Liveright and then with Random House.

In the years following *Tamar*, Jeffers was intensely productive. He explored the implications of his breakthrough in such pieces as *The Tower Beyond Tragedy*, a recasting of Aeschylus's *Oresteia*, and *Roan Stallion*, another narrative of the California coast. Jeffers' most ambitious project, though, was *The Women at Point Sur*. He apparently began working on early versions of it almost immediately after *Tamar* and struggled with what he hoped would be "the Faust of this generation" through early 1927. In *Point Sur* he explored a topic that would recur in a number of later poems, that of the savior who mistakenly turns from his vision of nature's power and beauty to seek control of disciples.

Jeffers' longest, and in many ways most complicated, poem, *The Women at Point Sur* was less favorably received than *Roan Stallion, Tamar and Other Poems*. But reviewers took his status as a major figure for granted, and his reputation remained strong through the rest of the 1920's and the early 1930's, as he produced *Cawdor and Other Poems* (1928), *Dear Judas and Other Poems* (1929), *Thurso's Landing and Other Poems* (1931), and *Give Your Heart to the Hawks and Other Poems* (1933). In these volumes Jeffers turned more to his characters' human dilemmas, the problems of guilt, of pain, of endurance. As a result, the narratives of this period tend to be more realistic, though less mythic, and to explore the characters' psychologies in more detail. These volumes, which refined and extended the directions implicit in his early work, have been among Jeffers' most popular.

After *Give Your Heart to the Hawks,* the narratives at least came more slowly. *Solstice and Other Poems* (1935), *Such Counsels You Gave to Me and Other Poems* (1937), and *Be Angry at the Sun* (1941), were generally less well received than the earlier volumes, though they contained some of Jeffers' finer short poems. Part of the problem may have been a kind of fatigue: Jeffers' work had consistently derived from his thematic perspective and formal principles of the early 1920's. Part of it may have been the Second World War. Jeffers saw it coming earlier than most, and if the First World War had helped precipitate his mature work, this impending conflict threatened his creative equilibrium. Even though his vision of nature argued that war was a fact of nature, a part of the order of things, and so essentially beautiful and inevitable, the suffering it would bring and its futility challenged the answers of the early 1920's. As a result his work increasingly took the form of shorter meditations on contemporary politics or addressed explicitly the tenets of what he came to call in 1948 "Inhumanism," "a philosophical attitude" that called for "a shifting of emphasis and significance from man to not-man; the rejection of human solipsism and recognition of the transhuman magnificence."*

A confirmed isolationist, Jeffers pleased few contemporary readers with his poems of this period, even though they have proved surprisingly prophetic. The war itself led to two of his most distinctive narratives, *The Love and the Hate* and *The Inhumanist.* The first, written at the end of the war, is perhaps Jeffers' most controversial narrative, tracing the revenge of a soldier who physically returns from the dead to punish those whose blindness and hypocrisy have sent him to die. The second, perhaps Jeffers' most philosophical and allegorical narrative, examines the attempts of an isolated old man to maintain his integrity and balance despite the threats of society and its violence. Together *The Love and the Hate* and *The Inhumanist* made up the title sequence of *The Double Axe and Other Poems* (1948), a volume whose references to contemporary po-

*Robinson Jeffers, "Preface," *The Double Axe and Other Poems* (New York, 1948), p. vi.

litical figures, especially in its short poems, so upset his editors at Random House that they insisted on including an editorial disclaimer. Whether the editors properly understood the poems or the politics, the fact that the volume was published at all, even under such circumstances, suggests Jeffers was still regarded as a major figure in the late 1940's, though an increasingly isolated and troubling one. His other major project of the 1940's was his adaptation of Euripides' *Medea*. He had prepared the text in 1945 at the request of the tragic actress Dame Judith Anderson. The play was produced in late 1947 and was, like *Roan Stallion*, a major critical and commercial success.

Jeffers continued to write after *The Double Axe*, but intermittently. Traveling in Ireland in 1948, he nearly died from pleurisy. Shortly after that Una Jeffers began her own battle; she died of cancer in 1950. Jeffers' last narrative, the brief and poignant *Hungerfield*, shows how devastating this loss was. It was collected, along with several short poems and an adaptation of Euripides' *Hippolytus*, in *Hungerfield and Other Poems* (1954), the last volume Jeffers published. Although *Hungerfield* was received more positively than *The Double Axe*, it was less popular than most of his earlier volumes—perhaps because he had, by and large, ceased to be a topic of discussion. The New Criticism of the 1950's had little patience for either narrative or direct statement, and critics such as Yvor Winters and R. P. Blackmur condemned both Jeffers' ideas and what they took to be his slack line and inflated rhetoric. The work of Jeffers' final years was compiled by Melba Berry Bennet, his biographer, and appeared as *The Beginning and the End* in 1963, the year after his death on January 20, 1962. In the 25 years since, Jeffers has attracted a steadily growing readership and renewed critical and scholarly interest.

Whatever future readers and historians may decide, it is clear that Jeffers made good his vow not to "be a 'modern,'" but it should also be clear that Jeffers, in his own quite different way, developed a distinctly modern poetry. Chance and decision led him to an alternative model to Pound's, one that owed more to Milton, Wordsworth, Darwin, and modern astronomy than to Coleridge, Mallarmé, Pater, and Hulme. Where the modernist aesthetic stressed the power of the imagination to transform perception, Jeffers' aesthetic stressed the paradoxical energy of consciousness and the way it allowed us to perceive our place in nature and yet, thereby, alienated us from it in self-consciousness. Where modernism emphasized the word as a thing to be valued for its own inherent properties, Jeffers treated it for its referential power. And where modernism viewed the poem as an aesthetic object, Jeffers viewed it as utterance, a kind of prophetic speech.

All of these matters reflect Jeffers' sense that poetry points to reality rather than transforming or replacing it and that poetry's task is to demonstrate the permanent and universal. At times these views give his work a didactic quality, but he saw no reason poems should not include direct statement. And if these attitudes placed him distinctly at odds with his modernist contemporaries and made his work, finally, technically more conservative than theirs, it may be that his sense of the interplay of culture and nature was in many ways more radical and forward looking. If Pound and others sought to make their poems permanent, Jeffers sought to make his reveal the permanence beyond the poem:

Permanent things are what is needful in a poem, things temporally
Of great dimension, things continually renewed or always present.

Grass that is made each year equals the mountains in her past and future;
Fashionable and momentary things we need not see nor speak of.

Man gleaning food between the solemn presences of land and ocean,
On shores where better men have shipwrecked, under fog and among
    flowers,

Equals the mountains in his past and future; that glow from the earth was
    only
A trick of nature's, one must forgive nature a thousand graceful subtleties.

"Point Joe"

I

Tamar

1920–1923

THE MAID'S THOUGHT

Why listen, even the water is sobbing for something.
The west wind is dead, the waves
Forget to hate the cliff, in the upland canyons
Whole hillsides burst aglow
With golden broom. Dear how it rained last month,
And every pool was rimmed
With sulphury pollen dust of the wakening pines.
Now tall and slender suddenly
The stalks of purple iris blaze by the brooks,
The pencilled ones on the hill;
This deerweed shivers with gold, the white globe-tulips
Blow out their silky bubbles,
But in the next glen bronze-bells nod, the does
Scalded by some hot longing
Can hardly set their pointed hoofs to expect
Love but they crush a flower;
Shells pair on the rock, birds mate, the moths fly double.
O it is time for us now
Mouth kindling mouth to entangle our maiden bodies
To make that burning flower.

DIVINELY SUPERFLUOUS BEAUTY

The storm-dances of gulls, the barking game of seals,
Over and under the ocean . . .
Divinely superfluous beauty
Rules the games, presides over destinies, makes trees grow
And hills tower, waves fall.
The incredible beauty of joy
Stars with fire the joining of lips, O let our loves too
Be joined, there is not a maiden
Burns and thirsts for love
More than my blood for you, by the shore of seals while the wings
Weave like a web in the air
Divinely superfluous beauty.

THE EXCESSES OF GOD

Is it not by his high superfluousness we know
Our God? For to equal a need
Is natural, animal, mineral: but to fling
Rainbows over the rain
And beauty above the moon, and secret rainbows
On the domes of deep sea-shells,
And make the necessary embrace of breeding
Beautiful also as fire,
Not even the weeds to multiply without blossom
Nor the birds without music:
There is the great humaneness at the heart of things,
The extravagant kindness, the fountain
Humanity can understand, and would flow likewise
If power and desire were perch-mates.

TO THE STONE-CUTTERS

Stone-cutters fighting time with marble, you foredefeated
Challengers of oblivion
Eat cynical earnings, knowing rock splits, records fall down,
The square-limbed Roman letters
Scale in the thaws, wear in the rain. The poet as well
Builds his monument mockingly;
For man will be blotted out, the blithe earth die, the brave sun
Die blind and blacken to the heart:
Yet stones have stood for a thousand years, and pained thoughts found
The honey of peace in old poems.

TO THE HOUSE

I am heaping the bones of the old mother
To build us a hold against the host of the air;
Granite the blood-heat of her youth
Held molten in hot darkness against the heart
Hardened to temper under the feet
Of the ocean cavalry that are maned with snow
And march from the remotest west.
This is the primitive rock, here in the wet
Quarry under the shadow of waves
Whose hollows mouthed the dawn; little house each stone
Baptized from that abysmal font
The sea and the secret earth gave bonds to affirm you.

SALMON FISHING

The days shorten, the south blows wide for showers now,
The south wind shouts to the rivers,
The rivers open their mouths and the salt salmon
Race up into the freshet.
In Christmas month against the smoulder and menace
Of a long angry sundown,
Red ash of the dark solstice, you see the anglers,
Pitiful, cruel, primeval,
Like the priests of the people that built Stonehenge,
Dark silent forms, performing
Remote solemnities in the red shallows
Of the river's mouth at the year's turn,
Drawing landward their live bullion, the bloody mouths
And scales full of the sunset
Twitch on the rocks, no more to wander at will
The wild Pacific pasture nor wanton and spawning
Race up into fresh water.

NATURAL MUSIC

The old voice of the ocean, the bird-chatter of little rivers,
(Winter has given them gold for silver
To stain their water and bladed green for brown to line their banks)
From different throats intone one language.
So I believe if we were strong enough to listen without
Divisions of desire and terror
To the storm of the sick nations, the rage of the hunger-smitten cities,
Those voices also would be found
Clean as a child's; or like some girl's breathing who dances alone
By the ocean-shore, dreaming of lovers.

CONSCIOUSNESS

I

What catches the eye the quick hand reaches toward
Or plotting brain circuitously secures,
The will is not required, is not our lord,
We seek nor flee not pleasure nor pain of ours.
The bullet flies the way the rifle's fired,
Then what is this unreasonable excess,
Our needless quality, this unrequired
Exception in the world, this consciousness?
Our nerves and brain have their own chemic changes,
This springs of them yet surely it stands outside.
It feeds in the same pasture and it ranges
Up and down the same hills, but unallied,
However symbiotic, with the cells
That weave tissues and lives. It is something else.

II

As if there were two Gods: the first had made
All visible things, waves, mountains, stars and men,
The sweet forms dancing on through flame and shade,
The swift messenger nerves that sting the brain,
The brain itself and the answering strands that start
Explosion in the muscles, the indrinking eye
Of cunning crystal, the hands and feet, the heart
And feeding entrails, and the organs that tie
The generations into one wreath, one strand;
All tangible things or chemical processes
Needs only brain and patience to understand:

Then the other God comes suddenly and says
"I crown or damn, I have different fire to add.
These forms shall feel, ache, love, grieve and be glad."

III

There is the insolence, there is the sting, the rapture.
By what right did that fire-bringer come in?
The uncalled for God to conquer us all and capture,
Master of joy and misery, troubler of men.
Still we divide allegiance: suddenly
An August sundown on a mountain road
The marble pomps, the primal majesty
And senseless beauty of that austerer God
Come to us, so we love him as men love
A mountain, not their kind: love growing intense
Changes to joy that we grow conscious of:
There is the rapture, the sting, the insolence.
. . . . . Or mourn dead beauty a bird-bright-May-morning:
The insufferable insolence, the sting.

AGE IN PROSPECT

Praise youth's hot blood if you will, I think that happiness
Rather consists in having lived clear through
Youth and hot blood, on to the wintrier hemisphere
Where one has time to wait and remember.

Youth and hot blood are beautiful, so is peacefulness.
Youth had some islands in it but age is indeed
An island and a peak; age has infirmities,
Not few, but youth is all one fever.

To look around and to love in his appearances,
Though a little calmly, the universal God's
Beauty is better I think than to lip eagerly
The mother's breast or another woman's.

And there is no possession more sure than memory's;
But if I reach that gray island, that peak,
My hope is still to possess with eyes the homeliness
Of ancient loves, ocean and mountains,

And meditate the sea-mouth of mortality
And the fountain six feet down with a quieter thirst
Than now I feel for old age; a creature progressively
Thirsty for life will be for death too.

WISE MEN IN THEIR BAD HOURS

Wise men in their bad hours have envied
The little people making merry like grasshoppers
In spots of sunlight, hardly thinking
Backward but never forward, and if they somehow
Take hold upon the future they do it
Half asleep, with the tools of generation
Foolishly reduplicating
Folly in thirty-year periods; they eat and laugh too,
Groan against labors, wars and partings,
Dance, talk, dress and undress; wise men have pretended
The summer insects enviable;
One must indulge the wise in moments of mockery.
Strength and desire possess the future,
The breed of the grasshopper shrills, "What does the future
Matter, we shall be dead?" Ah grasshoppers,
Death's a fierce meadowlark: but to die having made
Something more equal to the centuries
Than muscle and bone, is mostly to shed weakness.
The mountains are dead stone, the people
Admire or hate their stature, their insolent quietness,
The mountains are not softened nor troubled
And a few dead men's thoughts have the same temper.

TO THE ROCK THAT WILL BE A CORNERSTONE OF THE HOUSE

Old garden of grayish and ochre lichen,
How long a time since the brown people who have vanished from here
Built fires beside you and nestled by you
Out of the ranging sea-wind? A hundred years, two hundred,
You have been dissevered from humanity
And only known the stubble squirrels and the headland rabbits,
Or the long-fetlocked plowhorses
Breaking the hilltop in December, sea-gulls following,
Screaming in the black furrow; no one
Touched you with love, the gray hawk and the red hawk touched you
Where now my hand lies. So I have brought you
Wine and white milk and honey for the hundred years of famine
And the hundred cold ages of sea-wind.

I did not dream the taste of wine could bind with granite,
Nor honey and milk please you; but sweetly
They mingle down the storm-worn cracks among the mosses,
Interpenetrating the silent
Wing-prints of ancient weathers long at peace, and the older
Scars of primal fire, and the stone
Endurance that is waiting millions of years to carry
A corner of the house, this also destined.
Lend me the stone strength of the past and I will lend you
The wings of the future, for I have them.
How dear you will be to me when I too grow old, old comrade.

NOT OUR GOOD LUCK

Not our good luck nor the instant peak and fulfillment of time gives us to see
The beauty of things, nothing can bridle it.
God who walks lightning-naked on the Pacific has never been hidden from any
Puddle or hillock of the earth behind us.
Between the mean mud tenements and huddle of the filth of Babylon the river Euphrates;
And over the tiled brick temple buttresses
And the folly of a garden on arches, the ancienter simple and silent tribe of the stars
Filed, and for all her gods and the priests' mouths
God also moved on the city; or a certain young tribesman come down from the mountains of the north
Espied him in the eyes of a temple harlot;
Whom presently, as then, when the priests have choked him with perfume some prophet like a desert camel
Shall talk with in the ridges above the rock-tombs.

Dark ships drawing in from the sundown and the islands of the south, great waves with gray vapor in your hollows
And whitening of high heads coming home from the west,
From Formosa or the skerries of Siberia and the sight of the eyes that have widened for the sky-peaks of Asia:
That he touched you is no wonder, that you slid from his hand
Is an old known tale to our foreland cypresses, no news to the Lobos granite, no marvel
To Point Pinos Light and the beacon at Point Sur,

But here is the marvel, he is nowhere not present, his beauty, it is burning
in the midland villages
And tortures men's eyes in the alleys of cities.

Far-flown ones, you children of the hawk's dream future when you lean
from a crag of the last planet on the ocean
Of the far stars, remember we also have known beauty.

THE CYCLE

The clapping blackness of the wings of pointed cormorants, the great indolent planes
Of autumn pelicans nine or a dozen strung shorelong,
But chiefly the gulls, the cloud-calligraphers of windy spirals before a storm,
Cruise north and south over the sea-rocks and over
That bluish enormous opal; very lately these alone, these and the clouds
And westering lights of heaven, crossed it; but then
A hull with standing canvas crept about Point Lobos . . . now all day long the steamers
Smudge the opal's rim; often a seaplane troubles
The sea-wind with its throbbing heart. These will increase, the others diminish; and later
These will diminish; our Pacific have pastured
The Mediterranean torch and passed it west across the fountains of the morning;
And the following desolation that feeds on Crete
Feed here; the clapping blackness of the wings of pointed cormorants, the great sails
Of autumn pelicans, the gray sea-going gulls,
Alone will streak the enormous opal, the earth have peace like the broad water, our blood's
Unrest have doubled to Asia and be peopling
Europe again, or dropping colonies at the morning star: what moody traveller
Wanders back here, watches the sea-fowl circle
The old sea-granite and cemented granite with one regard, and greets my ghost,
One temper with the granite, bulking about here?

SHINE, PERISHING REPUBLIC

While this America settles in the mould of its vulgarity, heavily
thickening to empire,
And protest, only a bubble in the molten mass, pops and sighs out, and the
mass hardens,

I sadly smiling remember that the flower fades to make fruit, the fruit rots
to make earth.
Out of the mother; and through the spring exultances, ripeness and
decadence; and home to the mother.

You making haste haste on decay: not blameworthy; life is good, be it
stubbornly long or suddenly
A mortal splendor: meteors are not needed less than mountains: shine,
perishing republic.

But for my children, I would have them keep their distance from the
thickening center; corruption
Never has been compulsory, when the cities lie at the monster's feet there
are left the mountains.

And boys, be in nothing so moderate as in love of man, a clever servant,
insufferable master.
There is the trap that catches noblest spirits, that caught—they say—God,
when he walked on earth.

CONTINENT'S END

At the equinox when the earth was veiled in a late rain, wreathed with wet poppies, waiting spring,
The ocean swelled for a far storm and beat its boundary, the ground-swell shook the beds of granite.

I gazing at the boundaries of granite and spray, the established sea-marks, felt behind me
Mountain and plain, the immense breadth of the continent, before me the mass and doubled stretch of water.

I said: You yoke the Aleutian seal-rocks with the lava and coral sowings that flower the south,
Over your flood the life that sought the sunrise faces ours that has followed the evening star.

The long migrations meet across you and it is nothing to you, you have forgotten us, mother.
You were much younger when we crawled out of the womb and lay in the sun's eye on the tideline.

It was long and long ago; we have grown proud since then and you have grown bitter; life retains
Your mobile soft unquiet strength; and envies hardness, the insolent quietness of stone.

The tides are in our veins, we still mirror the stars, life is your child, but there is in me
Older and harder than life and more impartial, the eye that watched before there was an ocean.

That watched you fill your beds out of the condensation of thin vapor and
watched you change them,
That saw you soft and violent wear your boundaries down, eat rock, shift
places with the continents.

Mother, though my song's measure is like your surf-beat's ancient rhythm I
never learned it of you.
Before there was any water there were tides of fire, both our tones flow
from the older fountain.

TAMAR

I

A night the half-moon was like a dancing-girl,
No, like a drunkard's last half dollar
Shoved on the polished bar of the eastern hill-range,
Young Cauldwell rode his pony along the sea-cliff;
When she stopped, spurred; when she trembled, drove
The teeth of the little jagged wheels so deep
They tasted blood; the mare with four slim hooves
On a foot of ground pivoted like a top,
Jumped from the crumble of sod, went down, caught, slipped;
Then, the quick frenzy finished, stiffening herself
Slid with her drunken rider down the ledges,
Shot from sheer rock and broke
Her life out on the rounded tidal boulders.

The night you know accepted with no show of emotion the little accident; grave Orion
Moved northwest from the naked shore, the moon moved to meridian, the slow pulse of the ocean
Beat, the slow tide came in across the slippery stones; it drowned the dead mare's muzzle and sluggishly
Felt for the rider; Cauldwell's sleepy soul came back from the blind course curious to know
What sea-cold fingers tapped the walls of its deserted ruin. Pain, pain and faintness, crushing
Weights, and a vain desire to vomit, and soon again
The icy fingers, they had crept over the loose hand and lay in the hair now. He rolled sidewise
Against mountains of weight and for another half hour lay still. With a gush of liquid noises

The wave covered him head and all, his body
Crawled without consciousness and like a creature with no bones, a seaworm, lifted its face
Above the sea-wrack of a stone; then a white twilight grew about the moon, and above
The ancient water, the everlasting repetition of the dawn. You shipwrecked horseman
So many and still so many and now for you the last. But when it grew daylight
He grew quite conscious; broken ends of bone ground on each other among the working fibres
While by half inches he was drawing himself out of the sea-wrack up to sandy granite,
Out of the tide's path. Where the thin ledge tailed into flat cliff he fell asleep. . . .

Far seaward
The daylight moon hung like a slip of cloud against the horizon. The tide was ebbing
From the dead horse and the black belt of sea-growth. Cauldwell seemed to have felt her crying beside him,
His mother, who was dead. He thought "If I had a month or two of life yet
I would remember to be decent, only it's now too late, I'm finished, mother, mother,
I'm sorry." After that he thought only of pain and raging thirst until the sundown
Reddened the sea, and hands were reaching for him and drawing him up the cliff.

His sister Tamar
Nursed him in the big westward bedroom
Of the old house on Point Lobos. After fever
A wonderful day of peace and pleasant weakness

Brought home to his heart the beauty of things. "O Tamar
I've thrown away years like rubbish. Listen, Tamar,
It would be better for me to be a cripple,
Sit on the steps and watch the forest grow up the hill
Or a new speck of moss on some old rock
That takes ten years agrowing, than waste
Shame and my spirit on Monterey rye whiskey,
And worse, and worse. I shan't be a cripple, Tamar.
We'll walk along the blessed old gray sea,
And up in the hills and watch the spring come home."

Youth is a troublesome but a magical thing,
There is little more to say for it when you've said
Young bones knit easily; he that fell in December
Walked in the February fields. His sister Tamar
Was with him, and his mind ran on her name,
But she was saying, "We laugh at poor Aunt Stella
With her spirit visitors: Lee, something told her truth.
Last August you were hunting deer, you had been gone
Ten days or twelve, we heard her scream at night,
I went to the room, she told me
She'd seen you lying all bloody on the sea-beach
By a dead deer, its blood dabbling the black weeds of the ebb."
"I was up Tassajara way," he answered,
"Far from the sea." "We were glad when you rode home
Safe, with the two bucks on the packhorse. But listen,
She said she watched the stars flying over you
In her vision, Orion she said, and made me look
Out of her window southward, where I saw
The stars they call the Scorpion, the red bead
With the curling tail. 'Then it will be in winter,'
She whispered to me, 'Orion is winter.'" "Tamar, Tamar,

Winter is over, visions are over and vanished,
The fields are winking full of poppies,
In a week or two I'll fill your arms with shining irises."

The winter sun went under and all that night there came a roaring from the south; Lee Cauldwell
Lay awake and heard the tough old house creak all her timbers; he was miserably lonely and vacant,
He'd put away the boyish jets of wickedness, loves with dark eyes in Monterey back-streets, liquor
And all its fellowship, what was left to live for but the farm-work, rain would come and hinder?
He heard the cypress trees that seemed to scream in the wind, and felt the ocean pounding granite.
His father and Tamar's, the old man David Cauldwell, lay in the eastern chamber; when the storm
Wakened him from the heartless fugitive slumber of age he rose and made a light, and lighted
The lamp not cold yet; night and day were nearly equal to him, he had seen too many; he dressed
Slowly and opened his Bible. In the neighboring rooms he heard on one side Stella Moreland,
His dead wife's sister, quieting his own sister, the idiot Jinny Cauldwell, who laughed and chuckled
Often for half the night long, an old woman with a child's mind and mostly sleepless; in the other
Chamber Tamar was moaning, for it seemed that nightmare
Within the house answered to storm without.
To Tamar it seemed that she was walking by the seaside
With her dear brother, who said "Here's where I fell,
A bad girl that I knew in Monterey pushed me over the cliff,
You can see blood still on the boulders." Where he vanished to

She could not tell, nor why she was crying "Lee. No.
No dearest brother, dearest brother no." But she cried vainly,
Lee was not there to help her, a wild white horse
Came out of the wave and trampled her with his hooves,
The horror that she had dreaded through her dreaming
With mystical foreknowledge. When it wakened her,
She like her father heard old Jinny chuckling
And Stella sighing and soothing her, and the southwind
Raging around the gables of the house and through the forest of the cypresses.
"When it rains it will be quieter," Tamar thought. She slept again, all night not a drop fell.
Old Cauldwell from his window saw the cloudy light seep up the sky from the overhanging
Hilltops, the dawn was dammed behind the hills but overflowed at last and ran down on the sea.

II

Lee Cauldwell rode across the roaring southwind to the winter pasture up in the hills.
A hundred times he wanted Tamar, to show her some new beauty of canyon wildflowers, water
Dashing its ferns, or oaktrees thrusting elbows at the wind, black-oaks smouldering with foliage
And the streaked beauty of white-oak trunks, and redwood glens; he rode up higher across the rainwind
And found his father's cattle in a quiet hollow among the hills, their horns to the wind,
Quietly grazing. He returned another way, from the headland over Wildcat Canyon,
Saw the immense water possessing all the west and saw Point Lobos

Gemmed in it, and the barn-roofs and the house-roof
Like ships' keels in the cypress tops, and thought of Tamar.
Toward sundown he approached the house; Will Andrews
Was leaving it and young Cauldwell said, "Listen, Bill Andrews,
We've had gay times together and ridden at night.
I've quit it, I don't want my old friends to visit my sister.
Better keep off the place." "I will," said the other,
"When Tamar tells me to." "You think my bones
Aren't mended yet, better keep off." Lee Cauldwell
Rode by to the stable wondering why his lips
Twitched with such bitter anger; Tamar wondered
Why he went up-stairs without a word or smile
Of pleasure in her. The old man David Cauldwell,
When Lee had told him news of the herd and that Ramon
Seemed faithful, and the calves flourished, the old man answered:
"I hear that there's a dance at Notley's Landing Saturday. You'll be riding
Down the coast, Lee. Don't kill the horse, have a good time." "No, I've had all I want, I'm staying
At home now, evenings." "Don't do it; better dance your pony down the cliffs again than close
Young life into a little box; you've been too wild; now I'm worn out, but I remember
Hell's in the box." Lee answered nothing, his father's lamp of thought was hidden awhile in words,
An old man's words, like the dry evening moths that choke a candle. A space, and he was saying,
"Come summer we'll be mixed into the bloody squabble out there, and you'll be going headforemost
Unless you make your life so pleasant you'd rather live it. I mayn't be living
To see you home or hear you're killed." Lee, smiling at him,
"A soldier's what I won't be, father." That night
He dreamed himself a soldier, an aviator

Duelling with a German above a battle
That looked like waves, he fired his gun and mounted
In steady rhythm; he must have been winged, he suddenly
Plunged and went through the soft and deadly surface
Of the deep sea, wakening in terror.
He heard his old Aunt Jinny chuckling,
Aunt Stella sighing and soothing her, and the southwind
Raging around the gables of the house and through the forest of the cypresses.

III

They two had unbridled the horses
And tied them with long halters near the thicket
Under Mal Paso bridge and wandered east
Into the narrow cleft, they had climbed the summit
On the right and looked across the sea.
The steep path down, "What are we for?" said Tamar wearily, "to want and want and not dare know it."
"Because I dropped the faded irises," Lee answered, "you're unhappy. They were all withered, Tamar.
We have grown up in the same house." "The withered house
Of an old man and a withered woman and an idiot woman. No wonder if we go mad, no wonder."
They came to the hid stream and Tamar said, "Sweet, green and cool,
After the mad white April sun: you wouldn't mind, Lee?
Here where it makes a pool: you mustn't look; but you're my brother. And then
I will stand guard for you." The murmur and splash of water made his fever fierier; something
Unfelt before kept his eyes seaward: why should he dread to see the round arm and clear throat

Flash from the hollow stream? He trembled, thinking "O we are beasts, a beast, what am I for?
Was the old man right, I must be drunk and a dancer and feed on the cheap pleasures or it's dangerous?
Lovely and thoughtless, if she knew me how she'd loathe and avoid me. Her brother, brother. My sister.
Better the life with the bones, and all at once have broken." Meanwhile Tamar
Uneasily dipped her wrists, and crouching in the leaf-grown bank
Saw her breasts in the dark mirror, she trembled backward
From a long ripple and timidly wading entered
The quiet translucence to the thighs. White-shining
Slender and virgin pillar, desire in water
Unhidden and half reflected among the inter-branching ripples,
Arched with alder, over-woven with willow.
Ah Tamar, stricken with strange fever and feeling
Her own desirableness, half innocent Tamar
Thought, "If I saw a snake in the water he would come now
And kill the snake, he is keen and fearless but he fears
Me I believe." Was it the wild rock coast
Of her breeding, and the reckless wind
In the beaten trees and the gaunt booming crashes
Of breakers under the rocks, or rather the amplitude
And wing-subduing immense earth-ending water
That moves all the west taught her this freedom? Ah Tamar,
It was not good, not wise, not safe, not provident,
Not even, for custom creates nature, natural,
Though all other license were; and surely her face
Grew lean and whitened like a mask, the lips
Thinned their rose to a split thread, the little breasts
Erected sharp bright buds but the white belly
Shuddered, sucked in. The lips writhed and no voice

Formed, and again, and a faint cry. "Tamar?"
He answered, and she answered, "Nothing. A snake in the water
Frightened me." And again she called his name.
"What is it, Tamar?" "Nothing. It is cold in the water.
Come, Lee, I have hidden myself all but the head.
Bathe, if you mean to bathe, and keep me company.
I won't look till you're in." He came, trembling.
He unclothed himself in a green depth and dared not
Enter the pool, but stared at the drawn scars
Of the old wound on his leg. "Come, Lee, I'm freezing.
Come, I won't look." He saw the clear-skinned shoulders
And the hollow of her back, he drowned his body
In the watery floor under the cave of foliage,
And heard her sobbing. When she turned, the great blue eyes
Under the auburn hair, streamed. "Lee.
We have stopped being children; I would have drowned myself;
If you hadn't taught me swimming—long ago—long ago, Lee—
When we were children." "Tamar, what is it, what is it?"
"Only that I want . . . death. You lie if you think
Another thing." She slipped face down and lay
In the harmless water, the auburn hair trailed forward
Darkened like weeds, the double arc of the shoulders
Floated, and when he had dragged her to the bank both arms
Clung to him, the white body in a sobbing spasm
Clutched him, he could not disentangle the white desire,
So they were joined (like drowning folk brought back
By force to bitter life) painfully, without joy.
The spasm fulfilled, poor Tamar, like one drowned indeed, lay pale and quiet
And careless of her nakedness. He, gulfs opening
Between the shapes of his thought, desired to rise and leave her and was ashamed to.

He lay by her side, the cheek he kissed was cold like a smooth stone, the blue eyes were half open,
The bright smooth body seemed to have suffered pain, not love. One of her arms crushed both her breasts,
The other lay in the grass, the fingers clutching toward the roots of the soft grass. "Tamar,"
He whispered, then she breathed shudderingly and answered, "We have it, we have it. Now I know.
It was my fault. I never shall be ashamed again." He said, "What shall I do? Go away?
Kill myself, Tamar?" She contracted all her body and crouched in the long grass, shivering.
"It hurts, there is blood here, I am too cold to bathe myself again. O brother, brother,
Mine and twice mine. You knew already, a girl has got to learn. I love you, I chose my teacher.
Mine, it was my doing." She flung herself upon him, cold white and smooth, with sobbing kisses.
"I am so cold, dearest, dearest." The horses at the canyon mouth tugged at their halters,
Dug pits under the restless forehooves, shivered in the hill-wind
At sundown, were not ridden till dark, it was near midnight
They came to the old house.

IV

When Jinny Cauldwell slept, the old woman with a child's mind, then Stella Moreland
Invoked her childish-minded dead, or lying blank-eyed in the dark egged on her dreams to vision,
Suffering for lack of audience, tasting the ecstasy of vision. This was the vaporous portion

She endured her life in the strength of, in the sea-shaken loneliness, little loved, nursing an idiot,
Growing bitterly old among the wind-torn Lobos cypress trunks. (O torture of needled branches
Doubled and gnarled, never a moment of quiet, the northwind or the southwind or the northwest.
For up and down the coast they are tall and terrible horsemen on patrol, alternate giants
Guarding the granite and sand frontiers of the last ocean; but here at Lobos the winds are torturers,
The old trees endure them. They blew always thwart the old woman's dreams and sometimes by her bedside
Stood, the south in russety black, the north in white, but the northwest wave-green, sea-brilliant,
Scaled like a fish. She had also the sun and moon and mightier presences in her visions.) Tamar
Entered the room toward morning and stood ghost-like among the old woman's ghosts. The rolled-up eyes,
Dull white, with little spindles of iris touching the upper lids, played back the girl's blown candle
Sightlessly, but the spirit of sight that the eyes are tools of and it made them, saw her. "Ah Helen,"
Cried out the entranced lips, "We thought you were tired of the wind, we thought you never came now.
My sister's husband lies in the next room, go waken him, show him your beauty, call him with kisses.
He is old and the spittle when he dreams runs into his beard, but he is your lover and your brother."
"I am not Helen," she said, "what Helen, what Helen?" "Who was not the wife but the sister of her man,
Mine was his wife." "My mother?" "And now he is an old hulk battered ashore. Show him your beauty,

Strip for him, Helen, as when he made you a seaweed bed in the cave.
What if the beard is slimy
And the eyes run, men are not always young and fresh like you dead women." But Tamar clutching
The plump hand on the coverlet scratched it with her nails, the old woman groaned but would not waken,
And Tamar held the candle flame against the hand, the soot striped it, then with a scream
The old woman awoke, sat up, and fell back rigid on the bed. Tamar found place for the candle
On a little table at the bedside, her freed hands could not awaken a second answer
In the flesh that now for all its fatness felt like a warmed stone. But the idiot waked and chuckled,
Waved both hands at the candle saying, "My little star, my little star, come little star."
And to these three old Cauldwell sighing with sleeplessness
Entered, not noticed, and he stood in the open door. Tamar was bending
Over the bed, loose hair like burnished metal
Concealed her face and sharply cut across one rounded shoulder
The thin nightdress had slipped from. The old man her father
Feared, for a ghost of law-contemptuous youth
Slid through the chilly vaults of the stiff arteries,
And he said, "What is it, Tamar?" "She was screaming in a dream,
I came to quiet her, now she has gone stiff like iron.
Who is this woman Helen she was dreaming about?"
"Helen? Helen?" he answered slowly and Tamar
Believed she saw the beard and the hands tremble.
"It's too cold for you, Tamar, go back to bed
And I'll take care of her. A common name for women."
Old Jinny clapped her hands, "Little star, little star,
Twinkle all night!" and the stiff form on the bed began to speak,

In a changed voice and from another mode of being
And spirit of thought: "I cannot think that you have forgotten.
I was walking on the far side of the moon,
Whence everything is seen but the earth, and never forgot.
This girl's desire drew me home, we also had wanted
Too near our blood,
And to tangle the interbranching net of generations
With a knot sideways. Desire's the arrow-sprayer
And shoots into the stars. Poor little Tamar
He gave you a luckless name in memory of me
And now he is old forgets mine." "You are that Helen,"
Said Tamar leaning over the fat shape
The quiet and fleshless voice seemed issuing from,
A sound of youth from the old puffed lips, "What Helen? This man's . . .
Sister, this body was saying?" "By as much more
As you are of your brother." "Why," laughed Tamar trembling,
"Hundreds of nasty children do it, and we
Nothing but children." Then the old man: "Lies, lies, lies.
No ghost, a lying old woman. Your Aunt Helen
Died white as snow. She died before your mother died.
Your mother and this old woman always hated her,
This liar, as they hated me. I was too hard a nature
To die of it. Lily and Stella." "It makes me nothing,
My darling sin a shadow and me a doll on wires,"
Thought Tamar with one half her spirit; and the other half said,
"Poor lies, words without meaning. Poor Aunt Stella,
The voices in her have no minds." "Poor little Tamar,"
Murmured the young voice from the swollen cavern,
"Though you are that woman's daughter, if we dead
Could be sorrowful for anyone but ourselves
I would be sorrowful for you, a trap so baited
Was laid to catch you when the world began,

Before the granite foundation. I too have tasted the sweet bait.
But you are the luckier, no one came home to me
To say there are no whips beyond death—but only memory,
And that can be endured." The room was quiet a moment,
And Tamar heard the wind moving out-doors. Then the idiot Jinny Cauldwell
Whose mind had been from birth a crippled bird but when she was twelve years old her mind's cage
Was covered utterly, like a bird-cage covered with its evening cloth when lamps are lighted,
And her memory skipped the more than forty years between but caught stray gleams of the sun of childhood,
She in her crumpled voice: "I'd rather play with Helen, go away Stella. Stella pinches me,
Lily laughs at me, Lily and Stella are not my sisters." "Jinny, Jinny,"
Said the old man shaking like a thin brick house-wall in an earthquake, "do you remember, Jinny?"
"Jinny don't like the old man," she answered, "give me the star, give me my star,"
She whined, stretching from bed to reach the candle, "why have they taken my little star?
Helen would give it to Jinny." Then Stella waking from the trance sighed and arose to quiet her
According to her night's habit. Tamar said, "You were screaming in your sleep." "I had great visions.
And I have forgotten them. There Jinny, there, there. It'll have the candle, will it? Pretty Jinny.
Will have candle to-morrow. Little Jinny let Aunt Stella sleep now." Old Cauldwell tottering
Went to his room; then Tamar said, "You were talking about his sister Helen, my aunt Helen,

You never told me about her." "She has been dead for forty years, what should we tell you about her?
Now little Jinny, pretty sister." And laying her hands upon the mattress of the bed
The old woman cradled it up and down, humming a weary song. Tamar stood vainly waiting
The sleep of the monstrous babe; at length because it would not sleep went to her room and heard it
Gurgle and whimper an hour; and the tired litanies of the lullabies; not quiet till daylight.

V

O swiftness of the swallow and strength
Of the stone shore, brave beauty of falcons,
Beauty of the blue heron that flies
Opposite the color of evening
From the Carmel River's reed-grown mouth
To her nest in the deep wood of the deer
Cliffs of peninsular granite engirdle,
O beauty of the fountains of the sun
I pray you enter a little chamber,
I have given you bodies, I have made you puppets,
I have made idols for God to enter
And tiny cells to hold your honey.
I have given you a dotard and an idiot,
An old woman puffed with vanity, youth but botched with incest,
O blower of music through the crooked bugles,
You that make signs of sins and choose the lame for angels,
Enter and possess. Being light you have chosen the dark lamps,
A hawk the sluggish bodies: therefore God you chose

Me; and therefore I have made you idols like these idols
To enter and possess.

Tamar, finding no hope,
Slid back on passion, she had sought counsel of the dead
And found half scornful pity and found her sin
Fore-dated; there was honey at least in shame
And secrecy in silence, and her lover
Could meet her afield or slip to her room at night
In serviceable safety. They learned, these two,
Not to look back nor forward; and but for the hint
Of vague and possible wreck every transgression
Paints on the storm-edge of the sky, their blue
Though it dulled a shade with custom shone serene
To the fifth moon, when the moon's mark on women
Died out of Tamar. She kept secret the warning,
How could she color such love with perplexed fear?
Her soul walked back and forth like a new prisoner
Feeling the plant of unescapable fate
Root in her body. There was death; who had entered water
To compass love might enter again to escape
Love's fruit; "But O, but O," she thought, "not to die now.
It is less than half a year
Since life turned sweet. If I knew one of the girls
My lover has known
She'd tell me what to do, how to be fruitless,
How to be . . . happy? They do it, they do it, all sin
Grew nothing to us that day in Mal Paso water.
A love sterile and sacred as the stars.
I will tell my lover, he will make me safe,
He will find means . . .

Sterile and sacred, and more than any woman
. . . Unhappy. Miserable," she sobbed, "miserable,
The rough and bitter water about the cliff's foot
Better to breathe."

When Lee was not by her side
She walked the cliffs to tempt them. The calm and large
Pacific surge heavy with summer rolling southeast from a far origin
Battered to foam among the stumps of granite below.
Tamar watched it swing up the little fjords and fountain
Not angrily in the blowholes; a gray vapor
Breathed up among the buttressed writhings of the cypress trunks
And branches swollen with blood-red lichen. She went home
And her night was full of foolish dreams, two layers of dream, unrelative in emotion
Or substance to the pain of her thoughts. One, the undercurrent layer that seemed all night continuous,
Concerned the dead (and rather a vision than a dream, for visions gathered on that house
Like corposant fire on the hoar mastheads of a ship wandering strange waters), brown-skinned families
Came down the river and straggled through the wood to the sea, they kindled fires by knobs of granite
And ate the sea-food that the plow still turns up rotting shells of, not only around Point Lobos
But north and south wherever the earth breaks off to sea-rock; Tamar saw the huddled bodies
Squat by the fires and sleep; but when the dawn came there was throbbing music meant for daylight
And that weak people went where it led them and were nothing; then Spaniards, priests and horseback soldiers,

Came down the river and wandered through the wood to the sea, and hearing the universal music
Went where it led them and were nothing; and the English-speakers
Came down the river and wandered through the wood to the sea, among them Tamar saw her mother
Walking beside a nameless woman with no face nor breasts; and the universal music
Led them away and they were nothing; but Tamar led her father from that flood and saved him,
For someone named a church built on a rock, it was beautiful and white, not fallen to ruin
Like the ruin by Carmel River; she led him to it and made him enter the door, when he had entered
A new race came from the door and wandered down the river to the sea and to Point Lobos.
This was the undertow of the dream, obscured by a brighter surface layer but seeming senseless.
The tides of the sea were quiet and someone said "because the moon is lost." Tamar looked up
And the moon dwindled, rocketing off through lonely space, and the people in the moon would perish
Of cold or of a star's fire: then Will Andrews curiously wounded in the face came saying
"Tamar, don't cry. What do you care? I will take care of you." Wakening, Tamar thought about him
And how he had stopped coming to see her. Perhaps it was another man came through her dream,
The wound in the face disguised him, but that morning Lee having ridden to Mill Creek
To bargain about some fields of winter pasture
Now that the advancing year withered the hill-grass,

Tamar went down and saddled her own pony,
A four-year-old, as white as foam, and cantered
Past San Jose creek-mouth and the Carrows' farm
(Where David Carrow and his fanatical blue eyes,
That afterward saw Christ on the hill, smiled at her passing)
And three miles up the Carmel Valley came
To the Andrews place where the orchards ran to the river
And all the air was rich with ripening apples.
She would not go to the house; she did not find
Whom she was seeking; at length sadly she turned
Homeward, for Lee might be home within two hours,
And on the Carmel bridge above the water
(Shrunken with summer and shot with water lichen,
The surface scaled with minute scarlet leaves,
The borders green with slimy threads) met whom she sought.
"Tamar," he said, "I've been to see you." "You hadn't
For a long time." "I had some trouble with Lee,
I thought you didn't want me." While they talked
Her eyes tasted his face: was it endurable?
Though it lacked the curious gash her dream had given him . . .
"I didn't want you, you thought?" "Lee said so." "You might have waited
Till Tamar said so." "Well," he answered, "I've been,
And neither of you was home but now I've met you."
—Well-looking enough; freckles, light hair, light eyes;
Not tall, but with a chest and hard wide shoulders,
And sitting the horse well—"O I can do it, I can do it,
Help me God," murmured Tamar in her mind,
"How else—what else can I do?" and said, "Luck, isn't it?
What did you want to see me about?" "I wanted . . .
Because I . . . like you, Tamar."—"Why should I be careful,"
She thought, "if I frighten him off what does it matter,
I have got a little beyond caring." "Let's go down

Into the willow," she said, "we needn't be seen
Talking and someone tell him and make trouble
Here on the bridge." They went to the hidden bank
Under the deep green willows, colored water
Stagnated on its moss up to the stems,
Coarse herbage hid the stirrups, Tamar slid from the saddle
As quietly as the long unwhitening wave
Moulds a sunk rock, and while he tethered the horses,
"I have been lonely," she said. "Not for me, Tamar."
"You think not? Will, now that all's over
And likely we'll not see each other again
Often, nor by ourselves, why shouldn't I tell you . . ."
"What, Tamar?" "There've been moments . . . hours then . . .
When anything you might have asked me for
Would have been given, I'd have done anything
You asked me to, you never asked anything, Will.
I'm telling you this so that you may remember me
As one who had courage to speak truth, you'll meet
So many others." "But now" — he meant to ask,
"Now it's too late, Tamar?" and hadn't courage,
And Tamar thought "Must I go farther and say more?
Let him despise me as I despise myself.
I have got a little beyond caring." "Now?" she said.
"Do you think I am changed? You have changed, Will, you have grown
Older, and stronger I think, your face is firmer;
And carefuller: I have not changed, I am still reckless
To my own injury, and as trustful as a child.
Would I be with you here in the green thicket
If I weren't trustful? If you should harm me, Will,
I'd think it was no harm." She had laid her hand
On the round sunburnt throat and felt it throbbing,
And while she spoke the thought ran through her mind,

"He is only a little boy but if he turns pale
I have won perhaps, for white's the wanting color.
If he reddens I've lost and it's no matter." He did not move
And seemed not to change color and Tamar said,
"Now I must go. Lee will be home soon.
How soft the ground is in the willow shadow.
I have ended with you honestly, Will; remember me
Not afraid to speak truth and not ashamed
To have stripped my soul naked. You have seen all of me.
Good-bye." But when she turned he caught her by the arm,
She sickened inward, thinking, "Now it has come.
I have called and called it and I can't endure it.
Ah. A dumb beast." But he had found words now and said,
"How would you feel, Tamar, if all of a sudden
The bird or star you'd broken your heart to have
Flew into your hands, then flew away. O Tamar, Tamar,
You can't go now, you can't." She unresisting
Took the hot kisses on her neck and hair
And hung loose in his arms the while he carried her
To a clean bank of grass in the deep shadow.
He laid her there and kneeling by her: "You said you trusted me.
You are wise, Tamar; I love you so much too well
I would cut my hands off not to harm you." But she,
Driven by the inward spark of life and dreading
Its premature maturity, could not rest
On harmless love, there were no hands to help
In the innocence of love, and like a vision
Came to her the memory of that other lover
And how he had fallen a farther depth
From firmer innocence at Mal Paso, but the stagnant
Autumn water of Carmel stood too far
From the April freshet in the hills. Tamar pushed off

His kisses and stood up weeping and cried
"It's no use, why will you love me till I cry?
Lee hates you and my father is old and old, we can't
Sour the three years he has before he dies."
"I'll wait for you," said the boy, "wait years, Tamar." Then Tamar
Hiding her face against his throat
So that he felt the tears whispered, "But I . . ."
She sobbed, "Have no patience . . . I can't wait. Will . . .
When I made my soul naked for you
There was one spot . . . a fault . . . a shame
I was ashamed to uncover." She pressed her mouth
Between the muscles of his breast: "I want you and want you.
You didn't know that a clean girl could want a man.
Now you will take me and use me and throw me away
And I've . . . earned it." "Tamar, I swear by God
Never to let you be sorry, but protect you
With all my life." "This is our marriage," Tamar answered.
"But God would have been good to me to have killed me
Before I told you." The boy feeling her body
Vibrant and soft and sweet in its weeping surrender
Went blind and could not feel how she hated him
That moment; when he awakened she was lying
With the auburn hair muddied and the white face
Turned up to the willow leaves, her teeth were bared
And sunk in the under lip, a smear of blood
Reddening the corner of the lips. One of her arms
Crushed both her breasts, the other lay in the grass,
The fingers clutching toward the roots of the soft grass. "O Tamar,"
Murmured the boy, "I love you, I love you. What shall I do? Go away?
Kill myself, Tamar?" She contracted all her body and crouched in the long
grass, thinking

"That Helen of my old father's never fooled him at least," and said, "There is nothing to do, nothing.
It is horribly finished. Keep it secret, keep it secret, Will. I too was to blame a little.
But I didn't mean . . . this." "I know," he said, "it was my fault, I would kill myself, Tamar,
To undo it but I loved you so, Tamar." "Loved? You have hurt me and broken me, the house is broken
And any thief can enter it." "O Tamar!" "You have broken our crystal innocence, we can never
Look at each other freely again." "What can I do, Tamar?" "Nothing. I don't know. Nothing.
Never come to the farm to see me." "Where can I see you, Tamar?" "Lee is always watching me,
And I believe he'd kill us. Listen, Will. To-morrow night I'll put a lamp in my window,
When all the house is quiet, and if you see it you can climb up by the cypress. I must go home,
Lee will be home. Will, though you've done to me worse than I ever dreamed, I love you, you have my soul,
I am your tame bird now."

VI

This was the high plateau of summer and August waning; white vapors
Breathed up no more from the brown fields nor hung in the hills; daily the insufferable sun
Rose, naked light, and flaming naked through the pale transparent ways of the air drained gray
The strengths of nature; all night the eastwind streamed out of the valley seaward, and the stars blazed.

The year went up to its annual mountain of death, gilded with hateful
sunlight, waiting rain.
Stagnant waters decayed, the trickling springs that all the misty-hooded
summer had fed
Pendulous green under the granite ocean-cliffs dried and turned foul, the
rock-flowers faded,
And Tamar felt in her blood the filth and fever of the season. Walking
beside the house-wall
Under her window, she resented sickeningly the wounds in the cypress
bark, where Andrews
Climbed to his tryst, disgust at herself choked her, and as a fire by water
Under the fog-bank of the night lines all the sea and sky with fire, so her
self-hatred
Reflecting itself abroad burned back against her, all the world growing
hateful, both her lovers
Hateful, but the intolerably masculine sun hatefullest of all. The heat of
the season
Multiplied centipedes, the black worms that breed under loose rock, they
call them thousand-leggers,
They invaded the house, their phalloid bodies cracking underfoot with a
bad odor, and dropped
Ceiling to pillow at night, a vile plague though not poisonous. Also the
sweet and female sea
Was weak with calm, one heard too clearly a mounting cormorant's
wing-claps half a mile off shore;
The hard and dry and masculine tyrannized for a season. Rain in October
or November
Yearly avenges the balance; Tamar's spirit rebelled too soon, the female fury
abiding
In so beautiful a house of flesh. She came to her aunt the ghost-seer.
"Listen to me, Aunt Stella.

I think I am going mad, I must talk to the dead, Aunt Stella will you help
me?" That old woman
Was happy and proud, no one for years had sought her for her talent.
"Dear Tamar, I will help you.
We must go down into the darkness, Tamar, it is hard and painful for me."
"I am in the darkness
Already, a fiery darkness." "The good spirits will guide you, it is easy for
you; for me, death.
Death Tamar, I have to die to reach them." "Death's no bad thing," she
answered, "each hour of the day
Has more teeth." "Are you so unhappy, Tamar, the good spirits will help
you and teach you." "Aunt Stella,
To-night, to-night?" "I groan when I go down to death, your father and
brother will come and spoil it."
"In the evening we will go under the rocks by the sea." "Well, in the
evening." "If they talk to us
I'll buy you black silk and white lace."

In and out of the little fjord swam
the weak waves
Moving their foam in the twilight. Tamar at one flank, old Stella at the
other, upheld poor Jinny
Among the jags of shattered granite, so they came to the shingle. Rich,
damp and dark the sea's breath
Folding them made amend for days of sun-sickness, but Jinny among the
rubble granite
(They had no choice but take her along with them, who else would care for
the idiot?) slipped, and falling
Gashed knees and forehead, and she whimpered quietly in the darkness.
"Here," said Tamar, "I made you
A bed of seaweed under the nose of this old rock, let Jinny lie beside you
Aunt Stella,

I'll lay the rug over you both." They lay on the odorous kelp, Tamar squatted beside them,
The weak sea wavered in her rocks and Venus hung over the west between the cliff-butts
Like the last angel of the world, the crystal night deepening. The sea and the three women
Kept silence, only Tamar moved herself continually on the fret of her taut nerves,
And the sea moved, on the obscure bed of her eternity, but both were voiceless. Tamar
Felt her pulse bolt like a scared horse and stumble and stop, for it seemed to her a wandering power
Essayed her body, something hard and rounded and invisible pressed itself for entrance
Between the breasts, over the diaphragm. When she was forced backward and lay panting, the assault
Failed, the presence withdrew, and in that clearance she heard her old Aunt Stella monotonously muttering
Words with no meaning in them; but the tidal night under the cliff seemed full of persons
With eyes, although there was no light but the evening planet's and her trail in the long water.
Then came a man's voice from the woman, saying "Que quieres pobrecita?" and Tamar, "Morir,"
Trembling, and marvelling that she lied for no reason, and said, "Es porque no entiendo,
Anything but ingles." To which he answered, "Ah pobrecita," and was silent. And Tamar
Cried, "I will talk to that Helen." But instead another male throat spoke out of the woman's
Unintelligible gutturals, and it ceased, and the woman changing voice, yet not to her own:

"An Indian. He says his people feasted here and sang to their Gods and the tall Gods came walking
Between the tide-marks on the rocks; he says to strip and dance and he will sing, and his Gods
Come walking." Tamar answered crying, "I will not, I will not, tell him to go away and let me
Talk to that Helen." But old Stella after a silence: "He says No, no, the pregnant women
Would always dance here and the shore belongs to his people's ghosts nor will they endure another
Unless they are pleased." And Tamar said, "I cannot dance, drive him away," but while she said it
Her hands accepting alien life and a strange will undid the fastenings of her garments.
She panted to control them, tears ran down her cheeks, the male voice chanted
Hoarse discords from the old woman's body, Tamar drew her beauty
Out of its husks; dwellers on eastern shores
Watch moonrises as white as hers
When the half moon about midnight
Steps out of her husk of water to dance in heaven:
So Tamar weeping
Slipped every sheath down to her feet, the spirit of the place
Ruling her, she and the evening star sharing the darkness,
And danced on the naked shore
Where a pale couch of sand covered the rocks,
Danced with slow steps and streaming hair,
Dark and slender
Against the pallid sea-gleam, slender and maidenly
Dancing and weeping . . .
It seemed to her that all her body
Was touched and troubled with polluting presences

Invisible, and whatever had happened to her from her two lovers
She had been until that hour inviolately a virgin,
Whom now the desires of dead men and dead Gods and a dead tribe
Used for their common prey . . . dancing and weeping,
Slender and maidenly . . . The chant was changed,
And Tamar's body responded to the change, her spirit
Wailing within her. She heard the brutal voice
And hated it, she heard old Jinny mimic it
In the cracked childish quaver, but all her body
Obeyed it, wakening into wantonness,
Kindling with lust and wilder
Coarseness of insolent gestures,
The senses cold and averse but the frantic too-governable flesh
Inviting the assaults of whatever desired it, of dead men
Or Gods walking the tide-marks,
The beautiful girlish body as gracile as a maiden's
Gone beastlike, crouching and widening,
Agape to be entered, as the earth
Gapes with harsh heat-cracks, the inland adobe of sun-worn valleys
At the end of summer
Opening sick mouths for its hope of the rain,
So her body gone mad
Invited the spirits of the night, her belly and her breasts
Twisting, her feet dashed with blood where the granite had bruised them,
And she fell, and lay gasping on the sand, on the tide-line. Darkness
Possessed the shore when the evening star was down; old Stella
Was quiet in her trance; old Jinny the idiot clucked and parroted to herself,
there was none but the idiot
Saw whether a God or a troop of Gods came swaggering along the
tide-marks unto Tamar, to use her
Shamefully and return from her, gross and replete shadows, swaggering
along the tide-marks

Against the sea-gleam. After a little the life came back to that fallen flower; for fear or feebleness
She crept on hands and knees, returning so to the old medium of this infamy. Only
The new tide moved in the night now; Tamar with her back bent like a bow and the hair fallen forward
Crouched naked at old Stella's feet, and shortly heard the voice she had cried for. "I am your Helen.
I would have wished you choose another place to meet me and milder ceremonies to summon me.
We dead have traded power for wisdom yet it is hard for us to wait on the maniac living
Patiently, the desires of you wild beasts. You have the power." And Tamar murmured, "I had nothing,
Desire nor power." And Helen, "Humbler than you were. She has been humbled, my little Tamar.
And not so clean as the first lover left you, Tamar. Another, and half a dozen savages,
Dead, and dressed up for Gods." "I have endured it," she answered. Then the sweet disdainful voice
In the throat of the old woman: "As for me, I chose rather to die." "How can I kill
A dead woman," said Tamar in her heart, not moving the lips, but the other listened to thought
And answered "O, we are safe, we shan't fear murder. But, Tamar, the child will die, and all for nothing
You were submissive by the river, and lived, and endured fouling. I have heard the wiser flights
Of better spirits, that beat up to the breast and shoulders of our Father above the star-fire,
Say, 'Sin never buys anything.' " Tamar, kneeling, drew the thickness of her draggled hair

Over her face and wept till it seemed heavy with blood; and like a snake lifting its head
Out of a fire, she lifted up her face after a little and said, "It will live, and my father's
Bitch be proved a liar." And the voice answered, and the tone of the voice smiled, "Her words
Rhyme with her dancing. Tamar, did you know there were many of us to watch the dance you danced there,
And the end of the dance? We on the cliff; your mother, who used to hate me, was among us, Tamar.
But she and I loved each only one man, though it were the same. We two shared one? You, Tamar,
Are shared by many." And Tamar: "This is your help, I dug down to you secret dead people
To help me and so I am helped now. What shall I ask more? How it feels when the last liquid morsel
Slides from the bone? Or whether you see the worm that burrows up through the eye-socket, or thrill
To the maggot's music in the tube of a dead ear? You stinking dead. That you have no shame
Is nothing: I have no shame: see I am naked, and if my thighs were wet with dead beasts' drippings
I have suffered no pollution like the worms in yours; and if I cannot touch you I tell you
There are those I can touch. I have smelled fire and tasted fire,
And all these days of horrible sunlight, fire
Hummed in my ears, I have worn fire about me like a cloak and burning for clothing. It is God
Who is tired of the house that thousand-leggers crawl about in, where an idiot sleeps beside a ghost-seer,
A doting old man sleeps with dead women and does not know it,
And pointed bones are at the doors

Or climb up trees to the window. I say He has gathered
Fire all about the walls and no one sees it
But I, the old roof is ripe and the rafters
Rotten for burning, and all the woods are nests of horrible things, nothing would ever clean them
But fire, but I will go to a clean home by the good river." "You danced, Tamar," replied
The sweet disdainful voice in the mouth of the old woman, "and now your song is like your dance,
Modest and sweet. Only you have not said it was you,
Before you came down by the sea to dance,
That lit a candle in your closet and laid
Paper at the foot of the candle. We were watching.
And now the wick is nearly down to the heap,
It's God will have fired the house? But Tamar,
It will not burn. You will have fired it, your brother
Will quench it, I think that God would hardly touch
Anything in that house." "If you know everything,"
Cried Tamar, "tell me where to go.
Now life won't do me and death is shut against me
Because I hate you. O believe me I hate you dead people
More than you dead hate me. Listen to me, Helen.
There is no voice as horrible to me as yours,
And the breasts the worms have worked in. A vicious berry
Grown up out of the graveyard for my poison.
But there is no one in the world as lonely as I,
Betrayed by life and death." Like rain breaking a storm
Sobs broke her voice. Holding by a jag of the cliff
She drew herself full height. God who makes beauty
Disdains no creature, nor despised that wounded
Tired and betrayed body. She in the starlight
And little noises of the rising tide

Naked and not ashamed bore a third part
With the ocean and keen stars in the consistence
And dignity of the world. She was white stone,
Passion and despair and grief had stripped away
Whatever is rounded and approachable
In the body of woman, hers looked hard, long lines
Narrowing down from the shoulder-bones, no appeal,
A weapon and no sheath, fire without fuel,
Saying, "Have you anything more inside you
Old fat and sleepy sepulchre, any more voices?
You can do better than my father's by-play
And the dirty tricks of savages, decenter people
Have died surely. I have so passed nature
That God himself, who's dead or all these devils
Would never have broken hell, might speak out of you
Last season thunder and not scare me." Old Stella
Groaned but not spoke, old Jinny lying beside her
Wakened at the word thunder and suddenly chuckling
Began to mimic a storm, "whoo-whoo" for wind
And "boom-boom-boom" for thunder. Other voices
Wakened far off above the cliff, and suddenly
The farm-bell ringing fire; and on the rock-islets
Sleepy cormorants cried at it. "Why, now He speaks
Another way than out of the fat throat,"
Cried Tamar, and prayed, "O strong and clean and terrible
Spirit and not father punish the hateful house.
Fire eat the walls and roofs, drive the red beast
Through every wormhole of the rotting timbers
And into the woods and into the stable, show them,
These liars, that you are alive." Across her voice
The bell sounded and old Jinny mimicking it,
And shouts above the cliff. "Look, Jinny, look,"

Cried Tamar, "the sky'll be red soon, come and we'll dress
And watch the bonfire." Yet she glanced no thought
At her own mermaid nakedness but gathering
The long black serpents of beached seaweed wove
Wreaths for old Jinny and crowned and wound her. Meanwhile
The bell ceased ringing and Stella ceased her moan,
And in the sudden quietness, "Tamar," she said
In the known voice of Helen so many years
Dead, "though you hate me utterly, Tamar, I
Have nothing to give back, I was quite emptied
Of hate and love and the other fires of the flesh
Before your mother gave the clay to my lover
To mould you a vessel to hold them." Tamar, winding
Her mindless puppet in the sea-slough mesh
Said over her shoulder, hardly turning, "Why then
Do you trouble whom you don't hate?" "Because we hunger
And hunger for life," she answered. "Did I come uncalled?
You called me, you have more hot and blind, wild-blooded
And passionate life than any other creature.
How could I ever leave you while the life lasts?
God pity us both, a cataract life
Dashing itself to pieces in an instant.
You are my happiness, you are my happiness and death eats you.
I'll leave you when you are empty and cold and join us.
Then pity me, then Tamar, me flitting
The chilly and brittle pumice-tips of the moon,
While the second death
Corrodes this shell of me, till it makes my end."
But Tamar would not listen to her, too busily
Decking old Jinny for the festival fire,
And sighing that thin and envious ghost forsook

Her instrument, and about that time harsh pain
Wrung Tamar's loins and belly, and pain and terror
Expelled her passionate fancies, she cried anxiously,
"Stella, Aunt Stella, help me, will you?" and thinking,
"She hears when Jinny whimpers," twistingly pinched
Her puppet's arm until it screamed. Old Stella
Sat up on the seaweed bed and turned white eyes
No pupils broke the diffused star-gleam in
Upon her sixty-year-old babe, that now
Crouched whimpering, huddled under the slippery leaves
And black whips of the beach; and by it stood gleaming
Tamar, anguished, all white as the blank balls
That swept her with no sight but vision: old Stella
Did not awake yet but a voice blew through her,
Not personal like the other, and shook her body
And shook her hands: "It was no good to do too soon, your fire's out, you'd been patient for me
It might have saved two fires." But Tamar: "Stella.
I'm dying: or it is dying: wake up Aunt Stella.
O pain, pain, help me." And the voice: "She is mine while I use her. Scream, no one will hear but this one
Who has no mind, who has not more help than July rain." And Tamar, "What are you, what are you, mocking me?
More dirt and another dead man? O," she moaned, pressing her flanks with both her hands, and bending
So that her hair across her knees lay on the rock. It answered, "Not a voice from carrion.
Breaker of trees and father of grass, shepherd of clouds and waters, if you had waited for me
You'd be the luckier." "What shall I give you," Tamar cried, "I have given away—" Pain stopped her, and then

Blood ran, and she fell down on the round stones, and felt nor saw nothing.
A little later
Old Stella Moreland woke out of her vision, sick and shaking.

Tamar's
mind and suffering
Returned to her neither on the sea-rocks of the midnight nor in her own room; but she was lying
Where Lee her brother had lain, nine months before, after his fall, in the big westward bedroom.
She lay on the bed, and in one corner was a cot for Stella who nursed her, and in the other
A cot for the idiot, whom none else would care for but old Stella. After the ache of awakening
And blank dismay of the spirit come home to a spoiled house, she lay thinking with vacant wonder
That life is always an old story, repeating itself always like the leaves of a tree
Or the lips of an idiot; that herself like Lee her brother
Was picked up bleeding from the sea-boulders under the sea-cliff and carried up to be laid
In the big westward bedroom . . . was he also fouled with ghosts before they found him, a gang
Of dead men beating him with rotten bones, mouthing his body, piercing him? "Stella," she whispered,
"Have I been sick long?" "There, sweetheart, lie still; three or four days." "Has Lee been in to see me?"
"Indeed he has, hours every day." "He'll come, then," and she closed her eyes and seemed to sleep.
Someone tapped at the door after an hour and Tamar said, "Come, Lee." But her old father

Came in, and he said nothing but sat down by the bed; Tamar had closed her eyes. In a little
Lee entered, and he brought a chair across the room and sat by the bed. "Why don't you speak,
Lee?" And he said, "What can I say except I love you, sister?" "Why do you call me sister,
Not Tamar?" And he answered, "I love you, Tamar." Then old Aunt Stella said, "See, she's much better.
But you must let her rest. She'll be well in a few days; now kiss her, Lee, and let her rest."
Lee bent above the white pure cameo-face on the white pillow, meaning to kiss the forehead.
But Tamar's hands caught him, her lips reached up for his: while Jinny the idiot clapped and chuckled
And made a clucking noise of kisses; then, while Lee sought to untwine the arms that yoked his neck,
The old man, rising: "I opened the Book last night thinking about the sorrows of this house,
And it said, 'If a man find her in the field and force her and lie with her, nevertheless the damsel
Has not earned death, for she cried out and there was none to save her.' Be glad, Tamar, my sins
Are only visited on my son, for you there is mercy." "David, David
Will you be gone and let her rest now," cried old Stella, "do you mean to kill her with a bible?"
"Woman," he answered, "has God anything to do with you? She will not die, the Book
Opened and said it." Tamar, panting, leaned against the pillow and said, "Go, go. To-morrow
Say all you please; what does it matter?" And the old man said, "Come, Lee, in the morning she will hear us."

Tamar stretched out her trembling hand, Lee did not touch it, but went
out ahead of his father.
So they were heard in the hall, and then their foot-steps on the stair. Tamar
lay quiet and rigid,
With open eyes and tightening fists, with anger like a coiled steel spring in
her throat but weakness
And pain for the lead weights. After an hour she said, "What does he mean
to do? Go away?
Kill himself, Stella?" Stella answered, "Nothing, nothing, they talk, it's to
keep David quiet.
Your father is off his head a little, you know. Now rest you, little Tamar,
smile and be sleepy,
Scold them to-morrow." "Shut the sun out of my eyes then," Tamar said,
but the idiot Jinny
Made such a moaning when the windows were all curtained they needed to
let in one beam
For dust to dance in; then the idiot and the sick girl slept. About the hour
of sundown
Tamar was dreaming trivially—an axeman chopping down a tree and
field-mice scampering
Out of the roots—when suddenly like a shift of wind the dream
Changed and grew awful, she watched dark horsemen coming out of the
south, squadrons of hurrying horsemen
Between the hills and the dark sea, helmeted like the soldiers of the war in
France,
Carrying torches. When they passed Mal Paso Creek the columns
Veered, one of the riders said, "Here it began," but another answered, "No.
Before the granite
Was bedded to build the world on." So they formed and galloped north
again, hurrying squadrons,

And Tamar thought, "When they come to the Carmel River then it will
happen. They have passed Mal Paso."

Meanwhile—
Who has ever guessed to what odd ports, what sea buoying the keels, a
passion blows its bulkless
Navies of vision? High up in the hills
Ramon Ramirez, who was herdsman of the Cauldwell herds, stood in his
cabin doorway
Rolling a cigarette a half hour after sundown, and he felt puffs from the
south
Come down the slope of stunted redwoods, so he thought the year was
turning at last, and shortly
There would come showers; he walked therefore a hundred yards to
westward, where a point of the hill
Stood over Wildcat Canyon and the sea was visible; he saw Point Lobos
gemmed in the darkening
Pale yellow sea; and on the point the barn-roofs and the house-roof
breaking up through the blackness
Of twilight cypress tops, and over the sea a cloud forming. The evening
darkened. Southwestward
A half mile loop of the coast-road could be seen, this side Mal Paso.
Suddenly a nebular company
Of lights rounded the hill, Ramirez thought the headlights of a car
sweeping the road,
But in a moment saw that it was horsemen, each carrying a light, hurrying
northward,
Moving in squads he judged of twenty or twenty-five, he counted twelve or
thirteen companies
When the brush broke behind him and a horseman rode the headlong ridge
like level ground,

Helmeted, carrying a torch. Followed a squad of twelve, helmeted,
cantering the headlong ridge
Like level ground. He thought in the nervous innocence of the early war,
they must be Germans.

Tamar awoke out of her dream and heard old Jinny saying, "Dear sister
Helen, kiss me
As you kiss David. I was watching under a rock, he took your clothes off
and you kissed him
So hard and hard, I love you too, Helen; you hardly ever kiss me." Tamar
lay rigid,
Breathless to listen to her; it was well known in the house that under the
shell of imbecility
Speech and a spirit however subdued existed still; there were waking flashes,
and more often
She talked in sleep and proved her dreams were made out of clear
memories, childhood sights and girlhood
Fancies, before the shadow had fallen; so Tamar craving food for passion
listened to her,
And heard: "Why are you cross, Helen? I won't peek if you'd rather I
didn't. Darling Helen,
I love him, too; I'd let him play with me the way he does with you if he
wanted to.
And Lily and Stella hate me as much as they hate you." All she said after
was so mumbled
That Tamar could not hear it, could only hear the mumble, and old Aunt
Stella's nasal sleep
And the sea murmuring. When the mumbled voice was quiet it seemed to
Tamar
A strange thing was preparing, an inward pressure
Grew in her throat and seemed to swell her arms and hands
And join itself with a fluid power

Streaming from somewhere in the room—from Jinny?
From Stella?—and in a moment the heavy chair
That Lee had sat in, tipped up, rose from the floor,
And floated to the place he had brought it from
Five hours ago. The power was then relaxed,
And Tamar could breathe and speak. She awaked old Stella
And trembling told her what she had seen; who laughed
And answered vaguely so that Tamar wondered
Whether she was still asleep, and let her burrow
In her bed again and sleep. Later that night
Tamar too slept, but shudderingly, in snatches,
For fear of dreaming. A night like years. In the gray of morning
A horse screamed from the stableyard and Tamar
Heard the thud of hoofs lashing out and timbers
Splintering, and two or three horses broken loose
Galloped about the grounds of the house. She heard men calling,
And down-stairs Lee in a loud angry tone
Saying "Someone's pitched the saw-buck and the woodpile
Into the horse-corral." Then Tamar thought
"The same power moved his chair in the room, my hatred, my hatred,
Disturbing the house because I failed to burn it.
I must be quiet and quiet and quiet and keep
The serving spirits of my hid hatred quiet
Until my time serves too. Helen you shadow
Were never served so handily." Stella had awakened,
And Tamar asking for a drink of water
She waddled to fetch it and met Lee at the door.
"O Lee," she said, "that noise—whatever has happened?"
He: "I don't know. Some fool has pitched the whole woodpile
Into the horse-corral. Is Tamar awake?
I want to see Tamar." He entered the room
As Stella left it. Old withered Aunt Jinny

Sat up in her bed saying "David, David," but Lee
Kneeling at Tamar's bedside, "O Tamar, Tamar.
The old man's out-doors tottering after the horses
So I can see you a minute. O why, why, why,
Didn't you tell me Tamar? I'd have taken you up
In my arms and carried you to the end of the world."
"How it's turned sour," she thought, "I'd have been glad of this
Yesterday," and she clinched her finger-nails
Into her palms under the bed-covers,
Saying, "Tell you—what? What have they told you," she asked
With a white sidelong smile, "people are always lying?"
"Tamar, that you—that we . . . O I've lived hell
Four or five days now." "You look well enough,"
She answered, "put yours by mine," laying her white, lean,
And somewhat twitching hand on the counterpane,
"Mine used to manage a bridle as well as yours
And now look at them. I don't suppose you want me
Now, but it doesn't matter. You used to come to my bed
With something else than pity, convenient, wasn't it?
Not having to ride to Monterey?" He answered frowning,
"However much you hurt me I am very glad too
That all the joys and memories of a love
As great and as forbidden as ours are nothing to you
Or worse than nothing, because I have to go away,
Two days from now, and stay till the war's over
And you are married and father is dead. I've promised him
Never to see him again, never to see his face.
He didn't ask it because he thinks his Book
Told him I'm to be killed. That's foolishness,
But makes your peace with him and thank God for that.
What his Book told him." "So here's the secret
I wasn't strong enough yesterday to hear.

I thought maybe you meant to kill yourself."
"Thanks, Tamar. The old man thinks I don't need to." "O,
You beast," she said, "you runaway dog.
I wish you joy of your dirty Frenchwomen
You want instead of me. Take it, take it.
Old people in their dotage gabble the truth,
You won't live long." "What can I say, Tamar?
I'm sorry, I'm sorry, I'm sorry." "But go away,"
She said, "and if you'll come again to-night
Maybe I'll tell you mine, my secret."

That morning
Ramon Ramirez who watched the Cauldwell cattle
Up in the hills kept thinking of his vision
Of helmets carrying torches; he looked for tracks
On the ridge where he had seen the riders cantering,
And not a bush was broken, not a hoof-mark
Scarred the sear grass. At noon he thought he'd ride
To Vogel's place taking his lunch in the saddle
And tell someone about it. At the gap in the hill
Where storm-killed redwoods line both sides he met
Johnny Cabrera with a flaming bundle
Of dead twigs and dry grass tied with brown cord.
He smelled the smoke and saw the flame sag over
On a little wind from the east, and said in Spanish
"Eh Johnny, are you out of matches?" who answered flashing
His white teeth in a smile, "I'm carrying fire to Lobos
If God is willing," and walked swinging ahead,
Singing to himself the fool south-border couplet
"No tengo tabaco, no tengo papel,
No tengo dinero, God damn it to hell,"
And Ramon called "Hey Johnny," but he would not stop

Nor answer, and thinking life goes wild at times
Ramon came to the hill-slope under Vogel's
And smelled new smoke and saw the clouds go up
And this same Johnny with two other men
Firing the brush to make spring pasture. Ramon
Felt the scalp tighten on his temples and thought best
Not to speak word of either one of his visions,
Though he talked with the men, they told him Tamar Cauldwell
Was sick, and Lee had enlisted.

The afternoon
Was feverish for so temperate a sea-coast
And terribly full of light, the sea like a hard mirror
Reverberated the straight and shining serpents
That fell from heaven and Tamar dreamed in a doze
She was hung naked by that tight cloth bandage
Half way between sea and sky, beaten on by both,
Burning with light; wakening she found she had tumbled
The bed-clothes to the floor and torn her night-gown
To rags, and was alone in the room, and blinded
By the great glare of sun in the western windows.
She rose and shut the curtains though they had told her
She mustn't get out of bed, and finding herself
Able to walk she stood by the little window
That looked southeast from the south bay of the room
And saw the smoke of burning brushwood slopes
Tower up out of the hills in the windless weather
Like an enormous pinetree, "Everybody
But me has luck with fire," she thought to herself,
"But I can walk now," and returned to bed
And drew the sheets over her flanks, but leaving

The breasts and shoulders bare. In half an hour
Stella and old Jinny came into the room
With the old man David Cauldwell. Stella hastily
Drew up the sheet to Tamar's throat but Tamar
Saying, "You left the curtains open and the sun
Has nearly killed me," doubled it down again,
And David Cauldwell, trembling: "Will you attempt
Age and the very grave, uncovering your body
To move the old bones that seventy years have broken
And dance your bosoms at me through a mist of death?
Though I know that you and your brother have utterly despised
The bonds of blood, and daughter and father are no closer bound,
And though this house spits out all goodness, I am old, I am old, I am old,
What do you want of me?" He stood tottering and wept,
Covering his eyes and beard with shaken old hands,
And Tamar, having not moved, "Nothing," she said,
"Nothing, old man. I have swum too deep into the mud
For this to sicken me; and as you say, there are neither
Brother nor sister, daughter nor father, nor any love
This side the doorways of the damnable house.
But I have a wildbeast of a secret hidden
Under the uncovered breast will eat us all up
Before Lee goes." "It is a lie, it is a lie, it is all a lie.
Stella you must go out, go out of the room Stella,
Not to hear the sick and horrible imaginations
A sick girl makes for herself. Go Stella." "Indeed I won't,
David." "You—you—it is still my house." "To let you kill her with bad
    words
All out of the bible—indeed I won't." "Go, Stella," said Tamar,
"Let me talk to this old man, and see who has suffered
When you come back. I am out of pity, and you and Jinny

Will be less scorched on the other side of the door." After a third refusal
The old woman went, leading her charge, and Tamar: "You thought it was your house? It is me they obey.
It is mine, I shall destroy it. Poor old man I have earned authority." "You have gone mad," he answered.
And she: "I'll show you our trouble, you sinned, your old book calls it, and repented: that was foolish.
I was unluckier, I had no chance to repent, so I learned something, we must keep sin pure
Or it will poison us, the grain of goodness in a sin is poison. Old man, you have no conception
Of the freedom of purity. Lock the door, old man, I am telling you a secret." But he trembling,
"O God thou hast judged her guiltless, the Book of thy word spake it, thou hast the life of the young man
My son . . ." and Tamar said, "Tell God we have revoked relationship in the house, he is not
Your son nor you my father." "Dear God, blot out her words, she has gone mad. Tamar, I will lock it,
Lest anyone should come and hear you, and I will wrestle for you with God, I will not go out
Until you are His." He went and turned the key and Tamar said, "I told you I have authority.
You obey me like the others, we pure have power. Perhaps there are other ways, but I was plunged
In the dirt of the world to win it, and, O father, so I will call you this last time, dear father
You cannot think what freedom and what pleasure live in having abjured laws, in having
Annulled hope, I am now at peace." "There is no peace, there is none, there is none, there is no peace

But His," he stammered, "but God's." "Not in my arms, old man, on these two little pillows? Your son
Found it there, and another, and dead men have defiled me. You that are half dead and half living,
Look, poor old man. That Helen of yours, when you were young, where was her body more desirable,
Or was she lovinger than I? You know it is forty years ago that we revoked
Relationships in the house." "He never forgives, He never forgives, evil punishes evil
With the horrible mockery of an echo." "Is the echo louder than the voice, I have surpassed her,
Yours was the echo, time stands still old man, you'll learn when you have lived at the muddy root
Under the rock of things; all times are now, to-day plays on last year and the inch of our future
Made the first morning of the world. You named me for the monument in a desolate graveyard,
Fool, and I say you were deceived, it was out of me that fire lit you and your Helen, your body
Joined with your sister's
Only because I was to be named Tamar and to love my brother and my father.
I am the fountain." But he, shuddering, moaned, "You have gone mad, you have gone mad, Tamar,"
And twisted his old hands muttering, "I fear hell. O Tamar, the nights I have spent in agony,
Ages of pain, when the eastwind ran like glass under the peeping stars or the southwest wind
Plowed in the blackness of the trees. You—a little thing has driven you mad, a moment of suffering,
But I for more than forty years have lain under the mountains and looked down into hell."

"One word," she said, "that was not written in the book of my fears. I did indeed fear pain
Before peace found me, or death, never that dream. Old man, to be afraid is the only hell
And dead people are quit of it, I have talked with the dead." "Have you—with her?" "Your pitiful Helen?
She is always all about me; if you lay in my arms old man you would be with her. Look at me,
Have you forgotten—your Helen?" He in torture
Groaned like a beast, but when he approached the bed she laughed, "Not here, behind you." And he blindly
Clutching at her, she left the coverlet in his hands and slipping free at the other side
Saw in a mirror on the wall her own bright throat and shoulder and just beyond them the haggard
Open-mouthed mask, the irreverend beard and blind red eyes. She caught the mirror from its fastening
And held it to him, reverse. "Here is her picture, Helen's picture, look at her, why is she always
Crying and crying?" When he turned the frame and looked, then Tamar: "See that is her lover's.
The hairy and horrible lips to kiss her, the drizzling eyes to eat her beauty, happiest of women
If only he were faithful; he is too young and wild and lovely, and the lusts of his youth
Lead him to paw strange beds." The old man turned the glass and gazed at the blank side, and turned it
Again face towards him, he seemed drinking all the vision in it, and Tamar: "Helen, Helen,
I know you are here present; was I humbled in the night lately and you exulted?
See here your lover. I think my mother will not envy you now, your lover, Helen, your lover,

The mouth to kiss you, the hands to fondle secret places." Then the old
man sobbing, "It is not easy
To be old, mocked, and a fool." And Tamar, "What, not yet, you have not
gone mad yet? Look, old fellow.
These rags drop off, the bandages hid something but I'm done with them.
See . . . I am the fire
Burning the house." "What do you want, what do you want?" he said, and
stumbled toward her, weeping.
"Only to strangle a ghost and to destroy the house. Spit on the memory of
that Helen
You might have anything of me." And he groaning, "When I was young
I thought it was my fault, I am old and know it was hers, night after night,
night after night
I have lain in the dark, Tamar, and cursed her." "And now?" "I hate her,
Tamar." "O," said Tamar gently,
"It is enough, she has heard you. Now unlock the door, old father, and go,
and go." "Your promise,
Tamar, the promise, Tamar." "Why I might do it, I have no feeling of
revolt against it.
Though you have forgotten that fear of hell why should I let you
Be mocked by God?" And he, the stumpage of his teeth knocking together,
"You think, you think
I'll go to the stables and a rope from a rafter
Finish it for you?" "Dear, I am still sick," she answered, "you don't want to
kill me? A man
Can wait three days: men have lived years and years on the mere hope."

Meanwhile

the two old women
Sat in their room, old Stella sat at the window looking south into the
cypress boughs, and Jinny
On her bed's edge, rocking her little withered body backward and forward,
and said vacantly,

"Helen, what do you do the times you lock the door to be alone, and Lily and Stella
Wonder where David's ridden to?" After a while she said again, "Do tell me, sister Helen,
What you are doing the times you lock the door to be alone, and Lily and Stella wonder
Where David's ridden to?" And a third time she repeated, "Darling sister Helen, tell me
What you are doing the times you lock the door to be alone, and Lily and Stella wonder
Where David's riding?" Stella seemed to awake, catching at breath, and not in her own voice,
"What does she mean," she said, "my picture, picture? O! the mirror—I read in a book Jinny.
A story about lovers; I never had a lover, I read about them;—I won't look, though.
With all that blind abundance, so much of life and blood, that sweet and warming blaze of passion,
She has also a monkey in her mind." "Tell me the story about the picture." "Ugh, if she plans
To humble herself utterly . . . You may peek, Jinny,
Try if you can, shut both eyes, draw them back into your forehead, and look, look, look
Over the eyebrows, no, like this, higher up, up where the hair grows, now peek Jinny. Can't you
See through the walls? You can. Look, look, Jinny. As if they'd cut a window. I used to tell you
That God could see into caves: you are like God now: peek, Jinny." "I can see something.
It's in the stable, David's come from Monterey, he's hanging the saddle on a peg there . . ."
"Jinny, I shall be angry. That's not David,

It's Lee, don't look into the stable, look into the bedroom, you know, Jinny,
  the bedroom,
Where we left Tamar on the bed." "O that's too near, it hurts me, it hurts
  my head, don't scold me, Helen.
How can I see if I'm crying? I see now clearly."
"What do you see?" "I see through walls, O, I'm like God, Helen. I see the
  wood and plaster
And see right through them." "What? What are they doing?" "How can
  you be there and here, too, Helen?"
"It's Tamar, what is she doing?" "I know it's you Helen, because you have
  no hair
Under the arms, I see the blue veins under the arms." "Well, if it's me, what
  is she doing?
Is she on the bed? What is she saying?" "She is on fire Helen, she has white
  fire all around you
Instead of clothes, and that is why you are laughing with so pale a face."
  "Does she let him do
Whatever he wants to, Jinny?" "He says that he hates . . . somebody . . .
  and then you laughed for he had a rope
Around his throat a moment, the beard stuck out over it." "O Jinny it
  wasn't I that laughed,
It was that Tamar, Tamar, Tamar, she has bought him for nothing. She and
  her mother both to have him,
The old hollow fool." "What do they want him for, Helen?" "To plug a
  chink, to plug a chink, Jinny,
In the horrible vanity of women. Lee's come home, now I could punish her,
  she's past hurting,
Are they huddled together Jinny? What, not yet, not yet?" "You asked for
  the key but when he held it
You ran away from him." "What do I want, what do I want, it is frightful
  to be dead, what do I . . .

Without power, and no body or face. To kill her, kill her?
There's no hell and curse God for it . . ."

Lee Cauldwell childishly
Loved hearing the spurs jingle, and because he felt
"After to-morrow I shan't wear them again,
Nor straddle a pony for many a weary month and year,
Maybe forever," he left them at his heels
When he drew off the chaps and hung the saddle
On the oak peg in the stable-wall. He entered the house
Slowly, he had taken five drinks in Monterey
And saw his tragedy of love, sin, and war
At the disinterested romantic angle
Misted with not unpleasing melancholy,
Over with, new adventure ahead, a perilous cruise
On the other ocean, and great play of guns
On the other shore . . . at the turn of the stair he heard
Hands hammering a locked door, and a voice unknown to him
Crying, "Tamar, I loved you for your flame of passion
And hated you for its deeds, all that we dead
Can love or hate with: and now will you crust flame
With filth, submit? Submit? Tamar,
The defilement of the tideline dead was nothing
To this defilement." Then Lee jingling his spurs,
Jumped four steps to the landing, "Who is there? You,
Aunt Stella?" Old gray Aunt Jinny like a little child
Moaning drew back from him, and the mouth of Stella:
"A man that's ready to cross land and water
To set the world in order can't be expected
To leave his house in order." And Lee, "Listen, Aunt Stella,
Who are you playing, I mean what voice out of the world of the dead
Is speaking from you?" She answered, "Nothing. I was something

Forty years back but now I'm only the bloodhound
To bay at the smell of what they're doing in there."
"Who? Tamar? Blood?" "Too close in blood, I am the blood-stain
On the doorsill of a crime, she does her business
Under her own roof mostly." "Tamar, Tamar,"
Lee called, shaking the door. She from within
Answered "I am here, Lee. Have you said good-bye
To Nita and Conchita in Monterey
And your fat Fanny? But who is the woman at the door
Making the noise?" He said, "Open the door;
Open the door, Tamar." And she, "I opened it for you,
You are going to France to knock at other doors.
I opened it for you and others." "What others?" "Ask her,"
Said the young fierce voice from old Aunt Stella's lips,
"What other now?" "She is alone there," he answered,
"A devil is in you. Tamar," he said, "tell her
You are alone." "No, Lee, I am asking in earnest,
Who is the woman making the noise out there?
Someone you've brought from Monterey? Tell her to go:
Father is here." "Why have you locked it, why have you locked it?"
He felt the door-knob turning in his hand
And the key shook the lock; Tamar stood in the doorway
Wrapped in a loose blue robe that the auburn hair
Burned on, and beyond her the old man knelt by the bed,
His face in the lean twisted hands. "He was praying for me,"
Tamar said quietly. "You are leaving to-morrow,
He has only one child." Then the old man lifting a face
From which the flesh seemed to have fallen, and the eyes
Dropped and been lost: "What will you do to him, Tamar?
Tamar, have mercy.
He was my son, years back." She answered, "I am glad
That you know who has power in the house"; and he

Hid the disfigured face, between his wrists
The beard kept moving, they thought him praying to God.
And Tamar said, "It is coming to the end of the bad story,
That needn't have been bad only we fools
Botch everything, but a dead fool's the worst,
This old man's sister who rackets at the doors
And drove me mad, although she is nothing but a voice,
Dead, shelled, and the shell rotted, but she had to meddle
In the decencies of life here. Lee, if you truly
Lust for the taste of a French woman I'll let you go
For fear you die unsatisfied and plague
Somebody's children with a ghost's hungers
Forty years after death. Do I care, do I care?
You shan't go, Lee. I told the old man I have a secret
That will eat us all up . . . and then, dead woman,
What will you have to feed on? You spirits flicker out
Too speedily, forty years is a long life for a ghost
And you will only famish a little longer
To whom I'd wish eternity." "O Tamar, Tamar,"
It answered out of Stella's mouth, "has the uttermost
Not taught you anything yet, not even that extinction
Is the only terror?" "You lie too much," she answered,
"You'll enter it soon and not feel any stitch
Of fear afterwards. Listen, Lee, your arms
Were not the first man's to encircle me, and that spilled life
Losing which let me free to laugh at God,
I think you had no share in." He trembled, and said
"O Tamar have your sickness and my crime
Cut you so deep? A lunatic in a dream
Dreams nearer things than this." "I'd never have told you,"
She answered, "if his vicious anger—after I'd balanced
Between you a long time and then chose you—

Hadn't followed his love's old night-way to my window
And kindled fire in the room when I was gone,
The spite-fire that might easily have eaten up
And horribly, our helpless father, or this innocent
Jinny . . ." "He did it, he did it, forgive me, Tamar.
I thought that you gone mad . . . Tamar, I know
That you believe what you are saying but I
Do not believe you. There was no one." "The signal
Was a lamp in the window, perhaps some night
He'd come still if you'd set a lamp into my window.
And when he climbed out of the cypress tree
Then you would know him." "I would mark him to know.
But it's not true." "Since I don't sleep there now
You might try for the moth; if he doesn't come
I'll tell you his name to-morrow." Then the old man jerking
Like dry bones wired pulled himself half erect
With clutching at the bed-clothes: "Have mercy, Tamar.
Lee, there's a trick in it, she is a burning fire,
She is packed with death. I have learned her, I have learned her, I have learned her,
Too cruel to measure strychnine, too cunning-cruel
To snap a gun, aiming ourselves against us."
Lee answered, "There is almost nothing here to understand.
If we all did wrong why have we all gone mad
But me, I haven't a touch of it. Listen, dead woman,
Do you feel any light here?" "Fire—as much light
As a bird needs," the voice from the old woman
Answered, "I am the gull on the butt of the mast
Watching the ship founder, I'll fly away home
When you go down, or a swallow above a chimney
Watching the brick and mortar fly in the earthquake."
"I'll just go look at the young cypress bark

Under her window," he said, "it might have taken
The bite of a thief's hob-nails." When he was gone
And jingling down the stair, then Tamar: "Poor people,
Why do you cry out so? I have three witnesses,
The old man that died to-day, and a dead woman
Forty years dead, and an idiot, and only one of you
Decently quiet. There is the great and quiet water
Reaching to Asia, and in an hour or so
The still stars will show over it but I am quieter
Inside than even the ocean or the stars.
Though I have to kindle paper flares of passion
Sometimes, to fool you with. But I was thinking
Last night, that people all over the world
Are doing much worse and suffering much more than we
This wartime, and the stars don't wink, and the ocean
Storms perhaps less than usual." Then the dead woman,
"Wild life, she has touched the ice-core of things and learned
Something, that frost burns worse than fire." "O, it's not true,"
She answered, "frost is kind; why, almost nothing
You say is true. Helen, do you remember at all
The beauty and strangeness of this place? Old cypresses
The sailor wind works into deep-sea knots
A thousand years; age-reddened granite
That was the world's cradle and crumbles apieces
Now that we're all grown up, breaks out at the roots;
And underneath it the old gray-granite strength
Is neither glad nor sorry to take the seas
Of all the storms forever and stand as firmly
As when the red hawk wings of the first dawn
Streamed up the sky over it: there is one more beautiful thing,
Water that owns the north and west and south
And is all colors and never is all quiet,

And the fogs are its breath and float along the branches of the cypresses.
And I forgot the coals of ruby lichen
That glow in the fog on the old twigs. To live here
Seventy-five years or eighty, and have children,
And watch these things fill up their eyes, would not
Be a bad life . . . I'd rather be what I am,
Feeling this peace and joy, the fire's joy's burning,
And I have my peace." Then the old man in the dull
And heartless voice answered, "The strangest thing
Is that He never speaks: we know we are damned, why should He speak?
The book
Is written already. Cauldwell, Cauldwell, Cauldwell, Cauldwell.
Eternal death, eternal wrath, eternal torture, eternity, eternity, eternity . . .
That's after the judgment." "You needn't have any fear, old father,
Of anything to happen after to-morrow," Tamar answered, "we have turned
every page
But the last page, and now our paper's so worn out and tissuey I can read it
already
Right through the leaf, print backwards."

It was twilight in the room, the
shiny side of the wheel
Dipping toward Asia; and the year dipping toward winter encrimsoned the
grave spokes of sundown;
And jingling in the door Lee Cauldwell with the day's-death flush upon his
face: "Father:
There are marks on the cypress: a hell of a way to send your soldier off: I
want to talk to her
Alone. You and the women— " he flung his hand out, meaning "go." The
old man without speaking
Moved to the door, propping his weakness on a chair and on the
door-frame, and Lee entering

Passed him and the two women followed him—three, if Stella were one—
but when they had passed the doorway
Old Cauldwell turned, and tottering in it: "Death is the horror," he said,
"nothing else lasts, pain passes,
Death's the only trap. I am much too wise to swing myself in the stable on
a rope from a rafter. Helen, Helen,
You know about death." "It is cold," she answered from the hallway;
"unspeakably hopeless . . ." "You curse of talkers,
Go," he said, and he shut the door against them and said, "Slut, how many,
how many?" She, laughing,
"I knew you would be sweet to me: I am still sick: did you find marks in
the bark? I am still sick, Lee;
You don't intend killing me?" "Flogging, whipping, whipping, is there
anything male about here
You haven't used yet? Agh you mouth, you open mouth. But I won't touch
you." "Let me say something,"
She answered, standing dark against the west in the window, the death of
the winter rose of evening
Behind her little high-poised head, and threading the brown twilight of the
room with the silver
Exultance of her voice, "My brother can you feel how happy I am but how
far off too?
If I have done wrong it has turned good to me, I could almost be sorry that
I have to die now
Out of such freedom; if I were standing back of the evening crimson on a
mountain in Asia
All the fool shames you can whip up into a filth of words would not be
farther off me,
Nor any fear of anything, if I stood in the evening star and saw this dusty
dime's worth
A dot of light, dropped up the star-gleam. Poor brother, poor brother, you
played the fool too

But not enough, it is not enough to taste delight and passion and disgust
and loathing
And agony, you have to be wide alive, 'an open mouth' you said, all the
while, to reach this heaven
You'll never grow up to. Though it's possible if I'd let you go asoldiering,
there on the dunghills
Of death and fire . . . ah, you'd taste nothing even there but the officers'
orders, beef and brandy,
And the tired bodies of a few black-eyed French dance-girls: it is better for
you
To be lost here than there." "You are up in the evening star," he said, "you
can't feel this," flat-handed
Striking her cheek, "you are up on a mountain in Asia, who made you
believe that you could keep me
Or let me go? I am going to-morrow, to-night I set the house in order."
"There is nothing now
You can be sorry for," she answered, "not even this, it is out of the count,
the cup ran over
Yesterday." He turned and left the room, the foolish tune of the spurs
tinkled
Hallway and stair. Tamar, handling the fiery spot upon her cheek smiled in
the darkness,
Feeling so sure of the end. "Night after night he has ridden to the granite
at the rivermouth
And missed my light, to-night he will see it, the Lobos star he called it, and
look and look to be sure
It is not a ship's light nor a star's, there in the south, then he will come, and
my three lovers
Under one roof."

VII

Lee Cauldwell felt his way in the dark among the cypress trees, and turning
At the stable door saw the evening star, he felt for the lantern
Hung on the bent nail to the right of the door,
Lighted it, and in the sweet hay-dusty darkness
Found the black quirt that hung beside the saddle
And seemed a living snake in the hand, then he opened
A locker full of hunter's gear and tumbled
Leather and iron to the floor for an old sheath-knife
Under all the rest; he took the knife and whip
And Tamar in the dark of the westward bedroom heard him
Tinkle on the stair and jingle in the hall, slow steps
Moving to hers, the room that had been her room
Before this illness; she felt him as if she had been there
Lighting her lamp and setting it on the sill,
Then felt him look about the little room and feel it
Breathing and warm with her once habitancy
And the hours of hers and his there, and soften almost
To childish tears at trifles on the wall;
And then he would look at the bed and stiffen
In a brittle rage, feel with thrust under-lip
Virtuous, an outcrop of morality in him
To grow ridiculous and wish to be cruel,
And so return to her. Hastily, without light,
She redded up some of the room's untidiness,
Thrust into the stove the folds of bandage-cloth,
Straightened the bed a little, and laying aside
The loose blue robe lay down in the bed to await him,
Who, throwing open the door, "Tamar: I've got no right
To put my hands into your life, I see
That each of us lives only a little while

And must do what he can with it: so, I'm going
To-night; I'd nearly worked myself to the act
Of some new foolishness: are you there, Tamar?
The lamp?" He struck a match and saw her eyes
Shine on him from the pillow and when the lamp
Was lighted he began again: "It's all such foolishness.
Well, you and I are done. I set your lamp for a signal on the sill,
I'll take it away or help you to that room,
Whichever you like. That'll be my last hand in the game.
It won't take me ten minutes to pack and go, my plan's
Not to risk losing temper and have half decent
Thoughts of you while I'm gone, and you of me, Tamar."
She lay too quietly and the shining eyes
Seemed not to hide amusement, he waited for her
To acknowledge not in direct words perhaps
His generosity, but she silent, "Well, shall I leave the lamp?"
He said, not all so kindly, and Tamar, "I've no one else
If you are going. But if you'd stay I wouldn't
Touch you again, ever. Agh you can't wait
To get to France to crawl into strange beds,
But Monterey to-night. You—what a beast.
You like them dirty." He said, "You're a fool, Tamar.
Well, so I'll leave the lamp. Good-bye, Tamar."
"You said you'd help me down the hall." "Yes, even that.
What must I do, carry you?" "Is the bed together?
See whether there are sheets and covers on it."
He went, and returned icy-pale. "It hasn't been changed
Since I smelled fire and ran into the room
Six or eight days ago. The cupboard door-frame
Is all charcoal. By God, Tamar,
If I believed he'd done it—who is he, Andrews?—
You and your lies have made a horror in the house.

What, shall I go, shall I go?" "Me? who made *me*
Believe that I could keep you or let you go,
Didn't you say?" "You still believe it," he answered,
Doubling his fists to hold in anger, the passionate need
Of striking her like a torrent in his throat,
"Believe it, fool." "Poor brother. You will never see France,
Never wear uniform nor learn how to fasten
A bayonet to a gun-barrel." "Come. Stop talking.
Get up, come to your room." "Carry me," she answered.
"Though I am not really much too tired to walk.
You used to like me." "Well, to get done and be gone,"
He said, bending above her, she enlaced his neck
Softly and strongly and raised her knees to let
His arm slip under them, he like a man stung by a serpent
Felt weakness and then rage, panted to lift her
And staggered in the doorway and in the dark hallway
Grew dizzy, and difficultly went on and groaning
Dropped her on the bed in her own room, she did not move
To cover herself, then he drawing his palm
Across his forehead found it streaming wet
And said, "You whore, you whore, you whore. Well, you shall have it,
You've earned it," and he twisted himself to the little table
And took the whip, the oiled black supple quirt,
Loaded at the handle, that seemed a living snake in the hand,
And felt the exasperate force of his whole baffled
And blindfold life flow sideways into the shoulder
Swinging it, and half repenting while it dropped
Sickened to see the beautiful bare white
Blemishless body writhe under it before it fell,
The loins pressed into the bed, the breast and head
Twisting erect, and at the noise of the stroke
He made a hoarse cry in his throat but she

Took it silently, and lay still afterward,
Her head so stricken backward that the neck
Seemed strained to breaking, the coppery pad of her hair
Crushed on the shoulder-blades, while that red snake-trail
Swelled visibly from the waist and flank down the left thigh.
"O God, God, God," he groaned; and she, her whole body
Twitching on the white bed whispered between her teeth
"It was in the bargain," and from her bitten lip
A trickle of blood ran down to the pillow.

That one light in the room,
The lamp on the sill, did not turn redder for blood nor with the whip-stripe
But shone serene and innocent up the northward night, writing a long pale-golden track
In the river's arm of sea, and beyond the river's mouth where the old lion's teeth of blunted granite
Crop out of the headland young Will Andrews kissed it with his eyes, rode south and crossed the river's
Late-summer sand-lock. Figures of fire moved in the hills on the left, the pasture-fires and brush-fires
Men kindle before rain, on a southerly wind the smell of the smoke reached him, the sea on his right
Breathed; when he skirted the darkness of the gum-tree grove at San Jose creek-mouth he remembered
Verdugo killed there; Sylvia Vierra and her man had lived in the little white-washed farm-hut
Under the surf-reverberant blue-gums; two years ago they had had much wine in the house, their friend
Verdugo came avisiting, he being drunk on the raw plenty of wine they thought abused

Nine-year-old Mary, Sylvia's daughter, they struck him from behind and when he was down unmanned him
With the kitchen knife, then plotted drunkenly—for he seemed to be dead—where to dispose the body.
That evening Tamar Cauldwell riding her white pony along the coast-road saw a great bonfire
Perilling the gum-tree grove, and riding under the smoke met evil odors, turning in there
Saw by the firelight a man's feet hang out of the fire; then Tamar never having suffered
Fear in her life, knocked at the hut's door and unanswered entered, and found the Vierras asleep
Steaming away their wine, but little Mary weeping. She had taken the child and ridden homeward.
Young Andrews thinking of that idyll of the country gulped at the smoke from the hills and tethered
His horse in the hiding of a clump of pines, and climbed the line-fence.

Turning a cypress thicket
He saw a figure sway in the starlight, and stood still, breathless. A woman: Tamar? Not Tamar:
No one he knew: it faced the east gables of the house and seemed twisting its hands and suddenly
Flung up both arms to its face and passed out of the patch of starlight. The boy, troubled and cautious,
Turned the other way and circling to the south face of the house peered from behind the buttressed
Base of a seventy-year-old trunk that yellow light on the other side clothed, and he saw
A lamp on the table and three people sitting by it; the old man, stiff-jointed as a corpse,

Grotesquely erect, and old Aunt Stella her lips continually in motion, and old Jinny
Cross-legg'd having drawn up her ankles into her chair, nodding asleep. At length Aunt Stella
Ceased talking, none of the three stirred. Young Andrews backed into the wood and warily finishing
His circuit stood in the darkness under Tamar's window. The strong young tree to help him to it
Still wore on its boughs her lamplight, then he climbed and set his hands on the sill, his feet on the ledge
Under it, and Tamar came to the window and took up the lamp to let him enter. Her face
White in the yellow lamp's glow, with sharp shadows under the eyes and a high look of joy
He had never seen there frightened him, and she said, "I have been sick, you know." "I heard," he answered,
"O Tamar, I have been lonely. We must let them know, we can't go on, my place is with you
When you most need me." "We will tell them to-night," she said, and kissed his mouth and called, "Lee, Lee,
Come. He has come." "What? Now?" he said. "I have told Lee. I was sick, he was sorry for me, he is going
To camp to-morrow, he wants to see you and say good-bye." Lee entered while she spoke and quietly
Held out his hand and Andrews took it. "Talk to each other," Tamar said, "I am very tired
And must lie down." Lee muttered "She's been awfully sick, it scared us, you were lucky, Bill Andrews,
Not to be here." "I didn't think so," he answered, "what was it, Lee?" "Well, it's all over," Lee said
Shifting his feet, "I'm off to-morrow. I'm glad we're friends to say good-bye. Be good to her, won't you."

And the other, "O God knows I will. All I can do. But of course . . . Lee . . . if they need me
She knows I won't beg off because I'm . . . married . . . maybe I'll see you over there." "O," said Tamar
Laughing, "you too?" and she sat up on the bed saying, "Lee: go and call father if he's able.
We ought to tell him, he ought to meet my—husband." "I'll see if he can," Lee answered, "he was unwell
To-day, and if he's in bed . . ." He left the room, then Tamar: "Look. Bring the lamp. What Lee did to me."
She opened the blue robe and bared her flank and thigh showing the long whip-mark. "I have a story.
You must see this to believe it." He turned giddy, the sweet slenderness
Dazzling him, and the lamp shook in his hand, for the sharp spasm of physical pain one feels
At sight of a wound shot up his entrails. That long welt of red on the tender flesh, the blood-flecks
And tortured broken little channels of blood crossing it. "Tamar, Tamar!" "Put down the lamp,
And when they come I'll tell you the story." "What shall I do?" "Why, nothing, nothing. Poor boy," she said
Pityingly, "I think you are too glad of your life to have come
Into this house, you are not hard enough, you are like my mother, only stone or fire
Should marry into this house." Then he bewildered looking at the blackened door-frame, "Why yes,"
Laughed Tamar, "it is here, it has been here, the bridegroom's here already. O Will I have suffered . . .
Things I daren't tell." "What do you mean, Tamar?" "Nothing, I mustn't tell you, you are too high-tempered,
You would do something. Dear, there are things so wicked that nothing you can do can make them better,

So horrible now they are done that even to touch or try to mend or punish
them is only to widen
Horror: like poking at a corpse in a pool. And father's old and helpless."
"Your father, Tamar?"
"And not to blame. I think he hardly even knew what Lee— " "Lee?" "This
much I'll tell you,
You have to know it . . . our love, your love and mine, had . . . fruit,
would have been fruitful, we were going to have
A child, and I was happy and frightened, and it is dead. O God, O God, O
God, I wish
I too had been born too soon and died with the eyes unopened, not a cry,
darkness, darkness,
And to be hidden away. They did it to me; with other abuse, worse
violence." Meanwhile Lee Cauldwell
Finding his father with the two old women in the room down-stairs,
"Father," he said,
"Tamar was asking for you . . ." and Helen's voice through old Aunt Stella
answered, "She has enough,
Tell her she has enough." "Aunt Stella," he said, "how long will you keep it
up? Our trouble's clearing,
Let your ghosts be." "She has you and the other," she answered, "let me
have this one. Are we buzzards to quarrel
Over you dead, we ghosts?" Then Lee turning his shoulder at her, "You
must come up, father.
Do you remember the Andrews place that's up the valley? Young Andrews
is up-stairs with Tamar,
He wants to marry her. You know I have to go away to-morrow,
remember? and I'll go happier
To leave her . . . taken care of. So you'll see him, father?" "Who is it?"
asked the old man. "The bridegroom,"
Said Helen's voice, "a bridegroom for your Tamar, and the priest will be
fire and blood the witness,

And they will live together in a house where the mice are moles." "Why do you plague me," he answered
Plaintively, and Lee: "Come, father," and he lifting his face, "I have prayed to the hills to come and cover me,
We are on the drop-off cliff of the world and dare not meet Him, I with two days to live, even I
Shall watch the ocean boiling and the sea curl up like paper in a fire and the dry bed
Crack to the bottom: I have good news for her, I will see her." "And I to tell her she may take
Two but not three," said Helen. "Stay here, stay here, be quiet," Lee answered angrily, "can I take up
The whole menagerie, raving?" He turned in the door and heard his father move behind him and said,
"If you come up be quiet," and at the door up-stairs, "Father is tired and sick, he'll only
Speak to you, Andrews, and must go to bed; he's worried about my going away to-morrow.
This is Bill Andrews, father." And Tamar coming to the door, "Let him come in, it's dark here,
No, bring him in. Father come in. What, shall the men that made your war suck up their millions,
Not I my three?" Then Andrews: "If Tamar is well enough to go to-night I will take her to-night.
You will be well when you are out of this house." "You hate it still," said Tamar. "He hates the house,"
She said to Lee, leading his eyes with the significance in hers to the blackened door-frame,
"Well, I will go with you to-morrow." And Lee, "Listen, Will Andrews, I heard from somebody
You know who set the fire here." "No, not that," he answered, "but I know other worse things

That have been done here." "Fire, fire," moaned the old man, "the fire of the Lord coming in judgment. Tamar,
It is well with us, be happy, He won't torture the wicked, He will rub them out and suddenly
With instant fire. We shall be nothing." "Come, Tamar," Andrews cried, "to-night. I daren't leave you."
"For fear I ask her," said Lee. "You did it, then. You set the fire." "No, that's too idiot
A lie to answer," he said, "what do I know about your fires? I know something
Worse than arson. And saw the horrible new scar of a whip
Not to be paid—this way!" He felt the jerk of his arm striking
And his fist hitting the sharp edge of the jawbone, but yet
When Lee staggered and closed in with a groan,
Clutching him, fumbling for his throat, Will thought "What a fool
To make a nasty show of us before Tamar
And the others, why does he want to fight?" and indignantly
Pushed him off and struck twice, both fists, Lee dropped
And scrabbled on hands and knees by the little table.
Then the old man cried, "We shall be nothing, nothing.
O but that's frightful."
And Will turning to Tamar saw such hatred
Wrinkle her face he felt a horrible surge
Of nausea in him, then with bare teeth she smiled at him
And he believed the hate was for her brother
And said, "Ah Tamar, come." Meanwhile the Helen
That spoke out of the lungs and ran in the nerves
Of old Aunt Stella caught the old man David Cauldwell
By the loose flapping sleeve and the lean arm,
Saying in a clotted amorous voice, "Come, David,
My brother, my lover, O honey come, she has no eyes for you,
She feasts on young men. But you to me, to me,

Are as beautiful as when we dared
Desperate pleasure, naked, ages ago,
In the room and by the sea." "Father," said Tamar,
"It is only an hour to the end, whom do you want
To-night? Stay here by me." "I was hunting for something," said Lee
    Cauldwell,
"Here it is, here it is," and had the sheath-knife bared
And struck up from the floor, rising, the blade
Ripped cloth and skin along his enemy's belly
And the leather belt catching it deflected the point
Into the bowels, Andrews coughed and fell backward
And Lee falling across him stabbed at his throat
But struck too high and opened the right cheek,
The knife scraping on bone and teeth, then Tamar
In a sea-gull voice, "I dreamed it in his face,
I dreamed a T cut in his face— " "You and your dreams
Have done for us," Lee groaned answer. "Akh, all blood, blood.
What did you say to make him hit me?"

Though it is not thought
That the dead intervene between the minds
And deeds of the living, that they are witnesses,
If anything of their spirits with any memory
Survive and not in prison, would seem as likely
As that an exile should look longingly home:
And the mist-face of that mother at the window
Wavering was but a witness, could but watch,
Neither prevent nor cause: no doubt there are many
Such watchers in the world: the same whom Andrews,
Stepping like a thief among the cypress clumps an hour before
Saw twist her hands and suddenly fling up both vaporous arms and sway out
    of the starlight,

She now was watching at the down-stairs window
Old Jinny alone in the room, and saw, as the dead see, the thoughts
More clearly than the cloth and skin; the child mind
In that old flesh gathered home on itself
In coils, laboring to warm a memory,
And worked on by an effluence, petulantly pushing away
The easier memories of its open time
Forty years back, power flowing from someone in that house
Belting it in, pressing it to its labor,
Making it shape in itself the memory of to-day's
Vision, the watcher saw it, how could she know it
Or know from whence? a girl naked, no, wrapped in fire,
Filmed in white sheets of fire. "Why, I'm like God,"
Old Jinny had said, "I see through walls," a girl
Naked though clothed in fire, and under the arms
Naked, no hair, — "Ah to be like her, to be like her, probably
Cloth, hair, burned off": displaying herself before a wild old man
Who appeared part of the joy: "Ah to be like her,
Fire is so sweet, they never let me play with it,
No one loves Jinny, wouldn't fire be a father
And hold her in his arms? Fire is so sweet,"
She hovered the hot lamp, "sweet fire, sweet light,"
She held a rag of paper above it, "O dear, dear fire,
Come and kiss Jinny, no one's looking,
Jinny's alone. Dear star, dear light, O lovely fire
Won't you come out, why is it turning black,
Ah come, Ah come, hug Jinny." The hungry beautiful bird
Hopped from its bird-cage to her. "I've got my star,
Ah love, Ah love, and here's more paper
And a little of Jinny's dress, love, lovely light,
Jinny so loves you, Jinny's baby, Jinny's baby,
O," she screamed, "Oo, Oo, Oo," and ran to the window, folded

In a terrible wreath, and at her side the curtains
Danced into flame, and over her head; the gasp
That followed on a cry drew down a sword
Of flame to her lungs, pain ceased, and thinking "Father"
She dropped herself into the arms of the fire,
Huddling under the sill, and her spirit unprisoned
Filled all the room and felt a nuptial joy
In mixing with the bright and eager flame.
While from that blackened morsel on the floor
Fire spread to the wall and gnawed it through, and the window-glass
Crackling and tinkling a rush of south wind fed
The eagerness in the house. They heard up-stairs
That brutal arch of crying, the quick crescendo,
The long drop and the following moan, Will Andrews
Struggled to rise and like a gopher-snake that a child
Has mashed the head of with a stone, he waggled
The blood-clot of his head over the floor
Gulping "You devils, you devils." Lee would have run down
But Tamar clung to him, the old man on his knees
Muttered to God, and old Aunt Stella
In no voice but her own screamed, screamed. Then fire
Was heard roaring, the door leaked threads of smoke,
Lee caught up Tamar in his arms and turned
To the window, the cypress-ladder, but his first step,
Blind, with the burden in his arms, the smoke in his eyes,
Trampled his murdered man on the floor who turning
Caught the other ankle and Lee went down and Tamar
So lovingly wound him that he could not rise
Till the house was full of its bright death; then Tamar:
"I will not let you take me. Go if you want."
He answered, "You devil, shall I go?" "You wouldn't stay!

Think of your black-eyed French girls." "We are on the edge of it," he
answered,
"Tamar, be decent for a minute." "I have my three lovers
Here in one room, none of them will go out,
How can I help being happy? This old man
Has prayed the end of the world onto us all,
And which of you leaves me?" Then the old man: "O what mountain,
What mountain, what mountain?" And Lee, "Father. The window.
We'll follow you." But he kneeling would not rise,
While the house moved and the floor sagged to the south
And old Aunt Stella through the opening door
Ran into the red and black, and did not scream
Any more; then Tamar, "Did you think you would go
Laughing through France?" And the old man, "Fierce, fierce light,
Have pity, Christ have pity, Christ have pity, Christ have pity,
Christ have pity,
Christ have pity . . ."
And Tamar with her back to the window embraced
Her brother, who struggled toward it, but the floor
Turned like a wheel.

Grass grows where the flame flowered;
A hollowed lawn strewn with a few black stones
And the brick of broken chimneys; all about there
The old trees, some of them scarred with fire, endure the sea-wind.

POINT JOE

Point Joe has teeth and has torn ships; it has fierce and solitary beauty;
Walk there all day you shall see nothing that will not make part of a poem.

I saw the spars and planks of shipwreck on the rocks, and beyond the desolate
Sea-meadows rose the warped wind-bitten van of the pines, a fog-bank vaulted

Forest and all, the flat sea-meadows at that time of year were plated
Golden with the low flower called footsteps of the spring, millions of flowerets,

Whose light suffused upward into the fog flooded its vault, we wandered
Through a weird country where the light beat up from earthward, and was golden.

One other moved there, an old Chinaman gathering seaweed from the sea-rocks,
He brought it in his basket and spread it flat to dry on the edge of the meadow.

Permanent things are what is needful in a poem, things temporally
Of great dimension, things continually renewed or always present.

Grass that is made each year equals the mountains in her past and future;
Fashionable and momentary things we need not see nor speak of.

Man gleaning food between the solemn presences of land and ocean,
On shores where better men have shipwrecked, under fog and among flowers,

Equals the mountains in his past and future; that glow from the earth was only
A trick of nature's, one must forgive nature a thousand graceful subtleties.

GALE IN APRIL

Intense and terrible beauty, how has our race with the frail naked nerves,
So little a craft swum down from its far launching?
Why now, only because the northwest blows and the headed grass billows,
Great seas jagging the west and on the granite
Blanching, the vessel is brimmed, this dancing play of the world is too much passion.
A gale in April so overfilling the spirit,
Though his ribs were thick as the earth's, arches of mountain, how shall one dare to live,
Though his blood were like the earth's rivers and his flesh iron,
How shall one dare to live? One is born strong, how do the weak endure it?
The strong lean upon death as on a rock,
After eighty years there is shelter and the naked nerves shall be covered with deep quietness,
O beauty of things go on, go on, O torture
Of intense joy I have lasted out my time, I have thanked God and finished,
Roots of millennial trees fold me in the darkness,
Northwest wind shake their tops, not to the root, not to the root, I have passed
From beauty to the other beauty, peace, the night splendor.

POINT PINOS AND POINT LOBOS

I

A lighthouse and a graveyard and gaunt pines
Not old, no tree lives long here, where the northwind
Has forgot mercy. All night the light blinks north,
The Santa Cruz mountain redwoods hate its flashing,
The night of the huge western water takes it,
The long rays drown a little off shore, hopelessly
Attempting distance, hardly entering the ocean.
The lighthouse, and the gaunt boughs of the pines,
The carved gray stones, and the people of the graves.

They came following the sun, here even the sun is bitter,
A scant gray heartless light down wind, glitter and sorrow,
The northwind fog much kindlier. When shall these dead arise,
What day stand up from the earth among the broken pines?
A God rearisen will raise them up, this walking shadow?
Which tortured trunk will you choose, Lord, to be hewn to a cross?
I am not among the mockers Master, I am one of your lovers,
Ah weariest spirit in all the world, we all have rest
Being dead but you still strive, nearly two thousand years
You have wrestled for us against God, were you not conquered
At the first close, when the long horrible nails went home
Between the slender bones of the hands and feet, you frightfully
Heightened above man's stature saw the hateful crowd
Shift and sicken below, the sunburnt legionaries
Draw back out of the blood-drops . . . Far off the city
Slid on its hill, the eyes fainting. The earth was shaken
And the sun hid, you were not quieted. Men may never
Have seen you as they said in the inner room of the house,

Nor met you on the dusty suburb road toward Emmaus,
But nine years back you stood in the Alps and wept for Europe,
To-day pale ghost you walk among the tortured pines
Between the graves here and the sea.

Ah but look seaward,
For here where the land's charm dies love's chain falls loose, and the freedom of the eyes and the fervor of the spirit
Sea-hawks wander the huge gray water, alone in a nihilist simplicity, cleaner than the primal
Wings of the brooding of the dove on the waste of the waters beginning, perplexed with creation; but ours
Turned from creation, returned from the beauty of things to the beauty of nothing, to a nihilist simplicity,
Content with two elements, the wave and the cloud, and if one were not there then the other were lovelier to turn to,
And if neither . . . O shining of night, O eloquence of silence, the mother of the stars, the beauty beyond beauty,
The sea that the stars and the sea and the mountain bones of the earth and men's souls are the foam on, the opening
Of the womb of that ocean.

You have known this, you have known peace, and forsaken
Peace for pity, you have known the beauty beyond beauty
And the other shore of God. You will never again know them,
Except he slay you, the spirit at last, as more than once
The body, and root out love. Is it for this you wander
Tempting him through the thickets of the wolvish world?
O a last time in the last wrench of man made godlike
Shall God not rise, bitterly, the power behind power, the last star
That the stars hide, rise and reveal himself in anger—

Christ, in that moment when the hard loins of your ancient
Love and unconquerable will crack to lift up humanity
The last step heavenward — rise and slay, and you and our children
Suddenly stumble on peace? The oceans we shall have tamed then
Will dream between old rocks having no master, the earth
Forget corn, dreaming her own precious weeds and free
Forests, from the rivers upward; our tributary planets
Tamed like the earth, the morning star and the many-mooned
Three-belted giant, and those red sands of Mars between them,
Rust off the metal links of human conquest, the engines
Rust in the fields, and under that old sun's red waning
Nothing forever remember us.

And you at peace then
Not walk by a lighthouse on a wild north foreland
Choosing which trunk of the poor wind-warped pines
Will hew to a cross, and your eye's envy searching
The happiness of these bleak burials. Unhappy brother
That high imagination mating mine
Has gazed deeper than graves: is it unendurable
To know that the huge season and wheel of things
Turns on itself forever, the new stars pass
And the old return and find out their old places,
And these gray dead infallibly shall arise
In the very flesh . . . But first the camel bells
Tinkle into Bethlehem, the men from the east
Gift you sweet-bedded between Mary's breasts,
And no one in the world has thought of Golgotha.

II

Gray granite ridges over swinging pits of sea, pink stone-crop spangles
Stick in the stone, the stiff plates of the cypress-boughs divide the sea's breath,
Hard green cutting soft gray . . . I know the uplands
And windy pastures where the great globes of the oaks are like green planets
Each in his place; I know the scents and resonances of desolate hills,
The wide-winged shadows of the vultures wandering across them; and I have visited
Deserts and many-colored rocks . . . mountains I know
From the Dent d'Oche in Savoy and that peak of the south past St. Gingolphe
To Grayback and Tahoma . . . as for sea-borderers
The caverned Norman cliffs north of the Seine's mouth, the Breton sea-heads, the Cornish
Horns of their west had known me as a child before I knew Point Dume or Pinos
Or Sur, the sea-light in his forehead: also I heard my masters
Speak of Pelorum head and the Attic rocks of Sunium, or that Nymphaean
Promontory under the holy mountain Athos, a warren of monks
Walls in with prayer-cells of old stone, perpetual incense and religion
Smoke from it up to him who is greater than they guess, through what huge emptiness
And chasms above the stars seeking out one who is here already, and neither
Ahunting nor asleep nor in love; and Actium and the Acroceraunian
And Chersonese abutments of Greek ridges on the tideless wave
They named, my spirit has visited . . . there is no place
Taken like this out of deep Asia for a marriage-token, this planted
Asiaward over the west water. Our race nor the great springs we draw from,

Not any race of Europe, nor the Syrian blood from south of Lebanon
Our fathers drank and mixed with ours, has known this place nor its like
nor suffered
The air of its religion. The elder shapes and shows in extreme Asia,
Like remote mountains over immeasurable water, half seen, thought clouds,
Of God in the huge world from the Altai eagle-peaks and Mongol pastures
To the home of snow no wing inhabits, temples of height on earth,
Gosainthan
And Gaurisankar north of Ganges, Nanda Devi a mast of the ship
We voyage upon among the stars; and the earth-sprung multitudes of India,
Where human bodies grow like weeds out of the earth, and life is nothing,
There is so much life, and like the people the divinities of the people
Swarm, and the vulgar worship; thence far east to the islands of this ocean
Our sun is buried in, theirs born of, to the noble slope of the lone peak
Over Suruga Bay, and the headlands of Hai-nan: God without name,
God without form, the Lord of Asia, is here as there.

Serenely smiling
Face of the godlike man made God, who tore the web of human passions
As a yellow lion the antelope-hunter's net, and freeing himself made free
All who could follow, the tissue of new births and deaths dissolved away
from him,
He reunited with the passionless light sky, not again to suffer
The shame of the low female gate, freed, never to be born again,
Whom Maha Maya bore in the river garden, the Himalayan barrier
northward
Bounding the world: is it freedom, smile of the Buddha, surely freedom?
For someone
Whispered into my ear when I was very young, some serpent whispered
That what has gone returns; what has been, is; what will be, was; the future
Is a farther past; our times he said fractions of arcs of the great circle;

And the wheel turns, nothing shall stop it nor destroy it, we are bound on
the wheel,
We and the stars and seas, the mountains and the Buddha. Weary tidings
To cross the weary, bitter to bitter men: life's conqueror will not fear
Life; and to meditate again under the sacred tree, and again
Vanquish desire will be no evil.

The evening opens
Enormous wings out of the west, the sad red splendid light beats upward
These granite gorges, the wind-battered cypress trees blacken above them,
The divine image of my dream smiles his immortal peace, commanding
This old sea-garden, crumble of granite and old buttressed cypress trunks,
And the burnt place where that wild girl whose soul was fire died with her
house.

III

I have spoken on sea-forelands with the lords of life, the men wisdom made
Gods had nothing
So wise to tell me nor so sweet as the alternation of white sunlight and
brown night,
The beautiful succession of the breeding springs, the enormous rhythm of
the stars' deaths
And fierce renewals: O why were you rebellious, teachers of men, against
the instinctive God,
One striving to overthrow his ordinances through love and the other
crafty-eyed to escape them
Through patient wisdom: though you are wiser than all men you are
foolisher than the running grass,
That fades in season and springs up in season, praising whom you blame.

For the essence
and the end
Of his labor is beauty, for goodness and evil are two things and still variant,
but the quality of life as of death and of light
As of darkness is one, one beauty, the rhythm of that Wheel, and who can
behold it is happy and will praise it to the people.

THE TORCH-BEARERS' RACE

Here is the world's end. When our fathers forded the first river in Asia we crossed the world's end;
And when the North Sea throbbed under their keels, the world's end;
And when the Atlantic surge rolled English oak in the sea-trough: always there was farther to go,
A new world piecing out the old one: but ours, our new world?
Dark and enormous rolls the surf; down on the mystical tide-line under the cliffs at moonset
Dead tribes move, remembering the scent of their hills, the lost hunters
Our fathers hunted; they driven westward died the sun's death, they dread the depth and hang at the land's hem,
And are unavenged; frail ghosts, and ghostlike in their lives too,
Having only a simple hunger for all our complication of desires. Dark and enormous
Rolls the surf of the far storms of the heart of the ocean;
The old granite breaks into white torches the heavy-shouldered children of the wind . . . our ancient wanderings
West from the world's birth what sea-bound breaking shall flame up torchlike?
I am building a thick stone pillar upon this shore, the very turn of the world, the long migration's
End; the sun goes on but we have come up to an end.
We have climbed at length to a height, to an end, this end: shall we go down again to Mother Asia?
Some of us will go down, some will abide, but we sought
More than to return to a mother. This huge, inhuman, remote, unruled, this ocean will show us
The inhuman road, the unruled attempt, the remote lode-star.
The torch-bearers' race: it is run in a dusk; when the emptied racer drops unseen at the end of his course

A fresh hand snatches the hilt of the light, the torch flies onward
Though the man die. Not a runner knows where the light was lighted, not a runner knows where it carries fire to,
Hand kisses hand in the dark, the torch passes, the man
Falls, and the torch passes. It gleamed across Euphrates mud, shone on Nile shore, it lightened
The little homely Ionian water and the sweet Aegean.
O perfect breathing of the runners, those narrow courses, names like the stars' names, Sappho, Alcaeus,
And Aeschylus a name like the first eagle's; but the torch westering
The seas widened, the earth's bloom hardened, the stone rose Rome seeding the earth, but the torch northering
Lightened the Atlantic . . . O flame, O beauty and shower of beauty,
There is yet one ocean and then no more, God whom you shine to walks there naked, on the final Pacific,
Not in a man's form.

The torch answered: Have I kindled a morning?
For again, this old world's end is the gate of a world fire-new, of your wild future, wild as a hawk's dream,
Ways hung on nothing, like stars, feet shaking earth off; that long way
Was a labor in a dream, will you wake now? The eaglets rustle in the aerie, the red eyes of dawn stabbing up through the nest-side,
You have walked in a dream, consumed with your fathers and your mothers, you have loved
Inside the four walls of humanity, passions turned inward, incestuous desires and a fighting against ghosts, but the clarions
Of light have called morning.

What, not to be tangled any more in the blinding
Rays of reflected desire, the man with the woman, the woman with the child, the daughter with the father, but freed

Of the web self-woven, the burning and the blistering strands running
inward?
Those rays to be lightened awide, to shine up the star-path, subduing the
world outward? Oh chicks in the high nest be fledged now,
Having found out flight in the air to make wing to the height, fierce
eye-flames
Of the eaglets be strengthened, to drink of the fountain of the beauty of
the sun of the stars, and to gaze in his face, not a father's,
And motherless and terrible and here.

But I at the gate, I falling
On the gate-sill add this: When the ancient wisdom is folded like a
wine-stained cloth and laid up in darkness,
And the old symbols forgotten, in the glory of that your hawk's dream
Remember that the life of mankind is like the life of a man, a flutter from
darkness to darkness
Across the bright hair of a fire, so much of the ancient
Knowledge will not be annulled. What unimaginable opponent to end you?

There
is one fountain
Of power, yours and that last opponent's, and of long peace.

THE TREASURE

Mountains, a moment's earth-waves rising and hollowing; the earth too's an ephemerid; the stars—
Short-lived as grass the stars quicken in the nebula and dry in their summer, they spiral
Blind up space, scattered black seeds of a future; nothing lives long, the whole sky's
Recurrences tick the seconds of the hours of the ages of the gulf before birth, and the gulf
After death is like dated: to labor eighty years in a notch of eternity is nothing too tiresome,
Enormous repose after, enormous repose before, the flash of activity.
Surely you never have dreamed the incredible depths were prologue and epilogue merely
To the surface play in the sun, the instant of life, what is called life? I fancy
That silence is the thing, this noise a found word for it; interjection, a jump of the breath at that silence;
Stars burn, grass grows, men breathe: as a man finding treasure says "Ah!" but the treasure's the essence;
Before the man spoke it was there, and after he has spoken he gathers it, inexhaustible treasure.

II

Roan Stallion

1924-1925

GRANITE AND CYPRESS

White-maned, wide-throated, the heavy-shouldered children of the wind
  leap at the sea-cliff.
The invisible falcon
Brooded on water and bred them in wide waste places, in a bride-chamber
  wide to the stars' eyes
In the center of the ocean,
Where no prows pass nor island is lifted . . . the sea beyond Lobos is
  whitened with the falcon's
Passage, he is here now,
The sky is one cloud, his wing-feathers hiss in the white grass, my sapling
  cypresses writhing
In the fury of his passage
Dare not dream of their centuries of future endurance of tempest. (I have
  granite and cypress,
Both long-lasting,
Planted in the earth; but the granite sea-bowlders are prey to no hawk's
  wing, they have taken worse pounding,
Like me they remember
Old wars and are quiet; for we think that the future is one piece with the
  past, we wonder why tree-tops
And people are so shaken.)

WOODROW WILSON
(February, 1924.)

It said "Come home, here is an end, a goal,
Not the one raced for, is it not better indeed? Victory you know requires
Force to sustain victory, the burden is never lightened, but final defeat
Buys peace: you have praised peace, peace without victory."

He said "It seems I am traveling no new way,
But leaving my great work unfinished how can I rest? I enjoyed a vision,
Endured betrayal, you must not ask me to endure final defeat,
Visionless men, blind hearts, blind mouths, live still."

It said "Yet perhaps your vision was less great
Than some you scorned, it has not proved even so practicable; Lenine
Enters this pass with less reluctance. As to betrayals: there are so many
Betrayals, the Russians and the Germans know."

He said "I knew I have enemies, I had not thought
To meet one at this brink: shall not the mocking voices die in the grave?"
It said "They shall. Soon there is silence." "I dreamed this end," he said, "when the prow
Of the long ship leaned against dawn, my people

Applauded me, and the world watched me. Again
I dreamed it at Versailles, the time I sent for the ship, and the obstinate foreheads
That shared with me the settlement of the world flinched at my threat and yielded.
That is all gone. . . . Do I remember this darkness?"

It said "No man forgets it but a moment.
The darkness before the mother, the depth of the return." "I thought," he answered,
"That I was drawn out of this depth to establish the earth on peace. My labor
Dies with me, why was I drawn out of this depth?"

It said "Loyal to your highest, sensitive, brave,
Sanguine, some few ways wise, you and all men are drawn out of this depth
Only to be these things you are, as flowers for color, falcons for swiftness,
Mountains for mass and quiet. Each for its quality

Is drawn out of this depth. Your tragic quality
Required the huge delusion of some major purpose to produce it.
What, that the God of the stars needed your help?" He said "This is my last
Worst pain, the bitter enlightenment that buys peace."

BIRDS

The fierce musical cries of a couple of sparrowhawks hunting on the headland,
Hovering and darting, their heads northwestward,
Prick like silver arrows shot through a curtain the noise of the ocean
Trampling its granite; their red backs gleam
Under my window around the stone corners; nothing gracefuller, nothing
Nimbler in the wind. Westward the wave-gleaners,
The old gray sea-going gulls are gathered together, the northwest wind wakening
Their wings to the wild spirals of the wind-dance.
Fresh as the air, salt as the foam, play birds in the bright wind, fly falcons
Forgetting the oak and the pinewood, come gulls
From the Carmel sands and the sands at the river-mouth, from Lobos and out of the limitless
Power of the mass of the sea, for a poem
Needs multitude, multitudes of thoughts, all fierce, all flesh-eaters, musically clamorous
Bright hawks that hover and dart headlong, and ungainly
Gray hungers fledged with desire of transgression, salt slimed beaks, from the sharp
Rock-shores of the world and the secret waters.

FOG

Invisible gulls with human voices cry in the sea-cloud
"There is room, wild minds,
Up high in the cloud; the web and the feather remember
Three elements, but here
Is but one, and the webs and the feathers
Subduing but the one
Are the greater, with strength and to spare." You dream, wild criers,
The peace that all life
Dreams gluttonously, the infinite self that has eaten
Environment, and lives
Alone, unencroached on, perfectly gorged, one God.
Caesar and Napoleon
Visibly acting their dream of that solitude, Christ and Gautama,
Being God, devouring
The world with atonement for God's sake . . . ah sacred hungers,
The conqueror's, the prophet's,
The lover's, the hunger of the sea-beaks, slaves of the last peace,
Worshippers of oneness.

BOATS IN A FOG

Sports and gallantries, the stage, the arts, the antics of dancers,
The exuberant voices of music,
Have charm for children but lack nobility; it is bitter earnestness
That makes beauty; the mind
Knows, grown adult.

A sudden fog-drift muffled the ocean,
A throbbing of engines moved in it,
At length, a stone's throw out, between the rocks and the vapor,
One by one moved shadows
Out of the mystery, shadows, fishing-boats, trailing each other
Following the cliff for guidance,
Holding a difficult path between the peril of the sea-fog
And the foam on the shore granite.
One by one, trailing their leader, six crept by me,
Out of the vapor and into it,
The throb of their engines subdued by the fog, patient and cautious,
Coasting all round the peninsula
Back to the buoys in Monterey harbor. A flight of pelicans
Is nothing lovelier to look at;
The flight of the planets is nothing nobler; all the arts lose virtue
Against the essential reality
Of creatures going about their business among the equally
Earnest elements of nature.

HAUNTED COUNTRY

Here the human past is dim and feeble and alien to us
Our ghosts draw from the crowded future.
Fixed as the past how could it fail to drop weird shadows
And make strange murmurs about twilight?
In the dawn twilight metal falcons flew over the mountain,
Multitudes, and faded in the air; at moonrise
The farmer's girl by the still river is afraid of phantoms,
Hearing the pulse of a great city
Move on the water-meadow and stream off south; the country's
Children for all their innocent minds
Hide dry and bitter lights in the eye, they dream without knowing it
The inhuman years to be accomplished,
The inhuman powers, the servile cunning under pressure
In a land grown old, heavy and crowded.
There are happy places that fate skips; here is not one of them;
The tides of the brute womb, the excess
And weight of life spilled out like water, the last migration
Gathering against this holier valley-mouth
That knows its fate beforehand, the flow of the womb, banked back
By the older flood of the ocean, to swallow it.

VICES

Spirited people make a thousand jewels in verse and prose, and the restlessness of talent
Runs over and floods the stage or spreads its fever on canvas.
They are skilled in music too, the demon is never satisfied, they take to puppets, they invent
New arts, they take to drugs . . . and we all applaud our vices.
Mine, coldness and the tenor of a stone tranquillity; slow life, the growth of trees and verse,
Content the unagitable and somewhat earthfast nature.

PRACTICAL PEOPLE

Practical people, I have been told,
Weary of the sea for his waves go up and down
Endlessly to no visible purpose;
Tire of the tides, for the tides are tireless, the tides
Are well content with their own march-tune
And nothing accomplished is no matter to them.
It seems wasteful to practical people.
And that the nations labor and gather and dissolve
Into destruction; the stars sharpen
Their spirit of splendor, and then it dims, and the stars
Darken; and that the spirit of man
Sharpens up to maturity and cools dull
With age, dies, and rusts out of service;
And all these tidal gatherings, growth and decay,
Shining and darkening, are forever
Renewed; and the whole cycle impenitently
Revolves, and all the past is future: —
Make it a difficult world . . . for practical people.

SCIENCE

Man, introverted man, having crossed
In passage and but a little with the nature of things this latter century
Has begot giants; but being taken up
Like a maniac with self-love and inward conflicts cannot manage his
   hybrids.
Being used to deal with edgeless dreams,
Now he's bred knives on nature turns them also inward: they have thirsty
   points though.
His mind forebodes his own destruction;
Actaeon who saw the goddess naked among leaves and his hounds tore him.
A little knowledge, a pebble from the shingle,
A drop from the oceans: who would have dreamed this infinitely little too
   much?

PEOPLE AND A HERON

A desert of weed and water-darkened stone under my western windows
The ebb lasted all afternoon,
And many pieces of humanity, men, women, and children, gathering
   shellfish,
Swarmed with voices of gulls the sea-breach.
At twilight they went off together, the verge was left vacant, an evening
   heron
Bent broad wings over the black ebb,
And left me wondering why a lone bird was dearer to me than many
   people.
Well: rare is dear: but also I suppose
Well reconciled with the world but not with our own natures we grudge to
   see them
Reflected on the world for a mirror.

NIGHT

The ebb slips from the rock, the sunken
Tide-rocks lift streaming shoulders
Out of the slack, the slow west
Sombering its torch; a ship's light
Shows faintly, far out,
Over the weight of the prone ocean
On the low cloud.

Over the dark mountain, over the dark pinewood,
Down the long dark valley along the shrunken river,
Returns the splendor without rays, the shining of shadow,
Peace-bringer, the matrix of all shining and quieter of shining.
Where the shore widens on the bay she opens dark wings
And the ocean accepts her glory. O soul worshipful of her
You like the ocean have grave depths where she dwells always,
And the film of waves above that takes the sun takes also
Her, with more love. The sun-lovers have a blond favorite,
A father of lights and noises, wars, weeping and laughter,
Hot labor, lust and delight and the other blemishes. Quietness
Flows from her deeper fountain; and he will die; and she is immortal.

Far off from here the slender
Flocks of the mountain forest
Move among stems like towers
Of the old redwoods to the stream,
No twig crackling; dip shy
Wild muzzles into the mountain water
Among the dark ferns.

O passionately at peace you being secure will pardon
The blasphemies of glowworms, the lamp in my tower, the fretfulness
Of cities, the cressets of the planets, the pride of the stars.
This August night in a rift of cloud Antares reddens,
The great one, the ancient torch, a lord among lost children,
The earth's orbit doubled would not girdle his greatness, one fire
Globed, out of grasp of the mind enormous; but to you O Night
What? Not a spark? What flicker of a spark in the faint far glimmer
Of a lost fire dying in the desert, dim coals of a sand-pit the Bedouins
Wandered from at dawn . . . Ah singing prayer to what gulfs tempted
Suddenly are you more lost? To us the near-hand mountain
Be a measure of height, the tide-worn cliff at the sea-gate a measure of
continuance.

The tide, moving the night's
Vastness with lonely voices,
Turns, the deep dark-shining
Pacific leans on the land,
Feeling his cold strength
To the outmost margins: you Night will resume
The stars in your time.

O passionately at peace when will that tide draw shoreward?
Truly the spouting fountains of light, Antares, Arcturus,
Tire of their flow, they sing one song but they think silence.
The striding winter giant Orion shines, and dreams darkness.
And life, the flicker of men and moths and the wolf on the hill,
Though furious for continuance, passionately feeding, passionately
Remaking itself upon its mates, remembers deep inward
The calm mother, the quietness of the womb and the egg,
The primal and the latter silences: dear Night it is memory
Prophesies, prophecy that remembers, the charm of the dark.

And I and my people, we are willing to love the four-score years
Heartily; but as a sailor loves the sea, when the helm is for harbor.

Have men's minds changed,
Or the rock hidden in the deep of the waters of the soul
Broken the surface? A few centuries
Gone by, was none dared not to people
The darkness beyond the stars with harps and habitations.
But now, dear is the truth. Life is grown sweeter and lonelier,
And death is no evil.

AUTUMN EVENING

Though the little clouds ran southward still, the quiet autumnal
Cool of the late September evening
Seemed promising rain, rain, the change of the year, the angel
Of the sad forest. A heron flew over
With that remote ridiculous cry, "Quawk," the cry
That seems to make silence more silent. A dozen
Flops of the wing, a drooping glide, at the end of the glide
The cry, and a dozen flops of the wing.
I watched him pass on the autumn-colored sky; beyond him
Jupiter shone for evening star.
The sea's voice worked into my mood, I thought "No matter
What happens to men . . . the world's well made though."

JOY

Though joy is better than sorrow joy is not great;
Peace is great, strength is great.
Not for joy the stars burn, not for joy the vulture
Spreads her gray sails on the air
Over the mountain; not for joy the worn mountain
Stands, while years like water
Trench his long sides. "I am neither mountain nor bird
Nor star; and I seek joy."
The weakness of your breed: yet at length quietness
Will cover those wistful eyes.

PHENOMENA

Great-enough both accepts and subdues; the great frame takes all creatures;
From the greatness of their element they all take beauty.
Gulls; and the dingy freightship lurching south in the eye of a rain-wind;
The air-plane dipping over the hill; hawks hovering
The white grass of the headland; cormorants roosting upon the guano-
Whitened skerries; pelicans awind; sea-slime
Shining at night in the wave-stir like drowned men's lanterns; smugglers signaling
A cargo to land; or the old Point Pinos lighthouse
Lawfully winking over dark water; the flight of the twilight herons,
Lonely wings and a cry; or with motor-vibrations
That hum in the rock like a new storm-tone of the ocean's to turn eyes westward
The navy's new-bought Zeppelin going by in the twilight,
Far out seaward; relative only to the evening star and the ocean
It slides into a cloud over Point Lobos.

THE TOWER BEYOND TRAGEDY

I

You'd never have thought the Queen was Helen's sister—Troy's
burning-flower from Sparta, the beautiful sea-flower
Cut in clear stone, crowned with the fragrant golden mane, she the ageless,
the uncontaminable—
This Clytemnestra was her sister, low-statured, fierce-lipped, not dark nor
blonde, greenish-gray eyed,
Sinewed with strength, you saw, under the purple folds of the queen-cloak,
but craftier than queenly,
Standing between the gilded wooden porch-pillars, great steps of stone
above the steep street,
Awaiting the King.
Most of his men were quartered on the town; he,
clanking bronze, with fifty
And certain captives, came to the stair. The Queen's men were a hundred
in the street and a hundred
Lining the ramp, eighty on the great flags of the porch; she raising her
white arms the spear-butts
Thundered on the stone and the shields clashed; eight shining clarions
Let fly from the wide window over the entrance the wild-birds of their
metal throats, air-cleaving
Over the King come home. He raised his thick burnt-colored beard and
smiled; then Clytemnestra,
Gathering the robe, setting the golden-sandaled feet carefully, stone by
stone, descended
One half the stair. But one of the captives marred the comeliness of that
embrace with a cry
Gull-shrill, blade-sharp, cutting between the purple cloak and the bronze
plates, then Clytemnestra:

Who was it? The King answered: A piece of our goods out of the snatch of Asia, a daughter of the king,
So treat her kindly and she may come into her wits again. Eh, you keep state here my queen.
You've not been the poorer for me. — In heart, in the widowed chamber, dear, she pale replied, though the slaves
Toiled, the spearmen were faithful. What's her name, the slave-girl's?

AGAMEMNON
Come up the stair. They tell me my kinsman's
Lodged himself on you.

CLYTEMNESTRA
Your cousin Aegisthus? He was out of refuge, flits between here and Tiryns.
Dear: the girl's name?

AGAMEMNON
Cassandra. We've a hundred or so other captives; besides two hundred
Rotted in the hulls, — they tell odd stories about you and your guest: eh? no matter: — the ships
Ooze pitch and the August road smokes dirt, I smell like an old shepherd's goat-skin, you'll have bath water?

CLYTEMNESTRA
They're making it hot. Come, my lord. My hands will pour it.

(They enter the palace.)

CASSANDRA
In the holy city,
In Troy, when the stone was standing walls and the ash
Was painted and carved wood and pictured curtains,
And those lived that are dead, they had caged a den
Of wolves out of the mountain, and I a maiden
Was led to see them; it stank and snarled,
The smell was the smell here, the eyes were the eyes
Of steep Mycenae: O God guardian of wanderers
Let me die easily.

So cried Cassandra the daughter of King Priam, treading the steps of the palace at Mycenae,
Swaying like a drunken woman, drunk with the rolling of the ship, and with tears, and with prophecy.
The stair may yet be seen, among the old stones that are Mycenae; tall dark Cassandra, the prophetess,
The beautiful girl with whom a God bargained for love, high-nurtured, captive, shamefully stained
With the ship's filth and the sea's, rolled her dark head upon her shoulders like a drunken woman
And trod the great stones of the stair. The captives, she among them, were ranked into a file
On the flagged porch, between the parapet and the spearmen. The people below shouted for the King,
King Agamemnon, returned conqueror, after the ten years of battle and death in Asia.
Then cried Cassandra:
Good spearmen you did not kill my father, not you
Violated my mother with the piercing
That makes no life in the womb, not you defiled
My tall blond brothers with the masculine lust
That strikes its loved one standing,
And leaves him what no man again nor a girl
Ever will gaze upon with the eyes of desire:
Therefore you'll tell me
Whether it's an old custom in the Greek country
The cow goring the bull, break the inner door back
And see in what red water how cloaked your King
Bathes, and my brothers are avenged a little.
One said: Captive be quiet. And she: What have I to be quiet for, you will not believe me.

Such wings my heart spreads when the red runs out of any Greek, I must let the bird fly. O soldiers
He that mishandled me dies! The first, one of your two brute Ajaxes, that threw me backward
On the temple flagstones, a hard bride-bed, I enduring him heard the roofs of my city breaking,
The roar of flames and spearmen: what came to Ajax? Out of a cloud the loud-winged falcon lightning
Came on him shipwrecked, clapped its wings about him, clung to him, the violent flesh burned and the bones
Broke from each other in that passion; and now this one, returned safe, the Queen is his lightning.
While she yet spoke a slave with haggard eyes darted from the door; there were hushed cries and motions
In the inner dark of the great hall. Then the Queen Clytemnestra issued, smiling. She drew
Her cloak up, for the brooch on the left shoulder was broken; the fillet of her hair had come unbound;
Yet now she was queenly at length; and standing at the stairhead spoke: Men of Mycenae, I have made
Sacrifice for the joy this day has brought to us, the King come home, the enemy fallen, fallen,
In the ashes of Asia. I have made sacrifice. I made the prayer with my own lips, and struck the bullock
With my own hand. The people murmured together, She's not a priestess, the Queen is not a priestess,
What has she done there, what wild sayings
Make wing in the Queen's throat?

CLYTEMNESTRA I have something to tell you. Too much joy is a message-bearer of misery.
A little is good; but come too much and it devours us. Therefore we give of a great harvest

Sheaves to the smiling Gods; and therefore out of a full cup we pour the quarter. No man
Dare take all that God sends him, whom God favors, or destruction
Rides into the house in the last basket. I have been twelve years your shepherdess, I the Queen have ruled you
And I am accountable for you.

CASSANDRA

Why should a man kill his own mother?
The cub of the lion being grown
Will fight with the lion, but neither lion nor wolf
Nor the unclean jackal
Bares tooth against the womb that he dropped out of:
Yet I have seen—

CLYTEMNESTRA

Strike that captive woman with your hand, spearman; and then if the spirit
Of the she-wolf in her will not quiet, with the butt of the spear.

CASSANDRA —the blade in the child's hand
Enter the breast that the child sucked—that woman's—
The left breast that the robe has dropped from, for the brooch is broken,
That very hillock of whiteness, and she crying, she kneeling—

(The spearman who is nearest Cassandra covers her mouth with his hand.)

CLYTEMNESTRA

My sister's beauty entered Troy with too much gladness. They forgot to make sacrifice.
Therefore destruction entered; therefore the daughters of Troy cry out in strange dispersals, and this one
Grief has turned mad. I will not have that horror march under the Lion-gate of Mycenae
That split the citadel of Priam. Therefore I say I have made sacrifice; I have subtracted
A fraction from immoderate joy. For consider, my people,

How unaccountably God has favored the city and brought home the army.
King Agamemnon,
My dear, my husband, my lord and yours,
Is yet not such a man as the Gods love; but insolent, fierce, overbearing, whose folly
Brought many times many great evils
On all the heads and fighting hopes of the Greek force. Why, even before the fleet made sail,
While yet it gathered on Boeotian Aulis, this man offended. He slew one of the deer
Of the sacred herd of Artemis, out of pure impudence, hunter's pride that froths in a young boy
Laying nock to string of his first bow: this man, grown, a grave king, leader of the Greeks.
The angry Goddess
Blew therefore from the horn of the Trojan shore storm without end, no slackening, no turn, no slumber
Of the eagle bound to break the oars of the fleet and split the hulls venturing: you know what answer
Calchas the priest gave: his flesh must pay whose hand did the evil—his flesh! mine also. His? My daughter.
They knew that of my three there was one that I loved.
Blameless white maid, my Iphigeneia, whose throat the knife,
Whose delicate soft throat the thing that cuts sheep open was drawn across by a priest's hand
And the soft-colored lips drained bloodless
That had clung here—here—O! *(Drawing the robe from her breasts.)*
These feel soft, townsmen; these are red at the tips, they have neither blackened nor turned marble.
King Agamemnon hoped to pillow his black-haired breast upon them, my husband, that mighty conqueror,

Come home with glory. He thought they were still a woman's, they appear a woman's. I'll tell you something.
Since fawn slaughtered for slaughtered fawn evened the debt these that feel soft and warm are wounding ice,
They ache with their hardness . . .
Shall I go on and count the other follies of the King? The insolences to God and man
That brought down plague, and brought Achilles' anger against the army? Yet God brought home a remnant
Against all hope: therefore rejoice.
But lest too much rejoicing slay us I have made sacrifice. A little girl's brought you over the sea.
What could be great enough for safe return? A sheep's death? A bull's? What thank-offering?
All these captives, battered from the ships, bruised with captivity, damaged flesh and forlorn minds?
God requires wholeness in the victim. You dare not think what he demands. I dared. I, I,
Dared.
Men of the Argolis, you that went over the sea and you that guarded the home coasts
And high stone war-belts of the cities: remember how many spearmen these twelve years have called me
Queen, and have loved me, and been faithful, and *remain* faithful. What I bring you is accomplished.

VOICES

King Agamemnon. The King. We will hear the King.

CLYTEMNESTRA

What I bring you is accomplished.
Accept it, the cities are at peace, the ways are safe between them, the Gods favor us. Refuse it . . .
You will not refuse it . . .

VOICES The King. We will hear the King. Let us see the King.

CLYTEMNESTRA

You will not refuse it; I have my faithful. They would run, the red rivers,
From the gate and by the graves through every crooked street of the great city, they would run in the pasture
Outside the walls: and on this stair: stemmed at this entrance—

CASSANDRA

Ah, sister, do you also behold visions? I was watching red water—

CLYTEMNESTRA

Be wise, townsmen. As for the King: slaves will bring him to you when he has bathed; you will see him.
The slaves will carry him on a litter, he has learned Asian ways in Asia, too great a ruler
To walk, like common spearmen.

CASSANDRA Who is that, standing behind you, Clytemnestra? What God
Dark in the doorway?

CLYTEMNESTRA Deal *you* with your own demons. You know what I have done, captive. You know
I am holding lions with my two eyes: if I turn and loose them . . .

CASSANDRA It is . . . the King. There! There! Ah!

CLYTEMNESTRA

Or if I should make any move to increase confusion. If I should say for example, Spearman
Kill that woman. I cannot say it this moment; so little as from one spear wound in your body
A trickle would loose them on us.

CASSANDRA Yet he stands behind you. A-ah! I can bear it. I have seen much lately
Worse.

A CAPTAIN (*down the stair; standing forward from his men*)

O Queen, there is no man in the world, but one (if that one lives) may ask you to speak
Otherwise than you will. You have spoken in riddles to the people . . .

CASSANDRA

Not me! Why will you choose
Me! I submitted to you living, I was forced, you entered me . . .

THE CAPTAIN

Also there was a slave here,
Whose eyes stood out from his chalk face, came buzzing from the palace postern gate, whimpering
A horrible thing. I killed him. But the men have heard it.

CASSANDRA

You were the king, I was your slave.
Here, you see, here, I took the black-haired breast of the bull, I endured it, I opened my thighs, I suffered
The other thing besides death that you Greeks have to give us . . .

THE CAPTAIN

Though this one raves and you are silent,
O Queen, terrible-eyed . . .

CASSANDRA

That was the slave's part: but this time . . . dead King . . .
I . . . will . . . not submit. Ah! Ah! No!
If you will steal the body of someone living take your wife's, take that soldier's there—

THE CAPTAIN

I pray you Queen command the captive woman be quieted in a stone chamber; she increases confusion,
The soldiers cannot know some terrible thing may not have happened; your men and the King's grin
Like wolves over the kill, the whole city totters on a sword-edge over sudden—

CASSANDRA *(screaming)*

A-ai!

Drive him off me! Pity, pity!

I have no power; I thought when he was dead another man would use me, your Greek custom,

Not he, he, newly slain.

He is driving me out, he enters, he possesses, this is my last defilement. Ah . . . Greeks . . .

Pity Cassandra!

With the voice the spirit seemed to fly out. She upflung her shining

Arms with the dreadful and sweet gesture of a woman surrendering utterly to force and love,

She in the eyes of the people, like a shameless woman, and fell writhing, and the dead King's soul

Entered her body. In that respite the Queen:

Captain: and you, soldiers, that shift unsoldierly

The weapons that should be upright, at attention, like stiff grass-blades: and you, people of Mycenae:

While this one maddened, and you muttered, echoing together, and you, soldier, with anxious questions

Increased confusion: who was it that stood firm, who was it that stood silent, who was it that held

With her two eyes the whole city from splitting wide asunder? Your Queen was it? I am your Queen,

And now I will answer what you asked. . . . It is true. . . . He has died. . . . I am the Queen,

My little son Orestes will grow up and govern you.

While she spoke the body of Cassandra

Arose among the shaken spears, taller than the spears, and stood among the
waving spears
Stone-quiet, like a high war-tower in a windy pinewood, but deadly to look
at, with blind and tyrannous
Eyes; and the Queen: All is accomplished; and if you are wise, people of
Mycenae: quietness is wisdom.
No tumult will call home a dead man out of judgment. The end is the end.
Ah, soldiers! Down spears!
What, now Troy's fallen you think there's not a foreigner in the world
bronze may quench thirst on? Lion-cubs,
If you will tear each other in the lair happy the wolves, happy the
hook-nose vultures.
Call the eaters of carrion? I am your queen, I am speaking to you, you will
hear me out before you whistle
The foul beaks from the mountain nest. I tell you I will forget mercy if one
man moves now.
I rule you, I.
The Gods have satisfied themselves in this man's death; there shall not one
drop of the blood of the city
Be shed further. I say the high Gods are content; as for the lower,
And the great ghost of the King: my slaves will bring out the King's body
decently before you
And set it here, in the eyes of the city: spices the ships bring from the
south will comfort his spirit;
Mycenae and Tiryns and the shores will mourn him aloud; sheep will be
slain for him; a hundred beeves
Spill their thick blood into the trenches; captives and slaves go down to
serve him, yes all these captives
Burn in the ten-day fire with him, unmeasured wine quench it, urned in
pure gold the gathered ashes
Rest forever in the sacred rock; honored; a conqueror. . . . Slaves, bring the
King out of the house.

Alas my husband! she cried, clutching the brown strands of her hair in both her hands, you have left me
A woman among lions! Ah the King's power, ah the King's victories! Weep for me, Mycenae!
Widowed of the King!
The people stood amazed, like sheep that snuff at their dead shepherd, some hunter's
Ill handled arrow having struck him from the covert, all by mischance; he is fallen on the hill-side
Between the oak-shadow and the stream; the sun burns his dead face, his staff lies by him, his dog
Licks his hand, whining. So, like sheep, the people
Regarded that dead majesty whom the slaves brought out of the house on a gold bed, and set it
Between the pillars of the porch. His royal robe covered his wounds, there was no stain
Nor discomposure.
Then that captain who had spoken before: O Queen, before the mourning
The punishment: tell us who has done this. She raised her head, and not a woman but a lioness
Blazed at him from her eyes: Dog, she answered, dog of the army,
Who said Speak dog, and you dared speak? Justice is mine. Then he was silent; but Cassandra's
Body standing tall among the spears, over the parapet, her body but not her spirit
Cried with a man's voice: Shall not even the stones of the stair, shall not the stones under the columns
Speak, and the towers of the great wall of my city come down against the murderess? O Mycenae
I yearned to night and day under the tents by Troy, O Tiryns, O Mycenae, the door
Of death, and the gate before the door!

CLYTEMNESTRA That woman lies, or the spirit of a lie cries from her. Spearman,
Kill that woman!
But Cassandra's body set its back against the parapet, its face
Terribly fronting the raised knife; and called the soldier by his name, in the King's voice, saying
Sheathe it; and the knife lowered, and the soldier
Fell on his knees before the King in the woman's body; and the body of Cassandra cried from the parapet:
Horrible things, horrible things this house has witnessed: but here is the most vile, that hundreds
Of spears are idle while the murderess, Clytemnestra the murderess, the snake that came upon me
Naked and bathing, the death that lay with me in bed, the death that has borne children to me,
Stands there unslain.
CLYTEMNESTRA Cowards, if the bawling of that bewildered heifer from Troy fields has frightened you
How did you bear the horns of her brothers? Bring her to me.
THE BODY OF CASSANDRA Let no man doubt, men of Mycenae,
She has yet the knife hid in her clothes, the very blade that stabbed her husband and the blood is on it.
Look, she handles it now. Look, fellows. The hand under the robe. Slay her not easily, that she-wolf.
Do her no honor with a spear! Ah! If I could find the word, if I could find it,
The name of her, to say husband-slayer and bed-defiler, bitch and wolf-bitch, king's assassin
And beast, beast, beast, all in one breath, in one word: spearmen
You would heap your shields over this woman and crush her slowly, slowly, while she choked and screamed,

No, you would peel her bare and on the pavement for a bride-bed with a spear-butt for husband
Dig the lewd womb until it burst: this for Agamemnon, this for Aegisthus—Agh, cowards of the city
Do you stand quiet?

CLYTEMNESTRA Truly, soldiers,
I think it is he verily. No one could invent the abominable voice, the unspeakable gesture,
The actual raging insolence of the tyrant. I am the hand ridded the Argolis of him.
I, here, I killed him, I, justly.

THE BODY OF CASSANDRA You have heard her, you have heard her, she has made confession.
Now if she'll show you the knife too—

CLYTEMNESTRA Here. I kept it for safety.
And, as that beast said, his blood's yet on it.
Look at it, with so little a key I unlocked the kingdom of destruction. Stand firm, till a God
Lead home this ghost to the dark country
So many Greeks have peopled, through his crimes, his violence, his insolence, stand firm till that moment
And through the act of this hand and of this point no man shall suffer anything again forever
Of Agamemnon.

THE BODY OF CASSANDRA
I say if you let this woman live, this crime go unpunished, what man among you
Will be safe in his bed? The woman ever envies the man, his strength, his freedom, his loves.
Her envy is like a snake beside him, all his life through, her envy and hatred: law tames that viper:
Law dies if the Queen die not: the viper is free then,

It will be poison in your meat or a knife to bleed you sleeping. They fawn and slaver over us
And then we are slain.

CLYTEMNESTRA (*to one of the slaves that carried the King's body*)
Is my lord Aegisthus
Slain on the way? How long? How long?
(*To the people*) He came, fat with his crimes.
Greek valor broke down Troy, your valor, soldiers, and the brain of Odysseus, the battle-fury of Achilles,
The stubborn strength of Menelaus, the excellence of you all: this dead man here, his pride
Ruined you a hundred times: he helped nowise, he brought bitter destruction: but he gathered your glory
For the cloak of his shoulders. I saw him come up the stair, I saw my child Iphigeneia
Killed for his crime; I saw his harlot, the captive woman there, crying out behind him, I saw . . .
I saw . . . I saw . . . how can I speak what crowd of the dead faces of the faithful Greeks,
Your brothers, dead of his crimes; those that perished of plague and those that died in the lost battles
After he had soured the help of Achilles—for another harlot—those dead faces of your brothers,
Some black with the death-blood, many trampled under the hooves of horses, many spotted with pestilence,
Flew all about him, all lamenting, all crying out against him,—horrible—horrible—I gave them
Vengeance; and you freedom.
(*To the slave*) Go up and look, for God's sake, go up to the parapets,
Look toward the mountain. Bring me word quickly, my strength breaks,

How can I hold all the Argolis with my eyes forever? I alone? Hell cannot hold her dead men,
Keep watch there—send me word by others—go, go!
(To the people) He came triumphing.
Magnificent, abominable, all in bronze.
I brought him to the bath; my hands undid the armor;
My hands poured out the water;
Dead faces like flies buzzed all about us;
He stripped himself before me, loathsome, unclean, with laughter;
The labors of the Greeks had made him fat, the deaths of the faithful had swelled his belly;
I threw a cloak over him for a net and struck, struck, struck,
Blindly, in the steam of the bath; he bellowed, netted,
And bubbled in the water;
All the stone vault asweat with steam bellowed;
And I undid the net and the beast was dead, and the broad vessel
Stank with his blood.

THE BODY OF CASSANDRA
The word! the word! O burning mind of God,
If ever I gave you bulls teach me that word, the name for her, the name for her!

A SLAVE *(running from the door; to Clytemnestra)*
My lord Aegisthus has come down the mountain, Queen, he approaches the Lion-gate.

CLYTEMNESTRA It is time. I am tired now.
Meet him and tell him to come in the postern doorway.

THE CAPTAIN *(on the stair: addressing the soldiers and the people below)*
Companions: before God, hating the smell of crimes, crushes the city into gray ashes
We must make haste. Judge now and act. For the husband-slayer

I say she must die, let her pay forfeit. And for the great ghost of the King, let all these captives,
But chiefly the woman Cassandra, the crier in a man's voice there, be slain upon his pyre to quiet him.
He will go down to his dark place and God will spare the city.
(To the soldiers above, on the ramp and the porch) Comrades: Mycenae is greater
Than the Queen of Mycenae. The King is dead: let the Queen die: let the city live. Comrades,
We suffered something in Asia, on the stranger's coast, laboring for you. We dreamed of home there
In the bleak wind and drift of battle; we continued ten years, laboring and dying; we accomplished
The task set us; we gathered what will make all the Greek cities glorious, a name forever;
We shared the spoil, taking our share to enrich Mycenae. O but our hearts burned then, O comrades
But our hearts melted when the great oars moved the ships, the water carried us, the blue sea-waves
Slid under the black keel; I could not see them, I was blind with tears, thinking of Mycenae.
We have come home. Behold the dear streets of our longing,
The stones that we desired, the steep ways of the city and the sacred door-steps
Reek and steam with pollution, the accursed vessel
Spills a red flood over the floors.
The fountain of it stands there and calls herself the Queen. No queen, no queen, that husband-slayer,
A common murderess. Comrades join us
We will make clean the city and sweeten it before God. We will mourn together at the King's burying,
And a good year will come, we will rejoice together.

CLYTEMNESTRA Dog, you dare
something. Fling no spear, soldiers,
He has a few fools back of him would attempt the stair if the dog were slain: I will have no one
Killed out of need.

ONE OF HER MEN ON THE PORCH *(flinging his spear)*
Not at him: at you
Murderess!
But some God, no lover of justice, turned it; the great bronze tip grazing her shoulder
Clanged on the stones behind: the gong of a change in the dance: now Clytemnestra, none to help her,
One against all, swayed raging by the King's corpse, over the golden bed: it is said that a fire
Stood visibly over her head, mixed in the hair, pale flames and radiance.

CLYTEMNESTRA Here
am I, thieves, thieves,
Drunkards here is my breast, a deep white mark for cowards to aim at: kings have lain on it.
No spear yet, heroes, heroes?
See, I have no blemish: the arms are white, the breasts are deep and white, the whole body is blemishless:
You are tired of your brown wives, draw lots for me rabble, thieves there is loot here, shake the dice thieves, a game yet!
One of you will take the bronze and one the silver,
One the gold, and one me,
Me Clytemnestra a spoil worth having:
Kings have kissed me, this dead dog was a king, there is another
King at the gate: thieves, thieves, would not this shining
Breast brighten a sad thief's hut, roll in his bed's filth
Shiningly? You could teach me to draw water at the fountain,
A dirty child on the other hip: where are the dice? Let me throw first, if I throw sixes

I choose my masters: closer you rabble, let me smell you.
Don't fear the knife, it has king's blood on it, I keep it for an ornament,
It has shot its sting.

THE BODY OF CASSANDRA

Fools, fools, strike!
Are your hands dead?

CLYTEMNESTRA You would see all of me
Before you choose whether to kill or dirtily cherish? If what the King's used needs commending
To the eyes of thieves for thieves' use: give me room, give me room fellows, you'll see it is faultless.
The dress . . . there . . .

THE BODY OF CASSANDRA Fools this wide whore played wife
When she was going about to murder me the King; you, will you let her trip you
With the harlot's trick? Strike! Make an end!

CLYTEMNESTRA I have not my sister's, Troy's flame's beauty, but I have something.
This arm, round, firm, skin without hair, polished like marble: the supple-jointed shoulders:
Men have praised the smooth neck, too,
The strong clear throat over the deep wide breasts . . .

THE BODY OF CASSANDRA She is buying an hour: sheep: it may be Aegisthus
Is at the Lion-gate.

CLYTEMNESTRA If he were here, Aegisthus,
I'd not be the peddler of what trifling charms I have for an hour of life yet. You have wolves' eyes:
Yet there is something kindly about the blue ones there—yours, young soldier, young soldier. . . . The last,
The under-garment? You won't buy me yet? This dead dog,
The King here, never saw me naked: I had the night for nurse: turn his head sideways, the eyes

Are only half shut. If I should touch him, and the blood came, you'd say I had killed him. Nobody, nobody,
Killed him: his pride burst.
Ah no one has pity!
I can serve well, I have always envied your women, the public ones.
Who takes me first? Tip that burnt log onto the flagstones,
This will be in a king's bed then. Your eyes are wolves' eyes:
So many, so many, so famishing—
I will undo it, handle me not yet, I can undo it . . .
Or I will tear it.
And when it is off me then I will be delivered to you beasts . . .

THE BODY OF CASSANDRA

Then strip her and use her to the bone, wear her through, kill her with it.

CLYTEMNESTRA

When it is torn
You'll say I am lovely: no one has seen before . . .
It won't tear: I'll slit it with this knife—

(Aegisthus, with many spearmen, issues from the great door. Clytemnestra stabs right and left with the knife; the men are too close to strike her with their long spears.)

CLYTEMNESTRA

It's time. Cowards, goats, goats. Here! Aegisthus!

AEGISTHUS

I am here. What have they done?

CLYTEMNESTRA

Nothing: clear the porch: *I* have done something. Drive them on the stair!
Three of them I've scarred for life: a rough bridegroom, the rabble, met a fierce bride. *(She catches up her robe.)*
I held them with my eyes, hours, hours. I am not tired. . . . My lord, my lover:
I have killed a twelve-point stag for a present for you: with my own hands: look, on the golden litter.
You arrive timely.

THE BODY OF CASSANDRA

Tricked, stabbed, shamed, mocked at, the spoil of a lewd woman, despised
I lie there ready for her back-stairs darling to spit on. Tricked, stabbed, sunk in the drain
And gutter of time. I that thundered the assault, I that mustered the Achaeans. Cast out of my kingdom,
Cast out of time, out of the light.

CLYTEMNESTRA

One of the captives, dear. It left its poor wits
Over the sea. If it annoys you I'll quiet it. But post your sentinels.
All's not safe yet, though I am burning with joy now.

THE BODY OF CASSANDRA

O single-eyed glare of the sky
Flying southwest to the mountain: sun, through a slave's eyes,
My own broken, I see you this last day; my own darkened, no dawn forever; the adulterers
Will swim in your warm gold, day after day; the eyes of the murderess will possess you;
And I have gone away down: knowing that no God in the earth nor sky loves justice; and having tasted
The toad that serves women for heart. From now on may all bridegrooms
Marry them with swords. Those that have borne children
Their sons rape them with spears.

CLYTEMNESTRA

More yet, more, more, more, while my hand's in? It's not a little
You easily living lords of the sky require of who'd be like you, who'd take time in the triumph,
Build joy solid. Do we have to do everything? I have killed what I hated:
Kill what I love? The prophetess said it, this dead man says it: my little son, the small soft image
That squirmed in my arms be an avenger?—Love, from your loins'

Seed: I begin new, I will be childless for you. The child my son, the child my daughter!
Though I cry I feel nothing.

AEGISTHUS O strongest spirit in the world. We have dared enough, there is an end to it.
We may pass nature a little, an arrow flight,
But two shots over the wall you come in a cloud upon the feasting Gods, lightning and madness.

CLYTEMNESTRA
Dear: make them safe. They may try to run away, the children. Set spears to watch them: no harm, no harm,
But stab the nurse if they go near a door. Watch them, keep the gates, order the sentinels,
While *I* make myself queen over this people again. I can do it.

THE BODY OF CASSANDRA The sun's gone; that glimmer's
The moon of the dead. The dark God calls me. Yes, God,
I'll come in a moment.

CLYTEMNESTRA *(at the head of the great stairs)*
Soldiers: townsmen: it seems
I am not at the end delivered to you: dogs, for the lion came: the poor brown and spotted women
Will have to suffice you. But is it nothing to have come within handling-distance of the clear heaven
This dead man knew when he was young and God endured him? Is it nothing to you?
It is something to me to have felt the fury
And concentration of you: I will not say I am grateful: I am not angry: to be desired
Is wine even to a queen. You bathed me in it, from brow to foot-sole, I had nearly enough.

But now remember that the dream is over. I am the Queen: Mycenae is my city. If you grin at me
I have spears: also Tiryns and all the country people of the Argolis will come against you and swallow you,
Empty out these ways and walls, stock them with better subjects. A rock nest for new birds here, townsfolk:
You are not essential.

THE BODY OF CASSANDRA

I hear him calling through the she-wolf's noise, Agamemnon, Agamemnon,
The dark God calls. Some old king in a fable is it?

CLYTEMNESTRA So choose. What choices? To reenter my service
Unpunished, no thought of things past, free of conditions . . .
Or—dine at this man's table, have new mouths made in you to eat bronze with.

THE BODY OF CASSANDRA

Who is Agamemnon?

CLYTEMNESTRA

You letting go of the sun: is it dark the land you are running away to?

THE BODY OF CASSANDRA It is dark.

CLYTEMNESTRA

Is it sorrowful?

THE BODY OF CASSANDRA

There is nothing but misery.

CLYTEMNESTRA Has any man ever come back thence? Hear *me*, not the dark God.

THE BODY OF CASSANDRA No man has ever.

CLYTEMNESTRA

Go then, go, go down. You will not choose to follow him, people of the rock-city? No one

Will choose to follow him. I have killed: it is easy: it may be I shall kill nearer than this yet:
But not you, townsfolk, you will give me no cause; I want security; I want service, not blood.
I have been desired of the whole city, publicly; I want service, not lust. You will make no sign
Of your submission; you will not give up your weapons; neither shall your leaders be slain;
And he that flung the spear, I have forgotten his face.

AEGISTHUS (*entering*) Dearest, they have gone, the nurse and the children,
No one knows where.

CLYTEMNESTRA I am taming this people: send men after them. If any harm comes to the children
Bring me tokens. I will not be in doubt, I will not have the arch fall on us. I dare
What no one dares. I envy a little the dirty mothers of the city. O, O!
Nothing in me hurts. I have animal waters in my eyes, but the spirit is not wounded. Electra and Orestes
Are not to live when they are caught. Bring me sure tokens.

CASSANDRA Who is this woman like a beacon
Lit on the stair, who are these men with dogs' heads?
I have ranged time and seen no sight like this one.

CLYTEMNESTRA
Have you returned, Cassandra? . . . The dead king has gone down to his place, we may bury his leavings.

CASSANDRA
I have witnessed all the wars to be; I am not sorrowful
For one drop from the pail of desolation
Spilt on my father's city; they were carrying it forward
To water the world under the latter starlight.

CLYTEMNESTRA (*to her slaves*)

Take up the poles of the bed; reverently; careful on the stair; give him to the people. (*To the people*) O soldiers
This was your leader; lay him with honor in the burial-chapel; guard him with the spears of victory;
Mourn him until to-morrow, when the pyre shall be built. Ah King of men, sleep, sleep, sleep!
. . . But when shall I? . . . They are after their corpse, like dogs after the butcher's cart. Cleomenes, that captain
With the big voice: Neobulus was the boy who flung the spear and missed. *I* shall not miss
When spear-flinging-time comes. . . . Captive woman, you have seen the future, tell my fortune.

(*Aegisthus comes from the doorway.*)

Aegisthus,
Have your hounds got them?

AEGISTHUS I've covered every escape with men, they'll not slip through me. But commanded
To bring them here living.

CLYTEMNESTRA That's hard: tigresses don't do it: I have some strength yet: don't speak of it
And I shall do it.

AEGISTHUS It is a thing not to be done: we'll guard them closely: but mere madness
Lies over the wall of too-much.

CLYTEMNESTRA King of Mycenae, new-crowned king, who was your mother?

AEGISTHUS Pelopia.
What mark do you aim at?

CLYTEMNESTRA And your father?

AEGISTHUS Thyestes.

CLYTEMNESTRA And her
father?

AEGISTHUS The same man, Thyestes.

CLYTEMNESTRA

See, dearest, dearest? They love what men call crime, they have taken her crime to be the king of Mycenae.
Here is the stone garden of the plants that pass nature: there is no too-much here: the monstrous
Old rocks want monstrous roots to serpent among them. I will have security. I'd burn the standing world
Up to this hour and begin new. You think I am too much used for a new brood? Ah, lover,
I have fountains in me. I had a fondness for the brown cheek of that boy, the curl of his lip,
The widening blue of the doomed eyes . . . I will be spared nothing. Come in, come in, they'll have news for us.

CASSANDRA

If anywhere in the world
Were a tower with foundations, or a treasure-chamber
With a firm vault, or a walled fortress
That stood on the years, not staggering, not moving
As the mortar were mixed with wine for water
And poppy for lime: they reel, they are all drunkards,
The piled strengths of the world: no pyramid
In bitter Egypt in the desert
But skips at moonrise; no mountain
Over the Black Sea in awful Caucasus
But whirls like a young kid, like a bud of the herd,
Under the hundredth star: I am sick after steadfastness
Watching the world cataractlike
Pour screaming onto steep ruins: for the wings of prophecy
God once my lover give me stone sandals

Planted on stone: he hates me, the God, he will never
Take home the gift of the bridleless horse,
The stallion, the unbitted stallion: the bed
Naked to the sky on Mount Ida,
The soft clear grass there,
Be blackened forever, may vipers and Greeks
In that glen breed
Twisting together, where the God
Come golden from the sun
Gave me for a bride-gift prophecy and I took it for a treasure:
I a fool, I a maiden,
I would not let him touch me though love of him maddened me
Till he fed me that poison, till he planted that fire in me,
The girdle flew loose then.

The Queen considered this rock, she gazed on the great stone blocks of
Mycenae's acropolis;
Monstrous they seemed to her, solid they appeared to her, safe rootage for
monstrous deeds: Ah fierce one
Who knows who laid them for a snare? What people in the world's dawn
breathed on chill air and the vapor
Of their breath seemed stone and has stood and you dream it is established?
These also are a foam on the stream
Of the falling of the world: there is nothing to lay hold on:
No crime is a crime, the slaying of the King was a meeting of two bubbles
on the lip of the cataract,
One winked . . . and the killing of your children would be nothing: I tell
you for a marvel that the earth is a dancer,
The grave dark earth is less quiet than a fool's fingers,
That old one, spinning in the emptiness, blown by no wind in vain circles,
light-witted and a dancer.

CLYTEMNESTRA *(entering)*

You are prophesying: prophesy to a purpose, captive woman. My children, the boy and the girl,
Have wandered astray, no one can find them.

CASSANDRA Shall I tell the lioness
Where meat is, or the she-wolf where the lambs wander astray?

CLYTEMNESTRA But look into the darkness
And foam of the world: the boy has great tender blue eyes, brown hair, disdainful lips, you'll know him
By the gold stripe bordering his garments; the girl's eyes are my color, white her clothing—

CASSANDRA Millions
Of shining bubbles burst and wander
On the stream of the world falling . . .

CLYTEMNESTRA These are my children!

CASSANDRA I see mountains, I see no faces.

CLYTEMNESTRA

Tell me and I make you free; conceal it from me and a soldier's spear finishes the matter.

CASSANDRA

I am the spear's bride, I have been waiting, waiting for that ecstasy—

CLYTEMNESTRA *(striking her)* Live then. It will not be unpainful. *(Clytemnestra goes in.)*

CASSANDRA

O fair roads north where the land narrows
Over the mountains between the great gulfs,
O that I too with the King's children
Might wander northward hand in hand.
Mine are worse wanderings:
They will shelter on Mount Parnassus,

For me there is no mountain firm enough,
The storms of light beating on the headlands,
The storms of music undermine the mountains, they stumble and fall
  inward,
Such music the stars
Make in their courses, the vast vibration
Plucks the iron heart of the earth like a harp-string.
Iron and stone core, O stubborn axle of the earth, you also
Dissolving in a little time like salt in water,
What does it matter that I have seen Macedon
Roll all the Greek cities into one billow and strand in Asia
The anthers and bracts of the flower of the world?
That I have seen Egypt and Nineveh
Crumble, and a Latian village
Plant the earth with javelins? It made laws for all men, it dissolved like a
  cloud.
I have also stood watching a storm of wild swans
Rise from one river-mouth . . . O force of the earth rising,
O fallings of the earth: forever no rest, not forever
From the wave and the trough, from the stream and the slack, from growth
  and decay: O vulture-
Pinioned, my spirit, one flight yet, last, longest, unguided,
Try into the gulf,
Over Greece, over Rome, you have space O my spirit for the years

II

Are not few of captivity: how many have I stood here
Among the great stones, while the Queen's people
Go in and out of the gate, wearing light linen
For summer and the wet spoils of wild beasts
In the season of storms: and the stars have changed, I have watched

The grievous and unprayed-to constellations
Pile steaming spring and patient autumn
Over the enduring walls: but you over the walls of the world,
Over the unquieted centuries, over the darkness-hearted
Millenniums wailing thinly to be born, O vulture-pinioned
Try into the dark,
Watch the north spawn white bodies and red-gold hair,
Race after race of beastlike warriors; and the cities
Burn, and the cities build, and new lands be uncovered
In the way of the sun to his setting . . . go on farther, what profit
In the wars and the toils? but I say
Where are prosperous people my enemies are, as you pass them O my spirit
Curse Athens for the joy and the marble, curse Corinth
For the wine and the purple, and Syracuse
For the gold and the ships; but Rome, Rome,
With many destructions for the corn and the laws and the javelins, the insolence, the threefold
Abominable power: pass the humble
And the lordships of darkness, but far down
Smite Spain for the blood on the sunset gold, curse France
For the fields abounding and the running rivers, the lights in the cities, the laughter, curse England
For the meat on the tables and the terrible gray ships, for old laws, far dominions, there remains
A mightier to be cursed and a higher for malediction
When America has eaten Europe and takes tribute of Asia, when the ends of the world grow aware of each other
And are dogs in one kennel, they will tear
The master of the hunt with the mouths of the pack: new fallings, new risings, O winged one
No end of the fallings and risings? An end shall be surely,

Though unnatural things are accomplished, they breathe in the sea's depth,
They swim in the air, they bridle the cloud-leaper lightning to carry their messages:
Though the eagles of the east and the west and the falcons of the north were not quieted, you have seen a white cloth
Cover the lands from the north and the eyes of the lands and the claws of the hunters,
The mouths of the hungry with snow
Were filled, and their claws
Took hold upon ice in the pasture, a morsel of ice was their catch in the rivers,
That pure white quietness
Waits on the heads of the mountains, not sleep but death, will the fire
Of burnt cities and ships in that year warm you my enemies? The frost, the old frost,
Like a cat with a broken-winged bird it will play with you,
It will nip and let go; you will say it is gone, but the next
Season it increases: O clean, clean,
White and most clean, colorless quietness,
Without trace, without trail, without stain in the garment, drawn down
From the poles to the girdle. . . . I have known one Godhead
To my sore hurt: I am growing to come to another: O grave and kindly
Last of the lords of the earth, I pray you lead my substance
Speedily into another shape, make me grass, Death, make me stone,
Make me air to wander free between the stars and the peaks; but cut humanity
Out of my being, that is the wound that festers in me,
Not captivity, not my enemies: you will heal the earth also,
Death, in your time; but speedily Cassandra.
You rock-fleas hopping in the clefts of Mycenae,
Suckers of blood, you carrying the scepter farther, Persian, Emathian,
Roman and Mongol and American, and you half-gods

Indian and Syrian and the third, emperors of peace, I have seen on what stage
You sing the little tragedy; the column of the ice that was before on one side flanks it,
The column of the ice to come closes it up on the other: audience nor author
I have never seen yet: I have heard the silence: it is I Cassandra,
Eight years the bitter watch-dog of these doors,
Have watched a vision
And now approach to my end. Eight years I have seen the phantoms
Walk up and down this stair; and the rocks groan in the night, the great stones move when no man sees them.
And I have forgotten the fine ashlar masonry of the courts of my father. I am not Cassandra
But a counter of sunrises, permitted to live because I am crying to die; three thousand,
Pale and red, have flowed over the towers in the wall since I was here watching; the deep east widens,
The cold wind blows, the deep earth sighs, the dim gray finger of light crooks at the morning star.
The palace feasted late and sleeps with its locked doors; the last drunkard from the alleys of the city
Long has reeled home. Whose foot is this then, what phantom
Toils on the stair?

A VOICE BELOW Is someone watching above? Good sentinel I am only a girl beggar.
I would sit on the stair and hold my bowl.

CASSANDRA I here eight years have begged for a thing and not received it.

THE VOICE
You are not a sentinel? You have been asking some great boon, out of all reason.

CASSANDRA No: what the meanest
Beggar disdains to take.

THE GIRL-BEGGAR Beggars disdain nothing: what is it that they refuse you?

CASSANDRA What's given
Even to the sheep and to the bullock.

THE GIRL Men give them salt, grass they find out for themselves.

CASSANDRA Men give them
The gift that you though a beggar have brought down from the north to give my mistress.

THE GIRL You speak riddles.
I am starving, a crust is my desire.

CASSANDRA Your voice is young though winds have hoarsened it, your body appears
Flexible under the rags: have you some hidden sickness, the young men will not give you silver?

THE GIRL
I have a sickness: I will hide it until I am cured. You are not a Greek woman?

CASSANDRA But you
Born in Mycenae return home. And you bring gifts from Phocis: for my once master who's dead
Vengeance; and for my mistress peace, for my master the King peace, and, by-shot of the doom's day,
Peace for me also. But I have prayed for it.

THE GIRL I know you, I knew you before you spoke to me, captive woman,
And I unarmed will kill you with my hands if you babble prophecies.
That peace you have prayed for, I will bring it to you
If you utter warnings.

CASSANDRA To-day I shall have peace, you cannot tempt me, daughter of the Queen, Electra.
Eight years ago I watched you and your brother going north to Phocis: the Queen saw knowledge of you
Move in my eyes: I would not tell her where you were when she commanded me: I will not betray you
To-day either: it is not doleful to me
To see before I die generations of destruction enter the doors of Agamemnon.
Where is your brother?

ELECTRA Prophetess: you see all: I will tell you nothing.

CASSANDRA He has well chosen his ambush,
It is true Aegisthus passes under that house to-day, to hunt in the mountain.

ELECTRA Now I remember
Your name. Cassandra.

CASSANDRA Hush: the gray has turned yellow, the standing beacons
Stream up from the east; they stir there in the palace; strange, is it not, the dawn of one's last day's
Like all the others? Your brother would be fortunate if to-day were also
The last of his.

ELECTRA He will endure his destinies; and Cassandra hers; and Electra mine.
He has been for years like one tortured with fire: this day will quench it.

CASSANDRA They are opening the gates: beg now.
To your trade, beggar-woman.

THE PORTER *(coming out)* Eh, pillar of miseries,
You still on guard there? Like a mare in a tight stall, never lying down. What's this then?

A second ragged one? This at least can bend in the middle and sit on a stone.

ELECTRA Dear gentleman

I am not used to it, my father is dead and hunger forces me to beg, a crust or a penny.

THE PORTER

This tall one's licensed in a manner. I think they'll not let two bundles of rag

Camp on the stair: but if you'd come to the back door and please me nicely: with a little washing

It'd do for pastime.

ELECTRA I was reared gently: I will sit here, the King will see me,

And none mishandle me.

THE PORTER I bear no blame for you.

I have not seen you: you came after the gates were opened. *(He goes in.)*

CASSANDRA

O blossom of fire, bitter to men,
Watchdog of the woeful days,
How many sleepers
Bathing in peace, dreaming themselves delight,
All over the city, all over the Argolid plain, all over the dark earth,
(Not me, a deeper draught of peace
And darker waters alone may wash me)
Do you, terrible star, star without pity,
Wolf of the east, waken to misery.
To the wants unaccomplished, to the eating desires,
To unanswered love, to hunger, to the hard edges
And mould of reality, to the whips of their masters.
They had flown away home to the happy darkness,
They were safe until sunrise.

(King Aegisthus, with his retinue, comes from the great door.)

AEGISTHUS

Even here, in the midst of the city, the early day
Has a clear savor. *(To Electra)* What, are you miserable, holding the bowl out?
We'll hear the lark to-day in the wide hills and smell the mountain. I'd share happiness with you.
What's your best wish, girl-beggar?

ELECTRA It is covered, my lord, how should a beggar
Know what to wish for beyond a crust and a dark corner and a little kindness?

AEGISTHUS Why do you tremble?

ELECTRA

I was reared gently; my father is dead.

AEGISTHUS Stand up: will you take service here in the house? What country
Bred you gently and proved ungentle to you?

ELECTRA I have wandered north from the Eurotas, my lord,
Begging at farmsteads.

AEGISTHUS The Queen's countrywoman then, she'll use you kindly. She'll be coming
In a moment, then I'll speak for you.—Did you bid them yoke the roans into my chariot, Menalcas,
The two from Orchomenus?

ONE OF THE RETINUE Yesterday evening, my lord,
I sent to the stable.

AEGISTHUS They cost a pretty penny, we'll see how they carry it.—She's coming: hold up your head, girl.

(Clytemnestra, with two serving-women, comes from the door.)

CLYTEMNESTRA
Good hunt, dearest. Here's a long idle day for me to look to. Kill early, come home early.

AEGISTHUS
There's a poor creature on the step who's been reared nicely and slipped into misery. I said you'd feed her,
And maybe find her a service. Farewell, sweet one.

CLYTEMNESTRA Where did she come from? How long have you been here?

AEGISTHUS She says she has begged her way up from Sparta. The horses are stamping on the cobbles, good-bye, good-bye.

(He goes down the stair with his huntsmen.)

CLYTEMNESTRA Good-bye, dearest. Well. Let me see your face.

ELECTRA It is filthy to look at. I am ashamed.

CLYTEMNESTRA *(to one of her serving-women)* Leucippe do you think this is a gayety of my lord's, he's not used to be so kindly to beggars? —Let me see your face.

LEUCIPPE She is very dirty, my lady. It is possible one of the house-boys . . .

CLYTEMNESTRA I say draw that rag back, let me see your face. I'd have him whipped then.

ELECTRA It was only in hope that someone would put a crust in the bowl, your majesty, for I am starving. I didn't think your majesty would see me.

CLYTEMNESTRA Draw back the rag.

ELECTRA I am very faint and starving but I will go down; I am ashamed.

CLYTEMNESTRA Stop her, Corinna. Fetch the porter, Leucippe. You will not go so easily. *(Electra sinks down on the steps and lies prone, her head covered.)* I am aging out of queenship indeed, when even the beggars refuse my bidding. *(Leucippe comes in with the porter.)* You have a dirty stair, porter. How long has this been here?

THE PORTER O my lady it has crept up since I opened the doors, it was not here when I opened the doors.

CLYTEMNESTRA Lift it up and uncover its face. What is that cry in the city? Stop: silent: I heard a cry . . .
Prophetess, your nostrils move like a dog's, what is that shouting? . . .
I have grown weak, I am exhausted, things frighten me . . .
Tell her to be gone, Leucippe, I don't wish to see her, I don't wish to see her. *(Electra rises.)*

ELECTRA Ah, Queen, I will show you my face.

CLYTEMNESTRA No . . . no . . . be gone.

ELECTRA *(uncovering her face)*
Mother: I have come home: I am humbled. This house keeps a dark welcome
For those coming home out of far countries.

CLYTEMNESTRA I won't look: how could I know anyone? I am old and shaking.
He said, Over the wall beyond nature
Lightning, and the laughter of the Gods. I did not cross it, I will not kill what I gave life to.
Whoever you are, go, go, let me grow downward to the grave quietly now.

ELECTRA I cannot
Go: I have no other refuge. Mother! Will you not kiss me, will you not take me into the house,
Your child once, long a wanderer? Electra my name. I have begged my way from Phocis, my brother is dead there,
Who used to care for me.

CLYTEMNESTRA Who is dead, who?

ELECTRA My brother Orestes,
Killed in a court quarrel.

CLYTEMNESTRA *(weeping)* Oh, you lie! The widening blue blue eyes,
The little voice of the child . . . Liar.

ELECTRA It is true. I have wept long, on every mountain. You, mother,
Have only begun weeping. Far off, in a far country, no fit burial . . .

CLYTEMNESTRA And do you bringing
Bitterness . . . or lies . . . look for a welcome? I have only loved two:
The priest killed my daughter for a lamb on a stone and now you say the boy too . . . dead, dead?
The world's full of it, a shoreless lake of lies and floating rumors . . . pack up your wares, peddler,
Too false for a queen. Why, no, if I believed you . . . Beast, treacherous beast, that shouting comes nearer,
What's in the city?

ELECTRA I am a stranger, I know nothing of the city, I know only
My mother hates me, and Orestes my brother
Died pitifully, far off.

CLYTEMNESTRA Too many things, too many things call me, what shall I do? Electra,
Electra help me. This comes of living softly, I had a lion's strength
Once.

ELECTRA
Me for help? I am utterly helpless, I had help in my brother and he is dead in Phocis.
Give me refuge: but each of us two must weep for herself, one sorrow. An end of the world were on us
What would it matter to us weeping? Do you remember him,
Mother, mother?

CLYTEMNESTRA I have dared too much: never dare anything, Electra, the ache is afterward,
At the hour it hurts nothing. Prophetess, you lied.

You said he would come with vengeance on me: but now he is dead, this girl says: and because he was lovely, blue-eyed,
And born in a most unhappy house I will believe it. But the world's fogged with the breath of liars,
And if she has laid a net for me . . .
I'll call up the old lioness lives yet in my body, I have dared, I have dared, and tooth and talon
Carve a way through. Lie to me?

ELECTRA

Have I endured for months, with feet bleeding, among the mountains,
Between the great gulfs alone and starving, to bring you a lie now? I know the worst of you, I looked for the worst,
Mother, mother, and have expected nothing but to die of this home-coming: but Orestes
Has entered the cave before; he is gathered up in a lonely mountain quietness, he is guarded from angers
In the tough cloud that spears fall back from.

CLYTEMNESTRA

Was he still beautiful? The brown mothers down in the city
Keep their brats about them: what it is to live high! Oh!
Tell them down there, tell them in Tiryns,
Tell them in Sparta,
That water drips through the Queen's fingers and trickles down her wrists, for the boy, for the boy
Born of her body, whom she, fool, fool, fool,
Drove out of the world. Electra,
Make peace with me.
Oh, Oh, Oh!
I have labored violently all the days of my life for nothing—nothing—worse than anything—this death
Was a thing I wished. See how they make fools of us.
Amusement for them, to watch us labor after the thing that will tear us in pieces. . . . Well, strength's good.

I am the Queen; I will gather up my fragments
And not go mad now.

ELECTRA Mother, what are the men
With spears gathering at the stair's foot? Not of Mycenae by their armor, have you mercenaries
Wanting pay? Do they serve . . . Aegisthus?

CLYTEMNESTRA What men? I seem not to know . . .
Who has laid a net for me, what fool
For me, me? Porter, by me.
Leucippe, my guards; into the house, rouse them. I am sorry for him,
I am best in storm. You, Electra?
The death you'll die, my daughter. Guards, out! Was it a lie? No matter, no matter, no matter,
Here's peace. Spears, out, out! They bungled the job making me a woman. Here's youth come back to me,
And all the days of gladness.

LEUCIPPE *(running back from the door)*
O, Queen, strangers . . .

ORESTES *(a sword in his hand, with spearmen following, comes from the door)*
Where is that woman
The Gods utterly hate?

ELECTRA Brother: let her not speak, kill quickly. Is the other one safe now?

ORESTES That dog
Fell under his chariot, we made sure of him between the wheels and the hooves, squealing. Now for this one.

CLYTEMNESTRA
Wait. I was weeping, Electra will tell you, my hands are wet still,
For your blue eyes that death had closed she said away up in Phocis. I die now, justly or not
Is out of the story, before I die I'd tell you—wait, child, wait. Did I quiver

Or pale at the blade? I say, caught in a net, netted in by my enemies, my husband murdered,
Myself to die, I am joyful knowing she lied, you live, the only creature
Under all the spread and arch of daylight
That I love, lives.

ELECTRA The great fangs drawn fear craftiness now, kill quickly.

CLYTEMNESTRA As for her, the wife of a shepherd
Suckled her, but you
These very breasts nourished: rather one of your northern spearmen do what's needful; not you
Draw blood where you drew milk. The Gods endure much, but beware them.

ORESTES This, a God in his temple
Openly commanded.

CLYTEMNESTRA Ah, child, child, who has mistaught you and who has betrayed you? What voice had the God?
How was it different from a man's and did you see him? Who sent the priest presents? They fool us,
And the Gods let them. No doubt also the envious King of Phocis has lent you counsel as he lent you
Men: let one of them do it. Life's not jewel enough
That I should plead for it: this much I pray, for your sake, not with your hand, not with your hand, or the memory
Will so mother you, so glue to you, so embracing you,
Not the deep sea's green day, no cleft of a rock in the bed of the deep sea, no ocean of darkness
Outside the stars, will hide nor wash you. What is it to me that I have rejoiced knowing you alive
O child, O precious to me, O alone loved, if now dying by my manner of death
I make nightmare the heir, nightmare, horror, in all I have of you;

And you haunted forever, never to sleep dreamless again, never to see blue cloth
But the red runs over it; fugitive of dreams, madman at length, the memory of a scream following you houndlike,
Inherit Mycenae? Child, for this has not been done before, there is no old fable, no whisper
Out of the foundation, among the people that were before our people, no echo has ever
Moved among these most ancient stones, the monsters here, nor stirred under any mountain, nor fluttered
Under any sky, of a man slaying his mother. Sons have killed fathers—

ORESTES And
a woman her son's father—

CLYTEMNESTRA
O many times: and these old stones have seen horrors: a house of madness and blood
I married into: and worse was done on this rock among the older people before: but not this,
Not the son his mother; this the silent ones,
The old hard ones, the great bearers of burden have not seen yet,
Nor shall, to-day nor yet to-morrow, nor ever in the world. Let her do it, it is not unnatural,
The daughter the mother; the little liar there,
Electra do it. Lend her the blade.

ELECTRA Brother though the great house is silent hark the city,
That buzzes like the hive one has dipped a wand in. End this. Then look to our safety.

ORESTES Dip in my sword
Into my fountain? Did I truly, little and helpless,
Lie in the arms, feed on the breast there?

ELECTRA Another, a greater, lay in them,
another kissed the breast there,
You forget easily, the breaker of Asia, the over-shadower, the great
memory, under whose greatness
We have hung like hawks under a storm, from the beginning,—and he
when this poison destroyed him
Was given no room to plead in.

ORESTES Dip my wand into my fountain?

CLYTEMNESTRA Men
do not kill the meanest
Without defence heard—

ELECTRA Him—Agamemnon?

CLYTEMNESTRA But you, O my son,
my son,
Moulded in me, made of me, made of my flesh, built with my blood, fed
with my milk, my child
I here, I and no other, labored to bear, groaning—

ELECTRA This that makes
beastlike lamentation
Hunted us to slay us, we starving in the thicket above the stream three days
and nights watched always
Her hunters with spears beating the field: prophetess was it for love that she
looked after us?

CASSANDRA That love
The King had tasted; that was her love.

ELECTRA And mourning for our father on
the mountain we judged her;
And the God condemned her, what more, what more? Strike.

ORESTES If they'd
give me time, the pack there—how can I think,

And all the whelps of Mycenae yelling at the stair-foot? Decision: a thing to be decided:
The arm's lame, dip in, dip in? Shut your mouths, rabble.

CLYTEMNESTRA There is one thing no man can do.

ORESTES What, enter his fountain?

ELECTRA
O coward!

ORESTES I will be passive, I'm blunted. She's not this fellow's mother.

ELECTRA O spearman, spearman, do it!
One stroke: it is just.

THE SPEARMAN As for me, my lord . . .

CLYTEMNESTRA *(calling loudly)* Help, help, men of Mycenae, to your Queen. Break them.
Rush the stair, there are only ten hold it. Up, up, kill.

ORESTES I will kill.

CLYTEMNESTRA *(falling on her knees)* Child,
Spare me, let me live! Child! Ai! . . .

ELECTRA You have done well.

ORESTES I have done . . . I have done . . .
Who ever saw such a flow . . . was I made out of this, I'm not red, am I?
See, father?
It was someone else did it but I told him to. Drink, drink, dog. Drink dog.
He reaches up a tongue between the stones, lapping it. So thirsty old dog, uh?
Rich and sticky.

CLYTEMNESTRA *(raising herself a little)* Sleep . . . for me . . . yes.
Not you . . . any more . . . Orestes . . . I shall be there. You will beg death . . . vainly as I have begged . . . life. Ah . . . beast that I unkennelled! *(She dies.)*

ORESTES *(crouching by her)* Ooh . . . Ooh . . .

ELECTRA The face is lean and terrible. Orestes!

They are fighting on the stair. Man yourself. Come. Pick up the sword.

Let her be, two of ours are down, they yield on the stair. Stand up, speak or fight, speak to the people

Or we go where she is.

ORESTES There's a red and sticky sky that you can touch here.

And though it's unpleasant we are at peace.

ELECTRA *(catching up the sword)* Agamemnon failed here. Not in me. Hear, Mycenaeans.

I am Agamemnon's daughter, we have avenged him, the crime's paid utterly.

You have not forgotten the great King—what, in eight years? I am Electra, I am his daughter.

My brother is Orestes. My brother is your king and has killed his murderers. The dog Aegisthus is dead,

And the Queen is dead: the city is at peace.

ORESTES *(standing up)* Must I dip my wand into my fountain, give it to me.

The male plaything. *(He catches Electra's arm, snatching at the sword.)*

ELECTRA For what? Be quiet, they have heard me.

ORESTES You said I must do it, I will do it.

ELECTRA It is done!

Brother, brother? *(Orestes takes the sword from her by force.)* O Mycenae

With this sword he did justice, he let it fall, he has retaken it,

He is your King.

ORESTES Whom must I pierce, the girl that plotted with me in the mountain? There was someone to kill . . .

Sweet Electra?

ELECTRA It is done, it is finished!

CASSANDRA The nearest, the most loved,
her, truly. Strike! — Electra,
My father has wanted vengeance longer.

THE PEOPLE BELOW Orestes, Orestes!

ELECTRA *(pointing to Cassandra)* Her — your
mother — she killed him.

ORESTES *(turning and striking)*
How tall you have grown, mother.

CASSANDRA *(falling)* I . . . waited long for it . . .

ORESTES
I have killed my mother and my mother — two mothers — see, there they lie — I have gone home twice. You put it in
And the flesh yields to it . . . *(He goes down the stair.)* Now, to find her again
All through the forest . . .

ELECTRA Let him pass, Mycenaeans. Avoid his sword.
Let him pass, pass. The madness of the house
Perches on him.

A LEADER OF THE MYCENAEANS
Daughter of Agamemnon,
You with constancy and force
In the issueless thing have found an issue. Now it is for us the kingless city
To find a ruler. Rest in the house. As for the young man,
Though he has done justice, and no hand in Mycenae is raised against him, for him there is no issue.
We let him go on; and if he does not slay himself with the red sword he will die in the mountain.
With us be peace. Rest in the house, daughter of Agamemnon. The old madness, with your brother,
Go out of our gates.

ELECTRA A house to rest in! . . . Gather up the dead: I will go in; I have learned strength.

III

They carried the dead down the great stair; the slaves with pails of water and sand scoured the dark stains.
The people meeting in another place to settle the troubled city the stair was left vacant,
The porch untrampled, and about twilight one of the great stones: The world is younger than we are,
Yet now drawing to an end, now that the seasons falter. Then another, that had been spared the blood-bath:
What way do they falter?—There fell warm rain, the first answered, in the midst of summer. A little afterward
Cold rain came down; and sand was rubbed over me as when the winds blow. This in the midst of summer.
—I did not feel it, said the second sleepily. And a third: The noisy and very mobile creatures
Will be quieted long before the world's end.—What creatures?—The active ones, that have two ends let downward,
A mongrel race, mixed of soft stone with fugitive water. The night deepened, the dull old stones
Droned at each other, the summer stars wheeled over above them. Before dawn the son of Agamemnon
Came to the stair-foot in the darkness.

ORESTES O stones of the house: I entreat hardness: I did not live with you
Long enough in my youth. . . . I will go up to where I killed her. . . . We must face things down, mother,
Or they'd devour us. . . . Nobody? . . . Even the stones have been scrubbed. A keen housekeeper, sweet Electra. . . .
It would be childish to forget it; the woman has certainly been killed, and I think it was I

Her son did it. Something not done before in the world. Here is the penalty:
You gather up all your forces to the act, and afterward
Silence, no voice, no ghost, vacancy, but all's not expended. Those powers want bitter action. No object.
Deeds are too easy. Our victims are too fragile, they ought to have thousands of lives, you strike out once only
The sky breaks like a bubble. . . . No, wife of Aegisthus, — why should I mask it? — mother, my mother,
The one soft fibre that went mad yesterday's
Burnt out of me now, there is nothing you could touch if you should come; but you have no power, you dead
Are a weak people. This is the very spot: I was here, she here: and I walk over it not trembling,
Over the scrubbed stones to the door. *(He knocks with the sword-hilt.)* They sleep well. But my sister having all her desire
Better than any. *(He knocks again.)*

THE PORTER *(through the door)* Who is there?

ORESTES The owner of the house. Orestes.

THE PORTER Go away, drunkard.

ORESTES Shall I tell my servants to break in the door and whip the porter?

THE PORTER Oh, Oh! You men from Phocis, stand by me while I speak to the door. *(Having opened the door, holding a torch.)* Is it you truly, my lord? We thought, we thought . . . we pray you to enter the house, my lord Orestes.

ORESTES You are to waken my sister.
I'll speak with her here.

ELECTRA *(at the door)* Oh! You are safe, you are well! Did you think I could be sleeping? But it is true,
I have slept soundly. Come, come.

ORESTES A fellow in the forest

Told me you'd had the stone scrubbed . . . I mean, that you'd entered the house, received as Agamemnon's daughter
In the honor of the city. So I free to go traveling have come with — what's the word, Electra? — farewell.
Have come to bid you farewell.

ELECTRA It means — you are going somewhere?

Come into the house, Orestes, tell me . . .

ORESTES

The cape's rounded. I have not shipwrecked.

ELECTRA Around the rock we have

passed safely is the hall of this house,
The throne in the hall, the shining lordship of Mycenae.

ORESTES No: the open

world, the sea and its wonders.
You thought the oars raked the headland in the great storm — what, for Mycenae?

ELECTRA Not meanest of the Greek cities:

Whose king captained the world into Asia. Have you suddenly become . . . a God, brother, to over vault
Agamemnon's royalty? O come in, come in. I am cold, cold. I pray you.

ORESTES Fetch

a cloak, porter.
If I have outgrown the city a little — I have earned it. Did you notice, Electra, she caught at the sword
As the point entered: the palm of her right hand was slashed to the bone before the mercy of the point
Slept in her breast: the laid-open palm it was that undermined me . . . Oh, the cloak. It's a blond night,
We'll walk on the stones: no chill, the stars are mellow. If I dare remember
Yesterday . . . because I have conquered, the soft fibre's burnt out.

ELECTRA
You
have conquered: possess: enter the house,
Take up the royalty.

ORESTES
You were in my vision to-night in the forest,
Electra, I thought I embraced you
More than brotherwise . . . possessed, you call it . . . entered the fountain—

ELECTRA
Oh, hush. *Therefore* you would not kill her!

ORESTES
I killed. It is foolish to darken things with words. I was here, she there, screaming. Who if not I?

ELECTRA
The hidden reason: the bitter kernel of your mind that has made you mad: I that learned strength
Yesterday, I have no fear.

ORESTES
Fear? The city is friendly and took you home with honor, they'll pay
Phocis his wage, you will be quiet.

ELECTRA
Are you resolved to understand nothing, Orestes?
I am not Agamemnon, only his daughter. You are Agamemnon. Beggars and the sons of beggars
May wander at will over the world, but Agamemnon has his honor and high Mycenae
Is not to be cast.

ORESTES
Mycenae for a ship: who will buy kingdom
And sell me a ship with oars?

ELECTRA
Dear: listen. Come to the parapet where it hangs over the night:
The ears at the door hinder me. Now, let the arrow-eyed stars hear, the night, not men, as for the Gods

No one can know them, whether they be angry or pleased, tall and terrible, standing apart,
When they make signs out of the darkness. . . . I cannot tell you. . . . You will stay here, brother?

ORESTES I'll go
To the edge and over it. Sweet sister if you've got a message for them, the dark ones?

ELECTRA You do not mean
Death; but a wandering; what does it matter what you mean? I know two ways and one will quiet you.
You shall choose either.

ORESTES But I am quiet. It is more regular than a sleeping child's: be untroubled,
Yours burns, it is you trembling.

ELECTRA Should I not tremble? It is only a little to offer,
But all that I have.

ORESTES Offer?

ELECTRA It is accomplished: my father is avenged: the fates and the body of Electra
Are nothing. But for Agamemnon to rule in Mycenae: that is not nothing. O my brother
You are Agamemnon: rule: take all you will: nothing is denied you. The Gods have redressed evil
And clamped the balance.

ORESTES No doubt they have done what they desired.

ELECTRA And yours, yours? I will not suffer her
Justly punished to dog you over the end of the world. Your desire? Speak it openly Orestes.

She is to be conquered: if her ghost were present on the stones—let it hear you. I will make war on her
With my life, or with my body.

ORESTES What strange martyrdom, Electra, what madness for sacrifice
Makes your eyes burn like two fires on a watch-tower, though the night darkens?

ELECTRA What you want you shall have:
And rule in Mycenae. Nothing, nothing is denied you. If I knew which of the two choices
Would quiet you, I would do and not speak, not ask you. Tell me, tell me. Must I bear all the burden,
I weaker, and a woman? You and I were two hawks quartering the field for living flesh Orestes
Under the storm of the memory
Of Agamemnon: we struck: we tore the prey, that dog and that woman. Suddenly since yesterday
You have shot up over me and left me,
You are Agamemnon, you are the storm of the living presence, the very King, and I, lost wings
Under the storm, would die for you. . . . You do not speak yet? . . . Mine to say it all? . . . You know me a maiden, Orestes,
You have always been with me, no man has even touched my cheek. It is not easy for one unmarried
And chaste, to name both choices. The first is easy. That terrible dream in the forest: if fear of desire
Drives you away: it is easy for me not to be. I never have known
Sweetness in life: all my young days were given—

ORESTES I thought to be silent was better,
And understand you: afterwards I'll speak.

ELECTRA —to the noise of blood crying
for blood, a crime to be punished,
A house to be emptied: these things are done: and now I am lonely, and what becomes of me is not important.
There's water, and there are points and edges, pain's only a moment: I'd do it and not speak, but nobody knows
Whether it would give you peace or madden you again, I'd not be leagued with that bad woman against you
And these great walls sit by the crater, terrible desires blow through them. O brother I'll never blame you,
I share the motherhood and the fatherhood, I can conceive the madness, if you desire too near
The fountain: tell me: I also love *you*: not that way, but enough to suffer. What needs to be done
To make peace for you, tell me. I shall so gladly die to make it for you: or so gladly yield you
What you know is maiden. You are the King: have all your will: only remain in steep Mycenae,
In the honor of our father. Not yet: do not speak yet. You have said it is not
Remorse drives you away: monsters require monsters, to have let her live a moment longer
Would have been the crime: therefore it cannot be but desire drives you: or the fear of desire: dearest,
It is known horror unlocks the heart, a shower of things hidden: if that which happened yesterday unmasked
A beautiful brother's love and showed more awful eyes in it: all that our Gods require is courage.
Let me see the face, let the eyes pierce me. What dearest? Here in the stiff cloth of the sacred darkness
Fold over fold hidden, above the sleeping city,

By the great stones of the door, under the little golden falcons that swarm
before dawn up yonder,
In the silence . . . must I dare to woo you,
I whom man never wooed? to let my hand glide under the cloak. . . . O
you will stay! these arms
Making so soft and white a bond around you . . . I also begin to love—
that way, Orestes,
Feeling the hot hard flesh move under the loose cloth, shudder against
me. . . . Ah, your mouth, Ah,
The burning—kiss me—

ORESTES We shall never ascend this mountain. So it
might come true: we have to be tough against them,
Our dreams and visions, or they true themselves into flesh. It is sweet: I
faint for it: the old stones here
Have seen more and not moved. A custom of the house. To accept you
little Electra and go my journey
To-morrow: you'd call cheating. Therefore: we shall not go up this
mountain dearest, dearest,
To-night nor ever. It's Clytemnestra in you. But the dead are a weak tribe.
If I had Agamemnon's
We'd live happily sister and lord it in Mycenae—be a king like the
others—royalty and incest
Run both in the stream of the blood. Who scrubbed the stones there?

ELECTRA Slaves.
O fire burn me! Enter and lay waste,
Deflower, trample, break down, pillage the little city,
Make what breach you will, with flesh or a spear, give it to the spoiler. See,
as I tear the garment.
What if I called it cheating? Be cruel and treacherous: I'll run my chances
On the bitter mercies of to-morrow.

ORESTES Bitter they would be. No.

ELECTRA It's
clear that for this reason
You'd sneak out of Mycenae and be lost outward. Taste first, bite the apple, once dared and tried
Desire will be not terrible. It's dog like to run off whining. Remember it was I that urged
Yesterday's triumph. You: life was enough: let them live. I drove on, burning; your mind, reluctant metal,
I dipped it in fire and forged it sharp, day after day I beat and burned against you, and forged
A sword: I the arm. Are you sorry it's done? Now again with hammer and burning heat I beat against you,
You will not be sorry. We two of all the world, we alone
Are fit for each other, we have so wrought . . . O eyes scorning the world, storm-feathered hawk my hands
Caught out of the air and made you a king over this rock, O axe with the gold helve, O star
Alone over the storm, beacon to men over blown seas, you will not flee fate, you will take
What the Gods give. What is a man not ruling? An ant in the hill: ruler or slave the choice is,
—Or a runaway slave, your pilgrim portion, buffeted over the borders of the lands, publicly
Whipped in the cities. But you, you will bind the north-star on your forehead, you will stand up in Mycenae
Stone, and a king.

ORESTES I am stone enough not to be changed by words, nor by the sweet and burning flame of you,
Beautiful Electra.

ELECTRA Well then: we've wasted our night. See, there's the morning star
I might have draggled into a metaphor of you. A fool: a boy: no king.

ORESTES It
would have been better
To have parted kindlier, for it is likely
We shall have no future meeting.

ELECTRA You will let this crime (the God
commanded) that dirtied the old stones here
Make division forever?

ORESTES Not the crime, the wakening. That deed is past, it
is finished, things past
Make no division afterward, they have no power, they have become nothing
at all; this much
I have learned at a crime's knees.

ELECTRA Yet we are divided.

ORESTES Because I have
suddenly awakened, I will not waste inward
Upon humanity, having found a fairer object.

ELECTRA Some nymph of the field? I
knew this coldness
Had a sick root: a girl in the north told me about the hill-shepherds who
living in solitude
Turn beast with the ewes, their oreads baa to them through the matted
fleece and they run mad, what madness
Met you in the night and sticks to you?

ORESTES I left the madness of the house,
to-night in the dark, with you it walks yet.
How shall I tell you what I have learned? Your mind is like a hawk's or like
a lion's, this knowledge
Is out of the order of your mind, a stranger language. To wild-beasts and
the blood of kings
A verse blind in the book.

ELECTRA At least my eyes can see dawn graying: tell and not mock me, our moment
Dies in a moment.
ORESTES Here is the last labor
To spend on humanity. I saw a vision of us move in the dark: all that we did or dreamed of
Regarded each other, the man pursued the woman, the woman clung to the man, warriors and kings
Strained at each other in the darkness, all loved or fought inward, each one of the lost people
Sought the eyes of another that another should praise him; sought never his own but another's; the net of desire
Had every nerve drawn to the centre, so that they writhed like a full draught of fishes, all matted
In the one mesh; when they look backward they see only a man standing at the beginning,
Or forward, a man at the end; or if upward, men in the shining bitter sky striding and feasting,
Whom you call Gods . . .
It is all turned inward, all your desires incestuous, the woman the serpent, the man the rose-red cavern,
Both human, worship forever . . .
ELECTRA You have dreamed wretchedly.
ORESTES I have seen the dreams of the people and not dreamed them.
As for me, I have slain my mother.
ELECTRA No more?
ORESTES And the gate's open, the gray boils over the mountain, I have greater
Kindred than dwell under a roof. Didn't I say this would be dark to you? I have cut the meshes
And fly like a freed falcon. To-night, lying on the hillside, sick with those visions, I remembered

The knife in the stalk of my humanity; I drew and it broke; I entered the life of the brown forest
And the great life of the ancient peaks, the patience of stone, I felt the changes in the veins
In the throat of the mountain, a grain in many centuries, we have our own time, not yours; and I was the stream
Draining the mountain wood; and I the stag drinking; and I was the stars
Boiling with light, wandering alone, each one the lord of his own summit; and I was the darkness
Outside the stars, I included them, they were a part of me. I was mankind also, a moving lichen
On the cheek of the round stone . . . they have not made words for it, to go behind things, beyond hours and ages,
And be all things in all time, in their returns and passages, in the motionless and timeless centre,
In the white of the fire . . . how can I express the excellence I have found, that has no color but clearness;
No honey but ecstasy; nothing wrought nor remembered; no undertone nor silver second murmur
That rings in love's voice, I and my loved are one; no desire but fulfilled; no passion but peace,
The pure flame and the white, fierier than any passion; no time but spheral eternity: Electra,
Was that your name before this life dawned—

ELECTRA Here is mere death. Death like a triumph I'd have paid to keep you
A king in high Mycenae: but here is shameful death, to die because I have lost you. They'll say
Having done justice Agamemnon's son ran mad and was lost in the mountain; but Agamemnon's daughter
Hanged herself from a beam of the house: O bountiful hands of justice! This horror draws upon me
Like stone walking.

ORESTES What fills men's mouths is nothing; and your threat is nothing; I have fallen in love outward.
If I believed you—it is I that am like stone walking.

ELECTRA I can endure even to hate you,
But that's no matter. Strength's good. You are lost. I here remember the honor of the house, and Agamemnon's.

She turned and entered the ancient house. Orestes walked in the clear dawn; men say that a serpent
Killed him in high Arcadia. But young or old, few years or many, signified less than nothing
To him who had climbed the tower beyond time, consciously, and cast humanity, entered the earlier fountain.

ROAN STALLION

The dog barked; then the woman stood in the doorway, and hearing iron strike stone down the steep road
Covered her head with a black shawl and entered the light rain; she stood at the turn of the road.
A nobly formed woman; erect and strong as a new tower; the features stolid and dark
But sculptured into a strong grace; straight nose with a high bridge, firm and wide eyes, full chin,
Red lips; she was only a fourth part Indian; a Scottish sailor had planted her in young native earth,
Spanish and Indian, twenty-one years before. He had named her California when she was born;
That was her name; and had gone north.

She heard the hooves and wheels come nearer, up the steep road.
The buckskin mare, leaning against the breastpiece, plodded into sight round the wet bank.
The pale face of the driver followed; the burnt-out eyes; they had fortune in them. He sat twisted
On the seat of the old buggy, leading a second horse by a long halter, a roan, a big one,
That stepped daintily; by the swell of the neck, a stallion. "What have you got, Johnny?" "Maskerel's stallion.
Mine now. I won him last night, I had very good luck." He was quite drunk. "They bring their mares up here now.
I keep this fellow. I got money besides, but I'll not show you." "Did you buy something, Johnny,
For our Christine? Christmas comes in two days, Johnny." "By God, forgot," he answered laughing.

"Don't tell Christine it's Christmas; after while I get her something, maybe." But California:
"I shared your luck when you lost: you lost *me* once, Johnny, remember? Tom Dell had me two nights
Here in the house: other times we've gone hungry: now that you've won, Christine will have her Christmas.
We share your luck, Johnny. You give me money, I go down to Monterey to-morrow,
Buy presents for Christine, come back in the evening. Next day Christmas." "You have wet ride," he answered
Giggling. "Here money. Five dollar; ten; twelve dollar. You buy two bottles of rye whisky for Johnny."
"All right. I go to-morrow."

He was an outcast Hollander; not old, but shriveled with bad living.
The child Christine inherited from his race blue eyes, from his life a wizened forehead; she watched
From the house-door her father lurch out of the buggy and lead with due respect the stallion
To the new corral, the strong one; leaving the wearily breathing buckskin mare to his wife to unharness.

Storm in the night; the rain on the thin shakes of the roof like the ocean on rock streamed battering; once thunder
Walked down the narrow canyon into Carmel valley and wore away westward; Christine was wakeful
With fears and wonders; her father lay too deep for storm to touch him.

Dawn
comes late in the year's dark,

Later into the crack of a canyon under redwoods; and California slipped from bed
An hour before it; the buckskin would be tired; there was a little barley, and why should Johnny
Feed all the barley to his stallion? That is what he would do. She tip-toed out of the room,
Leaving her clothes, he'd waken if she waited to put them on, and passed from the door of the house
Into the dark of the rain; the big black drops were cold through the thin shift, but the wet earth
Pleasant under her naked feet. There was a pleasant smell in the stable; and moving softly,
Touching things gently with the supple bend of the unclothed body, was pleasant. She found a box,
Filled it with sweet dry barley and took it down to the old corral. The little mare sighed deeply
At the rail in the wet darkness; and California returning between two redwoods up to the house
Heard the happy jaws grinding the grain. Johnny could mind the pigs and chickens. Christine called to her
When she entered the house, but slept again under her hand. She laid the wet night-dress on a chair-back
And stole into the bed-room to get her clothes. A plank creaked, and he wakened. She stood motionless
Hearing him stir in the bed. When he was quiet she stooped after her shoes, and he said softly,
"What are you doing? Come back to bed." "It's late, I'm going to Monterey, I must hitch up."
"You come to bed first. I been away three days. I give you money, I take back the money
And what you do in town then?" She sighed sharply and came to the bed.

He reaching his hands from it
Felt the cool curve and firmness of her flank, and half rising caught her by the long wet hair.
She endured, and to hasten the act she feigned desire; she had not for long, except in dream, felt it.
Yesterday's drunkenness made him sluggish and exacting; she saw, turning her head sadly,
The windows were bright gray with dawn; he embraced her still, stopping to talk about the stallion.
At length she was permitted to put on her clothes. Clear daylight over the steep hills;
Gray-shining cloud over the tops of the redwoods; the winter stream sang loud; the wheels of the buggy
Slipped in deep slime, ground on washed stones at the road-edge. Down the hill the wrinkled river smothered the ford.
You must keep to the bed of stones: she knew the way by willow and alder: the buckskin halted mid-stream,
Shuddering, the water her own color washing up to the traces; but California, drawing up
Her feet out of the whirl onto the seat of the buggy swung the whip over the yellow water
And drove to the road.

All morning the clouds were racing northward like a river. At noon they thickened.
When California faced the southwind home from Monterey it was heavy with level rain-fall.
She looked seaward from the foot of the valley; red rays cried sunset from a trumpet of streaming

Cloud over Lobos, the southwest occident of the solstice. Twilight came soon, but the tired mare
Feared the road more than the whip. Mile after mile of slow gray twilight.

Then,
quite suddenly, darkness.
"Christine will be asleep. It is Christmas Eve. The ford. That hour of daylight wasted this morning!"
She could see nothing; she let the reins lie on the dashboard and knew at length by the cramp of the wheels
And the pitch down, they had reached it. Noise of wheels on stones, plashing of hooves in water; a world
Of sounds; no sight; the gentle thunder of water; the mare snorting, dipping her head, one knew,
To look for footing, in the blackness, under the stream. The hushing and creaking of the sea-wind
In the passion of invisible willows.

The mare stood still; the woman
shouted to her; spared whip,
For a false leap would lose the track of the ford. She stood. "The baby's things," thought California,
"Under the seat: the water will come over the floor"; and rising in the midst of the water
She tilted the seat; fetched up the doll, the painted wooden chickens, the woolly bear, the book
Of many pictures, the box of sweets: she brought them all from under the seat and stored them, trembling,
Under her clothes, about the breasts, under the arms; the corners of the cardboard boxes
Cut into the soft flesh; but with a piece of rope for a girdle and wound about the shoulders

All was made fast. The mare stood still as if asleep in the midst of the water. Then California
Reached out a hand over the stream and fingered her rump; the solid wet convexity of it
Shook like the beat of a great heart. "What are you waiting for?" But the feel of the animal surface
Had wakened a dream, obscured real danger with a dream of danger. "What for? For the water-stallion
To break out of the stream, that is what the rump strains for, him to come up flinging foam sidewise,
Fore-hooves in air, crush me and the rig and curl over his woman." She flung out with the whip then;
The mare plunged forward. The buggy drifted sidelong: was she off ground? Swimming? No: by the splashes.
The driver, a mere prehensile instinct, clung to the side-irons of the seat and felt the force
But not the coldness of the water, curling over her knees, breaking up to the waist
Over her body. They'd turned. The mare had turned up stream and was wallowing back into shoal water.
Then California dropped her forehead to her knees, having seen nothing, feeling a danger,
And felt the brute weight of a branch of alder, the pendulous light leaves brush her bent neck
Like a child's fingers. The mare burst out of water and stopped on the slope to the ford. The woman climbed down
Between the wheels and went to her head. "Poor Dora," she called her by her name, "there, Dora. Quietly,"
And led her around, there was room to turn on the margin, the head to the gentle thunder of the water.
She crawled on hands and knees, felt for the ruts, and shifted the wheels into them. "You can see, Dora.

I can't. But this time you'll go through it." She climbed into the seat and shouted angrily. The mare
Stopped, her two forefeet in the water. She touched with the whip. The mare plodded ahead and halted.
Then California thought of prayer: "Dear little Jesus,
Dear baby Jesus born to-night, your head was shining
Like silver candles. I've got a baby too, only a girl. You had light wherever you walked.
Dear baby Jesus give me light." Light streamed: rose, gold, rich purple, hiding the ford like a curtain.
The gentle thunder of water was a noise of wing-feathers, the fans of paradise lifting softly.
The child afloat on radiance had a baby face, but the angels had birds' heads, hawks' heads,
Bending over the baby, weaving a web of wings about him. He held in the small fat hand
A little snake with golden eyes, and California could see clearly on the under radiance
The mare's pricked ears, a sharp black fork against the shining light-fall. But it dropped; the light of heaven
Frightened poor Dora. She backed; swung up the water,
And nearly oversetting the buggy turned and scrambled backward; the iron wheel-tires rang on bowlders.

Then California weeping climbed between the wheels. Her wet clothes and the toys packed under
Dragged her down with their weight; she stripped off cloak and dress and laid the baby's things in the buggy;
Brought Johnny's whisky out from under the seat; wrapped all in the dress, bottles and toys, and tied them
Into a bundle that would sling over her back. She unharnessed the mare, hurting her fingers

Against the swollen straps and the wet buckles. She tied the pack over her shoulders, the cords
Crossing her breasts, and mounted. She drew up her shift about her waist and knotted it, naked thighs
Clutching the sides of the mare, bare flesh to the wet withers, and caught the mane with her right hand,
The looped-up bridle-reins in the other. "Dora, the baby gives you light." The blinding radiance
Hovered the ford. "Sweet baby Jesus give us light." Cataracts of light and Latin singing
Fell through the willows; the mare snorted and reared: the roar and thunder of the invisible water;
The night shaking open like a flag, shot with the flashes; the baby face hovering; the water
Beating over her shoes and stockings up to the bare thighs; and over them, like a beast
Lapping her belly; the wriggle and pitch of the mare swimming; the drift, the sucking water; the blinding
Light above and behind with not a gleam before, in the throat of darkness; the shock of the fore-hooves
Striking bottom, the struggle and surging lift of the haunches. She felt the water streaming off her
From the shoulders down; heard the great strain and sob of the mare's breathing, heard the horse-shoes grind on gravel.
When California came home the dog at the door snuffed at her without barking; Christine and Johnny
Both were asleep; she did not sleep for hours, but kindled fire and knelt patiently over it,
Shaping and drying the dear-bought gifts for Christmas morning.

She

hated (she thought) the proud-necked stallion.

He'd lean the big twin masses of his breast on the rail, his red-brown eyes
flash the white crescents,
She admired him then, she hated him for his uselessness, serving nothing
But Johnny's vanity. Horses were too cheap to breed. She thought, if he
could range in freedom,
Shaking the red-roan mane for a flag on the bare hills.

A man brought up
a mare in April;
Then California, though she wanted to watch, stayed with Christine
indoors. When the child fretted
The mother told her once more about the miracle of the ford; her prayer to
the little Jesus
The Christmas Eve when she was bringing the gifts home; the appearance,
the lights, the Latin singing,
The thunder of wing-feathers and water, the shining child, the cataracts of
splendor down the darkness.
"A little baby," Christine asked, "the God is a baby?" "The child of God.
That was his birthday.
His mother was named Mary: we pray to her too: God came to her. He
was not the child of a man
Like you or me. God was his father: she was the stallion's wife—what did I
say—God's wife,"
She said with a cry, lifting Christine aside, pacing the planks of the floor.
"She is called more blessed
Than any woman. She was so good, she was more loved." "Did God live
near her house?" "He lives
Up high, over the stars; he ranges on the bare blue hill of the sky." In her
mind a picture
Flashed, of the red-roan mane shaken out for a flag on the bare hills, and
she said quickly, "He's more

Like a great man holding the sun in his hand." Her mind giving her words the lie, "But no one
Knows, only the shining and the power. The power, the terror, the burning fire covered her over . . ."
"Was she burnt up, mother?" "She was so good and lovely, she was the mother of the little Jesus.
If you are good nothing will hurt you." "What did she think?" "She loved, she was not afraid of the hooves—
Hands that had made the hills and sun and moon, and the sea and the great redwoods, the terrible strength,
She gave herself without thinking." "You only saw the baby, mother?" "Yes, and the angels about him,
The great wild shining over the black river." Three times she had walked to the door, three times returned,
And now the hand that had thrice hung on the knob, full of prevented action, twisted the cloth
Of the child's dress that she had been mending. "Oh, Oh, I've torn it." She struck at the child and then embraced her
Fiercely, the small blond sickly body.

Johnny came in, his face reddened as if he had stood
Near fire, his eyes triumphing. "Finished," he said, and looked with malice at Christine. "I go
Down valley with Jim Carrier; owes me five dollar, fifteen I charge him, he brought ten in his pocket.
Has grapes on the ranch, maybe I take a barrel red wine instead of money. Be back to-morrow.
To-morrow night I tell you—Eh, Jim," he laughed over his shoulder, "I say to-morrow evening
I show her how the red fellow act, the big fellow. When I come home." She answered nothing, but stood

In front of the door, holding the little hand of her daughter, in the path of
sun between the redwoods,
While Johnny tied the buckskin mare behind Carrier's buggy, and bringing
saddle and bridle tossed them
Under the seat. Jim Carrier's mare, the bay, stood with drooped head and
started slowly, the men
Laughing and shouting at her; their voices could be heard down the steep
road, after the noise
Of the iron-hooped wheels died from the stone. Then one might hear the
hush of the wind in the tall redwoods,
The tinkle of the April brook, deep in its hollow.

Humanity is the start
of the race; I say
Humanity is the mould to break away from, the crust to break through, the
coal to break into fire,
The atom to be split.

Tragedy that breaks man's face and a white fire flies
out of it; vision that fools him
Out of his limits, desire that fools him out of his limits, unnatural crime,
inhuman science,
Slit eyes in the mask; wild loves that leap over the walls of nature, the wild
fence-vaulter science,
Useless intelligence of far stars, dim knowledge of the spinning demons
that make an atom,
These break, these pierce, these deify, praising their God shrilly with fierce
voices: not in a man's shape
He approves the praise, he that walks lightning-naked on the Pacific, that
laces the suns with planets,
The heart of the atom with electrons: what is humanity in this cosmos? For
him, the last

Least taint of a trace in the dregs of the solution; for itself, the mould to break away from, the coal
To break into fire, the atom to be split.

After the child slept, after the leopard-footed evening
Had glided oceanward, California turned the lamp to its least flame and glided from the house.
She moved sighing, like a loose fire, backward and forward on the smooth ground by the door.
She heard the night-wind that draws down the valley like the draught in a flue under clear weather
Whisper and toss in the tall redwoods; she heard the tinkle of the April brook deep in its hollow.
Cooled by the night the odors that the horses had left behind were in her nostrils; the night
Whitened up the bare hill; a drift of coyotes by the river cried bitterly against moonrise;
Then California ran to the old corral, the empty one where they kept the buckskin mare,
And leaned, and bruised her breasts on the rail, feeling the sky whiten. When the moon stood over the hill
She stole to the house. The child breathed quietly. Herself: to sleep? She had seen Christ in the night at Christmas.
The hills were shining open to the enormous night of the April moon: empty and empty,
The vast round backs of the bare hills? If one should ride up high might not the Father himself
Be seen brooding his night, cross-legged, chin in hand, squatting on the last dome? More likely
Leaping the hills, shaking the red-roan mane for a flag on the bare hills. She blew out the lamp.

Every fibre of flesh trembled with faintness when she came to the door; strength lacked, to wander
Afoot into the shining of the hill, high enough, high enough . . . the hateful face of a man had taken
The strength that might have served her, the corral was empty. The dog followed her, she caught him by the collar,
Dragged him in fierce silence back to the door of the house, latched him inside.

It was like daylight
Out-doors and she hastened without faltering down the foot-path, through the dark fringe of twisted oak-brush,
To the open place in a bay of the hill. The dark strength of the stallion had heard her coming; she heard him
Blow the shining air out of his nostrils, she saw him in the white lake of moonlight
Move like a lion along the timbers of the fence, shaking the night-fall
Of the great mane; his fragrance came to her; she leaned on the fence;
He drew away from it, the hooves making soft thunder in the trodden soil.
Wild love had trodden it, his wrestling with the stranger, the shame of the day
Had stamped it into mire and powder when the heavy fetlocks
Strained the soft flanks. "Oh if I could bear you!
If I had the strength. O great God that came down to Mary, gently you came. But I will ride him
Up into the hill, if he throws me, if he tramples me, is it not my desire
To endure death?" She climbed the fence, pressing her body against the rail, shaking like fever,
And dropped inside to the soft ground. He neither threatened her with his teeth nor fled from her coming,
And lifting her hand gently to the upflung head she caught the strap of the headstall

That hung under the quivering chin. She unlooped the halter from the high strength of the neck
And the arch the storm-cloud mane hung with live darkness. He stood; she crushed her breasts
On the hard shoulder, an arm over the withers, the other under the mass of his throat, and murmuring
Like a mountain dove, "If I could bear you." No way, no help, a gulf in nature. She murmured, "Come,
We will run on the hill. O beautiful, O beautiful," and led him
To the gate and flung the bars on the ground. He threw his head downward
To snuff at the bars; and while he stood, she catching mane and withers with all sudden contracture
And strength of her lithe body, leaped, clung hard, and was mounted. He had been ridden before; he did not
Fight the weight but ran like a stone falling;
Broke down the slope into the moon-glass of the stream, and flattened to his neck
She felt the branches of a buck-eye tree fly over her, saw the wall of the oak-scrub
End her world: but he turned there, the matted branches
Scraped her right knee, the great slant shoulders
Laboring the hill-slope, up, up, the clear hill. Desire had died in her
At the first rush, the falling like death, but now it revived,
She feeling between her thighs the labor of the great engine, the running muscles, the hard swiftness,
She riding the savage and exultant strength of the world. Having topped the thicket he turned eastward
Running less wildly; and now at length he felt the halter when she drew on it; she guided him upward;
He stopped and grazed on the great arch and pride of the hill, the silent calvary. A dwarfish oakwood
Climbed the other slope out of the dark of the unknown canyon beyond; the last wind-beaten bush of it

Crawled up to the height, and California slipping from her mount tethered him to it. She stood then,
Shaking. Enormous films of moonlight
Trailed down from the height. Space, anxious whiteness, vastness. Distant beyond conception the shining ocean
Lay light like a haze along the ledge and doubtful world's end. Little vapors gleaming, and little
Darknesses on the far chart underfoot symbolized wood and valley; but the air was the element, the moon-
Saturate arcs and spires of the air.

Here is solitude, here on the calvary, nothing conscious
But the possible God and the cropped grass, no witness, no eye but that misformed one, the moon's past fullness.
Two figures on the shining hill, woman and stallion, she kneeling to him, brokenly adoring.
He cropping the grass, shifting his hooves, or lifting the long head to gaze over the world,
Tranquil and powerful. She prayed aloud "O God I am not good enough, O fear, O strength, I am draggled.
Johnny and other men have had me, and O clean power! Here am I," she said, falling before him,
And crawled to his hooves. She lay a long while, as if asleep, in reach of the fore-hooves, weeping. He avoided
Her head and the prone body. He backed at first; but later plucked the grass that grew by her shoulder.

The small dark head under his nostrils: a small round stone, that smelt human, black hair growing from it:
The skull shut the light in: it was not possible for any eyes
To know what throbbed and shone under the sutures of the skull, or a shell full of lightning

Had scared the roan strength, and he'd have broken tether, screaming, and
run for the valley.

The atom bounds-breaking,
Nucleus to sun, electrons to planets, with recognition
Not praying, self-equaling, the whole to the whole, the microcosm
Not entering nor accepting entrance, more equally, more utterly, more
incredibly conjugate
With the other extreme and greatness; passionately perceptive of
identity. . . .

The fire threw up figures
And symbols meanwhile, racial myths formed and dissolved in it, the
phantom rulers of humanity
That without being are yet more real than what they are born of, and
without shape, shape that which makes them:
The nerves and the flesh go by shadowlike, the limbs and the lives
shadowlike, these shadows remain, these shadows
To whom temples, to whom churches, to whom labors and wars, visions
and dreams are dedicate:
Out of the fire in the small round stone that black moss covered, a crucified
man writhed up in anguish;
A woman covered by a huge beast in whose mane the stars were netted, sun
and moon were his eyeballs,
Smiled under the unendurable violation, her throat swollen with the storm
and blood-flecks gleaming
On the stretched lips; a woman—no, a dark water, split by jets of lightning,
and after a season
What floated up out of the furrowed water, a boat, a fish, a fire-globe?

It had
wings, the creature,

And flew against the fountain of lightning, fell burnt out of the cloud back to the bottomless water . . .
Figures and symbols, castlings of the fire, played in her brain; but the white fire was the essence,
The burning in the small round shell of bone that black hair covered, that lay by the hooves on the hill-top.

She rose at length, she unknotted the halter; she walked and led the stallion; two figures, woman and stallion,
Came down the silent emptiness of the dome of the hill, under the cataract of the moonlight.

The next night there was moon through cloud. Johnny had returned half drunk toward evening, and California
Who had known him for years with neither love nor loathing to-night hating him had let the child Christine
Play in the light of the lamp for hours after her bed-time; who fell asleep at length on the floor
Beside the dog; then Johnny: "Put her to bed." She gathered the child against her breasts, she laid her
In the next room, and covered her with a blanket. The window was white, the moon had risen. The mother
Lay down by the child, but after a moment Johnny stood in the doorway. "Come drink." He had brought home
Two jugs of wine slung from the saddle, part payment for the stallion's service; a pitcher of it
Was on the table, and California sadly came and emptied her glass. Whisky, she thought,
Would have erased him till to-morrow; the thin red wine. . . . "We have a good evening," he laughed, pouring it.
"One glass yet then I show you what the red fellow did." She moving toward the house-door his eyes

Followed her, the glass filled and the red juice ran over the table. When it struck the floor-planks
He heard and looked. "Who stuck the pig?" he muttered stupidly, "here's blood, here's blood," and trailed his fingers
In the red lake under the lamplight. While he was looking down the door creaked, she had slipped out-doors,
And he, his mouth curving like a faun's, imagined the chase under the solemn redwoods, the panting
And unresistant victim caught in a dark corner. He emptied the glass and went out-doors
Into the dappled lanes of moonlight. No sound but the April brook's. "Hey Bruno," he called, "find her.
Bruno, go find her." The dog after a little understood and quested, the man following.
When California crouching by an oak-bush above the house heard them come near she darted
To the open slope and ran down hill. The dog barked at her heels, pleased with the game, and Johnny
Followed in silence. She ran down to the new corral, she saw the stallion
Move like a lion along the timbers of the fence, the dark arched neck shaking the night-fall
Of the great mane; she threw herself prone and writhed under the bars, his hooves backing away from her
Made muffled thunder in the soft soil. She stood in the midst of the corral, panting, but Johnny
Paused at the fence. The dog ran under it, and seeing the stallion move, the woman standing quiet,
Danced after the beast, with white-tooth feints and dashes. When Johnny saw the formidable dark strength
Recoil from the dog, he climbed up over the fence.

The child Christine
waked when her mother left her
And lay half-dreaming, in the half-waking dream she saw the ocean come up out of the west
And cover the world, she looked up through clear water at the tops of the redwoods. She heard the door creak
And the house empty; her heart shook her body, sitting up on the bed, and she heard the dog
And crept toward light, where it gleamed under the crack of the door. She opened the door, the room was empty,
The table-top was a red lake under the lamplight. The color of it was terrible to her,
She had seen the red juice drip from a coyote's muzzle, her father had shot one day in the hills
And carried him home over the saddle: she looked at the rifle on the wall-rack: it was not moved:
She ran to the door, the dog was barking and the moon was shining: she knew wine by the odor
But the color frightened her, the empty house frightened her, she followed down hill in the white lane of moonlight
The friendly noise of the dog. She saw in the big horse's corral, on the level shoulder of the hill,
Black on white, the dark strength of the beast, the dancing fury of the dog, and the two others.
One fled, one followed; the big one charged, rearing; one fell under his fore-hooves. She heard her mother
Scream: without thought she ran to the house, she dragged a chair past the red pool and climbed to the rifle,
Got it down from the wall and lugged it somehow through the door and down the hill-side, under the hard weight
Sobbing. Her mother stood by the rails of the corral, she gave it to her. On the far side

The dog flashed at the plunging stallion; in the midst of the space the man,
slow-moving, like a hurt worm
Crawling, dragged his body by inches toward the fence-line. Then
California, resting the rifle
On the top rail, without doubting, without hesitance
Aimed for the leaping body of the dog, and when it stood, fired. It snapped,
rolled over, lay quiet.
"O mother you've hit Bruno!" "I couldn't see the sights in the moonlight,"
she answered quietly. She stood
And watched, resting the rifle-butt on the ground. The stallion wheeled,
freed from his torment, the man
Lurched up to his knees, wailing a thin and bitter bird's cry, and the roan
thunder
Struck; hooves left nothing alive but teeth tore up the remnant. "O
mother, shoot, shoot!" Yet California
Stood carefully watching, till the beast having fed all his fury stretched neck
to utmost, head high,
And wrinkled back the upper lip from the teeth, yawning obscene disgust
over—not a man—
A smear on the moon-lake earth: then California moved by some obscure
human fidelity
Lifted the rifle. Each separate nerve-cell of her brain flaming the stars fell
from their places
Crying in her mind: she fired three times before the haunches crumpled
sidewise, the forelegs stiffening,
And the beautiful strength settled to earth: she turned then on her little
daughter the mask of a woman
Who has killed God. The night-wind veering, the smell of the spilt wine
drifted down hill from the house.

III

The Women at Point Sur

1925–1926

THE BEACH

Moon-white dunes and the water like violets
The days of sun or like a dove's breast the dark ones: each year one bather
Dies in the violet beauty of the water.
Keeps the bay young. How did you fast when men were few and not
 playful?

No pits nor whirlpools in the violet water;
The tides are clear as breathing, the tall waves honest, the sun in their
 hollows;
No hidden currents nor secret suctions:
Every summer one bather: no secret currents but a secret desire.

I have seen a mother with the yellow-gray hair
Crossing in strings the convulsed face from the violet water go babbling
Up the white dune; I have seen a young wife
Scream on the beach, writhing among the bystanders, they held her with
 their hands.

It takes the gain and its face not changes;
It is fed; it is greater than man and much more beautiful: we that eat beeves
Accuse fair beauty if indeed it is fed
With the thin infusion of one young life in the water, each weary summer?

How did you fast, you water like violets,
When men were few and not playful, brown fishers of the ebb, not one in ten years?
How you will feast in the thronged years coming,
The exuberance of women makes you so many playfellows, you choose among thousands.

SUMMER HOLIDAY

When the sun shouts and people abound
One thinks there were the ages of stone and the age of bronze
And the iron age; iron the unstable metal;
Steel made of iron, unstable as his mother; the towered-up cities
Will be stains of rust on mounds of plaster.
Roots will not pierce the heaps for a time, kind rains will cure them,
Then nothing will remain of the iron age
And all these people but a thigh-bone or so, a poem
Stuck in the world's thought, splinters of glass
In the rubbish dumps, a concrete dam far off in the mountain . . .

NOON

The pure air trembles, O pitiless God,
The air aches with flame on these gaunt rocks
Over the flat sea's face, the forest
Shakes in gales of piercing light.

But the altars are behind and higher
Where the great hills raise naked heads,
Pale agonists in the reverberance
Of the pure air and the pitiless God.

On the domed skull of every hill
Who stand blazing with spread vans,
The arms uplifted, the eyes in ecstasy?

What wine has the God drunk, to sing
Violently in heaven, what wine his worshippers
Whose silence blazes? The light that is over
Light, the terror of noon, the eyes
That the eagles die at, have thrown down
Me and my pride, here I lie naked
In a hollow of the shadowless rocks,
Full of the God, having drunk fire.

POST MORTEM

Happy people die whole, they are all dissolved in a moment, they have had what they wanted,
No hard gifts; the unhappy
Linger a space, but pain is a thing that is glad to be forgotten; but one who has given
His heart to a cause or a country,
His ghost may spaniel it a while, disconsolate to watch it. I was wondering how long the spirit
That sheds this verse will remain
When the nostrils are nipped, when the brain rots in its vault or bubbles in the violence of fire
To be ash in metal. I was thinking
Some stalks of the wood whose roots I married to the earth of this place will stand five centuries;
I held the roots in my hand,
The stems of the trees between two fingers: how many remote generations of women
Will drink joy from men's loins,
And dragged from between the thighs of what mothers will giggle at my ghost when it curses the axemen,
Gray impotent voice on the sea-wind,
When the last trunk falls? The women's abundance will have built roofs over all this foreland;
Will have buried the rock foundations
I laid here: the women's exuberance will canker and fail in its time and like clouds the houses
Unframe, the granite of the prime
Stand from the heaps: come storm and wash clean: the plaster is all run to the sea and the steel
All rusted; the foreland resumes

The form we loved when we saw it. Though one at the end of the age and far off from this place
Should meet my presence in a poem,
The ghost would not care but be here, long sunset shadow in the seams of the granite, and forgotten
The flesh, a spirit for the stone.

CLOUDS AT EVENING

Enormous cloud-mountains that form over Point Lobos and into the sunset,
Figures of fire on the walls of to-night's storm,
Foam of gold in gorges of fire, and the great file of warrior angels:
Dreams gathering in the curded brain of the earth,
The sky the brain-vault, on the threshold of sleep: poor earth, you like your children
By inordinate desires tortured make dreams?
Storms more enormous, wars nobler, more toppling mountains, more jewelled waters, more free
Fires on impossible headlands . . . as a poor girl
Wishing her lover taller and more desirous, and herself maned with gold,
Dreams the world right, in the cold bed, about dawn.
Dreams are beautiful; the slaves of form are beautiful also; I have grown to believe
A stone is a better pillow than many visions.

OCTOBER EVENING

Male-throated under the shallow sea-fog
Moaned a ship's horn quivering the shorelong granite.
Coyotes toward the valley made answer,
Their little wolf-pads in the dead grass by the stream
Wet with the young season's first rain,
Their jagged wail trespassing among the steep stars.
What stars? Aldebaran under the dove-leash
Pleiades. I thought, in an hour Orion will be risen,
Be glad for summer is dead and the sky
Turns over to darkness, good storms, few guests, glad rivers.

PELICANS

Four pelicans went over the house,
Sculled their worn oars over the courtyard: I saw that ungainliness
Magnifies the idea of strength.
A lifting gale of sea-gulls followed them; slim yachts of the element,
Natural growths of the sky, no wonder
Light wings to leave sea; but those grave weights toil, and are powerful,
And the wings torn with old storms remember
The cone that the oldest redwood dropped from, the tilting of continents,
The dinosaur's day, the lift of new sea-lines.
The omnisecular spirit keeps the old with the new also.
Nothing at all has suffered erasure.
There is life not of our time. He calls ungainly bodies
As beautiful as the grace of horses.
He is weary of nothing; he watches air-planes; he watches pelicans.

APOLOGY FOR BAD DREAMS

I

In the purple light, heavy with redwood, the slopes drop seaward,
Headlong convexities of forest, drawn in together to the steep ravine.
Below, on the sea-cliff,
A lonely clearing; a little field of corn by the streamside; a roof under
spared trees. Then the ocean
Like a great stone someone has cut to a sharp edge and polished to shining.
Beyond it, the fountain
And furnace of incredible light flowing up from the sunk sun. In the little
clearing a woman
Is punishing a horse; she had tied the halter to a sapling at the edge of the
wood, but when the great whip
Clung to the flanks the creature kicked so hard she feared he would snap
the halter; she called from the house
The young man her son; who fetched a chain tie-rope, they working
together
Noosed the small rusty links round the horse's tongue
And tied him by the swollen tongue to the tree.
Seen from this height they are shrunk to insect size,
Out of all human relation. You cannot distinguish
The blood dripping from where the chain is fastened,
The beast shuddering; but the thrust neck and the legs
Far apart. You can see the whip fall on the flanks . . .
The gesture of the arm. You cannot see the face of the woman.
The enormous light beats up out of the west across the cloud-bars of the
trade-wind. The ocean
Darkens, the high clouds brighten, the hills darken together. Unbridled and
unbelievable beauty

Covers the evening world . . . not covers, grows apparent out of it, as
Venus down there grows out
From the lit sky. What said the prophet? "I create good: and I create evil: I
am the Lord."

II

This coast crying out for tragedy like all beautiful places,
(The quiet ones ask for quieter suffering: but here the granite cliff the
gaunt cypresses crown
Demands what victim? The dykes of red lava and black what Titan? The
hills like pointed flames
Beyond Soberanes, the terrible peaks of the bare hills under the sun, what
immolation?)
This coast crying out for tragedy like all beautiful places: and like the
passionate spirit of humanity
Pain for its bread: God's, many victims', the painful deaths, the horrible
transfigurements: I said in my heart,
"Better invent than suffer: imagine victims
Lest your own flesh be chosen the agonist, or you
Martyr some creature to the beauty of the place." And I said,
"Burn sacrifices once a year to magic
Horror away from the house, this little house here
You have built over the ocean with your own hands
Beside the standing boulders: for what are we,
The beast that walks upright, with speaking lips
And little hair, to think we should always be fed,
Sheltered, intact, and self-controlled? We sooner more liable
Than the other animals. Pain and terror, the insanities of desire; not
accidents but essential,
And crowd up from the core": I imagined victims for those wolves, I made
them phantoms to follow,

They have hunted the phantoms and missed the house. It is not good to forget over what gulfs the spirit
Of the beauty of humanity, the petal of a lost flower blown seaward by the night-wind, floats to its quietness.

III

Boulders blunted like an old bear's teeth break up from the headland; below them
All the soil is thick with shells, the tide-rock feasts of a dead people.
Here the granite flanks are scarred with ancient fire, the ghosts of the tribe
Crouch in the nights beside the ghost of a fire, they try to remember the sunlight,
Light has died out of their skies. These have paid something for the future
Luck of the country, while we living keep old griefs in memory: though God's
Envy is not a likely fountain of ruin, to forget evils calls down
Sudden reminders from the cloud: remembered deaths be our redeemers;
Imagined victims our salvation: white as the half moon at midnight
Someone flamelike passed me, saying, "I am Tamar Cauldwell, I have my desire,"
Then the voice of the sea returned, when she had gone by, the stars to their towers.
. . . Beautiful country burn again, Point Pinos down to the Sur Rivers
Burn as before with bitter wonders, land and ocean and the Carmel water.

IV

He brays humanity in a mortar to bring the savor
From the bruised root: a man having bad dreams, who invents victims, is only the ape of that God.

He washes it out with tears and many waters, calcines it with fire in the red
crucible,
Deforms it, makes it horrible to itself: the spirit flies out and stands naked,
he sees the spirit,
He takes it in the naked ecstasy; it breaks in his hand, the atom is broken,
the power that massed it
Cries to the power that moves the stars, "I have come home to myself,
behold me.
I bruised myself in the flint mortar and burnt me
In the red shell, I tortured myself, I flew forth,
Stood naked of myself and broke me in fragments,
And here am I moving the stars that are me."
I have seen these ways of God: I know of no reason
For fire and change and torture and the old returnings.
He being sufficient might be still. I think they admit no reason; they are
the ways of my love.
Unmeasured power, incredible passion, enormous craft: no thought
apparent but burns darkly
Smothered with its own smoke in the human brain-vault: no thought
outside: a certain measure in phenomena:
The fountains of the boiling stars, the flowers on the foreland, the
ever-returning roses of dawn.

OCEAN

It dreams in the deepest sleep, it remembers the storm last month or it feels the far storm
Off Unalaska and the lash of the sea-rain.
It is never mournful but wise, and takes the magical misrule of the steep world
With strong tolerance, its depth is not moved
From where the green sun fails to where the thin red clay lies on the basalt
And there has never been light nor life.
The black crystal, the untroubled fountain, the roots of endurance.

Therefore
I belted
The house and the tower and courtyard with stone,
And have planted the naked foreland with future forest toward noon and morning: for it told me,
The time I was gazing in the black crystal,
To be faithful in storm, patient of fools, tolerant of memories and the muttering prophets,
It is needful to have night in one's body.

LOVE-CHILDREN

The trail's high up on the ridge, no one goes down
But the east wind and the falling water the concave slope without a name to
  the little bay
That has no name either. The fish-hawk plunges
Beyond the long rocks, rises with streaming silver; the eagle strikes down
  from the ridge and robs the fish-hawk;
The stunted redwoods neither grow nor grow old
Up the steep slope, remembering winter and the sea-wind; the ferns are
  maiden green by the falling water;
The seas whiten on the reefs; nothing has changed
For a thousand years, ten thousand. It is not a thousand, it is only seventy,
  since man and woman came down
The untrampled slope, forcing a trail through lupine
And mountain laurel; they built a hut against the streamside; the coast
  cannot remember their names.
They had light eyes and white skins, and nobody knew
What they fled, why they came. They had children in this place; loved
  while they clung to the breast but later
Naked, untaught, uncared for, as wild as foxes,
A boy and a girl; the coast remembers they would squat beside a squirrel's
  earth until the furred thing
Crept out, then what the small hands caught the teeth
Would tear living. What implacable flame of passion I wonder left its
  children forgotten
To eat vermin and the raw mussels of the rock?
Love at the height is a bad hearth-fire, a wolf in the house to keep the
  children. I imagine languors,
Sick loathing, miserable renewals, blind insolence
In the eye of the noon sun. They'd stripped to bathe, desire on the salted
  beach between the skerries

Came bronze-clawed like a hawk; the children to see
Was the deep pearl, the last abandonment. They lived twelve years in the hut beside the stream, and the children
Died, and the hut is fallen and vanished, the paths
Filled with thicket and vanished utterly. Nothing remains. Certainly a flame burned in this place;
Its lamps wandered away, no one knows whither.
The flaming oil-drops fell and burned out. No one imagines that ghosts move here, at noon or at midnight.
I'm never sorry to think that here's a planet
Will go on like this glen, perfectly whole and content, after mankind is scummed from the kettle.
No ghost will walk under the latter starlight.
The little phials of desire have all been emptied and broken. Here the ocean echoes, the stream's like bird-song;
The stunted redwoods neither grow nor grow old
Up the steep slope, remembering winter and the sea-wind; the ferns are maiden green by the falling water;
The seas whiten on the reefs; the fish-hawk plunges
Beyond the long rocks, rises with streaming silver; the eagle strikes down from the ridge and robs the fish-hawk.

SOLILOQUY

August and laurelled have been content to speak for an age, and the ages that follow
Respect them for that pious fidelity;
But you have disfeatured time for timelessness.
They had heroes for companions, beautiful youths to dream of, rose-marble-fingered
Women shed light down the great lines;
But you have invoked the slime in the skull,
The lymph in the vessels. They have shown men Gods like racial dreams, the woman's desire,
The man's fear, the hawk-faced prophet's; but nothing
Human seems happy at the feet of yours.
Therefore though not forgotten not loved, in gray old years in the evening leaning
Over the gray stones of the tower-top,
You shall be called heartless and blind;
And watch new time answer old thought, not a face strange nor a pain astonishing:
But you living be laired in the rock
That sheds pleasure and pain like hail-stones.

HOME

She'd thrust the canyon out of her mind; she never thought of the whispering fall, the ferns, the hawk-haunted
Hills intense in the sun: no more than the child remembers uterine life: but after her mother
Died, and Phil Maybrick was holding her to the promised marriage; when time for some reason grew terrible:
"Why does it taste like ashes? Have children, begin it all over again, the anxious fable? Or have none,
Lie in his arms like stagnant water in the awful emptiness?" She was convinced that some insanity,
Obstruction in the mind, nothing in the nature of things, a wall of perverse thought that might be thrown down,
Threatened her away from normal happiness. "I've taught school three years and always hated it. I'll take
One month of perfect rest, away from the town, away from the people I know":—suddenly her mind
Was like a city built with towers, full of a vision
Of the heights that she was born under, hills like humped cattle herded to the ocean, south of Monterey—
"I shall come back and be myself, be human like the others." She wrote it all in a letter to him,
Except the place; and promising love forever, her name, Rachel Devine. If he were too angry
It was not, perhaps, paradise . . . would crumble.

She went to the place, and boarded at the farmer's below.
How long was it, nine years? These people had come since hers . . . departed: her name wasn't remembered.

The hills were undiminished, as great and sun-beaten and solitary as ever of old,
Though she'd been but a child, but twelve years old, last seeing them.
Three days she wandered on the great heights
Over the ocean. She wanted to enter the canyon; she was afraid; the fourth, she entered the canyon
With the shamed fear that a child feels
Who listens in the night to terrible sighs and whispers and the bed of her parents
Straining, the shame and fear: the paths were not much overgrown; though the dwelling she knew was ruinous
Men still drove cows through the deep canyon to the hills at the head. The creek sang the old music, the cresses
Were all in white flower. A mile up the deep cleft, in sight of the remembered roof, the path split.
One way led over the stream by the great blocks of stone to the clump of willows . . . her father, when the world
Darkened about him: she remembered his body
Brought from the blood-stained willows. She never had seen the puddle of blood; her mind had seen it so dreadfully
On the dead earth under the willows:
The red glaze blackening in from the edges was clearer than memory. She never had seen the wound; for his face
Had not been torn outward, he held the muzzle in his mouth. "Dear God no wonder," she thought "no wonder
With such wounds in my mind! Here is the place I should have fled from: I have come to this place." She lingered
At the split way, tasting the sickness high in her throat. The choked path to the house less painful,
She followed that path: no ghost: herself was the ghost: she'd thought it might have stood grizzled and blood-splotched:

But nothing came along the thick leaves. The gapped doorway and the
glassless windows. "Well: if I go in:
Because I've caught something from the lean hawks on the hillside. But
really I feel little, why almost
Nothing, feel nothing, that's wise. The coast's heavy with stone." She
entered the squalid rooms, the disgrace
And wreck of the house. Mice ran, and a linnet
Dodged out the far window. In the next room, one side of the cold hearth,
the floor was all rotted,
Some tribe of burrowers had heaped earth there, through the brown hole,
higher than the broken planks. She approaching
A rattle buzzed hard and she drew back from the planks. She thought of
finding a stick, but turned in the doorway
Happy with her new thought: "This is my house and you're my watchdog.
Meet strangers for me."

All night
In the farmhouse in the strain of the sea's voice, in dreams and waking she
was not unhappy, remotely consoled
By the utter ruin of what she had visited; most by the snake at the hearth.
Returning after two days
She heard one in the grass by the door and saw another in the house, by the
rotted planks. In the basket
The farmer's wife had given her, a little bottle of milk was packed with the
food; she found a cracked saucer
Back of the house, filled it with milk and crumbs of bread, she set it on the
floor, then heedfully pushed it
With the fork of a long rod to the edge of the planks, the ridged brown
opening. Had she read somewhere of pouring
Milk for the household spirit, the serpent? She seemed
remembering . . . that was no matter: if the act in itself

Gave pleasure: "I love their enemies." Then she remembered gently, with distant loneliness, her city lover.
"I'm out of the net. Something from the hills
Comes in here, cold strength." She was feebler than flesh and her heart knew it. At least not afraid of death she wandered
Outside the house, the dusty squalor within was too repulsive to suffer. Old oaks, the sweet leaves
Of alders, the polished fragrance the mountain laurels, and standing over a notch in the trees the tall dark
Mountain southward, an obelisk-shaped growth of deep redwoods heavy in the sun climbing the chief
Fold in the furrowed flank. She breathed with pleasure. "No humanity, no humanity at all.
Well done destruction."

Rachel returned to the farmhouse.
A horseman at the gate of the yard talked with the farmer. He was not a cowboy; clean cloth, bright leather,
Ruling the restless horse. She felt his eyes touch her approaching, saw him speak, imagined the farmer
Answering, "Young schoolteacher from town." She looked up frankly toward the rider as she entered the gate,
Question for question, she went on to the house feeling his eyes. Some troublesome spring of perplexed . . .
Memory perhaps? . . . had spoilt her confidence. A brutal face; sunburnt and strong, handsome you'd call it,
Older than she'd supposed, forty no doubt. How far from Philip's sensitive features, the charm
And the shy power. It came through her mind
That she was too coarse for Philip, a cattleman's daughter from the rough coast: Oh worse than that, or he'd not

Have gone down the red path. The farmer came in,
She asked who was that man on horseback? And pale, thinking "I should
have known, remembered, I am calm
As the hills themselves," heard the man's name: Charlie McCandless, the
man who'd pressed her father to the pit,
Who'd brought the charge against him. "They'd think it was strength,"
She thought, "this quietness. It's not: I feel nothing." Owned her father's
house now, this man, the shameful
Wreck of a house, and the sweet canyon. His own was over the ridge
southward; his hills, his ranges,
His prosperity. The one had killed himself and the other had prospered.
He was almost her father's murderer;
He had brought the charge that had brought death.

She thought in the
night it was soft folly to expect reason,
Justice or any human rightness in life. God, if there was one: the
rattlesnakes' God also.
The milk she poured them next day (she poured it again) was a libation.
Did they drink? The saucer was empty
But a sour crust at the edges. Perhaps the little lives that serve them for
food had lapped it, been caught,
Life for life, all's fair. "The thing is, to find one's meat. That's what they
know."

She went up stream, by the boulders
And the slip of shore. The cliff and the thick leaves enclosed the widened
creek, clear-currented cauldron,
One stone on the edge, the sun gilded. In the heat; by the stream; chiefly in
the clean deliverance from eyes:
She felt all thoughts dropping, all that disturbs quietness falling, peace
coming up, clear water.

She was not tired enough for peace, through the dark surface
Like a shark's fin, like a tower of white stone: whom would she wish come up from the water, naked companion?
A marble boy; minion not lover . . . Antinous . . . no one with personality, no one known to her;
Her own creature; she needed weakness to be strong with, coolness for fever, her own creature;
So shy that he'd need wooing, so young and soft that he'd need nursing, between the rose-crested hills,
Before some life of her own should filter into his arteries, the soft whiteness grow stronger, the child
Petted to life sharpen its softness to go home . . . "Ah, shame, shame,"
She felt her cheeks blazing, "you that were nerved for all the unreason, the savage energy, the snakes' God,
Hide in a cave to dream?" She thought "If I could give away my virginity, that's what weakens me.
That caution once lost: there's not a man: to the stone hills. Fool," she whispered to herself, and finding
A break in the cliff forced herself upward through the thicket, felt with sharp satisfaction the branches
Breaking, the twigs like thorns; in the midst it was a nightmare of heat and pressure; she crept beyond it,
Lay panting on the open slope; her clothes were scarred, her hands bleeding. She'd never go back: it was this
Was needed: harsh touches, steep freedom, recklessness. Labored up hill in the steep heat, gained the first summit,
Felt the great hills ringing like gongs in the universal sunlight, the bronze reverberance, the beating
Hammers of light. Then having to make water she looked for shelter and she thought, "No, here and publicly."
It gave her pleasure on the open height, she felt the shudder imagined of love, the consecration,

And dizzy with yearning toward no person wandered down westward; the ocean, taut blue, strung in the acute
V of the violent hills.

Phil Maybrick was at the farmhouse. "I knew you would go to this place, Rachel.
Oh I'm glad. I was afraid I'd not find you. I've waited hours here." The thin young face lighted with confidence,
The luminous eyes: her own hardened, her blue ones. "I asked for a month." "Dearest . . ." "Take the apple green then.
But come away from the house." His car was in the withering grass outside the gateway, they stood by it,
Then Rachel: "You've caught me honest. You came too soon Philip, you never needed to have known anything.
Dupes are happy." "What do you mean, what do you mean?" "I meant to cheat you happy. Push in
While the fire's roaring? Be burnt then. Your fault.
I would have fooled you." "You're not well, Rachel, you're pale, you've torn your clothes too, this insane talk
Has no meaning in the world." "Well it's a wonderful relief for me too, I was going to marry you;
Live in a coop, we'd know the smell of each other and you'd take me to shows
Once a week. That's finished." "I only know you're talking horribly, horrible things . . ." "If you want
Everything told plainly: I've got a man here, one that I want really, I meet him back here
At a dead house. You thought I was . . . white? He had me before I left here: I was twelve years old then: he had me.
So I came back for a month, Philip.
You'd kept away you might have had an eight-month baby next winter. People will take what they get.

I never *talked* shamelessly before: not till you came pushing in unwanted: now take it,
Shameless and all."
"Why," he said, "you're lying; that's all. You must come back with me."
She, trembling: "Bound to be cheated? I'll tell you more:
This was my father's enemy, the man that made him kill himself. That's something. Now he's got married, has children;
I'm the luxury." Philip began to tremble, but silent, and Rachel: "Probably you won't believe me
Until I hide you in a closet in the dead house. When you see the skirt lift."
Mumbling, he answered
With dead lips, "I believe you. Well. No," he shouted,
"I've got my mother to think of. You thought I'd let myself be tried for murder, for a whore's sake?" His dead-seeming
Lips mumbled so, she thought he was gathering slime behind them to spit in her face. He shuddered. "I'm not
The fool you think me. But," he said, "everything's horrible.
You've that much triumph. This'll never be wiped, never be wiped, I'll never look at the stars
But see dirt. Are you diseased yet? When't blotches your face
I'll pay the doctor." He frowned and coughed into his hand. "It's time to go back. Thanks for telling me.
I'd never have guessed, you know, Rachel." He stepped into the car and started the engine; the tires
Dug the dead grass.

She stood by the gateway, watched it slide up the coast-road, under the tawny-carpeted
Slopes: "Carefully he drives. Me to be like him, driving carefully. Not as if it had been
Worth anything: worth anything. What's to come. I'll get over. Nothing hurts." She thought "I'm not tired:

That's strange: I could begin the day again." She thought, "My enemy
Passes this way when he goes north, it's the only road." They had dinner at six, long daylight afterwards,
While Rachel wandered south on the road, she gathered sweet roses from a briar, the thorns were the best,
A rider came up the road but not McCandless, a Spanish cowboy. But about sunset McCandless
Came up the road as if he'd been sent. Rachel stepped into the road, he drew rein. "Mr. McCandless.
I wanted to ask you something." She'd made herself look as beautiful as she could, and some of the briars
Pinned at her breast, he appeared pleased to look at her. "Whether I might . . . You own the canyon back there":
It had been called by her father's name, her own, she'd not name it: "if I might camp up there for a week
In the ruined house." "What," he said, "all alone?" "Oh, I'd be careful of my fires." "But what for?
You're staying at Carter's, I saw you yesterday." "That's how I knew your name Mr. McCandless. You see,"
She said whitening, "I've spent most of my money, I can't stay there much longer. It's so beautiful here.
If I could stay a week longer." "Long as you like." He was so heavy, thick-necked, powerful, she thought
"The stick of dynamite that can blast the hill open." She trembled and looked down from his eyes.
The hooves were restless in the deep dust; she heard the horse mouthing its bit and the man saying
"Long as you like. I'll come up in a day or two, see how you get along." She answered trembling
"Oh thank you," and lifted her head by violence, and smiled.

In the morning
Rachel went up the creek and not pausing
At the split pathway crossed the ford to the clump of willows. There couldn't be any stain on the ground
After nine years. "It was here perhaps." "It was here perhaps, hid in this opening." "Father I seem
Not to feel anything at all. Makes three of us, for God doesn't: suppose there's one, the spirit of the serpents
And the cold stones. I've stepped over the edge to you, you cold spirits. They fooled us in school but I see
Nothing makes any difference, not really.
You wouldn't expect me to go through the world tearing, with this in my body?" She was cutting willows,
She'd brought a big knife she'd always kept because it had been her father's; it kept some edge yet; by sheaves
Cutting the long shoots with the foliage on them she carried them over the ford to the dead house,
Framed them with larger branches below and formed and wove them into a couch, like the nest of an eagle,
But low on the floor, by the mouldering boards, by the silent hearth-stones. No rattle had sounded to-day, though the saucer
Was half emptied. She formed the couch, lengthened it, narrowed it; drew a clean blanket from the farmhouse bed
Over the mound, "the snakes are all asleep," she was thinking,
"The cold bodies relaxed," it sang in her mind like an old tune, "I do the housework and the darting
Bodies relaxed in the hidden darkness." But when the room was cleaned, and the brown hole by the hearth
Stopped with sweet boughs that hid the wound, not closed it over: she dreaded quietness, she dared not linger,
Walked up and down the leafy canyon, down almost to the road, by the rustling water, and the sun

Stood south, she wandered back through the white patches, the flaming sunlight; she thought "I'll go up to the pool,
Bathe in the pool where I was yesterday." She thought that she knew nothing, "I know nothing. What horror
Comes up the canyon? What's it like, dying? being eaten by a worm?" She came to the clear pool that the leaves
And cliffs cavern with shadow. The bitter water made her tremble to see it: go in there naked,
The unprotected white shivering body?
She thought "They all suffer it: if the enemy's loved it's easier: means bondage afterwards." She looked at herself
With love and pity, shivering in the tent of dark leaves, the clear smooth arms and the long thighs,
Slight breasts, how could they endure the burden? Her mind was moving so much faster since yesterday, flooded
River streaming the strangest drift, the take of destruction, dead cattle rolling, dead father, in the yellow
Fall of the flayed hills: the gentle idyll of the widened brook,
The nuptial water: she hardly remembered
Entering, she lay in the pool and scoured herself with the clean sand and the water, and stood on the bank
Stroking the drops from the flushed skin. She dressed and hurried back to the house. No one was there.
He might have come and returned; he'd come on horseback; there were no hoof-marks.

He came when the coolness begins,
An hour sooner than sunset. The rushing flood of her mind stopped suddenly, froze dead. She went to meet him,
And at the stirrup: "I thought maybe you'd come. It's beautiful here, I'm glad to thank you." He answered,

Moving his head on the thick neck, "See whether you needed anything.
Everything's all right . . . Miss . . . Miss . . ."
"Rachel," she said pitiably shuddering,
Twisting her hands, "I'm on a holiday, last name's no matter." He stared down at her face, and dismounting
Darted quick eyes toward the house. She imagined he suspected she was not alone, there was someone hidden,
She said "I've seen no one all day. I haven't been lonely." "You'd rather I hadn't come then?" "My father's
Murderer," she thought pressing her thighs together; "ought to be charm in that knowledge: means nothing to me:
Why's everything without meaning?" "Well," he said sharply watching her, "I can go back." But he drew the reins
Over the pricked gray ears and let them trail from the bit. She answered "No . . . no . . ." And he: "I was thinking
Maybe I could help fix the place up. Aren't used to camping, are you?" "Oh. It doesn't matter. Nothing
Makes any difference. I fixed myself a place to sleep on." He undid the rope from the saddle-back. "I'll tie him,
Find some stones for the fire-place." She stood frozen watching him gather the reins and loop the halter,
And lead the horse to a clear tree. He was always looking sidelong toward her, and she thought "I can't bear
The preparation . . ." When the horse was tethered
She said and her mouth shuddering, "You needn't bother about a fire-place, I'll get breakfast at the farm,
Meals . . . at Carter's. I thought maybe you came to collect rent for the camp-site . . ." "Oh he'll understand me
Now, she thought, squeezing one hand in the other, arching her shoulders
As if to save the struck breasts. He turned a blank face of astonishment: "What are you talking about?

Rent?" So ridiculously astonished she couldn't help laughing, he peering under the eyebrows with lowered
Forehead saw twist like flame the slenderness under the earth-colored cloth, saw the eyes shining with terror,
The mouth with laughter, the arms straightened down at the sides and the face averted, flung upward, as of one defiant
Showing her desirableness, from throat to ankles, under green leaves: he said "What will you pay me?"
She felt her throat ache with stopped cries; she thought what she must answer, she was not able to, she murmured
"Nothing," and swayed a step into the foliage, then in trapped fear beat with her hands and her breasts
On the heavy buckthorn, silently. He came behind her
And when she felt his hand she was quiet. It lay like heated iron on her flank and she heard him hoarsely
Against her ear, and as if through waters: "What's wrong? Nobody's going to hurt you." The other hand grasped
The bent round of her shoulder, turned her to face him among the branches; the lines of her face confused him,
The under-lip held by the teeth, the half opened eyes and widened nostrils, a mask of wantonness
That changed his conception of why the body trembled so hard. He drew her in his arms against him; she twisted
Her face backward to avoid the kiss, and her neck
Under the ear felt the vile warmth and wetness. He lifted her out of the boughs and she felt her body
Jerking like a caught hare's, she labored so hard to quiet the muscles, she was not able to speak:
Though he carried her the wrong way, carried her up hill, she'd thought he'd take her to the house: struggling against him,
Striking his throat with the weak fists: she found his mouth, striking at random, felt the soft lip,

The hot breath on the teeth: when he groaned angrily and dropped her
She wrenched from his hand, ran down toward the dead house; he followed, not running; she avoided the clumps of deerweed
Thinking what spiral springs of poison might be hid in them, thinking the man, stiff leather to the knees,
Safe from the needles in the hard jaws: only his clutching hands and heavy-boned wrists were liable:
She entered the house, ran home, panting, home, home.

The flood of her mind
Ran faster than before he had come; the dead returned out of destruction, washed down from the mountain,
The beautiful chestnut horse her father had ridden, neck arched above the water and the withers floating,
The forehooves striking foam in the stream; the serpents in the swift water; the enormous cross of black cloud
She a child had seen over the canyon sunset: "Why it must be nearly sunset already," she thought
Standing in the midst of the room, "he's coming." She was her mother, frail and weary, and her father was coming;
The child's asleep: there's pleasure in being used to it, submitting willingly.

McCandless stood in the doorway
Darting quick eyes about the bare room, under drawn brows. He saw her in the midst of the square, standing
Erect, the dark hair turbulent, the wide blue eyes meek and submissive. She looked straight toward him, quiet eyes,
But the lips quivered. Her throat was flushed, the cloth was torn there, her cheeks were chalk white. She quietly and clearly:

"Where've you been? You were so long coming: I thought you'd got lost."
He astonished at her changes of mood:
"You wanted me to come . . . Rachel . . . why did you hit me?" "I had to go home." That would be dark to him: she added
"I had to go home." She crept backward he approaching, suddenly found herself trapped in the other corner,
No escape: "If I scream," she whispered, "someone might come and save me." He barred the corner with his arms, not touching her.
"Nobody'd hear you. You don't know what you want, little fool, is the trouble." She turning her body to the wall,
Her face over the shoulder: "I know what I want. I'm afraid: be kind to me. It's the first time. My father,"
She said stammering with eagerness, "hid some bottles under the floor by the hearth: ten years, they're still there.
I looked when I came. Get me some whiskey for the honeymoon to make me happy." He said, "Your father?
You used to live here, you're old Devine's girl?" "The thief's. That's why I'm shameless. I said I'll go for a holiday.
Get me the drink first. I broke up the boards by the hearth, they were all rotten, I dug for the bottles.
Push in your hand and get one: under the leaves there." "Afterwards," he said, "Oh" she said, "yes, yes, afterwards.
That's what I meant." "The old fellow has a beautiful daughter: dear girl, dear sweetheart." She unresisting
Felt his hands handle her, in the whirl of her mind
Praying to the secret serpents. She was on the couch, he was plucking anxiously about her clothing, her fingers
Remembered resistance, the rest of her body
Grown fatalist lay relaxed without imagination awaiting the event. The fingers grew tired.
She closed her eyes because his face became horrible. She watched the dead man walking through the dim house

Counting on his fingers . . . the calves misbranded, the stolen horses? Ah
never turn your back to me father,
For the gap under the gory gray hair . . . the pain, tearing . . . when the
bullet entered surely it was quiet,
The pain gorging the entrance,
Working the wound, and the earth over the grave was less heavy. Suddenly
her spirit
Like embers to flame, like a hawk flapping up,
Shot from the bitter seed of endurance: the orgy of martyrdom shook her
mind like a flag, no pleasure,
But the pain forgotten in the ecstasy of martyrdom: the dove of clear fire
That visited the saints on racks and gibbets, the spiritual joy, the splendor
of the dove.

In the rigid quietness
She lay wondering and burning. What had become of the gray old man?
Earthed again? Dig up, dig it up,
We must wash out the earth from the wound, the dirt-plug with the blood
from among the gray hair and the dirt
In the eye-lashes in the the eyes, the earth's bones
Relaxing, the mound of the grave softening and cracking make it easy to
dig treasure, the earth relaxing,
Dig up the bottles . . . but really there were no bottles . . . he had lifted
himself, she lay on the couch faintly
Moaning, but feeling extreme pleasure in the stone-quietness, the
self-abandonment, the knees to the waist
Uncovered made it most clear, a new corpse is not careful. The man had
taken her hand and was murmuring
Luke-warm love-words, his duty. Remembering a drunken girl in the night
street in front of the theatre
She essayed laughter, lewd answers, then lifting

Her face like a spear: "Listen. Will you serve the drinks? I came here for a holiday, I have to teach school
At home. Under the green there." Would the watch-dogs be faithful . . .
Was too lucky to hope for. Therefore she took the knife she'd cut the willows with, it hid by the couch-side
Under the folded blanket-edge; the man knelt down by the gapped planks;
His coat was off it was easy to see the blade's home, on the flank over the belt, the fat flesh bulged there,
He stooping, between the ribs and the belt: no bone in the blade's way:
But Rachel could not move her body from the couch; it did not tremble, it had turned stone, and she crouched
Stone, with the knife. The man fumbled in the opening. He muttered some question,
His chest on the floor, his arm strained sidewise under it. The following moment
Was blinding bright in Rachel's mind and instantly forgotten. The shoulder humping and twisting upward
From the struck arm: she knew as clearly as if she had eyes under the floor how the flat triangular
Barbed head hung to the hand's edge, the thin-drawn neck straining behind, it had struck without warning, was faithful
Beyond hope or reason: the victim's hoarse cough
Of pain sluiced fire through her flesh, he writhing to rise she felt the hard abundant fire of her body
Cross him like a wave, cover him. The imagination
Of her father's wound so bright in her mind she could not strike at the mark chosen but struck where the wound was,
Behind the neck, where the flesh was creased in the cropped hair. The point turned on the neck-bones, the edge
Gritted on the guiding bone, the big muscle part severed the head swung sidewise. The left arm yielding

The man rolled over on his left flank, the girl recovering the knife dipped
it in the soft belly
Twice, each time grunting like a woman in labor. He wailed in a high
childlike voice and she felt
With exultance for thought they had changed sexes; but he caught the
knife-wrist, she could not move it, and at the one time
Got his knees under her body and shot her off backward. He appeared not
to think of her again, he surged up
Like a mired bull, she crouching where fallen
Saw him rise and fill the room above her, his deformed bulk, red mists
about him, and the high unmanlike
Chirping of his pain. It seemed impossible that so great and distorted an
agony could pass the doorway,
He contracted himself toward it, ran outward, she following
Saw him trot under the trees, the head hung sidewise, both hands covering
the belly. She felt the white fire
Licking about the roots of her hair, she ran and screamed behind him, he
swerved to face her and she passed
Avoiding him; she reached the horse, cut the halter, pricked the rump with
the knife-point.

Remained no means of remembering
Why it was when a running horse went by her
A man dropped on his knees to her and bowing forward
Showed the gashed neck; nor why she felt pain
In a protected place, and her clothing disordered. Apparently she'd served
God with the empty body
And not the mind, not kept her mind on her prayers, but the wounded
neck
Was moaning where the solemn red sundown lay among the trees, and
when she approached it begged her get help,

It would soon die: "Oh yes you will die: you got the snake-bite for stealing horses," the lips answered it,
But the mind was not touching the words, the mind was thinking
Her baby was all alone in the house. It was getting dark in the house, the child not wakened, she remembered
The baby's cot was in the living-room by the hearthside: they had been so cold: but the fire had gone out:
She gathered the blanket from the bed and folded it for a child in her arms and the child's face
Was the dark stain. Standing in the door
She understood the vague pain that troubled her: because the child had just been born, the pain was quite natural,
A girl-baby named Rachel, Rachel Devine is a sweet name, "Oh hush little Rachel," she murmured
Swaying from the hips, folding her arms about the little delicate imagined body, and she watched
The rose-flowing sunset through the still trees. "Oh never run down to the ocean, Rachel."

Behind her happiness
Lay like a flood of misery—so the banked flood hangs on the dyke over the meadows—the dim
Thought that she'd done and suffered so much violence in vain, she had sharpened herself to compass deliverance
From the net of the mind, here she was netted the deeper, among delusions, among images, now nothing
Real in the world: this misery her dream
Resolved to a threat of the darkening forest against the baby, the beasts under the trees were its enemies,
Wolves with lit eyes, and the young mother
Held a wide door against the hunger of the world.

She lay on the bed of
boughs when the night darkened.
She brooded her more than life in her arms. She loosened the clothing
from her throat and brought out the small breasts,
Greedily the tiny warm lips . . .

In the night,
Wakening she knew there was no child, and that horrible things
Had been done easily. She had left him living, she must go and find him.
The journey in the darkness
Was worse than any suffering before. He had crept perhaps a few feet and
died in another place,
It needed many circuits among the trees by the path before she found him.
The flesh was wet-cold.
She dipped her finger into the wound in the neck: no warmth was hidden
there. After she had sat eternally
Came the gray light. After it was light
She saw that with his pocket-knife, with his left hand
He had slashed the blackening right one where the fangs had gone in: still
reaching at life, living to the end:
This dead man cutting himself for life's sake. The other dead man
Died in her mind; her father had been the wastrel, the fugitive; her lover
the brave one. She, sane and prepared,
Sat close by her chosen; she watched the dawn flower in the trees, the
intolerable beauty and the desolation.

GEORGE STERLING

I did not meet him in the gleaming years
That made the great friendships and the earlier fame,
The carnival time when wine was common as tears,
The fabulous dawn was darkened before I came.
The Carmel woods because he had wandered there
Were yet misted with gold when he returned.
The iron season had come, the iron was gray in his hair,
Yet in his heart the child and the song burned.
Who could have known he drew so near his November,
The power and the song not wearying; and now he is gone.
The Carmel woods are full of music to remember,
And my ears of a sad music; and mine to go on
To not so shining and not so swift an end,
Never to find nor lose so generous a friend.

GEORGE STERLING'S DEATH

Sorrows have come before and have stood mute
With blind implacable masks; when the eyes have endured them
They draw sidelong and stand
At the shoulder; they never depart.

The sweetest voice has desired silence, the eyes
Have desired darkness, the passion has desired peace.
He that gave, and not asked
But for a friend's sake, has taken

One gift for himself: he gives a greater, he goes
Remembered utterly generous, constraining sorrow
Like winter sundown, splendid
Memory to ennoble our nights.

The gray mothers of rain sail and glide over,
The rain has fallen, the deep-wombed earth is renewed;
Under the greening of the hills
Gulls flock in the black furrows.

And now it is hard to believe he will not return
To be our guest in the house, nor walk beside me
Again by the Carmel river
Or on the Sovranes reef.

ANTE MORTEM

It is likely enough that lions and scorpions
Guard the end; life never was bonded to be endurable nor the act of dying
Unpainful; the brain burning too often
Earns, though it held itself detached from the object, often a burnt age.
No matter, I shall not shorten it by hand.
Incapable of body or unmoved of brain is no evil, one always went envying
The quietness of stones. But if the striped blossom
Insanity spread lewd splendors and lightning terrors at the end of the forest;
Or intolerable pain work its known miracle,
Exile the monarch soul, set a sick monkey in the office . . . remember me
Entire and balanced when I was younger,
And could lift stones, and comprehend in the praises the cruelties of life.

CREDO

My friend from Asia has powers and magic, he plucks a blue leaf from the young blue-gum
And gazing upon it, gathering and quieting
The God in his mind, creates an ocean more real than the ocean, the salt, the actual
Appalling presence, the power of the waters.
He believes that nothing is real except as we make it. I humbler have found in my blood
Bred west of Caucasus a harder mysticism.
Multitude stands in my mind but I think that the ocean in the bone vault is only
The bone vault's ocean: out there is the ocean's;
The water is the water, the cliff is the rock, come shocks and flashes of reality. The mind
Passes, the eye closes, the spirit is a passage;
The beauty of things was born before eyes and sufficient to itself; the heart-breaking beauty
Will remain when there is no heart to break for it.

PRELUDE

I drew solitude over me, on the lone shore,
By the hawk-perch stones; the hawks and the gulls are never breakers of solitude.
When the animals Christ is rumored to have died for drew in,
The land thickening, drew in about me, I planted trees eastward, and the ocean
Secured the west with the quietness of thunder. I was quiet.
Imagination, the traitor of the mind, has taken my solitude and slain it.
No peace but many companions; the hateful-eyed
And human-bodied are all about me: you that love multitude may have them.

But why should I make fables again? There are many
Tellers of tales to delight women and the people.
I have no vocation. The old rock under the house, the hills with their hard roots and the ocean hearted
With sacred quietness from here to Asia
Make me ashamed to speak of the active little bodies, the coupling bodies, the misty brainfuls
Of perplexed passion. Humanity is needless.
I said "Humanity is the start of the race, the gate to break away from, the coal to kindle,
The blind mask crying to be slit with eye-holes."
Well now it is done, the mask slit, the rag burnt, the starting-post left behind: but not in a fable.
Culture's outlived, art's root-cut, discovery's
The way to walk in. Only remains to invent the language to tell it.
Match-ends of burnt experience
Human enough to be understood,

Scraps and metaphors will serve. The wine was a little too strong for the new wine-skins . . .

Come storm, kind storm.
Summer and the days of tired gold
And bitter blue are more ruinous.
The leprous grass, the sick forest,
The sea like a whore's eyes,
And the noise of the sun,
The yellow dog barking in the blue pasture,
Snapping sidewise.

When I remembered old rains,
Running clouds and the iron wind, then the trees trembled.
I was calling one of the great dancers
Who wander down from the Aleutian rocks and the open Pacific
Pivoting countersunwise, celebrating power with the whirl of a dance, sloping to the mainland.
I watched his feet waken the water
And the ocean break in foam beyond Lobos;
The iron wind struck from the hills.

You are tired and corrupt,
You kept the beast under till the fountain's poisoned,
He drips with mange and stinks through the oubliette window.
The promise-breaker war killed whom it freed
And none living's the cleaner. Yet storm comes, the lions hunt
In the nights striped with lightning. It will come: feed on peace
While the crust holds: to each of you at length a little
Desolation: a pinch of lust or a drop of terror:

Then the lions hunt in the brain of the dying: storm is good, storm is good, good creature,
Kind violence, throbbing throat aches with pity.

Onorio Vasquez,
Young seer of visions who lives with his six brothers
On the breast of Palo Corona mountain looking northward,
Watches his brother Vidal and Julio the youngest
Play with a hawk they shot from the mountain cloud,
The wing broken. They crucified the creature,
A nail in the broken wing on the barn wall
Between the pink splinters of bone and a nail in the other.
They prod his breast with a wand, no sponge of vinegar,
"Fly down, Jew-beak." The wind streams down the mountain,
The river of cloud streams over: Onorio Vasquez
Never sees anything to the point. What he sees:
The ocean like sleek gray stone perfectly jointed
To the heads and bays, a woman walking upon it,
The curling scud of the storm around her ankles,
Naked and strong, her thighs the height of the mountain, walking and weeping,
The shadow of hair under the belly, the jutting breasts like hills, the face in the hands and the hair
Streaming north. "Why are you sad, our lady?" "I had only one son.
The strange lover never breaks the window-latches again
When Joseph's at synagogue."

Orange eyes, tired and fierce,
They're casting knives at you now, but clumsily, the knives
Quiver in the wood, stern eyes the storm deepens.
Don't wince, topaz eyes.

The wind wearies toward evening,
Old Vasquez sends his boys to burn the high pastures
Against the rain: see the autumn fires on the mountain, creeping red lakes and crescents
Up the black slope in the slide of the year: that's Vasquez and his boys burning the mountain. The high wind
Holds, the low dies, the black curtain flies north.

Myrtle Cartwright
Locked the windows but forgot the door, it's a lonely canyon
When the waves flap in the creek-mouth. Andrew's driving
The calves to Monterey, he trusts her, he doesn't know
How all her flesh burned with lascivious desire
Last year, but she remembered her mother and prayed
And God quenched it. Prayer works all right: three times
Rod Stewart came down to see her, he might have been wood
For all she cared. She suffers with constipation,
Tired days and smothering dreams, she's young, life's cheerless,
God sent a little sickness to keep her decent
Since the great prayer. What's that in the west, thunder?
The sea rumbles like thunder but the wind's died down,
Soon it should rain.

Myrtle Cartwright
Could sleep if her heart would quit moving the bed-clothes;
The lighthouse-keeper's daughter little Faith Heriot
Says "Father the cow's got loose, I must go out
With the storm coming and bring her into the stable.
What would mother do without milk in the morning?"
(Clearly Point Pinos Light: stands back from the sea
Among the rolling dunes cupped with old pasture.

Nobody'd keep a cow on the rock at Point Sur.)
This girl never goes near the cowshed but wanders
Into the dunes, the long beam of the light
Swims over and over her head in the high darkness,
The spray of the storm strains through the beam but Faith
Crouches out of the wind in a hollow of the sand
And hears the sea, she rolls on her back in the clear sand
Shuddering, and feels the light lie thwart her hot body
And the sand trickle into the burning places.
Comes pale to the house: "Ah Bossy led me a chase,
Led me a chase." The lighthouse-keeper believes in hell,
His daughter's wild for a lover, his wife sickening toward cancer,
The long yellow beam wheels over the wild sea and the strain
Gathers in the air.

O crucified
Wings, orange eyes, open?
Always the strain, the straining flesh, who feels what God feels
Knows the straining flesh, the aching desires,
The enormous water straining its bounds, the electric
Strain in the cloud, the strain of the oil in the oil-tanks
At Monterey aching to burn, the strain of the spinning
Demons that make an atom, straining to fly asunder,
Straining to rest at the center,
The strain in the skull, blind strains, force and counterforce,
Nothing prevails . . .

Oh in storm: storm's kind, kind violence,
When the swollen cloud ached—suddenly
Her charge and agony condensed, slip, the thick dark
Whelps lightning; the air breaks, the twin birth rain falls globed

From the released blackness high up in the air
Ringing like a bell for deliverance.

Many-folded hills
Mouth the black voice that follows the white eye
Opening, universal white eye widening and shut. Myrtle Cartwright's
One of those whom thunder shakes with terror: head covered
Against the flashes: "If it should find me and kill me
What's life been worth? Nothing, nothing, nothing, death's horrible,"
She hears it like a truck driven jolting through heaven
Rumble to the north. "And if I die old:
Nothing, nothing."

Vasquez' boys have gone home.

Deep after
midnight the wind rises, turns iron again,
From east of south, it grinds the heads of the hills, the dunes move in the dark at Point Pinos, the sandstone
Lighthouse at Point Sur on the top of the rock is like an axhead held against a grindstone.
The high redwoods have quit roaring to scream. Oaks go down on the mountain. At Vasquez' place in the yellow
Pallor of dawn the roof of the barn's lifting, his sons cast ropes over the timbers. The crucified
Snaps his beak at them. He flies on two nails.
Great eyes, lived all night?
Onorio should have held the rope but it slid through his fingers. Onorio Vasquez
Never sees anything to the point. What he sees:
The planted eucalyptuses bent double

All in a row, praying north, "Why everything's praying
And running northward, old hawk anchored with nails
You see that everything goes north like a river.
On a cliff in the north
Stands the strange lover, shines and calls."

In the morning
The inexhaustible clouds flying up from the south
Stream rain, the gullies of the hills grow alive, the creeks flood, the summer sand-bars
Burst from their mouths, from every sea-mouth wedges of yellow, yellow tongues. Myrtle Cartwright
Hears the steep cataracts slacken, and then thunder
Pushes the house-walls. "Hear me God, death's not dreadful.
You heard before when I prayed. Now," she whispers,
"I'll make the bargain," thunder leans on the house-walls, "life's no value
Like this, I'm going to Stewart's, I can't live empty.
Now Andrew can't come home for every canyon
Vomits its bridge, judgment is yours only,
Death's in your hands." She opens the door on the streaming
Canyon-side, the desperate wind: the dark wet oak-leaves
All in a moment each leaf a distinct fire
Reflect the sharp flash over them: Myrtle Cartwright
Feels the sword plunge: no touch: runs tottering up hill
Through the black voice.

Black pool of oil hidden in the oil-tank
In Monterey felt the sword plunge: touched: the wild heat
Went mad where a little air was, metal curled back,
Fire leaped at the outlet. "Immense ages
We lay under rock, our lust hoarded,

The ache of ignorant desire, the enormous pressure,
The enormous patience, the strain, strain, the strain
Lightened we lay in a steel shell . . . what God kept for us:
Roaring marriage."

Myrtle Cartwright wins up hill through the oak-scrub
And through the rain, the wind at the summit
Knocks her breasts and her mouth, she crouches in the mud,
Feels herself four-foot like a beast and the lightning
Will come from behind and cover her, the wolf of white fire,
Force the cold flesh, cling with his fore-paws. "Oh, death's
What I was after." She runs on the road northward, the wind behind her,
The lightnings like white doves hovering her head, harmless as pigeons, through great bars of black noise.
She lifts her wet arms. "Come doves."

The oil-tank boils with joy in the north, one among ten, one tank
Burns, the nine others wait, feel warmth, dim change of patience. This one roars with fulfilled desire,
The ring-bound molecules splitting, the atoms dancing apart, marrying the air.

Myrtle Cartwright
Knocks on her door: "Oh, I've come. Here's what you wanted."

(In the yellow inland no rain but the same lightning,
And it lights a forest.) He leads her into the barn because there are people in the house.

In the north the oil-tanks
Catch from the first, the ring-bound molecules splitting, the atoms dancing apart, marrying the air.
The marriage-bound thighs opening, on the stiff white straw, the nerves of fire, the ganglia like stars.

Don't you see any vision Onorio Vasquez? "No, for the topazes
Have dulled out of his head, he soars on two nails,
Dead hawk over the coast. O little brother
Julio, if you could drive nails through my hands
I'd stand against the door: through the middle of the palms:
And take the hawk's place, you could throw knives at me.
I'd give you my saddle and the big bridle, Julio,
With the bit that rings and rings when the horse twirls it."
He smiles. "You'd see the lights flicker in my hair."
He smiles craftily. "You'd live long and be rich,
And nobody could beat you in running or riding."
He chatters his teeth. "It is necessary for someone to be fastened with nails.
And Jew-beak died in the night. Jew-beak is dead."

THE WOMEN AT POINT SUR

I

The Rev. Dr. Barclay outgrew his profession,
He stood on the platform, his hands like wires in a wind, silent, the eyes coals
In the dead face. "I have nothing for you." The face began twitching, he felt it. "I have something to tell you.
This place is dead, it is dead." He saw the narrow face of Audis his wife shine white by his child's.
"I am not a poor man, I haven't hung by the salary. I have served here ten years, I have made great friendships, I've honestly
Done what I thought was due. The creed died in my mind, I kept the pastorate, I thought the spirit,
The revolutionary spirit of Christ would survive, flame the more freely. There are many others
Leaders of churches have sunk the myths and swim by the ethic. Love: and not resist violence: which one of us
Holds to that now? Dared name it this time last year?" The assistant pastor
Was present, and suddenly standing in the aisle: "Dr. Barclay is ill.
The long strain of his pastorate, his labors and bereavement: he must rest . . ." But Barclay twitching his head, the lean face
Like white fire in the dimness through the colored windows: "I am well, and enough rested, this dim air
Has heard enough lies." The other one still attempting to speak, "Sit down will you, I am not patient."
And he said to the people: "You are kindly and simple, you made war when they told you to, you have made peace when they told you.
You obey the laws, you are simple people, you love authority. *I* have authority

Here, and no man will hinder me while I make my confession. I have been a blind man leading you blind,
Nobody can build the truth on lies. My blindness is not removed,
I have nothing true to tell you, no profession but ignorance, I can tell you what's false. Christianity is false.
The fable that Christ was the son of God and died to save you, died and lived again. Lies. You'd swallow
The yarns of idle fishermen, the wash of Syria? You are very simple people. It is time to scour off.
I tell you," he said: but the people were all moving, the great pipes of the organ
Poured into voice behind him, sonorous and ordered
Storm-fall roaring his words down, "repent, repent. Repent," through loops and moments of the noise they heard him
Crying, words glittered like hands through a net, having no meaning. Men moved in the aisles, Barclay remembered
The electric switch-board back of the platform, he strode to the back, threw the main switch, the organ groaned silent
Like a shot beast. Three men had mounted the platform steps, and Barclay
Fiercely and suddenly: "Go down, I am here!" they wavered backward
Unsure, shrinking from violence; they found the steps and went down. Barclay above them:
"Listen but once. To hear me again you'll have to follow me. Thought is not easy, I am giving you ten years'
Thought in a moment's words. It is not possible
To know anything while you eat lies: you half-believers, fog-people: leave that, wash the eyes, and who knows
Now the earth draws to maturity, has taken the bloody
Initiation of coming of age, you also grown adult
May fish some flaming gleam of knowledge out of the netted ocean, run down some deer of perception
In the dark wood: certainly it is hopeless, oh desperate; no man

Down all the blind millenniums has known anything, no not a scrap, not a dust-grain: I am calling you to that
Blind adventure, I call you to take despair by the throat: I know you are fools and soft, woman-brained,
I have lived among you, I have held my mouth not to despise you: I would set the sheep on the wolves to this end,
The doves at the hawk's nest . . . It is no alliance
And I am the hunter you shall not run as hounds for: but think you old men, you old women, if one of you
Should stumble over it by chance, you had cleaned the mind that you could see it, some instant pebble of perception
Glowing in the dust. Tell me if you find it, I am going away
And give the tag-end of my life to that purpose," he said quietly; and cried out
"I have been on the verge, these years. You with your monkey hubbub crossed me when I touched it.
When it lay in my hands: you with your marriages and your burials, your newspapers, the noise you keep up
Under the stars, your national quarrels and your observances,
Flags, fireworks, songs to dead gods: from moment to moment
While it knocked for entrance. I am going off alone and gather my mind, I have something fiery
Here that will burn the world down to significance." The aisle opened for him
Going down from the platform, passing alone to the doors.

II

He went alone to the vacation cottage near Monterey,
Thence wandered southward the coast. On the road crossing Sovranes Canyon despair covered him like water.

"I have broken my life like a dry stick and have come no nearer, in the city when I raged against time
It seemed in hand's reach." He thought of the house he had lived in. "Not that. Sticks plastered, cloth, books, what they call a home;
Framed to wall out the wild face of eternity."
He thought of Audis his wife. "Not her. If it were possible
I'd not go back there." He seemed to have passed into a vacuum, no means, no resistance, valueless freedom
Like a vain ghost's in the air. Nothing solid, the roots out. He climbed the small steep hill by the road,
He struck his hands against the rocks at the peak, the knuckles were bleeding: "All this energy to waste.
I am fifty years old and have this energy." The tide of high excitement returned, he unconscious of it,
Rising by waves. "Certainly I shall put out my hands and touch power. He is here, he is here." The sea's tide
Rose too, white-sheeting the dark reefs at the rock-foot, in the dark south the domed rock at Point Sur
Stood opposite the mainland wall of hills; clouds closed the sea-line; landward far down the hill-slope a hawk
Hung like a wind-vane, motionless with beating wings in the stream of the wind. A man tethered his mount
To the fence beneath it. Dr. Barclay felt in his forehead behind the eyes the ache of stored force
Beating against the sockets of the eyes. "When it finds release, when it finds it . . .
The vulture's got the sky of the hawk: you, brain, this power
Throngs you will not break through? There is a power behind the appearances, you will break through to it and touch it.
Death's got the sky of the vulture: the flaw in the story.
Fifty years old, facing the desperate . . . I shall not die blind. Jesus did: 'why hast thou forsaken me my God?'

I not his son take him by violence. This is that hybris in the tragedy, that
brings destruction.
Content. I will buy." It came to him like a whisper from outward: "Plow
the air, what harvest: take the earth in your hands.
God thinks through action, how shall a man but through action?" "I have
cut myself off, I acted when I cut myself off
From action: I am only a wandering mind reaching at knowledge." But he
thought "It is true that I have reached nothing.
The presence I almost touched in the crowds . . . what was it I sought?
. . . that came in flashes, vanishes derisive
When the eyes focus. To mould one's thoughts from action. Give up sanity
again, be mad enough to act.
This fellow that climbs up the hill to prick my solitude:
Kill him and hide the body, that would be action, not an inch more
monstrous
Than any other. I cannot think what it was that I was trying to discover, to
find out something,
I wrote it on paper yesterday. Here it is: Oh, these:
First, whether there's any . . . what the vulgar call God . . . spirit of the
universe.
But spirit's a more contaminated word than the other. Life then, one life
Informing . . . no, being: whether it's one being . . . why, this is evident.
Second, is anything left after we die but worm's meat? Third, how should
men live?
I have something to solve!

You want to speak to me?"
"Yes sir: you're Dr. Barclay? A letter for you."
"From Mrs. Barclay?" He read. "Have you got a knife, my pencil's broken.
Young man I'm curious to know what people believe.
Do you think there's a God?" He stared; and Barclay: "You think so:

You're ashamed to say so. What have we preachers done, how have we slandered him,
That people are ashamed to speak of him without laughing?
Must clean our conceptions. Well it's true, there is one.
If you define the word.
But the oyster wonders whether his element's conscious,
The great night-cored and storm-striped. You have no opinion?"
"I haven't." "The letter? It's absurd not to know anything.
You choose to ignore consciousness, incredible how quickly
The American mind short-circuits by ignoring its object.
Something in the gelded air of the country. Tell Mrs. Barclay,
No need of writing, if she pleases may follow me.
Do you know whether my daughter's with her, a girl
Twenty years old? Oh, you'd have noticed.
I shall have to do something, God thinks through action
And all this show is God's brain, the water, the cloud yonder,
The coast hills, thinking the thing out to conclusion.
Tell her that I'm walking southward.

It is certain," he thought after the man had gone down,
"The mind's powerless in vacuo, no one can dispense with disciples
And burn to the essence.
Those are the birds that are not caught but with confidence.
What's honesty, the end is honest. I should have taken him.
He serves the hotel, he is not proper to this earth
I shall crop the pure fruit of. If I must."

III

Going down he felt a dizziness, he stumbled, and the world
Dissolved in a moment. After a moment's horror in the gulf of emptiness

He leaned and touched the hill with his hand, he modelled with his hand
room enough to crouch on, and slowly,
Painfully, element by element, summoned the world back.
Willed it to being, and with the pain of creation.
Walked in his made world: some minutes that followed
Each footfall needed thought and creation to plant itself on
For the gaps in the dim fabric.

He stopped at a farmhouse about
sundown,
Bought food. The woman was severe and suspicious;
Not knowing what incredible guest . . . "I keep my secret,
I hide myself in the body of an old man.
Why should I be troubled with praise and thanksgiving?"

IV

The moon had stood on the hills like a domed mountain
Before sundown; he had walked in the night and slept by the roadside.
He remembered on a silver headland over black abysses
A multitude of people had followed him; he had stood
On raised ground by the roadside: "Oh faithful-hearted
The change of the world has come indeed and you do wisely to follow me.
Nevertheless the seed is not ripe. I am gathering seed in a great solitude, I
shall tell you everything
When I return, but not now. These little ones would faint on the way, it is
far and you cannot follow me."
He had left them there. He remembered enormous descents into the
darkness,
Interminable climbs through the rank night of the redwoods
On the north slopes.

He brushed his clothing at dawn,
And washed when he found water. At a prosperous farmhouse
Lodging was refused him, he went on southward
And saw from the road over the great bronze height
Eastward the mountain Pico Blanco, westward the rock at Point Sur
crowned with its lighthouse
Against great waters; a gated way dropped seaward,
He followed, he came to the gaunt farmhouse that stood
High over gap-roofed barns and broken wagons;
They had told him he might be given lodging at Morhead's.
High cube-shaped house, redwood logs squared and jointed,
Blackened with ancient weathers, chinked with white plaster,
Striped like a zebra with the white plaster, and the porch
Rotting under its rose-vine.

The young woman at the door
Needed persuasion, but now his mind was so clear
After the night's bewilderment, he understood
Perfectly. Her husband not yet back from the army,
The ranch was too much to manage, they were very poor
And lived poorly. Indeed the price of his lodging
Would help toward paying the cowboy.

He thought, could he hire
a horse
For Edward to ride? Edward was dead.
"My boy was only eighteen, he was killed in France
Two years ago." She answered, "My Rachel's four.
She had a fever two years ago." She took him up-stairs
Through the dark house and showed him the room.
He lived there quietly feeling the strings and tendons
Of his mind mend; he seemed remembering the sources,

The causes; he walked on the hillside over the great sand-flat
And the burnished ocean.

                                        The storms in his mind had had their signal,
When he had imagined, O corrupt fool, too near a friendship . . .
Should they not love each other, they were born twins.
That anger of his when Edward before his departure
Locked himself in the room with April to bid her farewell:
He had paced the hallway below, his mind boiling,
And suffered like a fainting-fit or a dizziness:
Sorrow at his son's departure: annihilating the world
A moment or more.

                                Annihilation, the beautiful
Word, the black crystal structure, prisms of black crystal
Arranged the one behind the other in the word
To catch a ray not of this world.

                                        Was it possible
His outburst against religion, against his ministry,
Dated from there, the public passionate resentment?
No; that was reasoned; having taught falsehoods, countenanced
Lies, must denounce them publicly. And the death of his son
Involved in the same texture; his own starved impotent
Desert of years.

                            Six came to table in the house.
Himself, and Mrs. Morhead; the four-year-old
Rachel her child; two farmhands; and the girl Faith Heriot
Who was certainly friend not servant, relative perhaps
Of Mrs. Morhead's, and nursed the old cripple up-stairs
On the third floor under the roof: old Morhead,

The absent husband's father, the owner of the farm
Probably; but never came down, sepulchred in bed
Under the roof while the place drifted to ruin.

What were they doing in the nights? No doubt the old cripple
Was restless, the girl Faith Heriot would move overhead
Barefoot or softly slippered; and she or another
Steal up and down the creaking stairs in the dark.

V

The fourth day of his lodging at Morhead's his mind
Was quieter, he wrote a brief letter to his wife.
"Dear Audis my mind is quieter. I repent nothing,
It was my duty to protest publicly.
I shall live here some months quieting my mind."
He was directing the bank to set to her account
(Three quarters, scored through and erased) one half his income
Monthly, enough he thought to keep up the house
For April and herself. And his love, he added,
To herself and April.

He wrote to the bank also.
A man would drive to the stage-road in the afternoon
And post them for him.

It was too easy to be at peace, quieting the mind.
Easily he could live here forever and build up peace like a fortress. "For this I have broken—to be quiet—
My life like a dry stick? That's to feed fire with." He hurried from the house and went up

Toward the bronze hills. "Die blind, die ignorant?" Ever at remembering
that he was fifty years old it pierced him
With stammering hurry and precipitance. He walked on the hill like one
carrying a torch in the wind on the hillside,
Seeking and seeking, the smoke and the flame blowing up the gray gullies,
twisted and flaring,
Nothing, nothing found. He sat in unbearable dejection
On the open starved earth. The power was all drained.
There was a time he had felt it in the skull
Like molten iron pushing for outlet.
Now emptiness, like a band over the coronal suture the ache of the
emptiness
In the bone vault below. Some buzzing arrowlets like stray electrons
In the void of space, gnats under a vault. Annihilation
Is the most beautiful word. "Edward my son
Feeds on the fruit of that bough."
He pushed his hand palm forward from the face outward.
"I will not touch peace." He rose and being for the time hopeless
Turned from himself, there was no help in that emptiness.
He saw over the triangle-shaped sand-flat the great black rock of Point Sur
against the blue water.
His mind relieved of vigilance instantly told him:
"God thinks through action. There are only two ways: gather disciples
To fling like bullets against God and discover him:
Or else commit an act so monstrous, so irreparable
It will stand like a mountain of rock, serve you for fulcrum
To rest the lever. In vacancy: nothing." He imagined
A priest by the yet-twitching carcass of sacrifice
Plunging his hands into the hot red cavern
Through the cut ribs and midriff, dragging out the heart,
Lifting it to the God of the sky, the thick blood

Rains on his face. "What is man? The filthiest of beasts;
But a discoverer, God sprouted him for the sake of discovery.
I have voyaged outside the maps, these waters not charted,"
He said exultantly. Going down the hill a company followed him,
His daughter April among them. "Do you love me April?"
"Dearest!" "I am going to war, we must be alone for farewell.
The people press me. — I have taken hold on the future, I see the future
Destructions," he said to the people, he waved his arms, "with a flail
Comes God smiting."

He stood on the hill by the house,
Then Mrs. Morhead looking up from below
Saw him shake his arms over the tops of the buck-eyes
Against the shining cloud and descend rapidly
Behind the trees. She was troubled to think of his passing
Her child by the old corral or beyond the pig-yard,
Yet did not call; she'd been much too indulgent
And little Rachel only came if she pleased.
Meeting the man she felt vaguely he was not alone,
What people were among the trees behind him? Oh, fancies.
"You didn't come in to lunch, you met some people?"
He answered coldly "It would be hard for you
To know what sort of people crying for my help.
As a man swimming dips the free hand forward
Into the wave that has not run by his mouth
I dipped my hand into the future, I was walking
With the people who have not been born yet." She thought "He is strange
And good, I cannot understand him, he is very learned."
She said "You must be very hungry and tired,
I'll have Maruca make you some tea." "Tired, what's tired?
There's power." They went toward the house. "How old is the house?
Sixty years old?" "My husband's father built it,"

She answered, "it is more than fifty." And Barclay, "It is sound, it will stand.
The old man up there?" "My father-in-law. He was strong as a redwood,
Everything thrived when he was riding. My husband
Needn't have gone," she said, "they'd never have drafted him.
He thought that his father'd manage the place. He was proud,"
She said bitterly. "Four months he had been away,
Grandfather's horse rolled over in a gully of bushes,
The old man has been dead from the chest downward. He chose
To lie at the top of the house." But Barclay answered,
"The old logs are solid as rock, they'll neither burn nor fall down.
This will be standing in the time that I saw
Come up like a red dawn twisted with storms."
She looked sideways with troubled eyes. "The chimney
Had to be propped" she said "against the south storms.
The brick would stagger, he ran a prop to the roof-beam."
He answered: "There is no strong tower that will not stagger in that time. I am telling you secrets.
I've learned something. It's certain that the world has changed. The war that your husband returns from
Was only the first blaze in the bark of the tree to mark it for the axes."
They stood by the stacked firewood
By the kitchen door, she thinking "A preacher and has read deep books.
He's looking at the oakwood." Then Barclay: "Not now,
I'll not go in yet. It's hard to hear the rustle and slip of the changing stars
Under a roof, I'm going to the sea." Then like a man stirring the dark seeking unconsciously
The word to earthquake her heart: "When you go in,
Kiss Faith Heriot and tell her that what was right is wrong, what was wrong's right, the old laws are abolished,
They cannot be crossed nor broken, they're dead. The sanction is dead.
This interval

There is nothing wicked, nothing strange in the world. What the heart desires or any part of the body
That is the law. The God of the stars has taken his hand out of the laws and has dropped them empty
As you draw your hand out of a glove. When I saw that he had withdrawn himself out of the churches
I left the church, I was a minister, I told them
God is not here. I came alone into the mountains by the sea. Tell your child, tell Faith Heriot.
Tell no one else, these things are secret." The cold core of his mind
Smiled at the rest, his mind was split into three parts, the cold core
Observing the others, the first in full faith clear-eyed in bitter earnestness riding the tides of prophecy,
The third watching the woman tremble and turn pale,
She had flinched the instant he named Faith Heriot, some nerve
Unknown to him was touched, she'd fled up the step to the doorway,
Stood pale and framed, her back to the door, between the great log-ends
That made the jambs and under the jutting lintel.
"I have knowledge and the world is changed. I have power to make you believe.
All that was true when you were a child is rubbed out." She wore the gesture
Of a woman standing naked in a door in a dream before the hot crowd, and Barclay gently:
"Don't fear. Did I forget to tell you there is nothing wicked in the world, no act is a sin?
Nothing you can do is wicked. I have seen God. He is there in the hill, he is here in your body. My . . . daughter,"
He said shaking, "God thinks through action, I have watched him, through the acts of men fighting and the acts of women
As much as through the immense courses of the stars; all the acts, all the bodies; who dares to enclose him

With *this is right* and *that's wrong*, shut his thought with scruples, blind him against discoveries, blind his eyes?" The brown-skinned
Vaquero with little Rachel beside had come down
Across the dooryard hearing the voice lifted;
And the kitchen door opening Rachel's mother
Drew down from the door-sill, Faith Heriot came out; the Indian house-girl
Maruca stood behind her in the door, the broad cheeks
Heavily smiling. Then Barclay, "Have you come to hear what I said? It is all secret." Faith Heriot
Caught her friend's hand; "Natalia: what was he saying?
What were you saying that frightened her?" He felt Natalia's
Dark eyes like a child's asking pity of his face,
It gave him pleasure, he had power to touch her where he pleased, he saw Faith Heriot's
Narrowing blue points of anger; here was the one to be humbled, the cut blond hair,
Haggard cheeks, outstretched throat: the cold core of his poised mind, without irony, without resentment,
Observed his sexual pleasure in making himself a prophet before them, "I am fifty years old!" and the competent
Storm of his power: "What was I telling her? You're right, it's a bad year for secrets, will yours be written,
Yours too over the towers of cities, and shot from hill-tops? Yours is so little Faith Heriot,
But how could I hide mine?" He looked sharply and the axe-formed
Young features not changed, not workable metal like the other. "Yours will not grow, yours not have children," the hard blue
Hardened, "but mine will fly over the world like sunrise. When the world changes and the tired soul
Of the earth drinks a new spring: someone is sent to tell men, I am sent to tell you": he said to the cowboy

"How long since you went to the priest and made confession?" Who
shifted his feet, smiling, shook his head, "Long time,"
And Barclay: "You never will need go back to him, there is no more sin,
nothing you could do will need confession.
Nothing is bad," and turned to Faith Heriot: "All the relations of the world
have changed in a moment.
If there was anything forbidden you may do it. Your father . . ." he saw the
lips twitching and he said
"Your father. Used pleasant sins in his youth . . ." the lips relaxing,
He said "and now old . . ." "Leave him alone." She thrust with the throat
like a held lance. "Because you have twisted
This girl with sly talk, scared her with tricks until she has told you
More than she knows . . ." "I didn't tell him anything at all," she whispered
trembling. "Listened at the keyhole
The two years back then. What is it, a sneaking evangelist?" It stood so
clearly in Barclay's mind what to answer,
Though it had no reason in his mind, he answered: "I know that what you
told her was lies." He thought of the woman
By the well-curb in Samaria, convert for having been told her own story. "I
have more power than I know."
But willing to use it further he doubted it, he feared the words would come
wrong, be merely ridiculous; he had touched
Something: and the torrent would serve: "Did you think who had seen into
the mind of God had not into yours?
The hill is gray with dead grass and the ocean
Blazing violet and blue, but a girl is clean white under the clothes, white as
milk, but under
The white skin, under the dead grass, in the blue crystal:
Red blood, white stone, black water: God is there also:
The same who is like a river swirling the stars like straws: I am telling you
the river
Turns sharp around the rock of this year. He gave a man laws on a
mountain, your old commandments,

Cut them in stone: I tell you that every letter of the laws is struck
backward, the stone tables turned over,
The stars are flowing another way and the people
Shall learn a new flight. I was a preacher in a church in the city: I knew all
the while
That God was not an old man in the sky saying like an old man
Be good my children: I knew that he was fiercer than a lion in the night and
lovelier than a girl
Alone and naked on the shore in the sea's breath, nearly too young to be
loved, yellow-haired: and I looked,
He let go the bent bough, he lifted his feet from the flattened grass, made
all the laws nothing. What purpose?
He will have confusion for its beauty, he is wild to walk in new ways, he
snatches at the rose of burning,
He stirs in the earth: Is a little freedom not worth destruction?" He
stopped, the five were silent, and he said
"Nothing is asked, what could be wanted? The whole earth will hear it."

VI

He rounded the house
toward the road seaward.
They saw him between the low oak-bush and the log wall
Moving his arms as if a multitude waited
Outside the gap-roofed sheds. When he was gone they were silent,
When he returned in the evening he also was silent.
He slept badly, he heard in the night the young child
Crying, he had thought that Rachel's mother Natalia
Slept in the same room, but the child cried
Uncomforted.

Came the thought "I am sterile as a bone
In lack of action: God thinks through action: akh, talk!

Talk and thoughts, though I felt a power straining within me.
And then I am emptied and lie in a bed like a pit
And have achieved nothing, all that I said
Was folly and there is no deliverance." He thought
"The act is deliverance. What act? . . . What are they doing
Lets the child cry and cry in the night?
I preached freedom and found none. Deliverance. Deliverance,"
He sighed and slept. He awoke thinking of April
His daughter, her purity and grace, named from the springtime,
And running his hand through the stiff growth on his chin
He thought "I am loathsome. God is in every creature,
In toads and curded excrement." He thought of Maruca,
The strong brown servant who fed the table: like a toad's
Her thick body and broad face. . . . "Oh! Back in adolescence?"
He cried to himself, a vision of the thick brown body
Rising against him like a giantess: no gesture,
Only the form, female as moist brown earth,
The heavy protuberances of breast and belly
And the idol thighs. Light had come, certainly she stirred
And was born from the stale bed. "Death is horrible," he thought,
"Rot in brown soil." He stretched himself stiffly in the bed,
Entered death, little arrows shook in his brain and were silent.
The years one by one, green in front, brown behind,
Passed and dropped grass-mold over. "Not dead, not yet,"
He cried to himself under the earth and thrust up
The burden for breath. That suffocation
Conquered him when he looked at Maruca, he came to her
After three days; she had fed the henyard and gone up
Among the twisted buck-eyes, he breathing with anguish,
The nightmare band around his chest: "I have money.
Dollars. I have come to buy deliverance. Listen Maruca,
I am Lazarus, I am Lazarus up from the dead,

Chastity has withered my bones, there is nothing I want
Less than you. How old are you, twenty?" She smiled under the stolid
cheek-bones,
Shook her head, the Asian-lidded eyes had no change.
He sobbing for breath: "How can I live unless you will do it?
It is not that I want anything, never, never want,
Clear-eyed as to that, not die blind as to that,
It is all," he said swaying drunkenly, "a matter of deliverance."
He fumbled his purse. "Here are ten dollars . . . four dollars.
Take them. You know that you are much stronger than I am,
How could you be afraid of me?" She clutched and nodded,
"To-night." "Oh" he cried gasping, "not in the house.
Oh!" and the hand shuddered to the face, "there is some
Reason against the . . . house. They walk all night there,
That's not the reason. The passions die in old age
But I have shot back to puberty." He said "It's a symbol,
Mode of deliverance." His hand, cold but quite dry,
Fastened on the warm brown wrist. She hung back, firm-planted,
Immovable. He said "I have more money I will give you,"
And drawing her along behind the twisted buck-eyes,
"You heard me that sin's abolished, it's not for that freedom.
As for desire there's nothing in the world Maruca
I desire less than you. Crack the diamond breast-plate,
Chastity that sucks the power of prophets." They left the buck-eyes,
And over a ridge of crumbled earth and dead grass
To a dry stream-bed stubbed with dwarf oaks. She halting
In the yellow pit that winter cataracts had sunk,
Hard green dry leaves shielded, "Now must go back
To work. Much work." He said "Here is too open.
Up farther. You want more money." He thought "She will follow,"
And broke up through the boughs to the next level,
"Must I kiss? Agh." He reached her hand, drew her up,

The anguish it was to draw breath had ceased and a flare
Lit in his brain. She seemed not to resent;
To invite. "I am of the higher race and perhaps
For that reason not horrible to her. If an angel
Came old, shaking and mad to someone of mine,"
He thought under the steady internal lightning,
"How my hand shakes." Though he was focussed on the act of deliverance
Disinterested voices in his brain all the while
Like insects back of a searchlight: "It is fifteen years.
I was thirty-five." The mass, hard thickness of her body
Astonished him. "To master the people, set myself free
To master the people. Pleasure would be contemptible."
The light waned, he despaired; suddenly a twitching
Vision of finer limbs, and he thought that the dead
Are dead forever, the inexorable seal across them.
The enduring animal, the God. To live, in itself's
A triumph. The light had grown vast, now suddenly and softly
It was extinguished. Kneeling to rise he thought "There is certainly
One power, and all its forms are equal before it.
I call it God to the people." The woman was asking him
To keep a promise about money and he doubled
What he had meant to give her. He was careless and freed.
She had to be reminded that it made eight dollars.
When she was gone: "I have bought salvation!" He broke
Another exit under the thicket branches.
Crossing the hill in the swirl and storm of sunlight,
Where were they? the invisible multitude he had felt following
Wherever he went? "They were a sign, now they peel off me
Against the instant fulfilment."

He saw from far up . . .
Maruca? in the form of his daughter? He peered under his hand against the wild sun. It gave him great happiness

To feel the visions kindle in his brain, the confusion of persons. "There is
no distinction, each individual
The one power fills and forms, bubbles of one breath. I lay in a woman's lap
uniting myself
With the infinite God." Maruca? She wrung her hands, didn't she, turning
and returning,
The vined porch and the road: the Indian woman would never
That side the house: gazed toward the sea and then gazed
Toward the hills. April. Why there was the car. He went down
Brushing the dusty and stained cloth with his hands,
He wore no hat, smoothing his hair and trembling.

VII

"Father." (I knew her when she was a baby, I fed her milk from the bottle.)
"You've come to see me?" Straining to adjust his mind
To new experience, and the actual reality her presence:
Wears blue, cut short: nearly as blonde as Faith Heriot: the infinite between
them,
The infinite distance. She's tired. "Yes," she answered, "*you* wouldn't come.
Mother's in the cottage at Point Pinos. I'll never ask you
Your reason, you've a good reason." "I have left reasons behind . . ."

"Oh,"

she answered,
"She's been sick, sick. Her suffering. When I tell you,
Then you'll come home." "I have come home out of death, I am Lazarus,
an hour ago, April,
I entered the dead." He trembled with exultance, he was telling her
everything, her maidenhood, "went down to the dead
And mixed myself with the dead race. I am out of the maps,
Breaking strange waves." "Death," she answered bitterly, "is what
I have had to listen to her crying for. Come sit in the car,

That woman is watching us from the rose-vines." He sat beside her,
He fancied she edged away from him. "It will look better when it's grown,"
He said touching his chin, "I had no razor.
There's not a gray hair." Vaguely in his mind it symbolized
The new growth of his life from the sharp break.
The head was gray, the old life was over, the brown beard
Like a new thundering of youth. But April: "The newspapers
Tormented her, she was ashamed to see friends, she couldn't live in the city.
Have you seen the papers?" "Why, no. It would make no difference.
You cannot understand April how utterly
The hive's hum's hushed. Papers." "She had nothing," she answered.
"You, I don't know what you have, some vision, some thunder
That drowns the noises. I'm not a Christian . . ." "I'm glad
My teaching," he said, "when I was a fool was fruitless.
No infection." "But mother had you and Christ. Edward was dead.
You took both in one day. Oh, she still tries
To imagine that her religion's a rock
And you appointed to punishment or repentance.
But the time has struck in. It's all shadows. You can see father,
She's like someone falling and snatching at the air.
Religion? She'd bought poison, I stole it from her
And hid it here under the seat of the car. I hardly
Dared leave her to-day." He moved his hand sidewise,
Palm downward, like one erasing a scripture. "Not lie,
To myself nor you." "Ah we're not friends then," she answered
Trembling. "Lives aren't split off so easily. If I must choose . . ."
"There's no distinction, choice is fantastic" he answered,
"No distinction of persons." April was silent
A little, and cold-eyed: "It doesn't much matter
That all you say's like a night fog where a torch
Sometimes passes but nobody sees the torch-bearer.
I came to ask you to come home, I only ask you

To go and see her and return. But now I must go up,
It will be night-time." "I'll give you something,"
He said "for Audis your mother. Tell her that the laws
Are abolished, let her cast out scruples like devils,
Tear down the walls, run naked, she has starved all her life.
And tell her to act, God thinks through action. You too April:
The act is deliverance: Oh it is more besides; discovery; I know, for I drank it
When you were on the road and while you came to the door: it has changed me
From a cold stone to a star: all the relations of the world have been changed in a moment, mine to her,
Yours to me April. Before, when I said freedom, I stammered." He descended from the car. "My people,"
He said, "must hear what I say." Though his voice was not raised
It made her shudder, his confidence of a multitude
Under the snake-limbed oaks leaning up canyon,
By the ruinous barns in the light of the bronze hills
Sun-beaten from seaward: though there was no one she also
Felt the spectral disciples gathered; and he said, "I held you in my arms,
There is no distinction of persons. . . . You were a baby, I held you in my arms, I fed you milk from the bottle,
God that grows up in trees and mountains, the same power
In the wrinkled limbs formed them and smoothed them, drew them long, polished them white and shining, mounded the low breasts,
Made beautiful the throat: he made you slender who made the servant Maruca like a pine block: the same power,
There is no distinction of persons, it is flame in all lamps: and blew a bone bubble on the head of the column
To hold his glory: yours he made beautiful with light brown
Hair, hers with dull black: I have light and fire to fill it with shining, as if the sun were shut up

In the little bone sky. . . . But you April I will tell you quietly,
You think me insane because I have learned something:
Does the mad father April not need your caring
As much as the bitter mother? Bring her to this hill,
I have what will heal it. I am not insane, I'd be content to be
To have learned causes and sources and have had the lightning
Lighten my thirst. I have many streams running in the mind,
They mingle on the lips, no matter, each one flows pure
And purest of all the one that I dare not think of.
But as for the people that I named: when you looked sideways
To see what multitude my madness invented
Under the oaks, by the ruinous barns, in the bronze hills:
Indeed there are minds knitted with mine, I have never met them,
When I send out my thought there are nerves to take it,
Yes, in these hills, and in that city: and they will come down,
They need not: they hear."

VIII

At the supper-table he asked Natalia
Whether she could make room for his wife and daughter,
"They are coming in a few days." "My husband's coming,"
She said, "next month. Almost a year they've kept him
Since the war came to an end." She looked at Faith Heriot,
Who suddenly rising and her face like the plaster
That striped the house outside between the black logs,
"Why shouldn't they come? Oh you'll be glad of company.
The girl who was here, that's his daughter, that came in the car,
Perhaps can earn her way keeping the old bones
Under the roof when I have gone out of this place.
She'll never take them out riding." Natalia: "Ah, Faith.
Are you so tired?" "Why should I wait for next month?"

She answered. Natalia half rose to follow her, then mournfully:
"Oh, there's still room in the house. Till Randal comes home."
They heard Faith Heriot move up-stairs like a restless
Fire in the hallway. "Before you take out the plates,
Maruca, fix a tray for my father." Then angrily
Regarding the two farmhands, the Spanish one and the other,
At the end of the table, "When my husband comes home
Things will get done on the place," she said to Barclay,
"The stock be saved, we shan't need to keep boarders.
The fields be plowed and planted, the horses not die."
She took the tray and went out to the stairway. Maruca
Gathering the plates leaned over Barclay's chair
So that the great breast through the oily brown cloth
Lay on his shoulder, he overlooked his repugnance,
Unmoved, secretly smiling: the symbolic flesh
Had served him: the value of the symbol secured,
By-product amorousness, the ridiculous female
After-glow had no finger on; "I have cast the last fear:
Of being ridiculous."

Later, he had walked in the twilight
Of the slight moon, he had peace and confidence, the sharp-tipped crescent
Reddened and fell in the sea beyond the Sur rock. Barclay returning
Felt someone meet him in the dark porch under the rose-vines, and a hand
touching him, he thought Maruca's,
He pushed it down, saying readily "What do you want? I have no love in
me."

Not the Indian's voice, though a whisper:
"You know something: tell me what I must do: come outside.
I've waited for you." She turned sharp to the left,
Too furtive to take the path, staying under the wall

Until they reached the windowless corner and had come
By the oak-bush; the face under the sky-gleam Natalia's,
But lamplike whitened and changed: "You are good: and I know
Your eyes can measure the hidden bones of one's trouble.
Nothing looks wicked to you, nothing looks loathsome,
I know you saw it."

That she had had a child was no matter.
The intoxicant slender body by him in the star-gleam,
Appealing to him, ready to make herself bare with confession:
That was one stream in the mind; it was most marvellous,
And not quite sanity, that he could see his own mind
Objectively, all the currents and courses at one moment:
That one, the sexual pleasure; this other, his authority
Acknowledged; he'd not been confident before: here, for this hunting,
Disciples, this one the first, lances to ambush
The power behind powers, bring down the mastodon: one current
Opaque yet, he understood it vortexed on April:
"And this when I have the time and have dared examine it
The earth will be crystal": he answered Natalia, "I told you
God turning like a quick seal under the water
Swims the other current: or like a snake has rubbed off
Old customs, the courts and churches sell the dry skin
Sloughed from the fire of his coils: there is nothing wicked
No sin, no wrong, no possible fountain of shame:
And the earth shines with aliveness: how could you be troubled?"
She trembled and said "The man that I love is coming."
"Are you not glad?" "I thought you had knowledge. Oh, no matter.
I'm glad," she said turning. He felt his authority
Slip in the dark like a rope slipping, and angrily:
"If it was only to say that you have more loves than that one: you needn't

Have crossed my evening of thought. Two are not too many, the man and his child, will three
Break down the basket? You are not a virgin to see the world through rainbows." She closed her eyes and he saw
The muscles of the face quiver. "Through nightmares." The mouth grinned like a mask. "I have kept her off for five days,"
She muttered against the teeth, "but I am afraid.
I took her in she was sick and helpless, she had nowhere to go." He answered "You may do anything.
If you have pleasure in being under two masters:
Choice is a fool. Why have you denied her?" She turned
Silently back toward the house. Then Barclay, "It is I
That am your master and I tell you play with your playmates.
Fear nothing for I will gather them also. I have strength.
And God is kindly, you may couple in his hands.
But if you fear the anger of lovers: only starved minds
Child the idiot jealousy: I have come to feed them." She went
Like one who in a famine has been given strange bread
And takes it home, hiding it under his coat,
Doubtful whether it is death or life that he carries
Hungering, and will lock the doors and perhaps
Not dare to be fed.

IX

Faith Heriot ranged the house like a fire.
In the afternoon Barclay, as his manner was, wandered
Up the hill to a certain rock, starved ledge of limestone
Breaking the slope above an abandoned cabin.
From here the great shed of the mountain shot in bronze folds
Seemed humming like bells under the strokes of the sun; in the creases the winter stream-beds

Haired with low oak, but higher between deep ridges spiring to redwood, netted the edge of the continent
With many-branching black threads; the wall steepened below and went down
To a sea like blue steel breakless to Asia, except the triangle-shaped sand-flat as low as the ocean
The lighthouse rock apexed, and the lesser morro
Flanked on the south; these two alone breaking the level
Opposite the straight sea-wall of the ended world.

Barclay was silent although his people
Expected words. He knew that this multitude
Was in a manner unreal . . . certainly the human
Earth knew its leader though not yet consciously; the deep
Layers of the islanded points of mind that are peaks
Risen from one base, thronged him from far, whose fatal
Perceptions and discoveries were making the future.
The future thronged him, the inevitable unborn
Inhabitants of this mountain, him making their lives—
He did not think expressly, it lay at the thought's root—
More than that Meccan camel-driver had made
The lands keyed on Arabia . . . he too was grown old
When revelation rained from the desert stars;
He too fled from his city and founded a church
On alien earth. . . . Were inhuman presences
Mixed in this people, beasts running, rocks moving,
Horned heads, heads of dark leaves? He stood up on the rock,
And quietly, hardly speaking aloud; but they all could hear him:
"What have I hidden, why do you still hang on my mind, will you have the perceptions
Embryo? My giants will all arise from their fountain

When time ripens. There are those among you that neither breathe nor feed, limestone fire-hardened, old lava,
Granite with the wet sea's growth; others that breathe through leaves and through roots
Milk the earth; those able to wait millenniums and these many green centuries: I am speaking to the one consciousness,
Modulated through wood and through stone, through the nerves of man, the flesh of cattle: you that wear horns
And suffer in this drought, but few seasons to live: that which suffers I tell you
Is not another thing from the disdain of the stones, not another
From the bull's joy dipping the blood-red whip-stock
In the honey of the womb: if this one thing enjoys and suffers, equally, equally at length, and in cool
Reclusion in the stone is utterly itself,
Then its existence, not its color in each form in each moment, not pain nor pleasure
That cancel each other . . ." He saw the horned foreheads
Turn down hill to watch someone approaching
His people from the low oaks, a woman, and he said:
"Though one had eighty years of delight and another
From birth to old age pain, pain: the one is the other, the delight
And pain are cancelled the one existence approving them,
The one consciousness: the one breath of the organ blown through innumerable
Conduits of sound; blessed are the ears that hear eternal music." She approached and he said "Maruca
I am speaking to those you cannot see: but stand among them."
She looked at the cattle thinking "They are steers and lean cows,
And now they are winding away over the hillside."
She stood before the limestone, smiling her lure, and Barclay:

"Nothing is ridiculous. Laughter and sentimentality
Are poured from the one pitcher, the pure in their minds
Taste all things, not those." She answered "Nobody saw me
Come up from the house, much work, soon must go back.
I thought it's not good for him to be alone
And talk to yourself. Nobody ever
Comes to the small dead house down here: soon must go back."
"There is nothing ridiculous: but I have emptied your cup,"
He answered; she approaching he said "Stand there!" and he said:
"What I did with this flesh is no importance:
Except I was lamed with a chain, the act filed it. But look at her,
Earth, and you trees that covered us, you lichen-sided
Boulders of the shore: you chiefly, air-wandering or time-traversing
presences of men,
Drift of the coast and drifted down from the future to hear me, worship
her a little, it is this that saves you.
Self-regardful humanity cutting itself away from the earth and the creatures,
gathered home on itself,
Digging a pit behind it and a gulf before it,
Cancerous, a growth that makes itself alien: how long would you be spared
before the knife rings you and the spreading
Ulcer scooped out, but this sound flesh solders you home to the beasts? It is
human yet of dark mind,
And never has cut the navel-string and draws from the mother, pleads
between you and destruction: this, here, your Savior:
Worship it a while.

I am not your savior, I have sharper gifts than
salvation."

The Indian perplexed and vacant
Looked sidelong, compelled in the net of imagination, darkly

Feeling multitude behind her, then clearly hearing
Motion on the hill: and Barclay across the steam of his people
Like a low ground-fog breaking to horns and branches
In the blinding sun, perceived two others; and the one:
"He preaches and your fat Maruca's the church,
That's why she slid away so quietly up hill."
He said "It is bitter herbs, Faith Heriot, God chooses.
The earth is full of sweet leaves: you for your bitterness.
I am speaking to those you cannot see: stand there among them."

X

The fog-bank that all day far off had lain slant
On the sea northward, perhaps indeed had drawn inland
And covered the shore like a flood and climbed up the hill-slope.
Though the sun blazed there came a ground-fog; and the wind
Was like the draught from a cellar, from the low sea
Sharp with its odors.

It was not the low fog.
The man had something in him, confidence, power . . . power? . . .
Enforced his own hallucination on his witnesses.
Then had he called, others to come up? For he was saying
"I believe faithfully that I was sent to you. What else then
Woke in me alone, me alone
The edged confidence, the perfect desire, one-eyed, thousand-handed
To conquer knowledge like a capital city taken in one storm,
One dawn, then all the provinces are flat? Others have trenched the suburbs and never an end: lance the heart:
Power is one power": while he was saying; and the three
Apart from each other, Natalia, Faith Heriot, the Indian,
Stared up through the incomprehensible torrent of prophecy

At him crowned with gray hair and sunlight, two horsemen
Rode through fog up the hill; they halted a little
At the spectral edge of his hallucination, the spurs
Clinked when they slid to the earth.

"Not for salvation,"
He said, "for perfection. I bring fire and not salt.
The time leaps at its end." If the half understood
Words alone enforced the vision then one of his hearers
Would have seen in her mind a cat spring at its prey but another a sea-wave
Shot at the rock: they all with one soul
Saw a naked child leap into fire; so clearly Natalia
Cried out thinking of her child; but one of the new-comers:
"I saw it yesterday!" And Barclay "What did you see
Yesterday?" "The blinded child." He answered "But the eyes
Ate the white heart before they blackened." Then the other horseman
(One saw his face flicker in the multitude, Joe Medina,
The dark one of the two vaqueroes at Morhead's)
Said "This my friend Vasquez, Onorio Vasquez
Who sees visions." Vasquez: "I live north
On Palo Corona mountain, I saw God at Point Sur
Flaming about this time yesterday." Then Barclay
Looking at Maruca, "It was immaculate of pleasure.
What form had the God?" "Master," he answered, "a flaming child.
But who are all these that hear you, thousands on the hillside?"
First after him for Natalia the fog
Organized into faces beyond faces, the doubled illusion
Enforcing itself against her; then the vaquero
Medina saw the heads and shoulders like waves of a sea
Break the plain gray; Maruca at that moment equally; Faith Heriot
Cried to herself "I am all alone, there is no one

On the hill," and angrily closed her eyes but had seen
Not human heads, hawks' heads and horned heads and sharp wings,
Stones and the peaks of redwoods.

Where yesterday
Only one visionary from Palo Corona Mountain
Felt Barclay's mind, to-day these five reverberating
The vision enforced and focussed it, so that whoever on the coast from the Carmel southward
Was vacant of desire a moment: one of the Victorines at Mal Paso, Woodfinn at Garapatas,
Myrtle Cartwright, Vogler's daughter up the Big Sur, Gonzalez on the hill far southward, Higuera
Under Pico Blanco: each without knowing a reason turned the eyes toward Point Sur: so that when word came
Of a man wielding powers and prophecies, they were not incredulous, they seemed to have known it before. But old Morhead,
The paralyzed old man under the farmhouse roof, imagined that lightning
Lay on the roof or fire was free in the house; he had no one by him,
And cried aloud in hollow loneliness.

Then Barclay:
"They are gathered to me. God is become a child: scimitar of light
On the dark rim in the evening. Not the power but the soul
Crescents or wanes between the nights of the centuries.
Can a child sin? What's done is that child doing it, and what has been done?
War, torture, famine; oppressions; the secret cruelties; the plague in the air that killed its millions; that child
Reaping a fly's wings, innocently laughing
From the rich heart? Oh it has no laughter though a child. It is tortured with its own earnestness, it is tortured.

It is lonely: what playmate? It has no mother.
The child that is the stars and the earth and men's bodies, and the hollow darkness
Outside the stars, and the dark hollow in the atom." (He thought, "What do I know? I speak of myself.
Am I that child?") "Hollow and hollow and dark, is there any substance?

There's
power. What does it want, power?
It tortures its own flesh to discover itself. Of humanity
What does it want? It desires monsters. I told you it had changed.
Once it commanded justice, charity, self-continence,
Love between persons, loyalty: it was wise then: what purpose?
To hold the pack together for its conquest of the earth.
Now the earth is conquered, there is room, you have built your mountain, there is no competitor,
It says *Flame!* it has sent me with fire, did you dream
That those were final virtues? your goodness, your righteousness,
Your love: rags for the fire."

He groaned in his heart,
Feeling himself like a shell hollowed, the weakness,
The diminution, the awful voice not his own
Blown through his void.

"I have come to establish you
Over the last deception, to make men like God
Beyond good and evil. There is no will but discovery,
No love but toward that tragic child, toward the motherless,
The unlaughing, the lonely."

The fog had climbed higher and his head
Was hidden, only they heard his voice falling from above them
Until it had ceased.

XI

Each one had stood lonely in a multitude.
Each felt about him the stir of multitude disparting,
The fog whitening in currents. They called to each other
Softly and afraid. When Joe Medina came out to the horses
One stood yet, Onorio's was gone. When he saw someone
Drift by him, it was Maruca, afraid of the steers.
She told him she had much work at the house but he answered
No one need work now, he left the horse tethered
And led her by the arm.

Over the mound of the slope
Faith Heriot found Natalia sobbing. She heard the fog-horn
Blow hoarse minutes from the lighthouse on the rock of Point Sur.
Her father whom she had left was the lighthouse-keeper,
She tenderly and fiercely: "Natalia, you hear him call me?
If you put me by, I will go back." Who, sobbing: "I love you."
"But now" she answered, "you've had a letter from Randal
And see eyes in the door." "He's coming, when he comes
What shall I do?" She trembled hearing far down
The hoarse throat from the rock. Faith Heriot stood rigid,
Her narrow face under the wet yellow hair
The fog's color, and said slowly "I am still good enough
To nurse the old dead man. Randal," she said against the set teeth,
"Will not be home always. Not days. The nights,"
She muttered shaking all rigid in the curded white
From the ground, like a stone pillar when the earth is shaken,

"Are your business"; the blue eyes ringed with dim white
Seemed shelterless of lids or lashes and the lips
Strained in a smile, "I have looked forward for a long time
To the midnights with hell opened under the floor.
I will be quiet." And Natalia: "Oh yes. Oh yes, yes.
Is that man crazy? What did he mean? Did we see people?"
"He means we must live as long and merrily as possible."

Barclay climbed upward the slope. High up the gray fog
Was split in tongues, and over the bald summit blue sky. A man approached him
And said "You've got outside humanity: you will not return.
Oh, let them feed and clothe you, you have money: but neither in love nor instruction
Lean to that breed." "Love?" he said, "what is love?" But the other: "To what purpose
Have you been dropping wine and fire in the little vessels?" When the buried sun
Rosed an arched banner of the mist, then Barclay saw the lean face, the stub of brown beard, the bar of the eye-brows,
His own mirrored; and the image: "If you did not love them would you labor to lead them?" He shaking and smiling:
"I see the devil is short of faces." It answered "You could not fool yourself utterly. Your very body
Cries for companions; you stood like a moose bellowing for love. I listened all the while with secret laughter
The time we persuaded ourself we wanted disciples to bait the God-trap: their sweet persons you wanted;
Their eyes on our eyes. A filthy breed to refer to." And Barclay, "Here you are, madness.
The Magus Zoroaster thy dead . . . Where else does consciousness

Burn up to a point but in the bone lamps? I should be lonely." It laughed,
"As the tragic child?" "He includes them.
And I though I choke, old portrait . . ."

In the ruinous cabin
Down the slope under the limestone ridge and the darkening fog
Medina said in his language, "If you'd go naked
And the face covered you'd have dozens of lovers.
Needs a strong man like me not to be frightened
By the face . . ." Maruca clinging and resisting: "Oh, Oh,
Let me alone." She clawed his cheek, then he dizzily
Feeling astonished with a splendor of happiness
Twisted her arm saying "Now will you let me? Now will you?
Will you? Now will you Maruca?" "Ao! Ay! Que si."

Barclay on the dome of the hill: "Old counterfeit,
Eye-thing, the hand would go through. Before I annul you
With one finger's experience: tell me what's the magic in bipeds? I see the stone and the tree
Through sheet crystal." "Ah that's our private impurity: but look at the majesty of things, a race of atomies
Obsess you? Except them till the stars are counted,
The bad crumb will digest, the apes that walk like herons
Nook themselves in." But Barclay looked at the sky, the long tassels of the fog reddening recurved;
At the earth, the bits of quartz in the stubble; and a shiver of laughter
Twitched in his nerves. "Oh that's," he said twitching, "confession.
Single-hearted is clean of laughter:
What is it that I dare not think of?" He thought Faith Heriot had moods of feature like April's . . . "Why," the image answered

"Of your own mind hypnotized by the accidents of birth and begetting.
Because you have coupled and are budded
Of couplers: humanity the only pillar on every horizon?"

Deep under the
darkening fog-sea
Natalia turned suddenly on her companion: "I am not ashamed
And if there were crowds: are there crowds on the hillside?
I'd do it in front of the cowboys, I'm full of cowardice,
The shining sacrifice." Faith Heriot regarded her with wonder
Through the gray plumes: "Long ago, when you were kind,
I used to lie awake in bed, the old log
Groaning past midnight, and dream wide awake
There were men tied to trees and you Natalia
All undressed in front of them and ashamed and afraid,
I saw their clothes humped with the hateful pillars,
When I came in, bare too, and we showed them . . . Oh,
The beasts not needed, the shining sacrifice . . .
They'd scream with desire, I'd say to you 'The trees are screaming,'
I'd strike them with my fists and return to you. I never told you."
"Dear," she answered trembling, "is the fog full of faces around us?"
"No," she answered. "Oh but I think it is full of watchers,
Dear hands, oh dear hands." The moving circle of starved sod
They trod in the dome of the fog suddenly was chorded
With a dark brink and a deep pit of drawn vapor.
They entered the dry stream-bed like entering a cavern
And wrestled together under the stub of dwarf oaks
With hoarse gaspings and little cries. Natalia
Imagined with fearful joy on both the clay banks
Watchers; but Faith Heriot was like a falcon
Wild with famine.

The mirror-image on the hill in the sundown: "Out of love destruction.
There was not one word but savored of sudden burning: but all for love's sake." And Barclay "Have it then, I love them."
"And feed the loved poison? You knew they were not stone but paper fagots to the fire of your saying.
Love that destroys?" Barclay looked right and left like an animal
Driven on a trap, the funnel of the high stockade narrowing. He muttered quickly, lowering his head:
"If they were finished: peace, peace. I have both the desires. May not one hate
The loved, love the hated, where does this fountain from?" When he looked
The inquisitor was dim; only the face, and that fading, hung opposite his eyes
On no stalk, and dissolved. There was a dizzy fugitive sickness at heart and the whirling had stopped,
So that he said gathering his functions to life "Love requires martyrs: seal it with martyrdom": he remembered
That both his father and his son were dead. "Love of humanity: the enormous picture of familiar passions.
I have conquered the tempter: who came in the image of the most hated: I am conquering the loved."

Onorio Vasquez rode out to a promontory:
The little seer of visions who never sees anything
But tangent to things: never worth seeing: and his pony
On the point of the hill, distrusting both declivities in the blind fog,
Stood; then the rider turned in the saddle and the hill
Was lit with arches: on the left a tender steep fog-bow
Footed about that desert cabin they had passed,

Pale-shining arc of a parabola drew upward;
On the right the like radiance, the equal steep fog-bow
Footed high up the gully that severed the hillside.
But where they crossed at the top was a shining trouble
In the strained fog as if a star had come down
To rest on the forked arcs; and the evening darkening
Onorio peered into the scars on his palms
And said "He is darker to himself than to men.
He is neither a child nor a man, he has no understanding.
He is terrible," he said with tranquil eyes.

He intended the multiform
God but it was Barclay on the hill-top.
Who feeling again his multitude gathered in the spectral glimmer: "Fear nothing: I have conquered: not a hair of your heads
Falls to the fire. O little ones, passionate maiden bodies and April faces if I had proved enemy
What power in the huge world . . ." He widened his arms opposite the flaring sun-fall. "I have chosen you for love."

XII

Here were new idols again to praise him;
I made them alive; but when they looked up at the face before they had seen it they were drunken and fell down.
I have seen and not fallen, I am stronger than the idols,
But my tongue is stone how could I speak him? My blood in my veins is sea-water how could it catch fire?
The rock shining dark rays and the rounded
Crystal the ocean his beam of blackness and silence
Edged with azure, bordered with voices;

The moon her brittle tranquillity; the great phantoms, the fountains of light, the seed of the sky,
Their plaintive splendors whistling to each other:
There is nothing but shines though it shine darkness; nothing but answers; they are caught in the net of their voices
Though the voices be silence; they are woven in the nerve-warp.
One people, the stars and the people, one structure; the voids between stars, the voids between atoms, and the vacancy
In the atom in the rings of the spinning demons,
Are full of that weaving; one emptiness, one presence: who had watched all his splendor
Had known but a little; all his night, but a little.
I made glass puppets to speak of him, they splintered in my hand and have cut me, they are heavy with my blood.
But the jewel-eyed herons have never beheld him
Nor heard; nor the tall owl with cat's ears, the bittern in the willows, the squid in the rock in the silence of the ocean,
The vulture that broods in the pitch of the blue
And sees the earth globed, her edges dripping into rainbow twilights: eyed hungers, blind fragments: I sometime
Shall fashion images great enough to face him
A moment and speak while they die. These here have gone mad: but stammer the tragedy you crackled vessels.

XIII

April had promised that if her mother wanted
They'd return the next day, but Audis Barclay
Each time they dropped south from a ridge felt gates
Close on the road; on the highest last hill-top
They left the road and dropped westward; then it was determined,

She thought, that having yielded and come barred the exit;
And all the road not a hill nor a tree remembered,
Lost in exhausting sleep. This was his lair:
Bronze hills, gray oaks. Then high over wrecked farm-sheds
The prison of black logs striped with white plaster, the flaring
Sea-fog of autumn sundown. They came to the porch
Rotting under its rose-vine, all the leaves fallen.
Barclay opened the door, someone behind him,
And said quietly "I knew it was you. Are you tired?
I have gained strange experience and felt you on the way.
Two hours ago I told you Natalia. Natalia Morhead.
My daughter April. My wife." Audis her slender
Cold hand touched Barclay's: "Are you well, Arthur?" Though indeed
It was touching a strange man's. April with her eyes
Assumed superiority over Natalia;
And Barclay: "At Sovranes Canyon the road
Cuts between hills, I saw you there in the car,
And like iron gates behind you on the hills for pillars
Closing behind you." Audis whitened and answered
"I remember nothing of the road, were there gates April?"
"No, mother." And Barclay: "I draw the region through my mind;
I have other streams in my mind." She felt herself taken
His prisoner; and pale, cold, silent, bitterly crying
To herself "Oh that I'd never come," she appeared
To the others in the house his prisoner. At the supper table
She murmured that she was too tired to eat and April
Followed her up the stairs. Her things had been carried
To Barclay's room, April's to the room beside it.
"I must sleep with you April, I have no other place."
She undressed and knelt by the bed, April regarded her
With curious pity. She prayed formally aloud,
And after she had lain down the lips kept moving

Without sound. April blew out the lamp,
Went slowly down to her father. "I think we'll go back
To-morrow morning, first I must talk to you. I brought
Mother: what will you do?" He was pacing the floor
In the big room, the door was open to the other,
He stopped and said loudly "Did that cost blood?
Brought her? I am making the world, I hold the intolerable weight
In my hands while I make it, I bear the strain, strain." She bitterly:
"I ought to have known. But is it needful
To tell the whole house how much we have to be sorry for?"
She thought anxiously "Oh, where?" and said "Let us go
And walk in the road, you walk in the night you told me
Often." He said "Decision?" and softly, "decision?
We'll talk on the road," he said quietly, she followed him
And saw the slit of a moon move in the leafless rose-vine
To die in a pearled cloud. He turned and walked fast
Down the hill, she thought "He wants to get by the farm-sheds."
She felt dwindled to early childhood, the strides
Rapid and long to follow, and breathless beside him,
"What is that taint, the odor?" "Coyotes," he answered,
"The men shoot them and hang them up on the fence,
Yesterday's by last year's. Come into the field rather than pass them.
Here there's a gap." He stood until she crept through,
Thinking "Yes: if she enters," and, "I am stone, stone, I have not trembled.
If I kept the bondage of common men": he breathed: "to whom this act would reek like the wire-hung carrion:
I have got outside of good and evil, it needs a symbol, God thinks through action: when I cried on the hill,
Love is more cruel than a wolf, hungrier than flame or the gape of water; your virtues, your nerves, your goodness,
Rags for that fire." He took April by the arm
Gently, to hasten her steps on the sloping stubble;

She felt herself diminished to helpless childhood, the ancient
Tower of authority, the trustfulness without thought
Long out of mind: yet the surface of her mind
Insisted "We have come far enough, father.
You were going to tell me . . ." He said eagerly "I'll tell you.
But all my thoughts are turbid, like a weighted river
Drops its grain standing, must walk, you'd never understand
Unless I tell you everything. I have given my mind to the future
In love, in love." She stumbled on a stone in the field,
Felt his hand bear her and saw the chip of bent moon
Slip like a silver feather between cloud and sea-fog.
He thought "She is weak and not strong," he said "But at best
You won't understand until you follow. I have gone out of the maps, it is
not written in a book.
I gave myself to find out God, I have found him.
There's yet one link to be filed. Filed." He walked faster. "You wouldn't
ask me
To love backward, back toward the dead, dead souls: April
There's an old dead man under the farmhouse roof,
His horse fell on him and broke him, he lies in bed there
Breathing and dead, they can't bury him still breathing.
To-night there are two corpses lying in the farmhouse.
There is nothing after death. Nothing. You put her to bed.
A man who can find God one moment, only one living moment, has lived
immortally—but how could you
Understand me?—the after is trash. I have come to that summit.
I have long ago forgotten sacking my fears
Like blind puppies, a stone for an anchor at the black bottom."
She thought "There is one man I never need fear,
Not though he runs mad," her hand nursing
The terrified quick clamor of her heart, and she said, "But, father,
You asked me to bring her." "I, summon the dead? Oh, I remember,

To the word with all the black crystals in it, what's the word? Annihilation,
the beautiful crystal contrivance
To catch rays from outside the stars in. We split the graves, April,
The stone has its nature, but a man
May become God. How could a man touch him or see him but becoming
him? I was on the mountain and I saw him."
She answered, the words tripping on breaths like sobs: "It is time.
What have you brought me out here for? I am frightened. Father.
We must go back. I'll take her back home." "Oh blind,"
He answered letting her arm free, "can't you see the ocean
Raised like a great black column opposite the hills . . ." "The rock of
Point Sur,
Father, the light above it . . ." "The ocean" he said "on one side, the hills
on the other, witnessing
The terrible honor, the sacrifice, the marriage of God. The stars over the
cloud-scud
Divided into two antiphonies: April the silver trumpets, the wailing and
singing, the waves
Of answers, the clear clear voices . . . There is nothing
To be kept and see him, but burn and flame and burn up
All the withdrawals, the evasions, all that feels pain or shame, the rags of
virtues, the dog's meat sanity,
The blood from the bitten-out arteries . . ." She twisting her hands,
Striking them together, the lips retracted, the teeth lightening in the dark
of her face,
The moon was down, under few stars: "Oh indeed, indeed father.
I know that it's all true but you will have pity
And tell me to-morrow, I'm tired, near fainting . . ." "Was I not tired
The time wandering I found him?" "Dear tired father"
She panted quickly "but now happy you have found him.
Now rest and sleep on the hill, I shall not be afraid
Walking alone, the way's easy to the house,

It's very near by, they could hear secrets." "Oh" he said opposing her,
"You never walked in a path, neither under walls,
Under still hills nor by shining water but hurried breathless
To this pole of the world, it was not possible for you
To turn out of it, not possible to flee away from it, did never voices
Tell you like singing fires, and you looked up at midnight and saw wings
astonishing the darkness?
As for me I remember drifting the stars before these
Into their ways to make this moment." He stood in her way
Seeming grown mountainous, such a great mask her fear
Projected on the pitiful human proportions.
She sobbing he said hoarsely "Panting and hot-blooded
What boy was it last, Edward's gone? You think me an old man
Daren't dabble in the honeycomb." The treacherous blood
Now when all needed draining down from her brain
Dimmed the eyes, all the peripheral field of vision
Drawn with a veined gray veil, the colored veins in it
Writhing like serpents, but in the midst as through water
The bearded mask darkening against the dim cloud
Was clear enough; she reeled turning but his power circled her,
And fallen on the dark, captive: "No matter what horror
Writhes in your mind like worms I am not afraid of you,
You will stop at madness. No matter if hell" she said faintly,
Leering faces, cold pads with no claws, soft hairless bodies,
Pale tongues bushed with wet hair passed in her mind
Processional, "had struck the gates with broken hinges
And snapped bolts of your mind and entered you like conquerors—"
She felt the degradation of resisting his hands,
Dimly, through waves of deep abominable water—
"It could not rule you, oh not to poison the innocent
Years before you went mad. Ah. No. Struck hatchet
In the new-born skull would have been gentle and fatherly;

But spit poison in the fountain": "God has come home to you,"
He said furiously, "to you that refused him
Faith, now you feel his power and believe. You laughed in your pride
But God is stronger." She struck at the beard, screaming,
And the night perished about her into horrible sleep
From which opening she watched a shadow pass crying
And the clouds gone, the gimlet stars all agleam,
And like waves in a grain-field alternate waves
Of bright and dim wore slowly over the whole sky,
Aldebaran, the anthill Pleiades; she felt dull pain
Like a close element, closed eyes, the waves continued
Audible, she hadn't known the sea was so near;
The night was so cold that she would turn on her side
And strive to creep a little toward the house. "I was unhappy
A long while before." The waves of starlight, the waves
Of sickness, the long waves of the surf's noise, the cold stubble
Undulating . . . When she got up she was able
To walk back to the house; the door was not locked;
No horror behind it. "I am not horrible if nobody
Knows that I am: if I keep it": her mind had not moved
From torpor before, flashed into bitter activity
Striking its length at random like a burnt snake.
A cataract of phantasmal images filled it
Between the door and the stair; two triumphed and remained:
A vision of her own naked body forever
Knotted on the secret scar, her hands crushing
The joined thighs, her nails entering the fruitlike flesh;
And out of the poisoned past of childhood her brother's,
Her dead brother's falsetto fury, "I'd like to kill him.
Oh, Oh if he'd die. I didn't ask to be born.
Be grateful for it, be grateful?"

Though her mother half awoke
April was able to gather her change of clothing
From the hand-bag in the darkness and hide the stained ones.

XIV

An old man on a tired pony rode down the coast
By the distant farms, he said that about midnight
Riding out of the redwoods up the Sur Hill,
Hoping to sleep with Johnny Allado at the shack
On the Hayworth ranch, he heard at a bend feet, hooves,
Hushed voices, a whole company marched in the dark.
He thought, smugglers of liquor bringing it north from a landing,
He'd best clear out of the road, and rammed his pony
Into the bushes; there might have been ten went by
Or hundreds, how could he tell, the twigs in his ears?
But someone called from the company "Oye Mendoza,"
In Spanish, "tell all you meet that our master goes up
To Pico Blanco to be united with God."
Another answered "Tell him to come"; but the first:
"We have messengers in the north." He heard afterwards
A voice in English, he could not tell what it said.
After they'd all gone by he rode to the ranch
And woke Allado. Johnny had gone in the morning
The trail up the South Fork, but himself had come south.

At Morhead's Joe Medina heard it and rode
To the ruinous cabin under the limestone ridge
Where his friend Onorio Vasquez the vision-seer
Had camped the nights of a week. The blanket and the tins
Were gone, Vasquez was gone. Medina rode home
To coax from the Indian housegirl, Maruca, who loved him,

Bread and cold meat; then followed toward the south fork
Of the Little Sur River, toward Pico Blanco.

Natalia Morhead

Eyed at noon his vacant place at the table,
"Where's Joe?" And the other farmhand wiping his mouth:
"Homesick I guess. Haven't seen him since breakfast."
"He needn't come back," she said angrily. "To-morrow
Randal comes home: Oh if I could have kept the place running
Till Randal . . ." She saw over the table Faith Heriot's
Eyes like light blue flints in the narrow whiteness,
And faltered, and then taking them fairly: "Is grandfather
Glad?" Faith, low-voiced: "He hasn't told me, but I think
Old grandfather loves Randal as much as I do.
Not any more." Natalia turned from her and anxiously
Fondling the child by her side, "Oh but he'll laugh
To see what a big girl it's grown to: sweetheart when he tells you
About the air-planes, the guns and all the soldiers.
Daddy coming to-morrow." Faith Heriot had laid
Iron on her nerves, and after a moment to April Barclay
Said quietly, but the lips like stretched threads, "Your father
Isn't at the table either; he wasn't at breakfast."
April, her wound much too deep to feel probing,
Her face not whitened a shade around the great bruise
On the right cheek: "He told me he had work to think out.
Any farm in the hills will feed him for money.
He walks and works instead of sleeping." She heard her own voice
Formed and steady as the slender shaft of a pillar
And felt her face like polished marble and felt perfectly
With quiet and secure attention the shambles under
The marble crust, explosive corruption vaulted with marble,
"If he were here I'd get him to fix the porch step
That's rotted away, I tripped on last night in the dark

Coming in, and struck my face on the post." Her mother
Trembled over her private cistern of bitterness,
Ignorant and afraid, feeling the strain, the strain,
The stone faces: "Oh, if Mr. Morhead's coming
We must go home April; though father's gone off
And I haven't seen him . . ." She imagined April had spoken
To her father about his madness; and he in what frenzy—
Ah, had he struck April?—had rushed off in the night . . .
"Though I haven't seen him . . ." But April unmoved: "Till father
Comes back, we'll not go away." She knew herself rock
To stay to the end: for what reason was dark:
No reason: it was resolved. "If Mr. Morhead
When he comes wants us to leave we'll get the Hayworths
To keep us." She thought "They'll wonder." She thought "My secret's
Horrible enough to be safe: and if it had happened
That's unbelievable: Oh clearly all one's desire
Would be to flee, to flee, to forget: to wait here
Locks it rather." She said "Here we must wait,
When he wants to see mother he'll find us." She felt
Unguessed continents of fortitude. But none was needed
Where nothing hurt much, nothing now was intolerable,
This puddle of slime and blood excessive, in the infinite ocean?
The shores had been set wider.
Whatever needed to be done would be done: herself
Not responsible: there stood a competent power
Running the machine. The world in a moment so changed
Utterly . . . She felt the sweat cold on her forehead,
The sight of the eyes narrowing again and the sweat
Trickle down from the throat between the two breasts . . .
She caught herself back: since no fortitude sufficed
Flayed with the nails of her right hand the wrist of her left
Under the table, caught herself back from falling
On faintness . . . not faintness, the silken-curtained, a new

State of consciousness, without brakes, without rudder,
Might have involved confession: she took it captive
And retained rule, thinking of Edward her brother,
Why did his face and shoulders rise up? She raised up
Her head, and her eyes warred on Faith Heriot's. Natalia's
Always went down humbled: Faith Heriot's went down
But not humbled. "We'll stay though."

At the foot of Pico Blanco
mountain
Barclay had stumbled on black exhaustion, he turned on his followers,
The five or six Onorio Vasquez had gathered to follow him: "It is finished.
Let me go. Nothing remains.
You have no conception," he cried striking his fists against his eyes, "of the
treachery of—what's his name?—God, God.
But if you have led me into this wilderness to kill me—do it quickly. Oh
mercy, mercy! I am not prepared.
Who knows there is nothing afterwards?" Onorio Vasquez
To the others: "He is only a man, he must see God.
No man could come to it and not go mad with terror.
Go down to the creek and make camp." Barclay had staggered
To his knees and babbled bending his forehead earthward, "Have pity. Oh,
Oh.
I was so hurried on from madness to madness
I never had choice, I was rushed down to destruction."
He said picking at the earth, "They wove it too loose,
All full of eye-holes, the horror steams up through it.
Hunted out of life. No refuge. Oh cheat, cheat!" They watched him,
And Vasquez took a fallen branch of dead oak
And struck at them though it broke in his hand, and drove them
Down hill from the path. "Go and make camp by the creek.
When it's time, then I will call you." He said "Master, my prophet,
Sleep." But he grovelling on the blind earth: "To murder me!

Oh, Oh, have mercy," and fought to rise and fell down
On the white trail under the high sun in the dust of limestone.
He seemed sleeping and moaning. Then Vasquez cut poles
And slanted them over his head from southward to the oak-bough
And spread the shelter of a blanket.

In the afternoon
Came a few riders from the coast and went down to the brook
At Vasquez' word. The sun approached the Sur Hill
Burning laces of cloud; eastward above the ridges mushroom-capped giants
Of cotton-white cloud piled and rose higher. Then Barclay
Moved and cried out under the tent of the blanket.
When Vasquez drew it down from the poles he said "I am Lazarus,
I was taking water to the women in the fire." Vasquez made haste
And brought him water in a can; he spilled it on the earth,
And the young man brought it again he drank and said quietly, "Nothing is forgotten.
The sun falls against evening and rain in November.
The dead are quiet, I was only dreaming."

The people
Had seen Vasquez go down for water and return.
They came from the creek saying "It is late. Has he wakened?"
Three others coming the trail from the coast each party in the other
Saw multitude at the mountain-foot.

XV

Then Barclay: "I have come to the mountain.
None of you knows over what pass I have come, over what white ridge . . . prone like a beast . . . clinging,

When I cast my hands and my love over the future in the ecstasy: threw forward: changed times like God . . . nor what
Sacrifice bled on the hill.
I told you what God requires: the tragic child gashing himself with knives in the ecstasy, to discover
New shores and there is nothing but himself: trying all the ways and chances forever, tortured from eternity;
Himself the furnace, himself the God, himself the burnt-offering: I will break up my memory, it is finished,
And not remember this thing, it is finished. . . . You scum of the coast
What wave carried you up here? How did the waters turn backward, you and the lean horses? I had many companions
Before."

And certainly when they looked about them
The ridges were filled, the woods in the south over the canyon
With listeners, the trail they had come from the ocean
With eyes and mouths, the long ridge eastward with erect
Multitude, men like trees against the standing
Domes and caverns of cloud; only the mountain-slope
Naked. And now the day's eye-ball was hidden,
The shadow of the Sur Hill lay over the valley,
The white peak blazed.

"But I will make promises for God. He desires not only
Destruction, but more than the fire feeding on the eyes, than the knives pastured on flesh: power, power, and the terrible
Buds of growth in the bone sepulchres the slime of your brains
Stuffs with lazy corruption: I tell you there is soil under the lock of those arches, spear-rooted fire
Will suck it and take heaven.

I have the burning to kindle you. I tell you that the brown bodies and the white bodies of you cheap counters,
You pawns, you unregarded droppets of chance-blown wombs, are the seeds of the world
I am planting between to-night and to-morrow: the hand plucking the sun for its apple, the bridle of the hand
Of a man on the last planet, the huge capture, humanity taking its house, the final possession."
They understood nothing but listened. It seemed to them all he was making magic in the shadow of the air
With speech incomprehensible and ancient gestures, and the hurricane his mind.

"Stopped eyes, me use you? I will tell you
In the talk that will touch you in the bone caves. I know that I stand near God and speak for him.
He brought me from the north; I was fifty years old, I am ageless.
He gave me sap of redwoods to drink, towers of millennial
Inexhaustible life, I shall be young still
A thousand years from this day, nothing can weary me.
He gave me the strength to endure . . . mountains: and the power
To move them: the power to take possession
Of the blind throats and stopped channels—
Brute material—that rages in the air over your heads like a wind
Nursing lightning. And knowledge he gave me, that stands against the fountain and touches the stir of currents
Before they are streams; the intent moves in his depth
And is born cauled in clear flame to be stars
And new structures of suns, and vermin on the planets; I tasted it
In the germ of the egg, I, here, I am his token
And symbol to you that he will give you these gifts,

Inexhaustible life, incomparable power, inhuman knowledge:
That he will make you Gods walking on the earth
And striking the sky.

I preach promises to rats: I will tell you in the squeak of your private voices: you are poor,
He will make you rich, give you the deeds to valleys of meat and cattle and mined gold in the mountains.
You love drunkenness: he will fill you with wine that never sickens nor runs empty. You want women: he will make you
All beautiful and young, sweet-smelling: carved and delicate girls of ivory and gold will creep to your feet
Trembling, begging to be loved. You will choose new for each night,
Virgins: and it will not be sin but honesty, you must people the earth
That shall be emptied to be new: I tell you I have seen in the fountain of God destruction standing
With stone hooves on the cities, he will trample and burst all but my chosen, he will sweep them with brooms of pestilence,
Scrub them with fire: I heard him whistle the black dog
Death to lick out the dish: but you that come to me
Shall watch from secure hills and not weep."

He thought in himself,
"Madness, madness,
And lies: it is put in my mouth."

He said: "I am taking up to this mountain the private
Desire like a jewel of each of you, to give to the infinite
Power and I know that he will give you fulfilment." He turned to go up the mountain. "But you Onorio

Shepherd them to-night." He walked upward in the shadow of the twilight,
limestone burned rose above him and faded,
The eagle light ebbed from the cloud.

XVI

April, in the house,
Had never moved but struck her forehead against imprisonment.
The presence of her mother was the most oppressive.
She would have walked alone in the fields but the field
Was Tarquin, and the small pain of walking a new deflowerment.
"Mother let's take the car and go down to the sea.
I am dead in this house." Audis would have refused,
But thought "If he should come back and I should be alone."
But April was thinking "If we should meet him on the road.
Or be together in the car and meet him by the sea."
Their eyes crossing it seemed to her struck a dull spark
Of loathsome shared wisdom, like the offspring monkey
Of old diseases, for she thought "We have shared
Knowledge of a man, were virgin under one violence,
We harem-sisters," the explosive corruption
Straining the polished vault-stones.

But the chief strain, the strain,
Was lower than consciousness, her mind was filmed over it.
"Only a maniac: not the same man: have been handled
By a mad beast and life will grow over the horror
Kept secret and sealed shut." They passed the thick-furred
Coyotes hung heads downward on the wire fence
Corrupting the air; the freshest corpse had its ears,
The heads of the others had been gnawed; two hawks hung by them.
And April easily: "Vermin they shoot and hang there

To warn the others I suppose." They came to the wide sand-flat
And looked across it at the great rock of Point Sur
That carries the little-seeming lighthouse buildings.
They found a track northward to a shore of cliffs
And inlet sands. Audis remained in the car,
April went down to a coved beach, the low sun
Burnt the sea gold. Lying on the pure sand
She felt the strain loosened, the strain slid over
Into sweet reveries.

She did not think to herself
These were new dreams and not a girl's dreams, an adolescent
Boy's, that made windy honey in her mind. A dark prow swung in the sun's track;
Erect sword-slender figure riding the plunge of the great prow toward Asia.
(Travelling needs money: a madman soon dies, I shall have money.) But why do you wander into wide Asia?
To ride the desert horses under the Mongol stars, all night to ride horses.
The enormous plain slips like a ribbon, the stars follow like birds in the trough of the sky, the flowing
Of the sheet muscles in the great shoulders. Dawn builds an awful flower at the world's end. I shake the black tents.
Again and again you desert horsemen
Have raided the world and there was nothing but fell down.
Wild riders you have forgotten Attila,
You have not forgotten Genghiz, is Tamerlane forgotten?
The world is full of filth and despair,
I am welding you tribes into the sword that will straighten it.
I have taken my inheritance from my father
To buy you guns, you will bring me the spoil of provinces.
My parents have eaten corrupt food and my throat was defiled, the man whom I called father had gone mad.

If I had a dog that was fallen into the pit would I not save him? *I ended my father's madness.*
I will tell you a secret.
That beast with the brown beard was not my father.
That dead man not my father: but he had gone mad,
He could not have lived. What wandering poet
In her bride youth in the moon of beauty
That shines once on every woman
Sang me into the womb of my mother?
They whispered in the garden. But I have a sword for a song, wild tribesmen . . .

Audis above
Stood on the cliff against the white cloud, and calling
"April, how long? April." But April to herself:
"She is calling my sister, I need not answer." And Audis,
"Are you asleep April? I see you on the sand."
Then April let the revery hang in suspense
And answered "It's me, mother, April's not here,
It's Edward" she was about answering, and suddenly
The strain and the desecration of being herself
Came like a wave. She rose and went up to her mother,
The earth and the sea swayed, she mounted the rocks.
When she remembered she thought she had been possessed
By her brother Edward's spirit returned from death.
The sun was like a red bead on a wire
Flat on the sea. The desecration; the strain,
The strain. "Though I am wrong-sexed, defenceless mother,
I'll be her sword and her son." To have thought so, eased
The strain, the strain; but nothing to be said out loud;
It was necessary to live in tunnels of secrecy.

"But I am new-sexed, mother needs help, Edward is dead,"
She confused Edward and her father, "he is dead."

XVII

And when Natalia came in the evening and spoke
Of Randal her husband coming to-morrow, released
From the dead war and service, April thought "Edward
Released from service: to-day Edward came back;
The other is coming to-morrow"; it was part of the strain
That strands tangled and metals melted together;
Nothing was ever pure in her mind, one wave at a time
Might be swum through, but always the battering alliance;
She kept herself calm in the face, paying silence for it,
Until she felt the tears flooding her eyelids,
Flowing down the bruised cheek and the other, then sobs
Wrenched her throat. "You are happy," she said. And the other,
"Oh what have I done to hurt you?" "Nothing, nothing.
My brother was killed. I cry easily, I'm tired to the bones . . ."
Natalia with a sudden pitying affection
Kissed her and stroked the short brown hair.

Faith Heriot
Stood on the stair and looked down, shaking, and the oval
Face like the foam-lantern on a night wave.
"You're soon friendly. Don't mind, Miss . . . Barclay, she always
Handles new-comers lovingly—me—me,
Two years ago. And her fellow's coming to-morrow,
It flows over all syrupy." Natalia drew back
Like guilt, and April gazing from one to the other
Thought of her father's horrible . . . love.

The air had flecks of fire in it and flecks of slime,
She thought how this one and the other drop dung in the mornings,
And yet affectionate animals . . . "Live in steel towers,"
She thought silently, "horrible to smell each other,
To touch each other," and said "I am not in your company,
Keep your endearments for each other," yet passing between them
She realized through the loathing the terrible beauty,
The white and moulded, the hot lightnings under the cloth,
The beastlike sucking bodies as beautiful as fire,
The fury of archangelic passions, her eyes
Having changed sex a moment. She whispered on the stair
"Oh burn, never grow old; burn, burn." The ungeared
Mind ran wild in the sad bed by her mother
Through phantasmal pollutions and lightning beauty
Like a child screaming in a labyrinth; toward dawn, sleep
Sealed it with lead.

I say that if the mind centers on humanity
And is not dulled, but remains powerful enough to feel its own and the others, the mind will go mad.
It is needful to remember the stone and the ocean, without the hills over the house no endurance,
Without the domed hills and the night. Not for quietness, not peace;
They are moved in their times. Not for repose; they are more strained than the mind of a man; tortured and twisted
Layer under layer like tetanus, like the muscles of a mountain bear that has gorged the strychnine
With the meat bait: but under their dead agonies, under the nightmare pressure, the living mountain
Dreams exaltation; in the scoriac shell, granites and basalts, the reptile force in the continent of rock

Pushing against the pit of the ocean, unbearable strains and weights,
inveterate resistances, dreams westward
The continent, skyward the mountain . . . The old fault
In the steep scarp under the waves
Melted at the deep edge, the teeth of the fracture
Gnashed together, snapping on each other; the powers of the earth drank
Their pang of unendurable release and the old resistances
Locked. The long coast was shaken like a leaf. April Barclay
Came from blind lakes of sleep, her mother was laboring
At the locked door, but April in the shaken darkness
Imagined her father breaking entrance and cried out
In a boy's voice, feeling in her hands already
The throat under the beard, but whispering "Oh mother,
Don't tremble so." She had slipped from the bed and she felt
The floor under her feet heave and be quieted.

But Audis through her terror had heard the sparrows
Cry out in the oak by the window, in the leonine roar
Of the strained earth, the clatter of bricks or small stones,
And the great timbers of the walls grind on their bearings.

XVIII

Barclay on the mountain.
He had climbed under the glaze of the last red sundown
And under the moments of the cloud-wandering moon; but after dense
cloud
Covered the mountain, was no recourse nor higher in the savage darkness.
He had found a ledge of slant rock
Where one could take three paces and return three paces, always fondling
the cliff, remembering the precipice.

Here his faith died. While the eyes of belief
Had fed him, standing above those followers at the foot of the mountain, he had almost believed
Power would indeed visit him, at night, on the mountain.
But now across the dreadful emptiness of sanity returned a moment, in the solid dark, the vertiginous
Absection, with clear weak voice only the mind,
That merest phantom, no power of the flesh supporting it, no emotion, repeated
That there is one Power, you may call it God to the vulgar,
Exists from eternity into eternity, all the protean phenomena, all forms, all faces of things,
And all the negligible lightnings of consciousness,
Are made of that Power. . . . What did it matter? outside communication, nowise adorable, not touchable
But in the minutest momentarily formed and dissolving fractions: rock . . . flesh . . . phenomena! the unhappy
Conception closes the circle back to its beginning,
Nothing discovered in all the vicious circumference.
"At least no guilt nor judgment discovered: I am free of the phantasy
That has wrecked giants. None. No regret. None."
But the mind with a twist of insane cunning: "There is one Power,
You may call it God to the vulgar. How shall men live
Without religion? All the religions are dead,
When it stank you denounced it. You are chosen to found the new one,
To draw from your own fountain the soul of the world.
What did you expect, the God would show himself visibly, his voice roar, his hand cover you in a cranny of the rock
Against the flaring eyes soul-eating terror the unbearable face,
And let you peep at his rump when the power passes?"
He crouched wearily at the end of the ledge. "This lie or a like one
To cram the mouth of credulity when I return to them.

One must paint pictures, no faith's honest at the stalk.
The night on the mountain will not be useless; the prophet
Not his own dupe." The clouds that drowned the starlight kept the night
warm.
The solid and secure darkness. He half slept, and April
Went by in a dream, the region and the blood of deflowerment
Bright through her torn clothing; she smiled with wise eye-lids.
Then Barclay felt the torpor drop off like a cloak,
Like a cloud split with lightning . . . certainly this cloud
Has lightning in it, he felt it tingle at the hair-roots,
And strain, the strain in the air . . . and he said "Oh Lord God
Why have you deceived me? Why turned me to these?
To be your gull and love them, I will not be your fool
And take their part against you and their part in destruction, they have had
their Jesus,
Me also to be hanged on Caucasus?"

The region people
Were present in him, his mind contained them, and the others,
Innumerable, covering the earth, cities and fields of humanity, the
Americas, Asia, the ravenous
Billion of little hungers, the choked obscene desires, the microscopic terrors
and pities,
All present in that intolerable symbol his daughter
With the bare bleeding wound in her.

"These? Against the stars? To
what end?
For either the ice will come back and bury them, or the earth-crust open
and fire consume them,
Or much more likely they will have died of slow-rotting age
Millions of years before." The God in his insane mind

Answered: "Is it nothing to you that I have given you
The love and the power? How many times earlier in bourneless eternity
Have they not flowered; and you from the violent bath heavy with the fury of the love stood evident above them,"
He had risen and stood on the rock, "the pillar of the bride humanity's desire. The explosion, the passion, repeated
Eternally: what if they rot after, you and they shall return again. The bride and the bridegroom: the unions of fire
Like jewels on a closed necklace burn holes through extinction." But he remembering
Crouched on the rock and whispered "There is pain, there is terror,
I have heard of torture. The inflictions of disease and of men that knot up
Muscles and the screaming nerves into one horror." The God in his mind answered "These also return."
It seemed to Barclay the cloud broke and he saw the stars,
Those of this swarm were many, but beyond them universe past universe
Flared to infinity, no end conceivable. Alien, alien, alien universes. At length, one similar
To this one; instantly his mind crying through the vastness
Pitched on the twin of this one, the intolerable identical
Face framed in the same disastrous galaxy: and if once repeated
Repeated forever. He heard the scream of suffered violence on the dark hill; he ate the miracle,
The closed serpent.

Consciousness drowned and sleep covered him.

In a dream a young man
Approached him, what was it they were saying? Edward, Edward,
Why does thy brand drip red with blood? "That's an old song
And this is a dream." He awoke. On the ledge a young man

Approached him. "We knew by wire, Edward. The telegram
Broke your mother's heart and my mind from that hour
Scrabbles at the doors, April seems not to care much."
Your hawk's blood was never so red . . .
"I am Christ, I have come to slay God who violated my mother
And streaked the earth with its pangs." "God has turned. God loves. O
    my son
He has taken the people's part against the wild stars."
"The agony" the young man answered
"I suffered grew from your mind but I will make an end.
My crucifixion a digging between the war-lines,
My death-wound in the belly, I licked the wound in my arm
Like a dog but in the anguish of thirst for three days."
Your hound's blood was never so dear . . . "That is not my reason
That I shall kill you." "What is it you are hiding Edward
In your hand behind your back?" "All the earth's agonies
Scream in my ears like famished eaglets in the aerie
Furious for the black flesh of annihilation.
To be ended and sleep, not to be renewed: that is not my reason
That I shall kill you." The old man: "O my son, my son,
The enormous beauty of the world!" "It is too much to pity,
Too heavy to endure" he answered, "I will make it peace;
Too many times having attempted atonement.
That is not my reason." Oh I will kill my father dear . . .
The old man: "God lifts his head and laughs in white heaven.
When have you considered the stars, what have you known of the streams
    in my soul,
And one lit point lost in the sky's eternity
A universe, millions of many-planeted suns, but another a universe
Of universes: they move in my mind, they shine within me, they eat infinite
    renewals." The young man:
"Nailed to the wood of groaning I meditated these things,

And seeing as in a vision all the vain bitterness.
I am one with my father, his equal in power, I have turned against him.
I did not ask for existence." And Barclay: "I gave you
The gift that the mouth was not yet moulded to ask for nor the heart to desire. I am changed, I have turned to love men.
I was like a furnace and a raging in the midst of the stars. I embraced the future, I came to a virgin . . ."
Oh I have killed my father dear. "I," the young man answered,
"To even that stabbing love of yours with steel." He approached and the hidden right hand
Was drawing from behind his loins, Barclay awoke from the dream
And knew it for one. There was nothing. The thick darkness
Was like annihilation. He crouched on the rock whispering
"No guilt, no judgment, no guilt, for I looked. There was renewal.
Will the dead not be quiet? Oh horrible, pursue
From one star-grain of sand to another through desert eternity?
And if the life is annihilated and memory
Lives . . ." He imagined the gray hair on his head
Lifting and blanched. "Having entered annihilation,
The terror at the shoulder after the shoulder has crumbled?"
Crouched on the rock he felt his knees knocking together
Against his will though he strove at quietness, and then
All his body trembling.

The strain, the strain in the air. Come lightning?

The sparrows in the oak at April's window
Cried out. The fault under the sea had slipped, and the people
Camping beside the creek under the mountain
Heard the hills move, heard the woods heaving, the boughs of the redwoods

Beating against each other from the southwest,
And the roaring earth. The earth swayed in waves like a bog
Under the strewn boughs they lay on and was quiet.
Certain among the frightened twenty remembered
Their new faith and believed that God had come down
To stand on the clouded mountain. They heard stones falling.

Barclay heard the forest and the stones falling
And the roaring earth. He felt the limestone mountain shaken
For a willow leaf in a light wind by the streamside.
When the mountain was quiet his body had ceased trembling.
He sat in the darkness exalted, shattered with exaltation,
Considering this thing, feeling his humanity slipped off
Lie on the rock like a skin, like a cast shirt.
"When I trembled in a bad dream: the earth shook when I trembled.
The dream knew me by name. It is true. I have touched truth."
He did not feel he had been received into communion,
But that he had realized his own members and functions . . . "All the life,
all the power.
All. All the orbits and times."

Silent lightning
Twitched curtains on the edges of heaven and over the mountain,
Few flashes, like forms of ceremony. No rain-drops.
Dawn lingered and then triumphed. Barclay came down,
His face livid against the streaming splendors of the mountain.
He had found the perfect confidence that controls
The faith of followers, but it was hard to remember
In the huge fenceless dispersion, in the torrent and weight
Of what appeared universal awareness,
These few followers. When he saw them he thought "My secret

Would set me away from them, outside the stars." Vasquez came upward
From the others grouped in the path or running among the trees, then
Barclay
Seemed to remember Vasquez and made movements of speech
Without a voice; he spoke again, audibly, and said:
"Multitude. But I will be with you. If sight or hearing Onorio,
Or vision, brings you the awful secret, lock it in your heart
Not to be spoken." He ate when they brought him food.

XIX

At Morhead's place the slender brick chimney
Propped to the roof against the south winds, had broken
Where the roof bound it; the bricks gashed the black roof
But slid on the sheathing and rained outward. Faith Heriot
Slept under the roof to nurse the bed-bound old man.
She stood on the rocking floor, when the match spurted
The earth had resumed its old passionate quietness.
The old man had his unimpaired; only the eyes
Moved, though the hands were able to. The bleached gray eyes
Danced in the matchlight to the dead motion of the earth,
And steadied. Faith lighted the lamp, listlessly saying
"The chimney went down," in the tone of a slack question.
He answered in the earthy and dim voice, "Go on down.
She dreamed her husband was home and it shook the bedstead.
The old walls I built have stood more shaking than this."
Faith lighted a candle for the stair and went down; there was long light
From the end of the hallway, the strangers had made a light
And had their door open; she entered Natalia's.
The bed was empty, she heard a murmuring like love
And spilled the grease from the candle turning on the darkness,
Her teeth bared. Natalia lay prone

On the child's narrower bed, her shielding body
Over the child's. The white legs and clear arms
Gleamed in the smoky flicker, the drawn night-dress
Moulded the loins, and the mass of black hair
Lay like a stain on the coverlet. Faith trembled and touched.
"Get up, it's over. What are you afraid of?" And then
Seeing in her mind the phallic shaft of the chimney,
And that it had had to be propped against the south storms,
"The chimney went down," she said exultantly, "no wonder."
Natalia sat up weeping. "Nothing will be left,
Everything had to be ruined before Randal comes home,
To-morrow: to-day." Faith, shaking, "Let him go back then
To the camp women. What he wants." She met the child's eyes
Like pools of blue shadow on the pillow and thought bitterly,
"If you'd die and be out of it." She said "I lied to you,
Long, long ago." Natalia seemed to grow conscious
Of Faith's presence, her lover's, "dearest, what lie?"
She drew the stretched linen from her knees, it had made a bad fold,
Smiled wistfully and straightened the dark forest of hair, when suddenly
the child
Wailed a long quaver of meaningless desolation,
Her eyes fixed on Faith Heriot. Natalia lifted her;
And Faith submissively: "It's almost morning, let me stay
Till the light comes; I never shall be able to again."
Natalia murmured to Rachel, who gripped a thick strand
Of her live hair in the little fingers and slept.
The child and the mother seemed to become one person
And Faith felt like a hawk blinded at night
Beating on glass. She screwed the hem of her garment
To a twist over the thigh, the stiff white tassel
Seemed to have pitiful significance, she tensed her body in the chair
With all the strain of writhing violence, not moving

The slender body. Natalia brooded on the child.
There were noises in the house; the mother and the girl, the strangers,
Must have dressed and gone down. Smells of wood-smoke and coffee
Cut the night air, the old Chinaman was up and at work,
Certainly the stove would smoke, was dangerous, no matter,
And when the window glimmered to grayness Faith said,
The child sleeping: "The day I came here
Rachel was sick with fever and you sat
Like this Natalia holding her. She was so little
She remembered the breasts and you had made yourself bare
To cool her face against them.—Oh," she thought shivering,
"To strangle the dawn, destroy movements and persons,
The strain," and she said quietly, "The earth finds happiness
When it stretches and shakes after it is tired being quiet. You smiled
pitifully
But all my blood ran on my heart when I saw you.
I couldn't have helped touching your shoulder dearest.
You said that when I touched you the baby's breathing
Changed and the forehead was wet, the fever was gone.
Yes, into *me*!" Natalia peacefully: "I loved you
Because Rachel got well after you touched me. What was the lie
You said you told me, was it then?" "If I tell you
You'd make me go away, I'll never go away."
She stood like a thin white pillar in the room. "What right have you
To be so rich and so happy? What right have you to have three? I had one,
And to-day takes you."
She moved in the room like a thin jet of white fire. "What time does he
come
And slobber on your mouth, morning?" Natalia
Turned ice answered "I don't want you in my room.
And if the house is hateful to you go out of it.
The rats feel the ship stagger; Medina went yesterday,

The ship will swim yet." Faith answered "I cannot endure to-day
But what shall I do when night comes?" She covered her face
With the hooked fingers. Natalia turning to pity
Laid down the child on the bed, but Faith: "When I felt it
I prayed it tremble harder and shake down the hung floors
And roll the old trees of the walls over us dead,
A butt on each brain. It was not my father."
Natalia, shrewd-eyed: "What was not?" "The man that had me.
I was ashamed that anyone else . . . Oh, be careful.
Have you forgotten that I had a softer sex
Before my misery, and might again." "Who was it?" "Be careful.
He had furred me inside with life, my mother had cancer
In the same fountain. She took me to Monterey,
Going to the hospital to be saved.
She lied to my father, she paid the doctor for mine,
Had *my* sickness clawed out. Something went wrong.
The smell of the ether makes me sick to remember."
"Why did you tell me the monstrous . . ." "My father came up
Unexpected: found me where my mother
Ought to have been. He took my mother and went home.
Now I don't know whether she lives or is dead.
I had to leave the hospital three days later,
The money was gone. I took the stage to go home,
I believed father would kill me. I had to walk
From where the stage left me." "You fell in the road
Outside the door. I made Maruca bring you in.
Little Rachel had the fever. Why did you make the lie
About your father?" "Not to go back to the lighthouse.
So that you wouldn't send me home to him, I hate him.
It came in my mind." "Then who was the man that— " "Ah no,"
She answered, the face wrinkling, "my shame's my own still."
Natalia trembled, she thought of Randal's absences,

Her husband's, the weeks before he entered the army,
When he used to wander seaward toward the rock at Point Sur,
Then suddenly without reason enough he enlisted,
They'd never have drafted him: Faith was in trouble at that time.
He'd not been gone two weeks and Rachel got sick;
He'd just been gone a month Faith Heriot fell fainting
In the road at the door.

Neither Natalia nor Faith
Understood how the anguish of desertion, and the mother's sacrifice,
The penalizing pain and weakness, had changed
Faith's nature, who'd been punished not be caught twice,
Not again suffer this misery. Drowned under consciousness
That resolution: and furious envy of the man,
The sex that only inflicted, not suffered: the tropic nature
Knowing that no fence would cage it found the other outlet.
She had found Natalia, young, hot, husband-forsaken,
Beautiful to be wooed: Faith had learned something
From school-girl friends in town, when her father kept the light at Point
Pinos:
And the sweet furnace painted with natural friendship,
And at the furnace heart the jewel sterility,
The love without fear.

Her nature sea-streams
Set in new ways poured on the openings of Eden,
She never had acknowledged happiness before.

But now she cried out
So that the child Rachel awoke on the bed
Sobbing. She cried: "I wish it had shaken the ocean
Over all standing heights and everything alive.

I wish the hills opened their doors and streamed fire, when it struck the ankles
The hands would fall in, and when the wrists were burnt through, the faces. I wish that it darkened
Toward the last night instead of pinching out the last day
Like a peeled snake." Natalia forgot the child sobbing
And ranged white through the room gathering her day-clothes
With picking fingers. She heaped them in a place. And Faith Heriot:
"It's good that he comes, time to give up and be quiet,
People can't live like this. Dear friend. Dear friend.
I could show you something.
If you'd a little knife and you'd nick me here
On the arm or anywhere: melted stone would run out.
There's no common red left. What it feels like." The child
Cried, and Natalia handled the heap of clothing.
But then with the gesture of a diver long balanced
Above chill water, who plunges, she slipped the night-dress
Over the dark-forested head, and Faith Heriot
Saw the arms lifted, the nippled moons, the white-moulded
Erect caryatid slenderness waver on slant dawn
A moment before it stooped to be clouded: she felt
A change like death and tears tracked the white cheeks,
She whispered "I will be quiet, Oh I'll be quiet.
I had no right." She leaned to the door and fumbled
The knob with shaking fingers. "Be happy. I'll stay up-stairs.
I haven't forgotten the old quietness up-stairs. *My* baby.
The only log of the house that needs feeding. Oh." She fled out.

XX

The day brought home Randal to the house and Barclay to the hill,
The one believing himself happy and the other

Believing himself God. Barclay remembered
The empty cabin under the limestone ridge;
There would abide a season; his following people
Took the hillside; they were not few, now the long coast
Was couriered north and south with extravagant stories
Of powers and wonders; he was said to have prophesied the earthquake,
Have foretold future destructions, and have healed sick folk.
But many during the next days came up to him
To find amusement, it was slack of the year on the steep farms,
The plows waiting for rain.

Onorio Vasquez
Passed among the hundred with screaming visions.
Onorio and one of his brothers, and two women
The madness touched, went in and out of the cabin
Seeing Barclay, who kept quietness, and feeding him. Toward evening the second day
Barclay went up among the people to the white ridge; and standing above them:
"I have sent the other multitude away. I have put them in my left hand. I will show you the face of God.
He is like a man that has an orchard, all the boughs from the river to the hill bending with abundance,
Apples like globes of sunset, apples like burnt gold from the broken mountain: . . . the man is a madman.
He has found a worm in one of the apples: he has turned from all the living orchard to love the white worm
That pricks one apple. I tell you," he said writhing above them, "that God has gone mad.
What, here on this one fruit, lump of earth-sprinkled stone
With the iron core, this earth you call it,

There's noble to love: if these mountains were not enough he has mountains under the south, the condor-
Nesting Andes, and in Asia Himalaya
Shining like candles before sunrise hung socketless
In the night of the air: he has turned away from them, he has gone mad, he has turned to love men. You greasy foreheads,
It is not for power nor beauty, what have you got under you that I should love you? The cut blue crystal the ocean
Has brilliance on its face and broken shadows and shinings, and in the heart silence: it is set in the continents
For the gold band, it is like the great jewel of the ring. He has turned and left it, he has turned to love men,
I tell you God has gone mad, he has broken
The ring not of the earth but eternity, he has broken his eternal nature: so a doomed man
Changes his mould of nature, a month before death, the miser scatters the gold counters, the coward
Eats courage somewhere. If he needed flesh
To spend that passion on . . ."

One of the women flung herself on the rock
Under his feet, crying "Lord I am here," and moaning anxiously. Her work-worn hands dug the rough stone;
Her prostrate body, ridged with the thrusting corset-bones, like a broken machine
Twitched out its passion.

Barclay continued not looking downward:
"Must he love cellular flesh, the hot quivering
Sheathed fibers, the blood in them,

And threaded lightning the nerves: had he no choice, are there not lions in the nights of Africa
Roar at his feet under the thunder-cloud manes? Not hawks and eagles, the hooked violence between
The indomitable eyes, storms of carnivorous desire drive over the huge blue? He has chosen insanely, he has chosen
The sly-minded, the cunning-handed, the talkative-mouthed,
The soft bodies go shelled in cloth: he has chosen to sheathe his power in women, sword-strike his passion
In the eyes of the sons of women. . . . I cannot tell you what madness covered him; he heard a girl's voice . . ." Barclay
Shook like a fire and cried out: "I am not ready to call you.
Let no one come to me, no one be moved." He stood rigid above them, like a man struck blind, feeling
The spheres of fire rushing through the infinite room in the bubble of his mind: but hearing inward his prophet
Onorio Vasquez, clamoring across the people:
"The April-eyed, the daughter," he cried in his vision,
"And the honey of God,
Walks like a maiden between the hills and high waters,
She lays her hand passing on the rock at Point Sur,
The petals of her fingers
Curve on the black rock's head, the lighthouse with lilies
Covered, the lightkeepers made drunken like bees
With her hand's fragrance . . ."

Faith Heriot had come up alone,
Her laughter like a knife ran over the people, "Old Heriot
My father in the lily fragrance, the cowhide face
Drunken in the lilies." And Onorio: "I see the long thighs,
Pillars of polished lightning, the marbled flanks
That God made to desire: she is not a maiden, she is all humanity,

The breasts nippled with faces, the blue eyes
Dizzy with starlight: Oh blue wells
Of sorrow he will brim you with rejoicing, Oh bruised lips
The God of the stars crushed with his kiss . . ."

Barclay like trumpets
Crossing a hawk's cry: "Only by force I have held off you
The meteor death plunging at the eyes that dared see and the mouth prophesy
What the stars cloud from. For your faith I saved you."
He said to the others: "It is true: I threw forward: he has seen.
I take youth to my age. I threw forward and struck talons in the future, I have spat out the mother
And left Eve in the dust of the garden. Where's Caesar, where is Jesus, what have I to do with dead men?
The unborn are my people and you are my people, Ah love,
I am breeding falcons. No fear that your new lover will expiate his passion
On lightning-prodded Caucasus under the vultures,
On the earthquake-rocked cross. The power and the love have joined, the great God is the lover, he has parted the stars
Like leaves to come at love. Be silent, stand quiet, I will not have you
Move till I call." He stood rigid above them,
His arms extended and fists clenched holding them to stillness,
Holding himself; his forehead grooved with bridling
The insane starts and dispersions of his mind. Some channel
He had formed for speech: now who could remember what course
He had meant to drive the wild horses of speech?
"You straws be quiet!" There were the stars rolling enormous
Courses, the unoriented void; the explosive poison in the house yonder; sundown; the flurry of the nations,
But that was over: death, death? He heard Onorio moaning a vision. He saw Faith Heriot, white fire,

Lean into flame, he cancelled her cry with: "You here, you chosen,
Are the opening of love, you are the wedge in the block, the blast in the quarry, power and fire have come down to you,
This poor crack of the coast, between the ocean and the earth, on these bare hills. God walking in you
Goes north and gathers multitude and takes the cities to give you. What does he require, there is no commandment?
For love, for the broken order of the universe: nothing but acceptance.
That you *be* your desires, break custom, flame, flame,
Enter freedom."

They, that had wished before to leap and cry out, were silent. A woman cried to him
"I flamed once in my life. I am dead." This was the woman Myrtle Cartwright who had run to her lover
Through a storm, the time Onorio had his palms pierced. Barclay not pausing for thought but seeing in his mind
Rain and thunder on the hills: "You lay under lightning
On the white straw: when your husband had died then the other
Never wanted you again . . ." He thought "It's my madness
Makes nonsense in the air." But she screaming and turning:
"He knows all I have done and what I have dreamed in the night!" He astonished with knowledge: "There is one lover
Brushed off the stars to reach down to you, this one will never leave you."
"Oh my hair" she cried "is the best part of me,"
She combed the heap with her hands and shook it on the air, then suddenly
Leaped up and down before him like flame. He commanded, "Flame, flame!"
And others were leaping. The first, feeling the breath
Choke in her throat, caught in her hands her clothing
And tore it from the throat to the midriff. When others
Disordered their garments Faith Heriot

Seized hers in her two hands at the neck and rigidly
Undid the hands. She spat on the earth and turned down
Toward the house having refused to be comforted.

XXI

She came to a point
Whence the house was visible: she was not wicked enough
To approach it, carrying a fire that the man had kindled
Would rage inside the black logs . . .
She saw the rock of Point Sur: she went down to the house
For fear of going to the rock.

She saw from the door, Randal
Talking with . . . not Natalia, with April. She thought,
"He had me and kept Natalia, he will have this one
And keep Natalia: no German had a bayonet.
Oh he chanced nothing, he stayed with the camp women."
She found Natalia on the second stairway; who wearily:
"Grandfather keeps calling me: and Rachel is sick:
I can't be in two places. Where have you been?"
"Looking at the horns. Oh, Rachel sick again?" Natalia
Sharply: "What do you mean by again? She's never
Since the week you came." But Faith: "The great horn
On the hill isn't so pretty as the little ivory
Fellow down-stairs, who do you think it's flourished at?
Maruca? No, nor the Chinaman." "I can't hear you,"
Natalia answered.

In the evening Randal followed
April from the table and said "I hated to come home.
I hate this place, I mean to sell it for a share of the world.

Your world. How could I know that you would be here
Making the place beautiful? When you go, what emptiness."
She heard him saying, but her mind gave him no heed,
She was always, these late days, vague with the day-dream
About making a weapon in Asia, wakening the nomads,
Or finding freedom in dim Asia, her father
Dying by the blight of some star, she inheriting his means
To seek freedom in Asia. That the dream was ridiculous
She knew, but she forgot the dream was her brother's
New-made in her mind from keeping memories;
And Randal, not perceiving her mind's distance
But only that her face was wistful like a boy's,
Continued and said: "Even before I went over
The sea and learned something, I knew all the while
There was much better in the world than anything I knew.
Oh, I've known women." She inclined her head, not hearing
But "over the sea," that meant escape and release,
"Better than I knew," that meant freedom. He emboldened:
"I knew breeding, knew what I'd never seen,
The bright lamp of the mind shine through the face.
It's like a story: to have gone over into hell
And fought with all the horrible faces of death
And lain among his loathsome pickings
Years, then come home and find my dream in my house.
High-bred, shining with mind, my ideal queen.
You know I am bound, you think I speak like a madman.
You don't know me . . . April . . . I have fighting spirit,
I was born a fighter, I went because I wanted to: I fight
For what I want." April perceived
Rather a bodily odor than the spoken words,
And whispered "My mother wants me." The extreme loathing and fear
Drew not from this man's vanities. He, handling her arm,

"Oh wait a little. What have I got out of the war?
This uniform and a pistol taken from a prisoner.
I kept the light of ideal love burning in my heart,
I knew there was a girl made for me to worship,
I'd never seen her, tant pis pour moi. But now, now,
I have climbed out of hell and found her."

Faith Heriot crossed over
The end of the room opposite the stair, and taking
Natalia's wrist with one hand pointed with the other.
Natalia gazed and thought of nothing but her child
Sick in the room up-stairs, but felt without thought
Like salt in the eyes those two talking: the young soldier
His handsome trivial face lifted in the shadow,
The lines of the uniform, his back was turned, flaring
From the loins to the straight shoulders; but April's face
In profile, like a boy's, eager and resolved.

She had changed, was answering: "You took a weapon
From the enemy? You must be proud of it." "The little automatic
Was all I could smuggle home." "Oh, may I see it? My brother,"
She said, "was killed." An old song
Beat her mind like a drum, "Edward, Edward,
Why does your breast—sword was it?—so drip wi' blood?
Why does your breast so drip with blood?" He, touching her,
"I have it up-stairs." They went up.

Natalia
Moved toward the stair thinking that little Rachel
Was sick, needed her mother, but like a dancer Faith Heriot
Prevented her and said "Ah no sweetheart, don't follow.
You must endure a little, I endured in the night,

Don't lie to me, when I bit my wrists lying in the bed—
Marks? Oh yes, look at them—
No wonder the child sickened, what you were doing.
Endure a little." Natalia, the face not changing,
Extended open hands like a blind person,
Touching Faith's breast with finger-tips, the obstacle
Soft and moving, she hardly imagined what obstacle
That blocked her way.

At the door up-stairs
Randal thought April would not enter, but she entered,
To see where he kept it. He took it from the drawer, blue steel,
Bigger than she'd imagined. Death. She remembered the poison
That she had taken from her mother and hidden in the car
Among the tools. Randal was saying "I've only
Five shells to fit the calibre, it's loaded with them.
My old revolver lay in the holster while I was gone
And rusted into a block, the leather draws damp."
"Your hawk's blood was never," it ran in her mind,
"Your hawk's blood was never so red, Edward, Edward."
She looked at Randal, smiling. "It doesn't seem terrible,
Because I can't imagine it, not really, a man
Killing a man." He put it in the drawer, his head
And hand certainly trembling. "That's clean and easy,"
He answered, "but what burst men to spatters . . . April,"
He said clutching her wrists; she writhed herself backward.
She'd thought the child would be in the room, it was not,
But in the next one; he said "Who's lived years
Between the teeth, takes his joy where he finds it.
Watching them grind his friends: we never counted
To-morrows, to-morrow we were mashed." He knelt suddenly

And whimpered, "Wolves it makes us. Oh pure and lovely
How could you know the terrible ferocity of men?
That all your clear bright beauty, shining with spirit,
Untouched, ideal . . . I can't bear it." He wept in his hands;
She, freed, stood gazing. The pistol in the second drawer.
This man appointed to outrage the abstraction of her mind
With comic attitudes. He said, "I kept my ideals
Bright and clean through it all, I believe in goodness,
In *ro*mance." She left the room and heard Faith Heriot down-stairs:
"No, no, but give them time. I give you the long nights.
Wait." At the stair-head she met Natalia and felt
Her eyes like rods in the dark: then they were drawn
Home like a snail's. No word; a tension, a violence
Passing, and then Faith's voice in the stair, her laughter.
Natalia went to the child's room and April to her mother's.

XXII

Faith mounted two flights, to old Morhead's. She heard a rhythmic
Swinging noise in the room before she entered, she found him
Swinging his arms—the left one full length, the other
Was lame at the shoulder, he swung it shortened—
So that the nerveless body was shaken on the bed.
She stood in the door, eyeing him for monstrous, in the dim lamplight.

She thought nothing, it drew through the mind under thought:
Embryo, waiting to be born,
Lying in the house his mother.
When he was young he made his own mother.
Being old he entered her, laid off
All faculties, all will,
To lie passive in the womb.

She has lost the medicine. He flaps in the womb
Like a child flapping in the womb.

"Ah what's the matter grandfather?" He did not hear
Until she spoke shrilly the second time.
The arms kept swinging; a hole in the white beard
Opened and babbled in the earthy voice: "Nothing.
Nothing but the arms to dance with." He let them fall.
"How did you know they're dancing on the hill, I didn't tell you?"
She turned the lamp up and saw the shame in his eyes.
"What hill? Uh," he coughed, twitching the arms, "who dancing?"
She cast her hands up to the throat of her dress,
Caught hold as if to tear it, her lips tortured
Away from the teeth. The hands relaxed. "A hairy old fellow
With a big horn, the women dancing around him.
Up on the hill toward Hayworth's." She saw the arms rising.
"Be quiet, little Rachel's sick, grandfather. That Barclay,
The same man that was here."

The monstrous foetus
Beating the walls of the womb.
Nothing can keep it from growing.
Nothing. Fatality. Moons
Up to the tenth have whetted
Their sickles on the rock at Point Sur.
The house shook in the little earthquake
Was the first pain.
It made its mother, her labor is upon her.
How shall I endure the day
Of the monstrous birth-pangs?

"Rachel is sick, we must be quiet, now it's bedtime."
She laid her hand on the arm and when it was quieted

Fished under the bed for the bottle with the wide neck
That lay by the flat pan; she drew the bed-covers
Down to the knees, and bending above the faint
Dry and inhuman odor of the bed drew over to its flank
The flattened body, joined it to the dull glass,
Her spirit raging on the hill, heard the vague rain.

XXIII

The child in the dim light twisted her little features,
Moaned in her sleep, drawing up the knees, and often
Sighing hopelessly pushed back the coverlet without awakening.
Her fever increased. Natalia replaced the coverlet.
Randal opened the door quietly. "She's better?
When are you coming?" She thought of her baby's
Pretty arrogance the days of her health, the pitiful
Self-confidence, nothing could hurt her. "I can't leave her,
Randal." The small, tired head twitched over on the pillow
The hundredth time, sighing. Randal returned
And lay on his bed. "I used to think of this place
Tenderly, all for Natalia's sake, in the packed entrainments
That drew toward hell; yes, and in the few hours
Of drunken happiness, remember thinking most tenderly
Of the pure woman to return to, I impure but her soldier.
And now there's nothing in the house but a sick child."
The old horror of death that might drop down in a moment,
And could it be heard coming? returned to forbid
Sleep: the mere phantasy of death excited again
Wrathful desire: risk dropping the unemptied wine-cup?
He had rights. He had made sacrifice for her and the child,
For the future, for their freedom and safety. He rose

And gazed toward April's door down the dark hallway
And turned softly the knob of the other. Natalia
Sat by the bed but certainly the child was quieter.
He embraced her arm with his fingers. "She doesn't wake up.
She doesn't need you." The trouble in her face angered him.
"You're troubled about nothing serious." She thought
If she could lead the intolerable whispers
Into the hallway and hide them. She held the latch
To keep it from clicking and attempted to tell him
About Rachel's illness. He thought of death
Comes down like a hawk—on the man. What did Natalia,
Inexhaustible fountain of life, know of death? He alone
Menaced in the house, "Come," he said, drawing at her arm,
Trembling, his habit of fear wearing desire for a wolf-skin
Not to know its own face. Suddenly her mind
Solved its distraction; in a moment, in white light,
Saw the slant eyes of terror and the thirsting mouth,
And her own motherhood, mother of this changeling also
Who had come to the house like a strange man: even to Faith Heriot
A sort of mother: they all drained her. Dear, if her pity
Could yield him peace. It was true the child slept, this other
Child was unable to sleep.

Undressing herself
In the next room, smiling wearily, she bared
The breasts before she thought of loosening the skirt.
More prominent and larger than the mould in his mind
They coarsened him with sudden anger and he took
Roughly, and still half clothed, what was about to be given,
Raging as over an enemy. Natalia kept patience,
He would rest soon, she could return to her vigil with the other.

But Randal imagined April Barclay humbled
By force, the proud and the pure: avenging his felt
Unacknowledged feebleness, dividing desire
Into imaginary violences; the strain-shocked mind
Returning on adolescence.

Some psychic remnant
Was it, that frustrate and perverse, wasting
From that incapable passion wandered in the house?
April Barclay feeling a phantom violence
Whined in her sleep and felt him—the monstrous father—
Hoop the earth with his will, the stars wavered in prison.
The bruise on her cheek awakened her, the hand had been clenched
Under the bruise and hurt it. She could not endure nightmare,
She got up and began to dress in the darkness.
He possessed all the region. His spirit.

It is not possible
A man's spirit possess more than his members; but the ocean soul of the world
Has whirlpools in its currents, knots in the tissue, ganglia that take
Personality, make temporal souls for themselves: may parallel a man's before they are melted. He, fooled,
Counts his great hour, he appears to have broken his limits, imposed himself outward. Without subjection no Caesar,
First the subjection. Without form first no phantom. I knew that it had a spirit,
This coast of savage hills impendent on the ocean, insecure on the ocean; and few and alien
Humanity reaping it and not loving it, rape and not marriage,
Dream a bad edge on the demon. They felt it in the night

Take flesh and be man; the man imagined himself God; the people were fooled,
Touching reality a little, simply not geared to engage reality; the cogs clash and withdraw,
Some impulse was caught, the noise and the spark of the steel kissing, a myth and a passion.

Barclay had bidden them
Build fires on the hill; they were like happy drunkards around the great fires, but Barclay
Entered the hut at nightfall and lay on the blanket.
He heard Onorio Vasquez prophesying and the women
Shout by the fires; he was perfectly convinced and at peace.
He awoke in an hour and thought "What shall I do?
The strain, the unendurable strain and deceit. Kill myself?"
He lay deprived in the awful return of sane thought,
Not daring to recall his evidences
Nor piece together the hollow miracles . . .
He knew in a flitting instantly forgotten moment
That sanity was too frightful to endure: and murmured to himself
"Why do I make pain? Why do I make death? I have turned to love men:
All for discovery." His mind unfolded into madness and resumed its glory, narrowed to a point
The innumerable stars. "I am also outside the stars," he thought in the wild hush, rising, "the infinite
Nothing outside them, the room . . . room . . . the firmament unreason
That has no wings. I do not myself
Know what I am . . . there. In the unconceived, the embryo *before* conception." Shaken with his own
Divine mystery, in sacred silence . . . When he came outside
A woman arose from the red coals and anxiously
Leaped up and down before him. He answered, "Unhappy,

I am in the young men, have you not found me?" She answered
"I have kept myself clean till now." "Change. God has changed."
She crouched by the coals, wept and would answer nothing.

He walked across the scattered people by the dying fires
Feeling the south wind in the stubble of his beard and thinking "I shall never
Sleep any more, I have all my desire." Of those by the red fires many were sleeping,
A few lifted to watch him. Down the hill in the dark
He heard murmurs of pleasure, he had commanded them to find God in each other; and voices of anger
One way in the dark; by one of the fires the stammering of happy drunkards. They hushed feeling him pass them,
The bottle was hidden. He angrily: "Nothing is denied you.
Why do you want forgetfulness, you are out of the net? Yet nothing is denied you." The woman among them, the puckered
Face and shawled head, she stood up swaying like a spurt of black fire: "I am old.
Have you changed that?" He felt the skies of his mind
Suddenly be turned and focus upon her, she also felt them
And slid to the earth. He said "I will change it. When I set you
Back of the bleeding womb and *before* conception."

XXIV

Faith Heriot had dreamed that she was buried in the earth,
Roofed in with terrible centuries of silent darkness,
On her back breathless: then a tall tree grew erect
Out of the middle of her body and towered on the soft air,
The pride, the enormous girth of the trunk . . . She heard old Morhead
Waken and wave his arms in the dark on his bed,

A little at first. She heard a wind gathering
Begin to push at the roof, the wind had wakened him.
The monstrous embryo be born?
The waking nightmare was less endurable, she rose
And found her hands clutching the throat of her night-dress.
She unclasped them by force, assuring herself Natalia
To-night would never lie down but sit by the child.
Perhaps Rachel was dying, she thought, with bitter
Unconfessed pleasure, now the seasons turned backward
And nothing remained rational, the mad God on the hill
Possessed the region. His spirit.

She felt him on the stairs
In the thick dark, she felt him crowding the hallway.
She entered the room they kept the child in. Natalia
Was not in the room, the child was beating the bed with its arms
In the lamplight, the eyelids lifted from blanks of fever.
Faith fixed her eyes on the partition, toward the next room,
Torturing her hands.

Natalia had whispered
Through the dim abstraction of her patience, "Dear are you done?
I should go back." He had ploughed and not sown, the ploughshare
Blunted and failed in the furrow "Ah you slack skin,"
He answered, "who wore you out when I was in hell?
Damn you go back to him." She answered "I haven't deserved . . .
Randal I haven't deserved . . ." He between shame
And obscure terror bending over the bedside
Took her throat in his nailed fingers, but sparing to stop the breath,
"It has to be settled, I'm the master in the house.
Say it, that I'm the master. You know that I loathe you,
But while I have to live with you. Say it." She clutching

His wrist with her hands, "Rachel is sick, let me go."
"First say it." She was mute, her face changing, and her eyes
Warred against his; but Randal's wavered, and Natalia:
"What happened to you to make you a fool and a coward,
What did they do to you?" He shuddered and struck
With the free hand, "Ah, that's what you want, what you want,"
He loosed the other, "want more?" She rose in the bed
Holding her hands before her face, whispering "Now I see clearly
That you're the master." She touched the corner of her lips
And stared down at the fingers. "Tell me sometime
What they did to you to make you . . . like this." He had turned,
She holding up at the waist her remnant clothing
Went from that room to the other and bent to the child's bed
With sharp quick breath, she had seen Faith Heriot but only
As one misery the more. Faith touched her head,
Not for disgust able to touch the bare shoulder,
And said "How horrible you are, you have to have him.
How many times again before morning? Ah, ah,"
The words crumbled in her mouth. Natalia bent lower
Over the child. From Faith the intolerable world
Drained like blood from a wound, life shallowed and thinned
Until it seemed a shining and blade-thin pool,
Like a flat moon hardly wetting her foot-soles,
She bloodless spired to a point from and spoke easily
Now it was drained, her purged consciousness
Had hardly a part in the saying, "It is time, dear.
I always loved you, it is time when it grows old and dirty,
There are too many people. I would go with you
And help you if you like. I am almost, already." Natalia
Saw the child's face ecstatic, blank-eyed,
But the mouth shrivelled and the arms swinging cramped arcs
Beyond her understanding, and Faith Heriot: "I think

She wants to be born, she too. That fellow's been calling
All over the world." Natalia quieted the arms
And bent her cheek to Rachel's. "You are right to hold her," Faith said,
"The first brings enough misery. More life, more misery.
I have been holding myself.
The thing would be to find out a way of getting *un*born.
I have found out a way."

Randal entered the room
Barefoot, in shirt and trousers, he had heard the trailing
Monotonous voice. He trembled still. "A great peace to come home to.
Tell it, let me hear." But Faith Heriot: "Oh wonderful, again?
All the long night, Natalia." Natalia not lifted
The cloud of her hair; Randal: "Go up you thin wire.
Dear," he said to Natalia, "I'm sorry. The nerves go bad.
I brought them home crackled: there's something in the air.
I came to tell you." No one answered, and the child
As if disturbed by silence moaned wearily and struggled to rise,
Thrusting with the hands. Natalia sobbed broken voices,
But Faith having her mind fixed on destruction:
"Oh cover her, it's the crazy God calling.
Don't let her be born again for once is bad enough. I tried to crawl home,
I stuck in the cancer. Listen Natalia,
Let it go in if you have to, never let it come out. Mouse-trap.
I had yours killed," she said to Randal, "my mother
Paid for it. Oh, I can think of anything. Your nerves
Cracked? Mine are wires." He approached her quietly and snatched
The thin arm with his hand. "You've got to go up.
You can't play mad here. If you've got to be taken
I'll take you, you've got to be quiet." She laughing
And twisting her lean shoulders, "Oh I'll be your April.
Natalia tell me where you keep the mouse-poison,

He thinks I'm a girl. He ought to know. Randal,
Do you remember the dune under the bushes?
We cheated you though." He drew her to the door. Natalia
Stood up, the look of patience had hardened to stone;
The firm breasts and firm flanks, a surface, the eyes even
Were surfaced, though they fixed themselves on the others
Were neither giving nor taking. Her giant self-enclosure
Dwarfed the others, all the balance was altered, the baby
Under the partial covering struggled on the bed
At the height of her knees little as if newly born.
And Faith at the door, straining to play a part
Under the surfaced eyes, dancing before the divine
Idol: "I made a pitiful boy, good-bye Natalia.
When an old lover takes you by the arm.
Here's the end of play-time, when the man comes women stop playing.
Oh you can do as you like." He thrust her outward
And locked the door. He turned inward, but rather
On the room than on Natalia. "Now I've found you out.
It took me two days. Oh well, you change easily.
By God I'll see you. Is Rachel better?" She answered
"I've thought of a medicine," she still was erect
In the same standing, but the stone surface and shine
Matted to soft and gray, all the height and majesty
Nulled, she was like a shadow in the room, all the weight
Disbodied that had seemed dangerous; whatever had enforced
The surface now drawn inward or dissolved away.
The child appeared quieter of pain.

XXV

Faith Heriot
Stood by the door, her hands gathered to her throat,

Saw April Barclay come through lamplight, through the open doorway
Of Randal's room. She thought "news for Natalia,"
Her mind fixed on destruction, and laughed "You missed him,
He's here with his wife," trembling and laughing, but certain
That what she thought of was false, herself was turned woman,
April held hidden under the coat something
That men have: "What are you carrying in front of you?" She answered like someone
Smiling in the good passage of a mixed dream,
"We'll be good friends," and passed her. Faith followed whispering:
"The fellow on the hill, you know him, he calls the dances.
What is he making you do?" But April had passed
With a boy's gesture and entered her mother's room,
Shutting the door softly.

XXVI

Randal came out to the hallway
Having heard passages by the door; he saw Faith Heriot
Mount the dim stair, he turned dully to sleep.
He awakened after an hour and some person
Stirred in the room: he lay happily attentive: perhaps Faith Heriot . . .
The world has turned strange but April would never.
When he turned over on the bed the fumbling was quiet.
He reached matches and when the motion again
Began its patience, lit one by flicking it on his thumb-nail
After a manner he used, and saw Natalia
Still bare to the loins turning from the chest of drawers,
The second drawer was open, she drew out her hand.
He thought she looked for a clean night-dress and had missed the drawer.
"Oh make a light, I'm awake." She turned and pushed home
That drawer and opened the one above it; the match

Died, and he heard in the darkness the drawers moving
Again, the blind noises of search. He got up
And lighted the lamp. Her eyes appeared lidless
And lacking iris, round vacant ports of a wrecked ship,
So big that the breasts looked little. She said quietly:
"Rachel has died. I have saved . . . she is saved everything.
Where does it go to, in the air? I was looking for a key . . .
Rachel has died." He cried like a child, "Oh. Oh.
Why did you not call me? Oh! You are lying,
By God," he ran to the next room and the lamp
Shone dimly there. The frightfully little
Blue doll's face on the bed: wet when he touched it,
Like wet putty; he shook his hand, moaning, and made more light.
The eyes half open, the nostrils pinched shut, the pillow
And the yellow hair darkened with moisture. A gasping
Hysteria like claws in his throat, all the house heard him
Controlless, lamenting more his own terror
And the general ruins of the earth.

Faith Heriot had heard a rasping
Whisper of dry boughs to a coming storm when she went up-stairs,
And bent above old Morhead's bed in the darkness,
"What's it now, old friend, not sleeping?" The earthy voice:
"Isn't my son enough for her but you must serve too?
Make light for me." She saw by matchlight the covers
Half off the bed, the flattened fork of the body;
By lamplight the hands against the thighs, rubbing them,
The dry and withered; and the earthy voice she had never
Heard tremble before was shaken: "They've got new feeling.
The pulse prickles. Look," he said, his lean finger
Shook like the compass-needle to a stand, pointing
The gnarled left foot, jointed and sinewed creature

Weak and white from deep sea, that while she watched it
Moved painfully, the tendons
Drawn, and the toes and the foot turned on the ankle,
Turned and returned.

The air about her head vibrated like fire,
The horror of birth: she confused in her mind
The log house with her mother
In whose womb putrescence
And old disease . . . who had kept the death in her womb
To pay the extinction of life
Out of her daughter's. The monstrous
Lump was ready to be born.
Death was ready to be born
And walk in the world, she thought not consciously, her fingers
Flew once more to the throat of her dress and clutched it,
"But I will be unborn and be still in the darkness,
Unbirth, to lie down with death, lie with death . . . My father in the lighthouse
Read the bible," she said, "when I was little,
King David was old and couldn't walk they gave him
A young girl for warmth. I'll warm you, in a minute
Death will get up and walk." She lying by his side
Chafed the dry skin on the concave thighs
Tenderly with her hands, because she loved death.
He was like a father, and when she heard Randal crying
Under the floor it was like a dream. She rose up
Vaguely and did not go to the crying but went down
The second stairway, holding the lamp in her hand,
Full of hatred of Natalia. She found her in the kitchen.
"You've done it, have you?" Who answered coldly, "Not yet.
He's hidden it out of its place." "What?" "Ah the tool,

The tool," but Faith, bewildered, "To think, my God,
I called those slack mounds beautiful! Get on some clothes
Before they take you." And Natalia: "Who has been with you
That your eyes shine . . ." The man's wailing through the open doorways
Covered the words, and Natalia again, her lips
Twisting over the teeth in the smoky lamplight:
"What a fool that is. Nothing, nothing." Faith, watching
Her right hand folded with some hidden utensil
In the cloth at her groin: "I hate you with all my heart.
I hate you with all my heart. A killer." She answered
Patiently: "Though you ought to be patienter with me.
Things you said gave me the thought . . . if I remember
What you said, it's no matter. I am not strong enough
To help you much. World's too stiff to help others,
Except one's own child. Own. You could use it after me,
Or find your own." But Faith approaching her she said
"Stop there. I should like first . . ." The servant Maruca
Came sloe-eyed from her kennel behind the kitchen,
Mazed at the voices. Natalia moved by the wall
And stood by the cold stove. "Stand there Maruca.
I ought to say first . . ." But Faith: "Why should you say
Anything? I saw him do it. He had the knife—
Was it a knife?" "I dropped a towel in the pitcher,
I took it and covered her face." "Oh Maruca," Faith said, "Rachel has died.
She was sick in the night and died. Did all we were able
And could not save her." Natalia said quietly, "I saw
What she had to grow up to, and she was in pain. We have to choose
For a wee helpless child. I'd done her a crime
In the conception, made it as right as I could.
For two minutes of hurt bought her eternal heaven.
There honey, there quietness.
I've not the strength to save anyone else

But only myself." She pressed her left hand
Under the left breast. "Oh, tell Randal
That cornered between the stove and the wall can still
Creep through the mouse-hole." She'd unwound the right hand
But Faith at the instant flash leaped for the wrist
And though it dodged her, breast to breast with Natalia
Closed and constrained. They wrestled, remembering their loves,
Groaning, Maruca across their shoulders
Cried like a fishing gull. When they fell, Natalia
Struck her head on the iron stove and was quiet, the little
Paring-knife clinked from her fingers.

When her mind returned
They had laid her on the bed in her own room, and Randal
Talked of a fire on the hill, "the whole hill is burning,
Fools, in this wind. They've fired the hill I must go.
My God is there no end?" For the poor remnant
Of the farm stock were fenced on the hill. The women
Heard him crying by the stables, toward the dark dawn.

XXVII

The south wind that in better winters blows rain on men's fields
This year blew fire, it rose in the night and snatched the embers of the fires
Across the sleeping people, it sowed them in the dry grass. The few that watched were not there, for Barclay
Had walked in the night southward the ridge, full of his exultations; a few followed him; Onorio
Vasquez the vision-seer was at his arm when he stumbled, Myrtle Cartwright was with him; three others
Followed, and all deranged with ecstasy but one with whiskey. Barclay, the stars forming and dying

In the measurelessness of his lost mind, stood on the hill's brow over Morhead's farmhouse and saw
Lights change in the little windows far down; and he saw
The great light glowing and lapsing on the rock of Point Sur, in the ocean loneliness; and the sea stars
Brighten and go out through the small cloud-scud, the wind increasing. "I am God: but I am secret": and he said:
"You are atoms of humanity and all humanity
A cell of my body: listen, I have turned all my lightnings of consciousness
On the one cell; I have turned to love men. I lift a handful from the ocean. What do you see in this house
Onorio, the lights change in the windows?" "The age of the world," he stammered, "the new world, power is turned backward.
They love pleasure and death." Then Barclay: "I pour my life into these bottles, that burst and the life
Spills on the ground, it is inexhaustible, I am the fountain." The drunkard swaying in the darkness, "Elijah
Pop out the cork, clock clock," plopping his thumb
From the sucked cheek; and Onorio Vasquez: "Master they prophesy the last days, they are drunk with confusion,
What people are these, the women make themselves men and the men are unable, the man plows and no seed,
Dreaming of the next field." Then Barclay answered "These are the people.
The times they command fate to serve them, then I lay waste their fountain. The useless function runs mad
Until power dies. Powers increase and power dies." The drunkard fell prone before him,
Having essayed to dance in the wind, tripped up by the earthling blackberry vines that trailed on the hill's brow,
And Vasquez cried out "No hope, see-saw forever?" He answered "Caesar is not born but the power perishes,

The life moves to the skin." And the drunkard: "Because I kissed my
mother
I have thorns in my skin, Oh that she doesn't love me" he wept; and
Vasquez: "Be quiet will you, I am asking
My lord is there any hope?" Barclay feeling the stars
Turn in his mind: "I have turned to love men. What does hope mean, ask
nothing foolishly, I take my remnant.
I have not done this before, not for the crown of the stars: you are out of
the net." And he cried suddenly:
"To-night my love for whom I turned to love men, the bride and the
equal-minded, whom I took like a tower
Taken by violence, the supreme sacrifice, the lamb of God
That bled," he said shuddering, "secretly, that moaned for love in the high
darkness, the spirit of splendor
Through whom the dark earth blinds Arcturus comes up to me: Onorio
The light of the foot-prints, the flute-music of the frightened breathing."
He shook like a tall pine, and the wind
Began to rage up hill in the darkness.

The wind glided from southward
In gusts, like a knife drawn against a whetstone, that glides and gives over,
so the great wind lay gustily
On the ocean, on the dark rocks of the shore, on the secret hills, pausing
and thrusting. It gathered the embers
Of Barclay's fires among his company to sow them
In grass gemless of dew that long had forgotten
Rain and the green; the white fibers of the hill whispered to each other: "A
holy spirit has come down
To one us with the God that we came from. Have courage," they cried
writhing like terror, "we were dead already."
The wind slackened, they erected themselves and trembled.

Under the third
gathering of wind
Randal Morhead began to cry out through the log house over the child that was dead: then April,
Who had sat without moving near the bed of her mother, holding the small engine of death
As it were a precious appendage of her own body . . . Natalia
Had sought it in vain, April had heard the secret
Comings and goings in the dense house, and suddenly
The man's voice in the bright hysteria wailing like a woman's . . . "Mother,
Get up and dress, it is time." She lighted the lamp.
"I have planned everything." When Audis Barclay
Sat up in the bed trembling, with useless questions,
April patiently: "Unless you come I must leave you.
Nobody here will hurt you . . . lock it behind me,
Lie still till morning." She hastily got up: then April
Averted her eyes, feeling not thinking herself
Boy-sexed in the woman's room, and with vague shame
And vague disgust stiffened by the window, her back
Turned on the woman dressing. She watched from the window
The lighthouse lighten and darken through the gross darkness on the rock of Point Sur,
She heard the womanish voice of lamentation
Lift and pause in the house. She cried "Are you ready?"
And swept her mother uselessly questioning
Out of the room by mere impetus of mind
To the stair-head and the turn of the stair and the door;
Then Audis would not go out; but April: "Come mother,
You have come this far. Death is up-stairs, I don't know who dead,
But not innocently, and there's more," she said pointing
Through the open doors to the far room. Faith Heriot

Came first, her thin back toward them, and Maruca behind her,
Carrying a third; Faith had the bare shoulders,
Maruca the knees, there was blood in the hair. Then April:
"Oh easily. Come. Here's only the wake of that ship
That wills horror on the hill. I'm going up, mother,
Against the stem and cutwater and change him. Unhappy April . . .
These things are not our miseries but unhappy April . . .
Had a sweet name." She drew the door open, the storm
Strained through the hollow of the house, the lamp behind them
Streamed up into death. She holding Audis erect,
Who bowed over the threshold in the rushing darkness,
Drew her through and drew the door home. "The electric torch,
Wait mother, in the pocket of my coat: I've something
In the hand: reach it."

XXVIII

Barclay cried on the hill "Where does my love linger?"
A moment the mill-race of the swirling galaxy parted in his mind, he saw through an island of peace
That who came up to find him would go to the fires to find him, how could one find another on the hill,
Even God on the dark hill? He turned quickly to go back to the fires, but Vasquez:
"What are they doing," unable to fetch his eyes from the farmhouse windows
Down the headlong wind, "killing their hope, one vessel they had made
To swim up time, one little quiverful
Of slender arrows to shoot the future: they have broken
The arrow-shafts in the bundle, what will stand up now?" Then Barclay: "Out of *me*

Destruction, out of me renewal, I preserve nothing: exult with me.
I take my chosen, I never said I would salvage you all
Out of the net of change and renewal: they climb out of the pit to the brink and suddenly they slay
The next step with their hands: I laugh in tempests over their heads in the air, and exult, and raise up
The old violence, the old mysticism, the old terror among them,
The resurrection of time among them." Myrtle Cartwright
To Vasquez: "Is the old man still living that lies like death
Under the roof?" He with fixed eyes not answered, but Barclay:
"It is time: I called him. Come quickly." They went to the fires,
The far hill like a burning mountain.

Audis Barclay
Sobbed on the dark slope "Has the father's madness
Burst out in the daughter? I cannot go up any farther,
April, April." Who answered "You are talking to the dead.
Now I can neither leave you here nor go back
It's likely I'll have to tell you . . . I'll have to . . .
That I mean patience. I had a sick thought
That looked red at the end but that's over. Use the torch mother.
Come this way from the bush, now's easier walking.
He . . . April . . ." She panted for breath. "Insane.
A red curtain hung over his mind . . . what beasts in the newspaper . . .
But this you must remember was her own father,
In whom she had natural confidence.
She fought hard, was betrayed by her own . . . soul . . .
Weakness of body." She cried against her mother's silence
"There was a bruise if you'll remember on the cheek!
That you saw. And others. He struck with the fists." Audis
Retractile and sad all her pale years, felt sudden
Calmness and power. "If this were the truth April."

Who answered "But you can see plainly it was not possible
To live the rest. It would be conceivable, if life
Had been too obstinate in her it might have nourished . . . succession . . .
nature
Goes very blindly. I keep locks on myself
To speak coldly of things in their nature unspeakable.
Because our nerves are like . . . wires in this wind
And have to be kept muted." "What do you mean to do?"
"It is not much higher though now so steep, mother.
And I feel perfectly sure of finding him here
On the next brow, and alone or nearly: that was my hurry:
We'll find him alone we can speak quietly
And use reason at the least, if possible: we couldn't hope to
There by the fires among the fooled people.
Having passed under death if that's a true dream
Cools me. I'd have been hastier. Dear mother,
If there's time afterwards . . . do you hear nothing at all
Known in my voice, mother? I cannot
Myself believe, though I remember the pain,
And then the faintness, of death: and the long homesick wandering:
That this terrible happiness has flowered
Out of my sister's misery: I Edward your son,
I died in France, hear your real voice and again
Touch you with living hands. *Living* is nothing
To make joy over. . . . It is really no matter
Whether you believe me or not, I have this gladness
Against this horror. . . . Would I dare to go up and face him
If I were that victim, mother, that stricken April?
I go coldly, having gone under death;
Nothing of vengeance although I loved her. . . . My aim
To bring him down and lay him under restraint
Quietly: I'm armed: you can't run to the law

In the infamous case: nothing but private recourse:
Even if the man were a stranger."

Audis stood, saying
"I have always been weak. . . . Oh this delusion," she thought,
"Of the strength that might have saved us come back to be alive:
She has courage from this. He's with God. Is it delusion?"
Feeling the strength draw from it. "Dear I have only
A measure of power: I must hold sane: it leaves me
The judge in the world. Armed, you said? Show me." She answered
"I stole a pistol in the house." She folded the cloak
Over her hand, she could not for shame make naked
The vital instrument and symbol of power
To another sex though her own mother. The hard
Hot grip burned in her hand. "I will not go up
Until you show me." "Then, mother," she answered swaying
With the great gusts of love warring on shame.
She held it bare in her hand, the sacramental
Exhibition, the awful witness of power.

XXIX

But Audis snatched for it. April caught back the hand
And the emblem, and shaking with white anger: "I have lucky parents.
Feel your own way." She climbed up the last slope
And on the brow the blackness of the night, the solitude, the streaming
Wind were alone. She stood astonished. "Not here?"
His dreadful and divine presence was yet so palpably
Covering the hill. Was it love . . . so impudently longed for his
presence . . .
"Then it needs killing, good-bye to reasonableness,
There's no escape but hold it straight-pointing, press here,

The little steel spring in the handle as he taught me,
Pull this one . . . what else did I fetch it up for?
Go on to the fire and find him." She had stood, and now heard
A voice from the earth, her mother's fallen to the earth
On the hill-top near her feet and thrusting a voice
Like a torn stalk up into the wind: "Ah dearie,
If ever it's fired fling it away, fling it away,
They couldn't trace it to you, not bought nor given.
Wait for me dear." She ran from the voice toward the fires,
The hillside over the saddle sheeted with fires,
And still heard crying: "April!" but afterwards, "Edward . . ."
That touched her, she turned and waited. "I am in the wave, mother,"
She thought to herself, "runs from the know-nothing ocean.
I feel it drawing and thrusting me up: all that I think
Or feel's less than the foam." She choked with fear.
"Doing has no thread to thinking, nobody knows
What's made in the dark water till it pops the surface."
The gliding earth-moon, the electric circle of the torch
Turned down for timid footing crept nearer. "Can I stand all night?"

In the house under the hillside Natalia
Rolled her head on the mats of her black hair, saying,
"It's early to dance. No, you must leave me to-day,
I've got a headache." Faith Heriot stared at the face,
That wore through its pain so wonderful a look of wantonness,
The slack lip and the teeth, the half-closure of the eyes,
And seeing the blood was oozing again through the black hair
She said "Maruca, get more water in the pitcher."
Who having gone down to fetch it came back trembling,
The pitcher empty in her hand. Meanwhile Faith Heriot
Had carried the wash-bowl with its ruddy water
And the dark clots at the bottom, to the window to empty.

She leaned from the window and saw the red sky streaming
Over the hill like dawn in the wrong quarter,
And heard what she supposed was the surf running
Under the distant rock of the lighthouse, it sounded
Like horses running. She turned, and Maruca
Stood trembling with the empty pitcher, the broad gray face
Lined with white streaks. "Well, what's the matter?" Who answered
That the big table in the dining-room had been thrown over
And the picture of a sail-ship on the wall was dancing,
"I came up-stairs then." Faith took the pitcher and went down,
And passing the overthrown table thought it was strange
That neither of the dogs had barked all night, not even when Randal
Went screaming toward the stable. She drew the water
And went up with the pitcher. Maruca placed the bowl,
Natalia rolled her head on the mats of black hair,
But when the wash-cloth wetted her face Natalia
Instantly ceased to breathe and fluttered both hands,
Making a coarse noise in the throat but still
Not breathing, and the lips blued. Faith dropped the wash-cloth,
Thrust hands under the shoulders and dragged up the body,
It would not breathe, she slapped the nipples of the breasts,
Then it bowed over and caught breath, and Natalia
Rose from the bed like a snapped-wing hawk that flops up
On the sound wing against the children tormenting it
And strikes this way and that way quicker than sight
With beak and talons, so that it seems not to have struck
Yet the hands and the cheeks are bleeding: then the snapped wing
Betrays it and it falls but the children are scattered:
She falling back on the bed had not the hawk's look
Nor silence but chattered inarticulate terror,
And Faith sullenly: "I only wanted to wash
The blood out of your hair." She chattered "I know these towels

With all the drowning ocean in them.
What blood, there was no blood, Oh you white liar
She died by herself." Faith said "There's nothing to be afraid of.
Lie still till morning, will you?"

But speaking, her lips
Twitched, and their pallor increased to her cheeks' whiteness:
The while Maruca tilted up the black beads
Between the folds of brow and cheek-bones and said smiling
"Old grandfather: he got up?" For the boards groaned
Over their heads, a noise of slow shuffling
Motion, and then like a load dragged on the floor
Under the roof. In Faith's mind
The womb's throes in waves
Of animal contraction
Thrust their object: she felt in her mind
Not the knives and grinding
Of the pain she'd never experienced, but sick thrust . . . thrust . . .
Complicating with stifling
Drunken abysses of remembered ether;
She felt the rings of flesh
Drawing and sucking
In waves on the bearded load, he had made his mother,
And she heard Natalia, who perceived nothing: "Oh no,
I did quiet her, the man on the hill called her,
She was too sick to dance I wanted to quiet her,
And I'd have fixed myself and Randal but he hid the gun,
We've got to go up." Faith from the sick vertigo
Gathering her native courage like a hand plucking
A dropped coin from a swirl of deep water: "*I've* got to go up.
But you lie quiet." But while she spoke slow foot-steps
Hung halt on the dull stairway, from tread to tread

Dropping, and the hand-rail creaked in the dark. The door of the room
Was open, they could hear clearly. It stopped at the stair-foot
While one breathed twice, then drew down the dark corridor,
And now he was heard breathing. He rested on the door-knob
Of the next room. Natalia rose naked from bed
As if she'd been awaiting him, and in the doorway:
"Go in grandfather. Grandfather look at Rachel.
She had a wound that would have poisoned her," she said,
"What all our misery comes out of." But Faith behind
Caught her by the arms above the elbows and jerked her
Sidelong against the bed, "Get cloth around you
You dough-image, this sort of game's finished.
We sailed up wind of the flesh before you were sleeping
And near the fires. She's been asleep, Lazarus,
And hasn't heard the world change. Where are you going?"
He answered calmly in the earthy voice: "The little one's dead.
I heard my son. Keep the quiet while I look at her."
He entered the dim room, the lamp had burned dim,
Faith cried behind him, "What quiet? There's none in the place.
They tip the tables over and dance the pictures,
And they'll have picked her out of the bed and hung her in the air
Shining: the quiet." But he sat where his son
Had sat crying by the bedside, and very gravely
Gazed at the face, the small gray and deformed
Features in the dim gold frame of the hair. Natalia
Entered the room, she had somewhat covered herself,
Maruca helping; but Faith stood by the door,
Her hands pressed on her thighs, visibly shaking,
Thrusting with the chin and the lean throat. Old Morhead
Said very gravely: "It is a pity. Good child.
Though all its playtime's over it was saved something.
We'll take it up with us." Natalia leaned over him

With insane picking fingers, twitched back the covers
Slid up the linen to the breast of the little body,
"See here, see here grandfather, I had good reason.
She had a wound do you see in the eye of the body,
When they grow up it turns a running ulcer
And all that have it are unhappy." He answered with patience,
Not restraining the crazy hands, "What you suffer Natalia,
Though two are worse than one for a woman, would seem
A very little toward the end. I have studied suffering
While I was dead up in the air, and before,
When I lived free: I have studied life and I find
Nothing ever very terrible. But now we've been called?"
Natalia pushing him with her shoulder leaned low
Over the bed and saw and smelled the wet stain
Under the little thighs, the bladder had emptied
In the struggle at death: the odor and the stain pierced
Like spears through her veiled brain, the child's dear babyhood,
Her own awed care and love remembered came flooding
Back on the broken mind and she flung herself
Like water on the dead, her wordless and wild crying
Like flesh torture-disjointed. Faith Heriot looked in
And called through it "Take off your hand Lazarus.
No fondling, we have nothing to do with each other, we are all turned up
Like needles to the north to the black may-pole
Stands on the mountain." He rose trembling, she saw
The waggle of the white beard against the dark lamplight,
And the drained eyes. As much as his were drained out
Hers filled with power, and her throat. "Come on old scarecrow,
Born at the wrong end of the horn, old baby,
You know what you were brought out for. And you Natalia,
I loved you once: but at the vile end, when it sticks,
Then we must turn to God. Take Rachel up to him,
He'll make it live, this old Lazarus was dead

Two or three years and look at him." Natalia looked up:
"Is he good, grandfather?" He answered groaning "No matter.
Starving people can't ask. Dawn's here." Faith Heriot
Exulted and cried: "He calls the dances, he is the column,
Come up to the stone on the hill. He is what women
And drained old men want in their dreams,
What the empty bodies howl for. I made a false one
And look at the woman!" Natalia stood up and said
With hollowed eyes across the twilights, the doubled
And mixed, the gray window and the murk lamp:
"I wish that the air were sudden poison, and the sun
Blind, and the black sea piled over the mountains.
I wish the wind that roars on the shaking glass
Were a sword in our throats. They ought to have it cut off them
When they're born, we'd be quieter. I wish that the rock
Would split and vomit, fountains of twisted fire
Catch the spirit with the life: that everything moving
Or feeling between the stars and the center were silent.
That every baby in the world were like this baby.
Take me to the God." Old Morhead, his face like scribbled paper
With three round holes burnt through it, leaned over on the bed,
On the head-boards of the bed, his left leg suddenly
Failing under him; he seemed to pray and it straightened,
And he said "We need saving." But Faith to Natalia,
Who stooped and gathered to her breast the dead child:
"I don't know you. I don't know what you are.
We're going to the hill. I've learned what *I* am." Maruca
Helped Natalia on the stairs; Faith helped old Morhead.

XXX

Back in the heart of the seamed mountain of the night Barclay
Returned to his awakened people. Some of the people

Were huddled in groups without a center, having no power to look to; others gathered their gear
Hastily, in fear the flame creep windward; a few ran on the mountain beating the fainter fire-lines
With broken branches, crying to each other through the red smoke in vain. Barclay leaped up to a broken
Farm-wagon on the bare hill crying, "I am all these things: I am the storm and the fire:
What ailed you to scatter? Because I was not here at your head? I was here at your head.
You blind saw but the fires and did not know me, you deaf heard but the wind, you ape-descended
Unable to see God but clothed in the contemptible body of the ape. I will take you and open you,
And when you see power you will know me, when you see peace, or beat your hands on the quietness of rock,
Me, the one power. Let it burn. How could I be God
But be the dregs of contempt, the uneasy slime under the glory, be you, you navelled sicknesses
That shiver in the wind: as well as the glory: as well as the sacred flesh and spirit that panting
Adorable terror, the young bride and not a maiden to the bridegroom waiting, the very daughter to the father,
Not virgin of him: I am God and the laws are mine and the times mine: comes up on the hill, the incarnate
And perfect April of the world, the shining
Foil for the love."

April stood under him and heard her own name
Sail on the storm: her teeth grated together and she saw in her mind
A naked white degrading image of herself
Spread out on the storm like a four-pointed star

Twirl down his torrent publicly: she turned on her mother,
And her words had no breath in them and fell like sparrows
In the battering wind, but Audis answered, and April:
"You still think that I'm April. Oh mother
April is dead. *I* paddled up out of darkness.
I know death. As for April she'll be safe though I send him.
The dead have nothing to do with each other, they're turned
Like needles to the north to the black may-pole . . ." She worked inward
Among the packed bodies. He stood culprit for all the streaming
Shadows of time: Oh with the small steel tool—the power without reason
  or pity, rogue elephant
Bayed on the world's end fires . . .

Barclay looked down
And saw the mask of her face lit by the fires.
The loins and shoulders parted out of her path;
She stood in the ring of people, the horror of his love
Came down from the height.

On the firelit side of the world Onorio
  Vasquez
With his eyes like desert caves dreamed atonement: the people
Never could make peace with God:
The son of man has gone up, the God of might has come down:
Onorio Vasquez has seen in all his visions
Not one relative to life, not one within light-years
Parallel to the nature of things, and the peace in his eyes
Is like the sun shining from desert caverns.
"Now I can see what all the cruelty was for
And why the stars were not blackened when they saw the people.
The giant Christ that brought fire to his tribe, he sneaked it from heaven
And hung on the mountain pierced with splinters of rock;

The Christ that brought us love and was punished on the tree
With piercing iron: he has come from the cave fortress, from the trees of
the forest,
He has risen like a comet streaming blood and bitterness for splendor,
Man has flung down the sword, God has ungated the garden,"
He cried with his face black against the red. "But I have been virgin
All night though God commanded me to take a woman.
I saved myself virgin for the sake of my visions."

Myrtle Cartwright

On the dark side of the world, her face fire-brightened,
Her eyes like red stones in the firelight: "What is the white light
Flutters four wings in the sky, lightens from four eyes?
The double-crested wonder, the double-throated,
The marriage of white falcons in the height of the air,
Here falls a feather as white as anguish.
The daughter of man has flown from the small planet
To be mated with God, here's a dropped flamelet.
She is crucified in the air with kisses for nails
Lining the palms and foot-soles, and the lance of delight,
The dear agony of women . . ."

April Barclay

Heard no one crying, she saw the dark mountain come down, she held her
soul's life
Under the storm of the cloak; the steel savior, the life of the male spirit of
her body; knowing clearly
That if she stumbled into the pit of womanhood there was no living.
"I am Edward, father, I have come." "My dream on the mountain," he
answered, "you act nothing but echoes me." She knew then
That the young man would desire to kill his father
And never could do it. The vault of the skies of her mind

Fell into fragments, through the streaming ruin she heard the scream of her mother: that was the signal
Of the act accomplished: both-sexed can love inward,
She turned the love inward, between the small breasts
Under the cloak, planted fire easily, fired twice
Falling. But after the shock, lying on the earth
With mind wasting at peace, feeling one thing done wisely
In the vast insanity of things . . .

Barclay bent over her
And opened the cloak; the body was there but not April; he smelled the gun's breath and lifted his face
Into abstract existence; consciousness abstracted from feeling; the wires of pain-pleasure
Burned out, the ways of consciousness cleared perfectly.
Himself was the desert that he had entered; these millions of millions
Were grains of sand of himself, all present, all counted,
All known. The thing can hardly be spoken further. April was dead:
But all that passion a fable: had served the purpose.
The dead have ears but no mouths, one's like another.
They are grains of sand on the sand; the living are grains of sand on the wind; the wind crying "I want nothing,"
Neither hot nor cold, raging across the sands, not shifting a point,
Wanting *nothing*: annihilation's impossible, the dead have none: it wants, actively, *nothing*:
Annihilation's impossible, the dead have none. "I am the desert.

You
living
That worry over this dead, this is the lamb of sacrifice, why do I do these things?
Let each one take a rope of the hair for long remembrance, and then be silent. Dawn has come in.

It is not as if the matter were important. Oh, if the old woman . . .
Audis I got two children on you in spite of you before I was God: where are your children?
You had poison hidden, you were not selfish with it, you fed it to the children . . . not soon enough, mostly
They catch them in the act under Mount Venus. Annihilation's impossible, the unborn have none."

XXXI

Faith Heriot had come
And said "The old man fell down after all. Oh here's another one, here's another, Natalia." And Barclay:
"Why should you riot over the child, hack her in pieces,
For each a mouthful." And wearily: "I will gather my desert dust over my shoulders. Being God must go on.
I never turn to love them but out the blood spurts.
Come north with me, I will tell you what it is to be God. North on the cities: go along with my wind
And shepherd my devouring fire."

Audis rose from the body of April
And stood with eyes like stab-wounds but with fawning shoulders
Giving him what she had found in the cloak. "It is not empty.
I am clean in this matter." He laughed and took it, saying "Look behind you." She thought
That when her head was turned he would give her instant
Deliverance, and then himself. She turned and stood waiting,
But fell in a moment, and had not seen Natalia,
Yielding the child out of her arms to a woman
Who thought that the child slept, stoop at the guardless
Body of April, and saying "Randal he told me

She has eyes in both the breasts," tear the light clothing
From the breast down to the belly, call the wounds eyes,
And beat the flesh with her hands. Faith Heriot cried out
"Oh yes it is time," and tore her own at the throat,
Feeling the pleasure all night refused fly through her body
Like fire eating white grass.

But Maruca: "You never tamed me,
The mountain-lion under the thick slow body,
The long cat of the woods: you made me serve in the kitchen.
God came secretly and gave me a child in my womb,
The Christ of the lions, for whom I shall kill fawns
And feed him on the young of the mountains." She fled from the rest,
And cried from the oaks over the rock against dawn
The cougar's cry, and said "He has turned to love lions,
We are wise to the catnipped baits and strychnine, we shall hunt men
After the kitten is grown."

None heard her; and Barclay
Passed from among the centered madness over dead April; he had dropped the pistol
Among the bacchanal feet; Myrtle Cartwright followed him, Vasquez remained; but after a little
Vasquez and certain of the others followed also, but like shells moving,
Having shed their spirits over the girl's body in the madness at dawn.

Barclay
went down to the embers
Of the oak fires, the coals yet glowing; the flame
Roared on the mountains northward. He gathered up in his hands a heap of red coals. "Never believe

That God sitting aloof inflicts on other flesh than his own experience and wounds. But at length
I grow weary of discovery." He spilled the fire on the earth and struck his hands together, then fragments
Of blackened flesh fell from the palms. "My strength's not tapped yet. But now I remember when the earth was innocent,
Before this heresy life celled the slime. Clean rock
Suffers no wrong. But even in the ages of the beasts, before I brought down
These tree-dwellers and made them like little towers walking, and sphered the brain-vault
To a bubble of fire: there was no cruelty, no traps, the suffering
Was tolerable. Heautontimoroumenos repents." He went northward
Across the blackened waste of the hill; who followed him
Ran with the feet ahead of the body, leaning backward
Against the wind's drive.

A string of scorched cattle
Ran down toward the ocean, crossing his path. He answered them,
"Eat flesh, I have burnt the pasture. The flesh-eater's
The only honesty, pays cash, peace for a price.
Learn to quarter your butchers."

The wind tumbled him, he fell on his hands,
The burnt palms cracked and blood ran down from the fingers.
He stood until they came up to him, the few
That still followed across the black hill. He had passed his hand over his brow, the short-bearded face
Was blood and ashes, they saw it without amazement. "Pain's," he said, "the foundation. I have turned to love men.
I have gathered the souls already, you've not a soul among you. Automatisms and gusts of the nerves

Plague you, but think on the nothing
Outside the stars, the other shore of me, there's peace.
I'll save the beasts, too."

He ran northward, his followers
Tired and fell off. He alone, like a burnt pillar
Smeared with the blood of sacrifice passed across the black hills,
And then the gray ones, the fire had stopped at a valley.
He came to the road and followed it, the waste vitality
Would not be spent. When the sun stood westward he turned
Away from the light and entered Mal Paso Canyon.
At the head of the steep cleft men had mined coal
Half a century before; acres of dry thistles
Covered the place where men had labored, and Barclay
Lay down in the mouth of the black pit. After three days,
Having not tasted water, he was dying and he said:
"I want creation. The wind over the desert
Has turned and I will build again all that's gone down.
I am inexhaustible."

IV

Cawdor

1926–1928

BIRTH-DUES

Joy is a trick in the air; pleasure is merely contemptible, the dangled
Carrot the ass follows to market or precipice;
But limitary pain—the rock under the tower and the hewn coping
That takes thunder at the head of the turret—
Terrible and real. Therefore a mindless dervish carving himself
With knives will seem to have conquered the world.

The world's God is treacherous and full of unreason; a torturer, but also
The only foundation and the only fountain.
Who fights him eats his own flesh and perishes of hunger; who hides in the grave
To escape him is dead; who enters the Indian
Recession to escape him is dead; who falls in love with the God is washed clean
Of death desired and of death dreaded.

He has joy, but joy is a trick in the air; and pleasure, but pleasure is contemptible;
And peace; and is based on solider than pain.
He has broken boundaries a little and that will estrange him; he is monstrous, but not
To the measure of the God. . . . But I having told you—
However I suppose that few in the world have energy to hear effectively—
Have paid my birth-dues; am quits with the people.

THE BROKEN BALANCE

I. Reference to a Passage in Plutarch's Life of Sulla

The people buying and selling, consuming pleasures, talking in the archways,
Were all suddenly struck quiet
And ran from under stone to look up at the sky: so shrill and mournful,
So fierce and final, a brazen
Pealing of trumpets high up in the air, in the summer blue over Tuscany.
They marvelled; the soothsayers answered:
"Although the Gods are little troubled toward men, at the end of each period
A sign is declared in heaven
Indicating new times, new customs, a changed people; the Romans
Rule, and Etruria is finished;
A wise mariner will trim the sails to the wind."

I heard yesterday
So shrill and mournful a trumpet-blast,
It was hard to be wise. . . . You must eat change and endure; not be much troubled
For the people; they will have their happiness.
When the republic grows too heavy to endure, then Caesar will carry it;
When life grows hateful, there's power . . .

II. To the Children

Power's good; life is not always good but power's good.
So you must think when abundance
Makes pawns of people and all the loaves are one dough.

The steep singleness of passion
Dies; they will say, "What was that?" but the power triumphs.
Loveliness will live under glass
And beauty will go savage in the secret mountains.
There is beauty in power also.
You children must widen your minds' eyes to take mountains
Instead of faces, and millions
Instead of persons; not to hate life; and massed power
After the lone hawk's dead.

III

That light blood-loving weasel, a tongue of yellow
Fire licking the sides of the gray stones,
Has a more passionate and more pure heart
In the snake-slender flanks than man can imagine;
But he is betrayed by his own courage,
The man who kills him is like a cloud hiding a star.

Then praise the jewel-eyed hawk and the tall blue heron;
The black cormorants that fatten their sea-rock
With shining slime; even that ruiner of anthills
The red-shafted woodpecker flying,
A white star between blood-color wing-clouds,
Across the glades of the wood and the green lakes of shade.

These live their felt natures; they know their norm
And live it to the brim; they understand life.
While men moulding themselves to the anthill have choked
Their natures until the souls die in them;
They have sold themselves for toys and protection:
No, but consider awhile: what else? Men sold for toys.

Uneasy and fractional people, having no center
But in the eyes and mouths that surround them,
Having no function but to serve and support
Civilization, the enemy of man,
No wonder they live insanely, and desire
With their tongues, progress; with their eyes, pleasure; with their hearts,
death.

Their ancestors were good hunters, good herdsmen and swordsmen,
But now the world is turned upside down;
The good do evil, the hope's in criminals; in vice
That dissolves the cities and war to destroy them.
Through wars and corruptions the house will fall.
Mourn whom it falls on. Be glad: the house is mined, it will fall.

IV

Rain, hail and brutal sun, the plow in the roots,
The pitiless pruning-iron in the branches,
Strengthen the vines, they are all feeding friends
Or powerless foes until the grapes purple.
But when you have ripened your berries it is time to begin to perish.

The world sickens with change, rain becomes poison,
The earth is a pit, it is time to perish.
The vines are fey, the very kindness of nature
Corrupts what her cruelty before strengthened.
When you stand on the peak of time it is time to begin to perish.

Reach down the long morbid roots that forget the plow,
Discover the depths; let the long pale tendrils
Spend all to discover the sky, now nothing is good

But only the steel mirrors of discovery . . .
And the beautiful enormous dawns of time, after we perish.

V

Mourning the broken balance, the hopeless prostration of the earth
Under men's hands and their minds,
The beautiful places killed like rabbits to make a city,
The spreading fungus, the slime-threads
And spores; my own coast's obscene future: I remember the farther
Future, and the last man dying
Without succession under the confident eyes of the stars.
It was only a moment's accident,
The race that plagued us; the world resumes the old lonely immortal
Splendor; from here I can even
Perceive that that snuffed candle had something . . . a fantastic virtue,
A faint and unshapely pathos . . .
So death will flatter them at last: what, even the bald ape's by-shot
Was moderately admirable?

VI. Palinode

All summer neither rain nor wave washes the cormorants'
Perch, and their droppings have painted it shining white.
If the excrement of fish-eaters makes the brown rock a snow-mountain
At noon, a rose in the morning, a beacon at moonrise
On the black water: it is barely possible that even men's present
Lives are something; their arts and sciences (by moonlight)
Not wholly ridiculous, nor their cities merely an offense.

VII

Under my windows, between the road and the sea-cliff, bitter wild grass
Stands narrowed between the people and the storm.
The ocean winter after winter gnaws at its earth, the wheels and the feet
Summer after summer encroach and destroy.
Stubborn green life, for the cliff-eater I cannot comfort you, ignorant which color,
Gray-blue or pale-green, will please the late stars;
But laugh at the other, your seed shall enjoy wonderful vengeances and suck
The arteries and walk in triumph on the faces.

HURT HAWKS

I

The broken pillar of the wing jags from the clotted shoulder,
The wing trails like a banner in defeat,
No more to use the sky forever but live with famine
And pain a few days: cat nor coyote
Will shorten the week of waiting for death, there is game without talons.
He stands under the oak-bush and waits
The lame feet of salvation; at night he remembers freedom
And flies in a dream, the dawns ruin it.
He is strong and pain is worse to the strong, incapacity is worse.
The curs of the day come and torment him
At distance, no one but death the redeemer will humble that head,
The intrepid readiness, the terrible eyes.
The wild God of the world is sometimes merciful to those
That ask mercy, not often to the arrogant.
You do not know him, you communal people, or you have forgotten him;
Intemperate and savage, the hawk remembers him;
Beautiful and wild, the hawks, and men that are dying, remember him.

II

I'd sooner, except the penalties, kill a man than a hawk; but the great
redtail
Had nothing left but unable misery
From the bones too shattered for mending, the wing that trailed under his
talons when he moved.
We had fed him six weeks, I gave him freedom,
He wandered over the foreland hill and returned in the evening, asking for
death,

Not like a beggar, still eyed with the old
Implacable arrogance. I gave him the lead gift in the twilight. What fell was relaxed,
Owl-downy, soft feminine feathers; but what
Soared: the fierce rush: the night-herons by the flooded river cried fear at its rising
Before it was quite unsheathed from reality.

THE HUMANIST'S TRAGEDY

Not like a beast borne on the flood of passion, boat without oars, but mindful of all his dignity
As human being, a king and a Greek, King Pentheus: "Tell him that we will reverence the Gods we have,
But not minded to increase the burden. What new ones ship raging like beasts from Asia by the islands
We've whips for, here in Thebes. Tell him to take his magic-drunken women and be off." The messenger
Went up to the mountain wood; needles of pine stuck in the sandal-straps of the man returning
At noon and saying: "He could not hear me O King. I shouted aloud, clothed in the king's authority,
Showing him the wand I carried; the God's . . . I say the stranger's . . . eyes like blue ice looked through my body
As if I had been an open window in the breast of a wall. He bored through me toward Thebes and answered
Not me, the raging laughing women: 'They have Isemenus to drink of and Dirce and all the fountains,
Must they have wine too?' What more he said, my lord, I cannot remember. But I, having seen more
Than I dare tell, turned home." "Ten spearmen" the king answered biting the bearded lip, "will do it.
What more saw you? Dread not to tell, obscene or magic. We are master of ourself as of this people.
Not like a beast borne on the flood of passion, boat without oars, but mindful of all our dignity
As human being, a king and a Greek: no random lightning of anger will stab the messenger. We're sane still
Though the air swarms." The messenger: "My lord, my lord . . ." And the king: "Out with it." "The lady Agave my lord."

"Our mother," the king answered frowning. " — Was in the mountain with
the other women, dancing adoring."

King Pentheus' knuckles, of the hand that held the long
Smooth-shaven staff tipped with the head of a man carved in pale ivory,
whitened, and the hand reddened
Under the scant stipple of black hair. More than that was no motion.
"Well, she was in the mountain,"
He answered, "my mother was there," the king housing his wrath in hard
self-mastery. He had the chariot
Horsed, and rode swiftly toward Cythaeron; the glens and slope bristled
with forest. In a glade he found them.
He had come alone; the charioteer stayed by the sweating horses.

Without
awe, without pleasure,
As a man spies on noxious beasts, he standing hidden spied on the rabid
choir of the God.
They had pine-cone-tipped wands, they went half naked, they were hoarse
with insane song; foam from their mouths, mingled
With wine and sweat, ran down their bodies. O fools, boats without oars
borne on the flood of passion,
Forgetting utterly all the dignity of man, the pride of the only
self-commanding animal,
That captains his own soul and controls even
Fate, for a space. The only animal that turns means to an end. "What end?
Oh, but what end?"
It cried under his mind, "Increase the city? Subdue the earth? Breed slaves
and cattle, and one's own
Off-shots, fed and secure? Ah fruitful-fruitless
Generations forever and ever. . . . For pleasure" — he spat on the earth —
"the slight collectible pleasure

Surplus to pain?" Then recollecting all his dignity as human being, a king and a Greek,
He heard with hostile ears the hoarse and beastlike choir of the worshippers: "O sisters we have found an opening,
We have hewn in the stone and mortar
A wild strait gate-way;
Slit eyes in the mask, sisters,
Entered the mountain.
We shall be sad to-morrow when the wine dies,
The God dies from our blood;
To-day in the forest
We are fire and have found an opening."
His own mother Agave singing. Endure a little. If one could understand their fountain
Of madness. Her shame to-morrow: not punishment enough: prison in the house. "O sisters we have found an opening":
What opening?

The boys from Thebes to be whipped, the Theban women shut up a fortnight, the God and his Thracian
Satyrs and women . . . "The generations," he thought suddenly, "aspire. They better; they climb; as I
Am better than this weak suggestible woman my mother. Had I forgotten a moment the end
Of being? To increase the power, collectedness and dignity of man. — A more collected and dignified
Creature," he groaned, "to die and stink."

That moment like a tall ship breasting through water the God
Passed, the high head, the shining hair and the blond shoulders, trailing a wake of ecstasy like foam

Across the multitude of faces like waves, his frantic worshippers. He anchored among them smiling
In the wild midst, and said softly: "When you are dead you become part of peace; let no man
Dream more of death; there is neither sight nor hearing nor any wonder; none of us Gods enters it.
You become part of peace, part of the sacred beauty, but *having* no part: as if a flute-player
Should make beauty but hear none, being deaf and senseless. But living if you will
It is possible for you to break prison of yourselves and enter the nature of things and use the beauty.
Wine and lawlessness, art and music, love, self-torture, religion,
Are means but are not needful, contemplation will do it. Only to break human collectedness.
The least shepherd on Cythaeron, if he dares, might do it. But you being neophyte all, Thracians and Thebans,
Are indeed somewhat wild, somewhat too drunken."

King Pentheus then,
seeing his enemy, but ever
Stately mindful of all his dignity, as human being, a king and a Greek, entered among them
Angrily to fetch his mother. Agave cried out,
"Sisters: a lion stalking us, a wild beast of the pinewood, or is it a wolf?" She leading eagerly,
Full of the courage that the God had taught them, rushed on her son not known, and the others raging
Joined her; the frantic voices, the tearing fingers, the teeth and the madness . . .

The God and his people went down
Toward Thebes, Agave dancing before them, the head of her son the
triumph in her hands, the beard and the blood:
"A lion I have killed in the mountain,
Thebans the head of a lion my own hands hunted,
With my hands, a lion!"

THE DEAD MEN'S CHILD

The track across the desert runs vague toward the north star and then more firmly
Along the clipped butt of the mountain; it curves into a bay of the cliff, where natural cisterns
Keep water in the streaked rock; the people call them *las tinajas altas* — the high water-jars —
Which every second or third summer a thunderstorm
Fills with clear life; if the lowest is empty one must climb to the next. There is a worked-out silver-mine
Gouged in the cliff beyond them; a single ironwood tree lives on the leakage below them, and here
Men used to camp, coming up from Mexico.

A train of smugglers was lost here long ago. It is said
The tanks were dry then except the highest, and men who wanted the smugglers' goods bailed that one empty,
And ambushed up the mountain, defended it with their rifles. For half the furnace morning the thirsty
Fought up to reach it; when they won it at length it was found dry. The horses could not go on,
They died, and the men died, of thirst and their wounds.

Across the trail, opposite the ironwood tree,
Stands a low mound of rock and sand, where later travellers
Deposited the parched and mummied companions and spread them over with a sheet of sand; there had been already
Two or three graves dug in that barrow. The desert wind respected none of these burials, the sun

And wind played with the bones and flesh until they were dust of the barrow.

A good while later, men found
A vein of silver in the cliff and opened the mine. A little encampment grew up, Mexican laborers
Came with their wives and black-eyed children. One saint's day evening some of the younger people of the camp
Made fire on the mound of half forgotten dead men, opposite the ironwood tree. They ate and drank there
In a circle about the flame, under the desert stars. Rosaria Rivas was one of the girls
In that company; after some months she was found pregnant. She told her parents that when the fire
Died down and the others departed she had remained on the place. In the night chill she had drawn her skirt
(Being all alone) above her knees to warm them at the red embers, then suddenly a swirl of wind
From the east blew dust and ashes into her unsheltered body. So by mere ignorant accident Rosaria
Conceived a child, neither for pleasure nor kindness, only by the innocent malice of the dark wind
Driving the dust of the dead. Her story was easily
Believed; the more because she had little reason for lying. Morality was not so enviously strict
Among them that love had to go masked. Her child was born the due tenth moon after that saint's day,
And she was much pitied, having the pain without the pleasure. But people soon perceived that her son
Was only a little different from other children; they all are mongrels between the present and the past,

Their natures drawing as much from men and beasts long dead as from
either parent. Yet in time this child
Of the dust of dead men proved his quality. He throve in fortune; he was
never duped nor reckless; his life
Ran smooth because he had nothing *future* about him. Men do not stumble
on bones mostly but on seeds,
And this young man was not of the sad race of Prometheus, to waste
himself in favor of the future.

FAWN'S FOSTER-MOTHER

The old woman sits on a bench before the door and quarrels
With her meagre pale demoralized daughter.
Once when I passed I found her alone, laughing in the sun
And saying that when she was first married
She lived in the old farmhouse up Garapatas Canyon.
(It is empty now, the roof has fallen
But the log walls hang on the stone foundation; the redwoods
Have all been cut down, the oaks are standing;
The place is now more solitary than ever before.)
"When I was nursing my second baby
My husband found a day-old fawn hid in a fern-brake
And brought it; I put its mouth to the breast
Rather than let it starve, I had milk enough for three babies.
Hey how it sucked, the little nuzzler,
Digging its little hoofs like quills into my stomach.
I had more joy from that than from the others."
Her face is deformed with age, furrowed like a bad road
With market-wagons, mean cares and decay.
She is thrown up to the surface of things, a cell of dry skin
Soon to be shed from the earth's old eye-brows,
I see that once in her spring she lived in the streaming arteries,
The stir of the world, the music of the mountain.

BIXBY'S LANDING

They burned lime on the hill and dropped it down here in an iron car
On a long cable; here the ships warped in
And took their loads from the engine, the water is deep to the cliff. The car
Hangs half way over in the gape of the gorge,
Stationed like a north star above the peaks of the redwoods, iron perch
For the little red hawks when they cease from hovering
When they've struck prey; the spider's fling of a cable rust-glued to the pulleys.
The laborers are gone, but what a good multitude
Is here in return: the rich-lichened rock, the rose-tipped stone-crop, the constant
Ocean's voices, the cloud-lighted space.
The kilns are cold on the hill but here in the rust of the broken boiler
Quick lizards lighten, and a rattle-snake flows
Down the cracked masonry, over the crumbled fire-brick. In the rotting timbers
And roofless platforms all the free companies
Of windy grasses have root and make seed; wild buckwheat blooms in the fat
Weather-slacked lime from the bursted barrels.
Two duckhawks darting in the sky of their cliff-hung nest are the voice of the headland.
Wine-hearted solitude, our mother the wilderness,
Men's failures are often as beautiful as men's triumphs, but your returnings
Are even more precious than your first presence.

THE SUMMIT REDWOOD

Only stand high a long enough time your lightning will come; that is what blunts the peaks of redwoods;
But this old tower of life on the hilltop has taken it more than twice a century, this knows in every
Cell the salty and the burning taste, the shudder and the voice.

The fire
from heaven; it has felt the earth's too
Roaring up hill in autumn, thorned oak-leaves tossing their bright ruin to the bitter laurel-leaves, and all
Its under-forest has died and died, and lives to be burnt; the redwood has lived. Though the fire entered,
It cored the trunk while the sapwood increased. The trunk is a tower, the bole of the trunk is a black cavern,
The mast of the trunk with its green boughs the mountain stars are strained through
Is like the helmet-spike on the highest head of an army; black on lit blue or hidden in cloud
It is like the hill's finger in heaven. And when the cloud hides it, though in barren summer, the boughs
Make their own rain.

Old Escobar had a cunning trick when he stole
beef. He and his grandsons
Would drive the cow up here to a starlight death and hoist the carcass into the tree's hollow,
Then let them search his cabin he could smile for pleasure, to think of his meat hanging secure
Exalted over the earth and the ocean, a theft like a star, secret against the supreme sky.

AN ARTIST

That sculptor we knew, the passionate-eyed son of a quarryman,
Who astonished Rome and Paris in his meteor youth and then was gone, at his high tide of triumphs,
Without reason or good-bye: I have seen him again lately, after twenty years, but not in Europe.

In desert hills I rode a horse slack-kneed with thirst. Down a steep slope a dancing swarm
Of yellow butterflies over a shining rock made me hope water. We slid down to the place,
The spring was bitter but the horse drank. I imagined wearings of an old path from that wet rock
Ran down the canyon; I followed, soon they were lost, I came to a stone valley in which it seemed
No man nor his mount had ever ventured, you wondered whether even a vulture'd ever spread sail there.
There were stones of strange form under a cleft in the far hill; I tethered the horse to a rock
And scrambled over. A heap like a stone torrent, a moraine,
But monstrously formed limbs of broken carving appeared in the rock-fall, enormous breasts, defaced heads
Of giants, the eyes calm through the brute veils of fracture. It was natural then to climb higher and go in
Up the cleft gate. The canyon was a sheer-walled crack winding at the entrance, but around its bend
The walls grew dreadful with stone giants, presences growing out of the rigid precipice, that strove
In dream between stone and life, intense to cast their chaos . . . or to enter and return . . . stone-fleshed, nerve-stretched

Great bodies ever more beautiful and more heavy with pain, they seemed leading to some unbearable
Consummation of the ecstasy . . . but there, troll among Titans, the bearded master of the place accosted me
In a cold anger, a mallet in his hand, filthy and ragged. There was no kindness in that man's mind,
But after he had driven me down to the entrance he spoke a little.

The
merciless sun had found the slot now
To hide in, and lit for the wick of that stone lamp-bowl a sky almost, I thought, abominably beautiful;
While our lost artist we used to admire: for now I knew him: spoke of his passion.

He said, "Marble?
White marble is fit to model a snow-mountain: let man be modest. Nor bronze: I am bound to have my tool
In my material, no irrelevances. I found this pit of dark-gray freestone, fine-grained, and tough enough
To make sketches that under any weathering will last my lifetime. . . .

The town is eight miles off, I can fetch food and no one follows me home. I have water and a cave
Here; and no possible lack of material. I need, therefore, nothing. As to companions, I make them.
And models? They are seldom wanted; I know a Basque shepherd I sometimes use; and a woman of the town.
What more? Sympathy? Praise? I have never desired them and also I have never deserved them. I will not show you
More than the spalls you saw by accident.

What I see is the enormous
beauty of things, but what I attempt
Is nothing to that. I am helpless toward that.
It is only to form in stone the mould of some ideal humanity that might be
worthy to *be*
Under that lightning. Animalcules that God (if he were given to laughter)
might omit to laugh at.

Those children of my hands are tortured because they feel," he said, "the
storm of the outer magnificence.
They are giants in agony. They have seen from my eyes
The man-destroying beauty of the dawns over their notch yonder, and all
the obliterating stars.
But in their eyes they have peace. I have lived a little and I think
Peace marrying pain alone can breed that excellence in the luckless race
might make it decent
To exist at all on the star-lit stone breast.

I hope," he said, "that when I
grow old and the chisel drops,
I may crawl out on a ledge of the rock and die like a wolf."

These
fragments are all I can remember,
These in the flare of the desert evening. Having been driven so brutally
forth I never returned;
Yet I respect him enough to keep his name and the place secret. I hope that
some other traveller
May stumble on that ravine of Titans after their maker has died. While he
lives, let him alone.

JULY FOURTH BY THE OCEAN

The continent's a tamed ox, with all its mountains,
Powerful and servile; here is for plowland, here is for park and playground, this helpless
Cataract for power; it lies behind us at heel
All docile between this ocean and the other. If flood troubles the lowlands, or earthquake
Cracks walls, it is only a slave's blunder or the natural
Shudder of a new made slave. Therefore we happy masters about the solstice
Light bonfires on the shore and celebrate our power.
The bay's necklaced with fire, the bombs make crystal fountains in the air, the rockets
Shower swan's-neck over the night water. . . . I imagined
The stars drew apart a little as if from troublesome children, coldly compassionate;
But the ocean neither seemed astonished nor in awe:
If this had been the little sea that Xerxes whipped, how it would have feared us.

THE MACHINE

The little biplane that has the river-meadow for landing-field
And carries passengers brief rides,
Buzzed overhead on the tender blue above the orange of sundown.
Below it five troubled night-herons
Turned short over the shore from its course, four east, one northward.
  Beyond them
Swam the new moon in amber.
I don't know why, but lately the forms of things appear to me with time
One of their visible dimensions.
The thread brightness of the bent moon appeared enormous, unnumbered
Ages of years; the night-herons
Their natural size, they have croaked over the shore in the hush at sundown
Much longer than human language
Has fumbled with the air: but the plane having no past but a certain future,
Insect in size as in form,
Was also accepted, all these forms of power placed without preference
In the grave arrangement of the evening.

ON BUILDING WITH STONE

To be an ape in little of the mountain-making mother
Like swarthy Cheops, but my own hands
For only slaves, is a far sweeter toil than to cut
Passions in verse for a sick people.
I'd liefer bed one boulder in the house-wall than be the time's
Archilochus: we name not Homer: who now
Can even imagine the fabulous dawn when bay-leaves (to a blind
Beggar) were not bitter in the teeth?

TO A YOUNG ARTIST

It is good for strength not to be merciful
To its own weakness, good for the deep urn to run over, good to explore
The peaks and the deeps, who can endure it,
Good to be hurt, who can be healed afterward: but you that have whetted consciousness
Too bitter an edge, too keenly daring,
So that the color of a leaf can make you tremble and your own thoughts like harriers
Tear the live mind: were your bones mountains,
Your blood rivers to endure it? and all that labor of discipline labors to death.
Delight is exquisite, pain is more present;
You have sold the armor, you have bought shining with burning, one should be stronger than strength
To fight baresark in the stabbing field
In the rage of the stars: I tell you unconsciousness is the treasure, the tower, the fortress;
Referred to that one may live anything;
The temple and the tower: poor dancer on the flints and shards in the temple porches, turn home.

MEDITATION ON SAVIORS

I

When I considered it too closely, when I wore it like an element and smelt it like water,
Life is become less lovely, the net nearer than the skin, a little troublesome, a little terrible.

I pledged myself awhile ago not to seek refuge, neither in death nor in a walled garden,
In lies nor gated loyalties, nor in the gates of contempt, that easily lock the world out of doors.

Here on the rock it is great and beautiful, here on the foam-wet granite sea-fang it is easy to praise
Life and water and the shining stones: but whose cattle are the herds of the people that one should love them?

If they were yours, then you might take a cattle-breeder's delight in the herds of the future. Not yours.
Where the power ends let love, before it sours to jealousy. Leave the joys of government to Caesar.

Who is born when the world wanes, when the brave soul of the world falls on decay in the flesh increasing
Comes one with a great level mind, sufficient vision, sufficient blindness, and clemency for love.

This is the breath of rottenness I smelt; from the world waiting, stalled between storms, decaying a little,

Bitterly afraid to be hurt, but knowing it cannot draw the savior Caesar but out of the blood-bath.

The apes of Christ lift up their hands to praise love: but wisdom without love is the present savior,
Power without hatred, mind like a many-bladed machine subduing the world with deep indifference.

The apes of Christ itch for a sickness they have never known; words and the little envies will hardly
Measure against that blinding fire behind the tragic eyes they have never dared to confront.

II

Point Lobos lies over the hollowed water like a humped whale swimming to shoal; Point Lobos
Was wounded with that fire; the hills at Point Sur endured it; the palace at Thebes; the hill Calvary.

Out of incestuous love power and then ruin. A man forcing the imaginations of men,
Possessing with love and power the people: a man defiling his own household with impious desire.

King Oedipus reeling blinded from the palace doorway, red tears pouring from the torn pits
Under the forehead; and the young Jew writhing on the domed hill in the earthquake, against the eclipse

Frightfully uplifted for having turned inward to love the people: — that root was so sweet O dreadful agonist? —

I saw the same pierced feet, that walked in the same crime to its expiation;
I heard the same cry.

A bad mountain to build your world on. Am I another keeper of the people, that on my own shore,
On the gray rock, by the grooved mass of the ocean, the sicknesses I left behind me concern me?

Here where the surf has come incredible ways out of the splendid west, over the deeps
Light nor life sounds forever; here where enormous sundowns flower and burn through color to quietness;

Then the ecstasy of the stars is present? As for the people, I have found my rock, let them find theirs.
Let them lie down at Caesar's feet and be saved; and he in his time reap their daggers of gratitude.

III

Yet I am the one made pledges against the refuge contempt, that easily locks the world out of doors.
This people as much as the sea-granite is part of the God from whom I desire not to be fugitive.

I see them: they are always crying. The shored Pacific makes perpetual music, and the stone mountains
Their music of silence, the stars blow long pipings of light: the people are always crying in their hearts.

One need not pity; certainly one must not love. But who has seen peace, if he should tell them where peace

Lives in the world . . . they would be powerless to understand; and he is not willing to be reinvolved.

IV

How should one caught in the stone of his own person dare tell the people anything but relative to that?
But if a man could hold in his mind all the conditions at once, of man and woman, of civilized

And barbarous, of sick and well, of happy and under torture, of living and dead, of human and not
Human, and dimly all the human future: — what should persuade him to speak? And what could his words change?

The mountain ahead of the world is not forming but fixed. But the man's words would be fixed also,
Part of that mountain, under equal compulsion; under the same present compulsion in the iron consistency.

And nobody sees good or evil but out of a brain a hundred centuries quieted, some desert
Prophet's, a man humped like a camel, gone mad between the mud-walled village and the mountain sepulchres.

V

Broad wagons before sunrise bring food into the city from the open farms, and the people are fed.
They import and they consume reality. Before sunrise a hawk in the desert made them their thoughts.

VI

Here is an anxious people, rank with suppressed bloodthirstiness. Among the mild and unwarlike
Gautama needed but live greatly and be heard, Confucius needed but live greatly and be heard:

This people has not outgrown blood-sacrifice, one must writhe on the high cross to catch at their memories;
The price is known. I have quieted love; for love of the people I would not do it. For power I would do it.

— But that stands against reason: what is power to a dead man, dead under torture? — What is power to a man
Living, after the flesh is content? Reason is never a root, neither of act nor desire.

For power living I would never do it; they are not delightful to touch, one wants to be separate. For power
After the nerves are put away underground, to lighten the abstract unborn children toward peace . . .

A man might have paid anguish indeed. Except he had found the standing sea-rock that even this last
Temptation breaks on; quieter than death but lovelier; peace that quiets the desire even of praising it.

VII

Yet look: are they not pitiable? No: if they lived forever they would be pitiable:

But a huge gift reserved quite overwhelms them at the end; they are able
then to be still and not cry.

And having touched a little of the beauty and seen a little of the beauty of
things, magically grow
Across the funeral fire or the hidden stench of burial themselves into the
beauty they admired,

Themselves into the God, themselves into the sacred steep unconsciousness
they used to mimic
Asleep between lamp's death and dawn, while the last drunkard stumbled
homeward down the dark street.

They are not to be pitied but very fortunate; they need no savior, salvation
comes and takes them by force,
It gathers them into the great kingdoms of dust and stone, the blown
storms, the stream's-end ocean.

With this advantage over their granite grave-marks, of having realized the
petulant human consciousness
Before, and then the greatness, the peace: drunk from both pitchers: these
to be pitied? These not fortunate?

But while he lives let each man make his health in his mind, to love the
coast opposite humanity
And so be freed of love, laying it like bread on the waters; it is worst turned
inward, it is best shot farthest.

Love, the mad wine of good and evil, the saint's and murderer's, the mote
in the eye that makes its object
Shine the sun black; the trap in which it is better to catch the inhuman
God than the hunter's own image.

THE BIRD WITH THE DARK PLUMES

The bird with the dark plumes in my blood,
That never for one moment however I patched my truces
Consented to make peace with the people,
It is pitiful now to watch her pleasure in a breath of tempest
Breaking the sad promise of spring.
Are these that morose hawk's wings, vaulting, a mere mad swallow's,
The snow-shed peak, the violent precipice?
Poor outlaw that would not value their praise do you prize their blame?
"Their liking" she said "was a long creance,
But let them be kind enough to hate me that opens the sky."
It is almost as foolish my poor falcon
To want hatred as to want love; and harder to win.

CONTRAST

The world has many seas, Mediterranean, Atlantic, but here is the shore
  of the one ocean.
And here the heavy future hangs like a cloud; the enormous scene; the
  enormous games preparing
Weigh on the water and strain the rock; the stage is here, the play is
  conceived; the players are not found.

I saw on the Sierras, up the Kaweah valley above the Moro rock, the
  mountain redwoods
Like red towers on the slopes of snow; about their bases grew a bushery of
  Christmas green,
Firs and pines to be monuments for pilgrimage
In Europe; I remembered the Swiss forests, the dark robes of Pilatus, no
  trunk like these there;
But these are underwood; they are only a shrubbery about the boles of the
  trees.

Our people are clever and masterful;
They have powers in the mass, they accomplish marvels. It is possible Time
  will make them before it annuls them, but at present
There is not one memorable person, there is not one mind to stand with
  the trees, one life with the mountains.

ASCENT TO THE SIERRAS

Beyond the great valley an odd instinctive rising
Begins to possess the ground, the flatness gathers to little humps and barrows, low aimless ridges,
A sudden violence of rock crowns them. The crowded orchards end, they have come to a stone knife;
The farms are finished; the sudden foot of the sierra. Hill over hill, snow-ridge beyond mountain gather
The blue air of their height about them.

Here at the foot of the pass
The fierce clans of the mountain you'd think for thousands of years,
Men with harsh mouths and eyes like the eagles' hunger,
Have gathered among these rocks at the dead hour
Of the morning star and the stars waning
To raid the plain and at moonrise returning driven
Their scared booty to the highlands, the tossing horns
And glazed eyes in the light of torches. The men have looked back
Standing above these rock-heads to bark laughter
At the burning granaries and the farms and the town
That sow the dark flat land with terrible rubies . . . lighting the dead . . .

It is not true: from this land
The curse was lifted; the highlands have kept peace with the valleys; no blood in the sod; there is no old sword
Keeping grim rust, no primal sorrow. The people are all one people, their homes never knew harrying;
The tribes before them were acorn-eaters, harmless as deer. Oh fortunate earth: you must find someone
To make you bitter music; how else will you take bonds of the future, against the wolf in men's hearts?

A REDEEMER

The road had steepened and the sun sharpened on the high ridges; the stream probably was dry,
Certainly not to be come to down the pit of the canyon. We stopped for water at the one farm
In all that mountain. The trough was cracked with drought, the moss on the boards dead, but an old dog
Rose like a wooden toy at the house-door silently. I said "There will be water somewhere about,"
And when I knocked a man showed us a spring of water. Though his hair was nearly white I judged him
Forty years old at most. His eyes and voice were muted. It is likely he kept his hands hidden,
I failed to see them until we had dipped the spring. He stood then on the lip of the great slope
And looked westward over an incredible country to the far hills that dammed the sea-fog: it billowed
Above them, cascaded over them, it never crossed them, gray standing flood. He stood gazing, his hands
Were clasped behind him; I caught a glimpse of serous red under the fingers, and looking sharply
When they drew apart saw that both hands were wounded. I said "Your hands are hurt." He twitched them from sight,
But after a moment having earnestly eyed me displayed them. The wounds were in the hearts of the palms,
Pierced to the backs like stigmata of crucifixion. The horrible raw flesh protruded, glistening
And granular, not scabbed, nor a sign of infection. "These are old wounds."
He answered, "Yes. They don't heal." He stood
Moving his lips in silence, his back against that fabulous basin of mountains, fold beyond fold,

Patches of forest and scarps of rock, high domes of dead gray pasture and gray beds of dry rivers,
Clear and particular in the burning air, too bright to appear real, to the last range
The fog from the ocean like a stretched compacted thunderstorm overhung; and he said gravely:
"I pick them open. I made them long ago with a clean steel. It is only a little to pay—"
He stretched and flexed the fingers, I saw his sunburnt lips whiten in a line, compressed together,
"If only it proves enough for a time—to save so many." I searched his face for madness but that
Is often invisible, a subtle spirit. "There never," he said, "was any people earned so much ruin.
I love them, I am trying to suffer for them. It would be bad if I should die, I am careful
Against excess." "You think of the wounds," I said, "of Jesus?" He laughed angrily and frowned, stroking
The fingers of one hand with the other. "Religion is the people's opium. Your little Jew-God?
My pain" he said with pride "is voluntary.
They have done what never was done before. Not as a people takes a land to love it and be fed,
A little, according to need and love, and again a little; sparing the country tribes, mixing
Their blood with theirs, their minds with all the rocks and rivers, their flesh with the soil: no, without hunger
Wasting the world and your own labor, without love possessing, not even your hands to the dirt but plows
Like blades of knives; heartless machines; houses of steel: using and despising the patient earth . . .

Oh as a rich man eats a forest for profit and a field for vanity, so you came west and raped
The continent and brushed its people to death. Without need, the weak skirmishing hunters, and without mercy.
Well, God's a scare-crow, no vengeance out of old rags. But there are acts breeding their own reversals
In their own bellies from the first day. I am here" he said—and broke off suddenly and said "They take horses
And give them sicknesses through hollow needles, their blood saves babies: I am here on the mountain making
Antitoxin for all the happy towns and farms, the lovely blameless children, the terrible
Arrogant cities. I used to think them terrible: their gray prosperity, their pride: from up here
Specks of mildew.

But when I am dead and all you with whole hands think of nothing but happiness,
Will you go mad and kill each other? Or horror come over the ocean on wings and cover your sun?
I wish," he said trembling, "I had never been born."

His wife came from the door while he was talking. Mine asked her quietly, "Do you live all alone here,
Are you not afraid?" "Certainly not," she answered, "he is always gentle and loving. I have no complaint
Except his groans in the night keep me awake often. But when I think of other women's
Troubles: my own daughter's: I'm older than my husband, I have been married before: deep is my peace."

TOR HOUSE

If you should look for this place after a handful of lifetimes:
Perhaps of my planted forest a few
May stand yet, dark-leaved Australians or the coast cypress, haggard
With storm-drift; but fire and the axe are devils.
Look for foundations of sea-worn granite, my fingers had the art
To make stone love stone, you will find some remnant.
But if you should look in your idleness after ten thousand years:
It is the granite knoll on the granite
And lava tongue in the midst of the bay, by the mouth of the Carmel
River-valley, these four will remain
In the change of names. You will know it by the wild sea-fragrance of wind
Though the ocean may have climbed or retired a little;
You will know it by the valley inland that our sun and our moon were born
from
Before the poles changed; and Orion in December
Evenings was strung in the throat of the valley like a lamp-lighted bridge.
Come in the morning you will see white gulls
Weaving a dance over blue water, the wane of the moon
Their dance-companion, a ghost walking
By daylight, but wider and whiter than any bird in the world.
My ghost you needn't look for; it is probably
Here, but a dark one, deep in the granite, not dancing on wind
With the mad wings and the day moon.

CAWDOR

I

In nineteen-nine a fire swept our coast hills,
But not the canyons oceanward; Cawdor's ranges
And farm were safe. He had posted sentinels,
His son George and his man Jesus Acanna,
On two hills and they watched the fire all night
Stream toward Cachagua; the big-coned inland pines
Made pillars of white flame.

Cawdor at dawn
Stood by his door and saw in the bronze light
That leaked through towers of smoke windowed with sanguine
Reflections of the burning, two does and a fawn
Spring down the creek-bed stones of his ravine
Fleeing from their terror, and then a tawny mountain-lion
With no eyes for the deer. Next walked a lame
Gray horse, a girl led it, a broken old man,
His face bound with a dirty cloth, clung weakly
To the limping withers. Cawdor recognized him
Though he was faceless, old Martial, who had got a place
In the hills two years before, a feeble old man
Marked for misfortune; his stock, the first year, sickened
With lump-jaw; when a cow died in the creek
Martial had let her lie there. Then Cawdor had ridden
And cursed him, and Cawdor with his man Acanna
Roped the horns to draw the carcass out of the stream,
But when they drew, it burst.
Now Martial came, he and his daughter Fera,

For refuge, having saved from the fire nothing
But their own lives and the lame horse.

The old man
Reeled and was dumb with pain, but the girl asked
For Hood Cawdor, and Cawdor said "Not here.
He left last winter." Hood was his second son,
The hunter, with whom he had quarrelled. And Fera Martial:
"We've come," she pointed toward the smoke-towers, "from that.
You are Hood's father. You've the same drooping eyes, like a big animal's
That never needs look sideways. I'm sorry, you'll have to take us in. My father is burnt, he is blinded.
The fire was on us before we awoke. He tried to fetch a bridle out of the burning stable.
There was a drum of coal-oil against the wall exploded and blew fire over his face.
I dragged him out of the fire." He said "Bring him in." "It wasn't dark," she answered, "the oaks were like torches
And all the hill roared like a wave. He says we can go in, father, here is the door-step."
The old man groaned, lifting his hand to his face but not touching it, and hung back from the door.
"I wish to God you had left me at home." She said "Your home?" "To be a blackened log with the others
Lying quiet," he said, "in the burnt hollow under the hill, and not have any care and not come
Blind and crying to my enemy's place." He turned in her hands and said "Oh Fera, where is the sun?
Is it afternoon?" She stood and held him. "Dear, only dawn. I think it must have come up, it's hidden
In the hell of smoke." "Turn me that way before I go in,

To the good light that gave me so many days. I have failed, and failed, and failed. Now I'll go in
As men go into the grave, and not fail any more."

He was in fact passive from that time on,
Except the restlessness of pain in bed
While his face scarred and the eyes died in the dark.
After the pain was lulled he seemed content
With blindness, it made an end of labor.

Cawdor meanwhile
Would somehow have sent him up coast to Monterey
To find other charity; but the girl Fera
Coming ragged and courageous out of the fire
With cool gray eyes, had troubled his tough heart.
He'd not seen her before that dawn; and the image
Of the young haggard girl streaked with the dirt of the fire
And her skirt torn to bandage her father's face
Lived like a plant in his blood. He was fifty years old,
And mocked at himself; she was nineteen, she said.
But being a beggar really, under the burden
Of that blind man to care for, discounted youth;
And Cawdor, whatever the next ten years might bring him,
Felt no weight in the fifty. He had been stronger
From his youth up than other men, and still
The strength seemed to increase, the only changes
Toward age were harder lines in the shaven face
And fewer ferocities; the black passions of anger
That used to blind him sometimes had almost ceased.
Perhaps for lack of cause, now the few people
He dealt with knew him too well to cross him. And he'd security
And rough abundance to offer.

When Martial was able
Fera led him out-doors about the house
To feel the sun. He said it had no solidness
So near the ocean. "At home in the dear cup of the hills it used to come down
Like golden hammers, yet I'm content. Now it's dulled. Is there a cloud?" She answered, "Cypresses planted
Around the house, but the wind has broken them so . . . Sit on this bench by the door, here it beats golden."
He sat, and soon handled a thing beside him on the warm plank. "What's this thing on the bench,
Like a saucer with little holes?" "An old sea-shell," she answered, "an abalone's. They grow on the ocean-reef;
All this black soil's full of their shells, the Indians brought up." He said: "Fera: while we stay here
Will you do something to lengthen the life you saved? When's the new moon? Go down when the tides drain out
In the dark of the moon and at full moon, gather me mussels and abalones, I'll drink the broth
And eat the meat, it is full of salts and nourishment. The ancestors of our life came from the sea
And our blood craves it, it will bring me years of health." She answered "He wants us to go to-morrow." "Go, where?"
"That I can't tell. Is the sun pleasant?" "Oh, we can't go," he said, "you needn't be troubled. The sun
Is faint but pleasant. Now is that Cawdor passing?" "No. Concha Rosas," she answered. "She helps the cook.
She helped me when you were sick."

Fera with private thoughts
Watched the Indian-blooded woman about her work
Pass in the dooryard, and go after a moment,

Carrying a pan under her arm, to the halved cask
Against the lift of the hill, where water trickled
From a wood pipe; tall weeds and calla lilies
Grew in the mud by it; the dark fat woman
Sat on a stone among them, paring and washing
Whatever was in the pan; and Fera said carefully:
"She has a child with blue eyes and she is an Indian.
She and the boy had their rooms in the house
When we came here, but Mr. Cawdor has moved them
To the old adobe out-building where Acanna
Lives with his wife." Her father listened or not, and answered: "Fera,
Am I still in the sun?" "Oh? Yes." "It is faint," he said, "but pleasant. I
suppose now you can see the ocean
With golden scales on the broad blue?" "No," she answered, "we face up
the canyon, toward the dark redwoods."

Cawdor's daughter Michal came by,
A blue-eyed girl of fourteen, nearly as tall as Fera.
She had a trap in her hand, and a live ground-squirrel
Dangled from it by the crushed paws. Then Fera
Left her father a moment to go with Michal
To the eagle's cage, to watch the captive be fed.
Against a cypress, a wide wire-screened box; no perch in it
But a wood block, for the bird's wing was broken.
Hood Cawdor, Michal's brother, had shot it, the autumn
Before he went away, and Michal had kept it alive.

She laid the squirrel inside and opened the trap.
The girls, their arms lacing each other's shoulders,
Set their faces against the wire to watch
The great dark-feathered and square-shouldered prisoner
Move in his corner. One wide wing trailed through filth

Quickening a buzz of blow-flies; the fierce dark eyes
Had dropped their films, "He'll never be tame," Michal said sadly.
They watched the squirrel begin to drag its body
On the broken fore-paws. The indomitable eyes
Seemed never to have left the girls' faces but a grim hand
Came forward and gathered its prey under its talons.
They heard a whispering twitter continue
Below the hover of the dark plumes, until
The brown hackles of the neck bowed, the bleak head
Stooped over and stilled it.

Fera turned at a shadow
And saw Cawdor behind her, who said "One thing it's good for,
It makes Michal catch squirrels. Well, Fera, you're ready to go to-morrow?"
"Let me go back to my father,"
She said, "I've left him alone too long. No, we're not ready." He followed her; Michal remained.
She touched her father's hand and spoke of the sun.
Old Martial lifted his cloth face, that he wore
To hide the scars; his voice dulled through the cloth:
"It is faint but very pleasant. I've been asleep."
She said "Mr. Cawdor's here." And Cawdor: "How are you. Now that he's better, Fera, little Romano
(That's Concha Rosas' boy) could take him walking in the afternoons and let you have a free time
To ride with Michal. If you could stay here. It's pitiful to see youth chained to helpless old age.
However, I have to drive to Monterey in the morning. I've put it off as long as I could,
And now he's able." She looked at Cawdor's face and his hands, and said "He means, father, that we
Must go to-morrow. I told you." Who sighed and answered, "That would be a long journey for nothing at all.

Are people more kind there? Wherever an old pitiful blind man goes
Someone will have to lead him and feed him and find him a bed. The world is not so made, Fera,
That he could starve. There *is* a God, but in human kindness." Cawdor said gravely: "Now's the other fool's turn
To speak: it makes me mad to have to spread out my foolishness.
I never had time to play with colored ribbons, I was brought up hard. I did a man's work at twelve
And bossed a gang at eighteen. That gets you nowhere. I learned that ruling poor men's hands is nothing,
Ruling men's money's a wedge in the world. But after I'd split it open a crack I looked in and saw
The trick inside it, the filthy nothing, the fooled and rotten faces of rich and successful men.
And the sons they have. Then I came down from the city.
I saw this place and I got it. I was what you call honest but I was hard; the little Mexican
Cried when I got it. A canyon full of redwoods and hills guaranteed not to contain gold.
I'd what I wanted, and have lived unshaken. My wife died when Michal was born; and I was sorry,
She seemed frightened at the end; but life was not changed.
I am fifty years old, the boys have grown up; and now I'm caught with wanting something and my life is changed.
I haven't slept for some nights. You'd think I might have been safe at fifty. Oh, I'm still my own master
And will not beg anything of you. Old blind man your girl's beautiful, I saw her come down the canyon
Like a fawn out of the fire. If she is willing: if you are willing, Fera, this place is yours.
It's no palace and no kingdom: but you are a beggar. It might be better for you to live
In a lonely place than lead your old blind-man up the cold street

And catch dimes in his hat. If you're not willing:
I'll tell you something. You are not safe here, by God you're not. I've been my own master;
But now I'm troubled with two wolves tearing each other: to kneel down like a fool and worship you,
And the other thing." She whitened and smiled. "I'm not afraid: but I'm not experienced. Marriage you mean?
There's no security in anything less. We are, as you say, beggars: we want security." Old Martial
Groped and muttered against her. She laughed: "I'm driving a bargain: be quiet father." Cawdor said sadly:
"I think that I am the one being made a fool of, old man, not you. Fera if you were willing
We'd drive up and be married to-morrow. And then . . . there must be something . . . clothes, clothes: you look ridiculous
Bursting through Michal's like the bud of a poppy." She stood quietly and looked over the dooryard
At Concha Rosas peeling potatoes beside the fountain. "Who's that wide-lapped dark o' the moon
Among the lilies?" He said, "Why: Concha. You know her." "Oh, Concha. And now you've moved her out of the house."
"Yes," he said angrily. And Fera laughing: "There is nothing under the sun worth loving but strength: and I
Had some but it's tired, and now I'm sick of it. I want you to be proud and hard with me; I'm not tame
If you ever soften. Oh, yes, to your offer. I'd a friend once that had fine dreams, she didn't look forward
Into her mist of moon on the roses—not Rosas—you remember Edith,
Father?—with half the heart that races me to meet to-morrow." Then Cawdor shuddered with hope of love;
His face relaxing began to look like an old man's. He stooped toward Fera, to fondle or kiss,
She drew herself back. "Not now. Oh, I'll be honest

And love you well." She took her father by the arm. "The sun's passed from
the bench, father, come in.
I'll build a fire on the hearth if you want." And Cawdor: "That's it! You like
horses, that's what I'll give you.
You liked mine but I'll buy you better; Morales has a pair of whites as
beautiful as flowers.
We'll drive by there to-morrow. Like kittens they are." He followed her
in-doors.

Blue kingfisher laughing laughing in the lit boughs
Over lonely water,
Is there no man not duped and therefore you are laughing?
No strength of a man
But falls on folly before it drops into dust?
Go wicked arrow down to the ocean
And learn of gulls: they laugh in the cloud, they lament also.
The man who'd not be seduced, not in hot youth,
By the angel of fools, million-worshipped success,
The self-included man, the self-armored,
And never beguiled as to a bull nor a horse,
Now in his cooled and craglike years
Has humbled himself to beg pleasure: even power was better.
Laugh kingfisher, laugh, that is their fashion.
Whoever has discerned the vanity of water will desire wind.

II

The night of Cawdor's marriage, his son
Hood Cawdor lay in the north on the open sand-beach
Of a long lake. He was alone; his friend in that country
Who hunted with him, had gone to the Indian camp.
Hood slept beside his fire and seemed to awake
And hear the faint ripple, and wind in far firs,

Then all at once a voice came from the south
As if it had flown mountains and wide valleys yet clearly heard
And like a dying man's, "Hood, Hood. My son." He saw
His father's face clearly a moment after
Distorted either with pain or approach of death.
But then the actual stars of the night came through it,
Like those of a winter evening, Orion rising,
Altair and Vega going west. When he remembered
It was early autumn, he knew it must be past midnight.
He laid a flare of twigs on the live coals
Before he lay down; eyes on the opposite shore
Would have seen the sharp stars in the black crystal
Of the lake cancelled by a red comet's tail.

That night and in the morning Hood had no doubt
His father had just died or approached death;
But dreams and visions are an obscure coinage
No sane person takes faithfully. He thought of writing
To his sister Michal; he had no habit of writing.
Months later, after the rains began and cramped
His migrant hunting, he thought not with much sorrow
Yet mournfully, of his father as dead; and thought
That he'd a share in the place unless he'd been,
As appeared likely, cut off by a written will.
No doubt it was too late to see the old man,
Yet he'd go south. He sold his horse and shot-gun, took his rifle and
went south.

He approached home
Over the hills, not by the coast-road from Monterey. Miles beyond miles a
fire had devoured

Until he looked from the height into the redwood canyons pitching to the ocean, these were unhurt,
Dark green and strong. Then he believed his father could not have died.

The first canyon he entered
A mountain-lion stood stilted on a bare slope between alder and redwood watching him come down:
Like the owner of the place: he slid the rifle-stock to his cheek thinking "The hills have not been hunted
Since I've been gone"; he fired, and the lank August-pasture-colored body somersaulted
Over the ridge; he found it lying under a laurel-bush. The skinning was a long toil; Hood came
Burdened across the fall of twilight to the great dome of high-cliffed granite, they call it the Rock,
That stands out of the hill at the head of Cawdor's canyon.

Here, after the trivial violent quarrel
That sped him from home the year before, he had built a fire at dusk hoping Michal would see it
And come to bid him good-bye; she had seen and come. He stood now and saw, down the great darkening gorge,
The reddish-yellow windows glimmer in his father's house, the iron-dark ocean a bank beyond,
Pricked at the gray edge with one pin-point ship's light. Deep, vast, and quiet and sad. After a little
He gathered sticks under the oaks and made a fire on the Rock's head, wishing Michal might see it.

If not, he could go down in the morning, (he'd blanket and food) and see whether the place was changed.

Michal had gone in-doors but Acanna saw it,
A bright high blood-drop under the lump-shaped moon,
When he was stamping stable-yard muck from his boots
Before he went in to supper. He said to the new farmhand
Dante Vitello, the Swiss whom Cawdor had brought
From Monterey: "You seen strangers go through?
Some fellow's got a fire on the Rock." Then Michal
Hurried her meal and went out. The fire waned,
Rayless red star up the blue-shadow-brimming
Moon-silver-lipped gorge. Michal went doubtfully
Up the dim moon-path by the lone redwood that lately
Excited by her father's marriage
She'd made a secret marriage with, and a law
That she must always touch it in passing. She touched it
Without much ceremony, and climbed, and peered
Under the oaks at the man out on the Rock's head.
Oh, it was Hood, in the red ember-glow. They met gladly;
The edge of shadow and moongleam down the gulf of the canyon crept up out of sight
Under the Rock before she went home. Hood said "You'll ask the old man whether he'd like to see me.
But tell him that I'll not stay. No plowing, I'm not a farmer." "You're still only a hunter" she answered.

By the house under the broken cypresses;
The saffron dawn from which Hood had descended
Still hung in the V of the canyon; Cawdor with morning friendliness, "Stay for a week if you like. Don't fear,

I won't set you at plowing, we've done the plowing. My wife's father," he said, "has your old room,
But you can have the one on the north, used to be Concha's." Fera Martial came out; she had changed
Amazingly from the sallow girl that Hood
Had seen two years ago at the lean farm. The eyes had not changed. A wind blew from her eyes
Like sea-wind from the gray sea. "Here's Hood," said Cawdor. "He looks more like you," she said, "than either of the others."
"As long as you don't ask him to work. George works, but this
Is only a hunter. Let him have the little north room for a week." Hood unstrapped the raw stiffening
Puma-skin from his pack. "I owe you a wedding-present," he said to Fera, "if you'll take this
I'll get it tanned. I shot it yesterday." Fera took in both hands the eight-foot trophy, she made
To draw it over her shoulders, "Stop. It's not dry, you'll stain your dress." "Who am I," she said impatiently,
"Not to be stained?" She assumed it like a garment, the head with the slits for eyes hung on her breast,
The moonstone claws dangling, the glazed red fleshy under-side
Turned at the borders, her bare forearm crossing it. "Sticky," she said and took it in-doors. "Come in."
He carried his pack, she led him up-stairs to the north room. "This was not yours when you used to live here."
"No. Mine was where your father is now." "Then who had this one?"
He answered "I don't remember: nobody: I guess it was empty." "That Rosas woman," she answered, "had it.
But the bed's aired." She left him there and went down.

He went out-doors to find Michal again
And couldn't find her; he wandered about and played with the horses,

Then Michal was coming up from the field seaward.
She carried a trap in her hand, and a live ground-squirrel
Dangled from it by the crushed paws, the white-rimmed
Eyes dull with pain, it had lain caught all night.
"What's that, Michal, why don't you kill it?" "A treat for the eagle.
I've taught him to eat beef but he loves to kill.
Oh squirrels are scarce in winter." "What, you've still got the eagle?"
"Yes. Come and watch."

Hood remembered great sails
Coasting the hill and the redwoods. He'd shot for the breast,
But the bird's fate having captivity in it
Took in the wing-bone, against the shoulder, the messenger
Of human love; the broad oar of the wing broke upward
And stood like a halved fern-leaf on the white of the sky,
Then all fell wrecked. He had flung his coat over its head,
Still the white talon-scars pitted his forearm.

The cage was not in the old place. "Fera," she said,
"She made me move it because it smells. I can't
Scrape the wood clean." Michal had had it moved
To the only other level on the pitch of the hill;
The earth-bench a hundred feet above the house-roof,
An old oak's roots partly upheld; a faint
Steep path trailed up there. One side of the low leaning
Bole of the tree was the eagle's cage, on the other
A lichened picket-fence guarded two graves,
Two wooden head-boards. Cawdor's dead wife was laid here
Beside a child that had died; an older sister
Of Hood's and Michal's.

They stood and watched
The dark square-shouldered prisoner, the great flight-feathers
Of the dragged wing were worn to quills and beetles
Crawled by the weaponed feet, yet the dark eyes
Remembered their pride. Hood said "You ought to kill him.
My God, nearly two years!" She answered nothing,
But when he looked at her face the long blue eyes
Winked and were brimmed. The grim hand took the squirrel,
It made a whispering twitter, the bleak head tore it,
And Michal said "George wanted to kill him too.
I can't let him be killed. And now, day after day
I have to be cruel to bring him a little happiness."
Hood laughed; they stood looking down on the house,
All roof and dormers from here, among the thirteen
Winter-battered cypresses planted about it.

III

The next day's noon Michal said, "Her old father
Believes that food from the sea keeps him alive.
The low tides at full moon we always go down."
When Fera came they took sacks for the catch
And brown iron blades to pry the shells from the rock.
They went to the waste of the ebb under the cliff,
Stone wilderness furred with dishevelled weed, but under each round black-shouldered stone universes
Of color and life, scarlet and green sea-lichens, violet and rose anemones, wave-purple urchins,
Red starfish, tentacle-rayed pomegranate-color sun-disks, shelled worms tuft-headed with astonishing
Flower-spray, pools of live crystal, quick eels plunged in the crevices . . . the three intrusive atoms of humanity

Went prying and thrusting; the sacks fattened with shell-vaulted meat.
Then Fera said "Go out on the reef,
Michal, and when you've filled the sack with mussels call Hood to fetch it."
"Why should I go? Let *him*."
"Go Michal, I need Hood to turn over the stones." When Michal was gone
And walked beyond hearing on the low reef, dim little remote figure between the blind flat ocean
And burning sky, Fera stood up and said suddenly: "Judge me, will you. Kindness is like . . .
The slime on my hands, I want judgment. We came out of the mountain fire beggared and blinded,
Nothing but a few singed rags and a lame horse
That has died since. Now you despise me because I gave myself to your father. Do then: I too
Hate myself now, we've learned he likes dark meat—that Rosas—a rose-wreath of black flesh for his bride
Was not in the bargain. It leaves a taste." Hood steadied himself against the wind of her eyes, and quietly:
"Be quiet, you are telling me things that don't concern me, true or not. I am not one of the people that live
In this canyon." "You can be cold, I knew that, that's Cawdor. The others have kindly mother in them.
Wax from the dead woman: but when I saw your face I knew it was the pure rock. I loved him for that.
For I did love him, he is cold and strong. So when you judge me, write in the book that she sold herself
For someone to take care of her blind father, but not without love. You had better go out on the reef
And help Michal."

He went, and kneeling beside his sister to scrape the stiff brown-bearded lives

From the sea face of the rock, over the swinging streaks of foam on the
water, "Michal" he said
"I wish you could get free of this place. We must think what we can do.
God knows I wouldn't want you
Like the girls in town, pecking against a shop-window." "What did she
want to tell you?" "Nothing at all.
Only to say she loves the old man. Michal, keep your mind clean, be like a
boy, don't love.
Women's minds are not clean, their mouths declare it, the shape of their
mouths. They want to belong to someone.
But what do I know? They are all alike to me as mussels." The sack was
filled; reluctance to return
Had kept him hewing at the thick bed of mussels, letting them slide on the
rock and drop in the water,
When he looked up Fera had come. "Why do you waste them?" she said.
"You're right, waste is the purpose
And value of . . . Look, I've something to waste." She extended her hand
toward him, palm downward, he saw bright blood
Trickle from the tips of the brown fingers and spot the rock. "You're hurt?"
"Oh, nothing. I turned a stone,
A barnacle cut me, you were so long coming I thought I could do without
you. Well, have you judged me,
With Michal to help?" "Let me see the cut," he said angrily. She turned
the gashed palm cup-shape upward
On purpose to let a small red pool gather. She heard his teeth grating, that
pleased her. He said
"I can't see," then she flung it on the ocean. "But you're a hunter, you must
have seen many a wild creature
Drain, and not paled a shade." He saw the white everted lips of the cut and
suffered a pain
Like a stab, in a peculiar place. They walked

And were silent on the low reef; Hood carried the sea-lymph-streaming sack on his shoulder. Every third step
A cold and startling shadow was flung across them; the sun was on the horizon and the tide turning
The surf mounted, each wave at its height covered the sun. A river of gulls flowed away northward,
Long wings like scythes against the face of the wave, the heavy red light, the cold pulses of shadow,
The croaking voice of a heron fell from high rose and amber.

There were three sacks to bring up the cliff.
Hood sent his sister to fetch a horse to the cliffhead to carry them home, but Michal without an answer
Went home by herself, along the thread of gray fog
That ran up the great darkening gorge like the clue of a labyrinth. Hood, climbing, saw on the cliffhead, unreal
To eyes upward and sidelong, his head cramped by the load, like a lit pillar Fera alone
Waiting for him, flushed with the west in her face,
The purple hills at her knees and the full moon at her thigh, under her wounded hand new-risen.
He slid the sack on the grass and went down. His knees wavered under the second on the jags of rock,
Under the third he stumbled and fell on the cliffhead. They were not too heavy but he was tired. Then Fera
Lay down beside him, he laughed and stood up. "Where's Michal? I sent her to fetch a horse." And Fera shivering:
"I waited for you but Michal went on. My father says that life began in the ocean and crept
Like us, dripping sea-slime up the high cliff. He used to be a schoolmaster but mother left him,

She was much younger than he. Then he began to break himself on bad liquor. Our little farm
Was the last refuge. But he was no farmer. We had utterly failed
And fallen on hollow misery before the fire came. That sort of thing builds a wall against recklessness.
Nothing's worth risk; now I'll be mean and cautious all the rest of my life, grow mean and wrinkled
Sucking the greasy penny of security. For it's known beforehand, whatever I attempt bravely would fail.
That's in the blood. But see," she looked from the ocean sundown to the violet hills and the great moon,
"Because I choose to be safe all this grows hateful. What shall I do?" He said scornfully: "Like others,
Take what you dare and let the rest go." "That is no limit. I dare," she answered. He looked aside
At the dark presence of the ocean moving its foam secretly below the red west, and thought
"Well, what does she want?" "Nothing," she said as if she had heard him. "But I wish to God
I were the hunter." She went up to the house,
And there for days was silent as a sheathed knife,
Attending her sick father and ruling the housework
With bitter eyes. At night she endured Cawdor if he pleased
As this earth endures man.

A morning when no one
Was in the house except her father in his room,
She stole to Hood's room on the north to fall
On the open bed and nuzzle the dented pillow
With a fire face; but then sweating with shame
Rose and fetched water for some menial service

About her father's body; he had caught cold
And was helplessly bedfast again.

Meanwhile Hood Cawdor
With hunting deer at waterheads before dawn,
Evening rides with Michal, lucky shots at coyotes
And vain lying-wait and spying of creekside pad-prints
For the great mountain-lion that killed a calf,
Contentedly used six days of his quick seven
And would have gone the eighth morning. But the sixth night
The farm-dogs yelled furious news of disaster,
So that Hood snatched up half his clothes and ran out
Barefoot; George came behind him; they saw nothing.
The dogs were silent, two of them came at call
Under the late moonrise cancelled with cloud,
But would not quest nor lead. Then the young men
Returned to bed. In the white of dawn they found
The dog that had not come in the night, the square-jawed
Fighter and best of the dogs, against the door
So opened with one stroke of an armed paw
That the purple entrails had come out, and lay
On the stone step, speckled with redwood needles.

That postponed Hood's departure, he was a hunter
And took the challenge. He found the fighting-spot,
Scratched earth and the dog's blood, but never the slayer.

IV

A sudden rainstorm
Beat in from the north ocean up a blue heaven and spoiled his hunting.
The northwest wind veered east,

The rain came harder, in heavy falls and electric pauses. Hood had come home, he sat with Michal
Playing checkers; Fera was up-stairs with her father.
The blind man had grown feebler; he had been in fact dying since the fire; but now two days he had eaten
Nothing, and his lungs clogged. Most of the daytime
And half the night Fera'd spent by his bedside. He had lain deeply absorbed in his own misery,
His blindness concentrating his mood, until the electric streams and hushes of the rain vexed him,
Toward evening he fell into feverish talk of trivial
Remembered things, little dead pleasures. Fera gave patient answers until he slept. She then
Left him and slept heavily beside her husband.

The rain had ceased,

Hood saw a star from his window
And thought if the rain ceased he might give over his hunting and go to-morrow. But out of doors
Was little promise of the rain ceasing; the east wind had slipped south, the earth lay expectant. The house
Wore an iron stub for some forgotten purpose
Fixed upward from the peak of the roof; to one passing out-doors at midnight the invisible metal
Would have shown a sphered flame, before the thunder began.

Fera

before the first thunderclap
Dreaming imagined herself the mountain-lion that had killed the dog; she hid in leaves and the hunter
Aimed at her body through a gap in the green. She waited the fire, rigid, and through closed lids

Saw lightning flare in the window, she heard the crash of the rifle. The enthralling dream so well interpreted
The flash and the noise that she was not awakened but slept to the second thunder. She rose then, and went
To her father's room for he'd be awakened. He was not awakened.
He snored in a new manner, puffing his cheeks. Impossible to wake him. She called Cawdor. In the morning
They sent Acanna, for form's sake, not hope's, to fetch a doctor. Hood offered to ride, Acanna was sent.
The torrents of rain prevented his return, and the doctor's coming, to the third day. But northward
He rode lightly, the storm behind him.

The wind had shifted before dawn and grooved itself
A violent channel from east of south, the slant of the coast; the house-roof groaned, the planted cypresses
Flung broken boughs over the gables and all the lee slope of the gorge was carpeted green
With the new growth and little twigs of the redwoods. They bowed themselves at last, the redwoods, not shaken
By common storms, bowed themselves over; their voice and not the ocean's was the great throat of the gorge
That roared it full, taking all the storm's other
Noises like little fish in a net.

On the open pasture
The cattle began to drift, the wind broke fences.
But Cawdor, although unsure and thence in his times
Violent toward human nature, was never taken
Asleep by the acts of nature outside; he knew
His hills as if he had nerves under the grass,

What fence-lengths would blow down and toward what cover
The cattle would drift. He rode with George, and Hood
Rode after, thwart the current in the cracked oaks
To the open mercy of the hill. They felt the spray
And sharp wreckage of rain-clouds in the steel wind,
And saw the legs of the others' horses leaning
Like the legs of broken chairs on the domed rims
On the running sky.

In the house Fera
Sat by her father's bed still as a stone
And heard him breathe, that was the master-noise of the house
That caught the storm's noises and cries in a net,
And captured her mind; the ruling tenth of her mind
Caught in the tidal rhythm lay inert and breathing
Like the old man's body, the deep layers left unruled
Dividing life in a dream. She heard not the roof
Crying in the wind, nor on the window
The endless rattle of earth and pebbles blasted
From the hill above. For hours; and a broken cypress bough
Rose and tapped the strained glass, at a touch the pane
Exploded inward, glass flew like sparks, the fury of the wind
Entered like a wild beast. Nothing in the room
Remained unmoved except the old man on the bed.

Michal Cawdor had crawled up the hill four-foot
To weight her eagle's cage with heavier stones
Against the storm, and creeping back to the house
Heard the glass crash and saw the gapped window. She got up-stairs
And saw in the eddying and half blinded glimmer
Fera's face like an axe and the window blocked

With a high wardrobe that had hidden the wall
Between the two windows, a weight for men
To strain at, but Fera whose nerves found action before
Her mind found thought had wrestled it into service
Instead of screaming, the instant the crash snapped her deep trance. When Michal came Fera was drawing
The table against the wardrobe to hold it firm, her back and shoulders flowing into lines like fire
Between the axe face and the stretched arms: "Ah shut the door," she said panting, "did Hood go with them?
He hasn't *gone*?" "Who? Hood?" "Coo if you like: has he gone?" "He went with father," she answered trembling,
"To herd the cows . . ." "Why are your eyes like eggs then, for he'll come back, Michal?" She went to the bedside
And murmured "He hasn't moved, it hasn't hurt him." But Michal: "Did you want Hood?" "Want him? I wanted
Someone to stop the window. Who could bear life
If it refused the one thing you want? I've made a shutter to hold although it sings at the edges.
Yet he felt nothing. Michal, it doesn't storm for a sparrow's death. You and I, Michal, won't have
A stir like this to speed us away in our times. He is dying." Michal answered "Dante Vitello's
Roping the hay-stacks, I'll fetch him Fera?" "What could he do while the wind continues, more than I've done?
We can stand draughts. Oh Michal, a man's life and his soul
Have nothing in common. You never knew my father, he had eagle imaginations. This poor scarred face
For whose sake neither nature nor man have ever stepped from the path while he was living: his death
Breaks trees, they send a roaring chariot of storm to home him.

Hood wouldn't leave without his rifle," she said,
"He didn't take the rifle when he went up?"
"Why no, not in this wind."

In the afternoon the wind
Fell, and the spray in the wind waxed into rain.
The men came home, they boarded the broken window.
The rain increased all night. At dawn a high sea-bird,
If any had risen so high, watching the hoary light
Creep down to sea, under the cloud-streams, down
The many canyons the great sea-wall of coast
Is notched with like a murderer's gun-stock, would have seen
Each canyon's creek-mouth smoke its mud-brown torrent
Into the shoring gray; and as the light gained
Have seen the whole wall gleam with a glaze of water.

V

There was a little acre in Cawdor's canyon
Against the creek, used for a garden, because they could water it
In summer through a wood flume; but now the scour
Devoured it; and after Cawdor had ditched the barns
Against the shoreless flood running from the hill,
In the afternoon he turned to save this acre.
He drove piling to stay the embankment; Hood pointed
The beams, and Cawdor drove them with the great sledge-hammer,
Standing to his knees in the stream.

Then Fera Cawdor
Came down the bank without a cloak, her hair
Streaming the rain, and stood among the brown leafless
And lavender shoots of willow. "Oh come to the house, Hood."

She struck her hands together. "My father is conscious,
He wants to speak to Hood, wants Hood." Who wondering
Gave the axe to his brother and went up.

They came to the room off the short hallway; he heard
Through the shut door before they reached it the old man's breathing: like nothing he'd ever heard in his life:
Slime in a pit bubbling: but the machine rhythm, intense and faultless. She entered ahead
And drew a cloth over the wrinkled eye-pits; the bald scars in the beard and the open mouth
Were not covered. "Ah shut the door," she said, "against the wind on the stairway." He came reluctantly
Into the dreadful rhythm of the room, and said "When was he conscious? He is not now." And Fera:
"He is in a dream: but *I* am in a dream, between blackness and fire, my mind is never gathered,
And all the years of thoughtful wonder and little choices are gone. He is on the shore of what
Nobody knows: but *I* am on that shore. It is lonely. I was the one that needed you. Does he feel anything?"
He thought, this breathing-machine? "Why no, Fera."
"It is only because I am cold," she said wringing her hands, violently trembling, "the cold rain-water
Rains down from my hair.
I hated my loose mother but this old man was always gentle and good even in drunkenness.
Lately I had true delight in doing things for him, the feeding, cleaning, we'd travelled so far together,
So many faces of pain. But now he has flown away, where is it?" She mastered her shuddering and said

"All that I loved is here dying: and now if you should ask me to I would strike his face
While he lies dying." But he bewildered in the ice-colored wind of her eyes stood foolish without an answer,
And heard her: "Do you understand?" He felt the wind tempered, it fell in tears, he saw them running
By the racked mouth; she ceased then to be monstrous and became pitiful. Her power that had held him captive
Ceased also, and now he was meanly afraid of what she might do. He went through the house and found Michal,
And brought her up to the room. Then Fera lifted her face from the bed, and stood, and answered "Come Michal.
This is the place. Come and look down and despise us. Oh, we don't mind. You're kind: I am wicked perhaps
To think that he is repulsive as well as pitiful to you. You hunter with a rifle, one shot's
Mercy in the life: but the common hunter of the world uses too many; wounds and not kills, and drives you
Limping and bleeding, years after years,
Down to this pit. One hope after another cracked in his hands; the school he had; then the newspaper
He labored day and night to build up, over in the valley. His wife my shameful mother abandoned him.
He took whiskey for a friend, it turned a devil. He took the farm up here, hunted at last
To the mountain, and nothing grew, no rain fell, the cows died
Before the fire came. Then it took his eyes and now it is taking his life. Now it has taken
Me too, that had been faithful awhile. For I have to tell you, dear dear Michal, before he dies,
I love you—and Hood for your sake, Michal—
More than I do this poor old man. He lies abandoned." She stood above him, her thin wet clothing

In little folds glued to the flesh, like one of the girls in a Greek frieze, the air of their motion
Moulds lean in marble; Michal saw her through mist in the eyes and thought how lovely she was, and dimly
Heard her saying: "Do you not wish you were like this man, Hood? *I* wish I were like this man.
He has only one thing left to do. It is great and maybe dreadful to die, but nothing's easier.
He does it asleep. Perhaps we *are* like this man: we have only one thing left to do, Hood,
One burning thing under the sun. I love you so much, Michal, that you will surely forgive
Whatever it is. You'll know it is not done wickedly, but only from bitter need, from bitter need . . ."
She saw him frowning, and Michal's wonder, and cried quickly:
"You needn't pity him! For even in this deformity and shame of obscure death he is much more fortunate
Than any king of fat steers: under the bone, behind the burnt eyes
There have been lightnings you never dreamed of, despairs and exultations and hawk agonies of sight
That would have cindered your eyes before the fire came.
Now leave me with him. If I were able I would take him up, groaning to death, to the great Rock
Over your cramp cellar of a canyon, to flame his bitter soul away like a shot eagle
In the streaming sky. I talk foolishly. Michal you mustn't come back until he has died, death's dreadful.
You're still a child. Stay, Hood." But he would not.

He heard in the evening
The new farmhand talking with Concha Rosas,

His Alp-Italian accent against her Spanish-
Indian like pebbles into thick water. "This country
You cannot trust, it never need any people.
My old country at home she is not so kind
But always she need people, she never kill all.
She is our mother, can't live without us. This one not care.
It make you fat and soon it cutting your neck."
Concha answered inaudibly, and the other: "You Indian.
Not either you. I have read, you come from Ah-sia.
You come from Ah-sia, us from Europa, no one from here.
Beautiful *matrigna* country, she care for Indian
No more nor white nor black, how have she help you?"
Their talk knotted itself on miscomprehension
Until *matrigna* shaped into *madrastra*.
"Beautiful stepmother country."

Hood ceased to hear them.
Why, so she was. He saw as if in a vision
The gray flame of her eyes like windows open
To a shining sky the north wind sweeps, and wind
And light strain from the windows. What wickedness in the fabric
Was driving her mad with binding her to old men?
He went to the door to look at the black sky.
He'd leave the house to-night but pity and the rain held him.
He heard the eaves gutter in their puddles and rush
Of rivulets washing the dark.

While he was there
She came from the stair and whispered: for they were alone
In the dark room, the others in the lamplit room
At the table: "If I were hurt in the hills,
Dying without help, you'd not sneak off and leave me.

Oh, nobody could do that. Pull the door to
On that black freedom. Perhaps my father will die
This drowning night, but can't you see that I am a prisoner
Until he does: the wrists tied, the ankles:
I can neither hold nor follow.
No, no, we have to let them take their time dying.
Why, even on Cawdor's, on your father's account
It would be wicked to call despair in here
Before it must come. I might do strangely
If I were driven. You'll promise. Put your hand here."
She caught it and held it under the small breast
Against the one dry thinness of cloth. She had changed then.
He felt it thudding. "I am being tortured you know."
He shook and said "Until he dies I'll not go.
Dear child, then you'll be quieter." "When you said *child*,
Your voice," she answered, "was as hard as your father's.
Hood, listen, all afternoon
I have been making a dream, you know my two white horses,
They are like twins, they mustn't be parted.
One for you, one for me, we rode together in the dream
Far off in the deep world, no one could find us.
We leaned and kissed . . ." He thrust her off, with violent fear,
And felt her throat sob in his hand, the hot slender
Reed of that voice of hers, the drumming arteries
Each side the reed flute. She went crouching and still
To the stair; he stood in the dark mourning his violence.

But she had gone up into the snoring rhythm
Neither day nor night changed. Cawdor had asked her
Whom she would have to watch with her all night,
"For you must sleep a little." She had chosen Concha
Rosas; and that was strange, he thought she had always

Hated Concha. He came at the end of evening
And brought the brown fat silent woman.

Then Fera
Looked up, not rising from the chair by the bed
And said with a difficult smile over the waves of noise:
"I was thinking of a thing that worried my father, in the old days. He made a bargain with a man
To pasture his horse, the horse died the first week. The man came asking pay for a year's pasture
For a dead horse. My father paid it at last, I wouldn't have paid it." "No, hardly," he answered. And Fera:
"The bargain ends when the man dies—when the horse dies." She looked at her dying father and said
Shuddering: "I'm sorry to keep you up all night, Concha; but you can sleep in your chair. He was always
A generous fool, he wasn't made for this world." Cawdor looked down at the bed through the dull noise
Like surf on a pebble shore, and said that he'd been out to look at the bridge; it was still standing.
The rain would break to-night, the doctor would come to-morrow. "That would be late, if there were hope,"
She answered, "no matter." "Dear child," he said hoarsely, "we all die."
"Those that have blood in us. When you said *child*,
Your voice," she answered, "was as hard as a flint. We know that you and the Rock over the canyon
Will not die in our time. When they were little children
Were you ever kind?" "Am I not now?" "Oh, kind." She leaned sidewise and smoothed
The coverlet on the bed, but rather as a little hawk slips sidelong from its flapping vantage

In the eye of the wind to a new field. "But about blood in the stone veins, could Concha tell me?
Look, his face now Concha, pure rock: a flick and it shows. Oh," she said and stood up, "forgive me.
For I am half mad with watching him
Die like an old steer the butcher forgot. It makes me
Mad at your strength. He had none: but his mind had shining wings, they were soon broken."

When Cawdor went out
She said to Concha "It is growing cold. Wrap yourself in the blanket before you sleep in the chair."
When Concha nodded she went and shook her awake, by the fat shoulder. "Did Hood make love to anyone
In those old days? They're hot at sixteen." "He never. Oh no." "You didn't serve the father and the sons?
Whom did he love?" "Nobody. He love the deer.
He's only a boy and he go hunting." Fera whispered from the throat: "I wish to God, you brown slug,
That I had been you, to scrape the mud from his boots when he came in from hunting; or Ilaria Acanna
Cooking him little cakes in the oak-smoke, in the white dawns when the light shakes like water in a cup
And the hills are foam: for now who knows what will happen?
Oh sleep, cover your head with the blanket, nothing has changed."

She went about the room and rested in her chair.
The snoring rhythm took her mind captive again,
And in a snatch of sleep she dreamed that Michal
Had stolen her lion-skin, the one that Hood had given her,
And wore it in the hills and was shot for a lion.

Her dead body was found wrapped in the skin.
There was more, but this was remembered.

Perhaps the minds
That slept in the house were wrought to dreams of death
By knowledge of the old man's ebbing. Hood Cawdor
Dreamed also of a dead body; he seemed a child; at first
He dreamed it was his father lay dead in the house,
But afterwards his father held him by the hand
Without a break in the dream. They looked through a door
Into the room in which his mother lay dead.
There an old woman servant, who had now been gone
These many years, prepared his mother's body
For burial; she was washing the naked corpse.
Matrigna; madrastra. He awoke and lay in the dark
Gathering his adult mind, assuring himself
The dream grew from no memory; he remembered
His mother living, nothing of seeing her dead.
Yes, of the burial a little; the oak on the hill,
And the red earth. His thought of the grave calmed him
So that he was falling asleep.

But Fera remained awake
After her dream. How could one drive a wedge
Between the father and the son? There was not now
Any affection: but Hood was loyal: or afraid.
They had quarrelled the time before. The snatch of sleep
Had cleared her mind.

She heard the snoring rhythm
Surely a little slower and a little slower,
Then one of the old hands drew toward the breast.

The breathing failed; resumed, but waning to silence.
The throat clicked when a breath should have been drawn.
A maze of little wrinkles, that seemed to express
Surprised amusement, played from the hollow eye-pits
Into the beard.

VI

The window was black still.
No cock had cried, nor shiver of dawn troubled the air.
The stale lamp shone and smelled. Ah, what a silence.
She crossed the room and shook Concha. "Get up, Concha.
He has died. I was alone and have closed his mouth.
Now I'll go out." She thought in the hallway,
"Besides, I am greedy to be caught in Hood's room.
We can but die, what's that. Where did this come from?"
She whispered, staring at the candle she held
Without a memory of having found nor lighted it.
She opened Hood's door and shut it behind her.

"He has died!"
No answer. Then Fera felt the tears in her eyes
Dried up with fear. "You haven't gone? Are you here Hood?"
She saw him lifting his face from the shadows like a sea-lion from the wave. "I dreaded
You'd slip away from here in my night. It is finished and I
Alone was by him, your father's flitch of dark meat snored in a corner. He has died. All the wild mind
And jagged attempts are sealed over." Her voice lifted and failed, he saw her sleep-walker face
Candle-lighted from below, the shadow of the chin covering the mouth and of the cheek-bones the eyes

To make it the mask of a strained ecstasy, strained fleshless almost. Herself was wondering what sacred fear
Restrained her, she'd meant to go touch, but here desire at the height burned crystal-separate. He said, staring:
"Have you called my father? I'll dress and come, what can I do?" "Do you think I will call," she said quietly,
"Cawdor?" She stopped and said: "Death is no terror, I have just left there. Is there anything possible to fear
And not take what we want, openly with both hands? I have been unhappy but that was foolish
For now I know that whatever bent this world around us, whether it was God or whether it was blind
Chance piled on chance as blind as my father,
Is perfectly good, we're given a dollar of life to gamble against a dollar's worth of desire
And if we win we have both but losers lose nothing,
Oh, nothing, how are they worse off than my father, or a stone in the field? Why, Hood, do you sleep naked?"
She asked him, seeing the candle's gleam on the arm and shoulder. "I brought no night-clothes with me," he sullenly
Answered, "I didn't expect people at night. What do you want?" "Nothing. Your breast's more smooth
Than rubbed marble, no hair like other men in the groove between the muscles, it is like a girl's
Except the hardness and the flat strength. No, why do you cover it, why may I not look down with my eyes?
I'd not hide mine. No doubt I'll soon die,
And happy if I could earn that marble to be my gravestone. You might cut letters in it. I know
It never would bleed, it would cut hard. *Fera Martial* you'd carve, the letters of a saved name,

Why should they fall like grains of sand and be lost forever
On the monstrous beach? But while I breathe I have to come back and beat against it, that stone, for nothing,
Wave after wave, a broken-winged bird
Wave after wave beats to death on the cliff. Her blood in the foam. If I were another man's wife
And not Cawdor's you'd pity me." "Being what you are," he answered: he rose in the bed angrily, her eyes
Took hold like hands upon the beautiful bent shoulders plated from the bone with visible power,
Long ridges lifting the smooth skin, the hunter slenderness and strength: "being what you are you will gather
The shame back on your mind and kill it. We've not been made to touch what we would loathe ourselves for
To the last drop." She said "What were you saying? Do you think I should be shameless as a man making
Love to reluctance, the man to you for a woman, if I had time, if you were not going to-morrow?
If I just had time, I'd use a woman's cunning manners, the cat patience and watchfulness: but shame
Dies on the precipice lip." "I hear them stirring in the house," he answered. "You lie, Hood. You hear nothing.
This little room on the north is separate and makes no sound, your father used to visit his thing here,
You children slept and heard nothing. You fear him of course. I can remember having feared something . . .
That's long ago. I forget what. Look at me once,
Stone eyes am I too horrible to look at? If I've no beauty at all, I have more than Concha had
When she was more fawn than sow, in her lean years, did your father avoid her? I must have done something

In ignorance, to make you hate me. If I could help it, would I come
Fresh from the death of the one life I have loved to make myself
Your fool and tell you I am shameless, if I could help it? Oh that's the misery: you look at me and see death,
I am dressed in death instead of a dress, I have drunk death for days, makes me repulsive enough,
No wonder, but you too Hood
Will drink it sometime for all your loathing, there are two of us here
Shall not escape.

Oh, but we shall though, if you are willing. There is one clean way. We'll not take anything
Of Cawdor's, I have two horses of my own. And you can feed us with the rifle. Only to ride beside you
Is all I want. But I would waken your soul and your eyes, I could teach you joy.

I know that you love
Liberty, I'd never touch your liberty. Oh let me ride beside you a week, then you could leave me.
I'd be your . . . whatever you want, but you could have other women. That wouldn't kill me; but not to be with you
Is death in torture." Her hope died of his look. "I know we came from the fire only to fail,
Fail, fail, it's bred in the blood. But," she cried suddenly, "you lie when you look like that. The flesh of my body
Is nothing in my longing. What you think I want
Will be pure dust after hundreds of years and something from me be crying to something from you
High up in the air."

She heard the door open behind her, she turned on the door. Cawdor had come.
She cried "Have you waked at last? You sleep like logs, you and your son. He has died. I can wake nobody.
I banged your door, but this one was unlatched and when I knocked it flew open. Yet I can't wake him.
Is it decent to leave me alone with the sow Concha in the pit of sorrow?"
His confused violent eyes
Moved and shunned hers and worked the room, with the ancient look of men spying for their own dishonor
As if it were a lost jewel. "How long ago did you knock? I have been awake." "What do I know
Of time? He has died." She watched him tremble, controlling with more violence the violence in him; and he said:
"I know he has died. I came from that room." Then Fera, knowing
That Hood looked like a boy caught in a crime but herself like innocence: "How did you dare to go in?
Oh yes, the dead never stand up. But how did you dare? You never once hid your contempt
While he was living. You came and cursed him because our cow died in the creek. Did he want it to die?
Then what have you done just now, spat in his face? I was not there, he lay at your mercy." She felt
Her knees failing, and a sharp languor
Melt through her body; she saw the candle-flame (she had set the candle on the little table) circling
In a short orbit, and Cawdor's face waver, strange heavy face with the drooping brows and confused eyes,
Said something heavily, unheard, and Fera answered: "Certainly I could have gone in and called you, but I
Was looking about the house for someone that loved him. You were one of the hunters that hunted him down.

I thought that Hood . . . but no, did he care? I couldn't awake him. This
flesh will harden, I'll be stone too
And not again go hot and wanting pity in a desert of stones. But you . . .
you . . . that old blind man
Whom you despised, he lived in the house among you a hawk in a
mole-hill. And now he's flown up. Oh, death
Is over life like heaven over deep hell." She saw Michal in the door.
"You're here too, Michal?
My father has died. *You* loved him."

She said in the hallway,
"Are you well, Michal? I'm not; but when I slept
A snatch of the early night I dreamed about you.
You wrapped yourself in the mountain-lion skin
That Hood gave me, and Jesus Acanna shot you for a lion."

VII

Cawdor remained behind in the room,
But Hood pretended to have been asleep and hardly
Awakened yet. Certainly he'd not betray
The flaming-minded girl his own simplicity
Imagined a little mad in her sorrow. He answered
Safe questions, but the more his intent was innocent
The more his looks tasted of guilt. And Cawdor:
"When are you going?" "To-day." "That's it? By God
You'll wait until the old blind man is buried.
What did she call you for,
Yesterday in the rain?" "She said her father
Was conscious, but when I came he was not conscious."
"Well, he's not now," he answered, his brows drooping
Between the dawn and the candle. Dawn had begun,

And Cawdor's face between the pale window
And the small flame was gray and yellow. "Get dressed," he said.
He turned to go, and turned back. "You were such friends
With that old man, you'll not go till he's buried."

He went and found Fera, in the room with the dead.
But seeing her bloodless face, and the great eyes
Vacant and gray, he grew somberly ashamed
Of having thought her passion was more than grief.
He had meant to charge Concha to watch her
While Hood remained in the house. He forgot that, he spoke
Tenderly, and persuaded Fera to leave
Concha to watch the dead, and herself rest
In her own room. Michal would sit beside her
All morning if she were lonely. "And Hood," he said,
Spying on her face even against his own will,
"Wanted to go to-day, I told him to wait.
Why did you call him, yesterday in the rain?"
"Yesterday?" "You came in the rain." "If that was yesterday:
Our nights have grown long. I think my father called him,
(My father was then alive) wishing to talk
Of the Klamath country. He too had travelled. He despised people
Who are toad-stools of one place." "Did they talk long?"
"I can't remember. You know: now he has died.
Now the long-laboring mind has come to a rest.
I am tired too. You don't think that the mind
Goes working on? That would be pitiful. He failed in everything.
After we fail our minds go working under the ground, digging, digging . . .
we talk to someone,
The mind's not there but digging around its failure. That would be
dreadful, if even while he lies dead

The painful mind's digging away . . ." Cawdor for pity
Of the paper-white face shrunk small at dawn
Forbore then, he folded his doubts like a man folding
A live coal in his hand.

Fera returned
To her father's room; she said, "Concha, go down to breakfast. Michal,
Leave me alone for God's sake." Being left alone she knelt by the bed: "In that dim world, in that
Dim world, in that dim world, father? . . . there's nothing. *I* am between the teeth still but you are not troubled.
If only you could *feel* the salvation."

She was mistaken. Sleep and delirium are full of dreams;
The locked-up coma had trailed its clue of dream across the crippled passages; now death continued
Unbroken the delusions of the shadow before. If these had been relative to any movement outside
They'd have grown slower as the life ebbed and stagnated as it ceased, but the only measure of the dream's
Time was the dreamer, who geared in the same change could feel none; in his private dream, out of the pulses
Of breath and blood, as every dreamer is out of the hour-notched arch of the sky. The brain growing cold
The dream hung in suspense and no one knew that it did. Gently with delicate mindless fingers
Decomposition began to pick and caress the unstable chemistry
Of the cells of the brain; Oh very gently, as the first weak breath of wind in a wood: the storm is still far,

The leaves are stirred faintly to a gentle whispering: the nerve-cells, by what would soon destroy them, were stirred
To a gentle whispering. Or one might say the brain began to glow, with its own light, in the starless
Darkness under the dead bone sky; like bits of rotting wood on the floor of the night forest
Warm rains have soaked, you see them beside the path shine like vague eyes. So gently the dead man's brain
Glowing by itself made and enjoyed its dream.

The nights of many years before this time
He had been dreaming the sweetness of death, as a starved man dreams bread, but now decomposition
Reversed the chemistry; who had adored in sleep under so many disguises the dark redeemer
In death across a thousand metaphors of form and action celebrated life. Whatever he had wanted
To do or become was now accomplished, each bud that had been nipped and fallen grew out to a branch,
Sparks of desire forty years quenched flamed up fulfilment.
Out of time, undistracted by the nudging pulse-beat, perfectly real to itself being insulated
From all touch of reality the dream triumphed, building from past experience present paradise
More intense as the decay quickened, but ever more primitive as it proceeded, until the ecstasy
Soared through a flighty carnival of wines and women to the simple delight of eating flesh, and tended
Even higher, to an unconditional delight. But then the interconnections between the groups of the brain

Failing, the dreamer and the dream split into multitude. Soon the altered
cells became unfit to express
Any human or at all describable form of consciousness.

Pain and pleasure
are not to be thought
Important enough to require balancing: these flashes of post-mortal felicity
by mindless decay
Played on the breaking harp by no means countervalued the excess of
previous pain. Such discords
In the passionate terms of human experience are not resolved, nor worth it.

The
ecstasy in its timelessness
Resembled the eternal heaven of the Christian myth, but actually the
nerve-pulp as organ of pleasure
Was played to pieces in a few hours, before the day's end. Afterwards it
entered importance again
Through worms and flesh-dissolving bacteria. The personal show was over,
the mountain earnest continued
In the earth and air.

But Fera in her false earnestness
Of passionate life knelt by the bed weeping.
She ceased when Michal returned. Later in the morning
She sent Michal to look for Hood and ask him
Whether he would surely stay as Cawdor had said
Until they buried her father. "Tell him to come
Himself and tell me." Michal came back: "He said
That he was not able to come; but he would stay."
At noon she saw him. She dressed and went to the table,

Where Cawdor sat and watched them. Hood shunned her eyes;
She too was silent.

In the afternoon Cawdor came up
And said "The doctor has come." "Why Michal," she said, "but that's a pity.
Came all the sloppy way for nothing, the doctor." "No," Cawdor said. "I want you to see him, Fera.
You are not well." She went and saw him, in her father's room, where Concha with some childhood-surviving
Belief in magic had set two ritual candles burning by the bed of death. The doctor hastily
Covered the face, the candle-flames went over in the wind of the cloth. Fera stood quietly and said
She had no illness, and her father was dead. "I'm sorry you've come so far for nothing." "Oh, well," he answered,
"The coast's beautiful after the rain. I'll have the drive." "Like this old man," she said, "and the other
Millions that are born and die; come all the sloppy way for nothing and turn about and go back.
They have the drive." The young doctor stared; and Cawdor angrily
Wire-lipped like one who hides a living coal
In the clenched hand: "What more do you want?" "Oh," she answered,
"I'm not like that"; and went out.

After the doctor had gone
She vomited, and became so weak afterwards
That Michal must call Concha to help undress her.
After another spasm of sickness her dream
Was like a stone's; until Cawdor awakened her
In the night, coming to bed. She lay rigid
And saw the fiery cataracts of her mind
Pour all night long. Before the cock crew dawn
Sea-lions began barking and coughing far off

In the hollow ocean; but one screamed out like torture
And bubbled under the water. Then Fera rose
With thief motions. Cawdor awoke and feigned sleep.
She dressed in the dark and left the room, and Cawdor
Followed silently, the black blood in his throat
Stood like a knotted rope. She entered, however,
Her father's room.

She was not surprised, no one was there
And Concha's candles had died. She fingered the dark
To find her father, the body like a board, the sheeted face,
And sat beside the bed waiting for dawn.
Cawdor, returned to his room, left the door open
To hear the hallway; he dressed, and waiting for dawn
Now the first time knew clearly for what reason
He had made Hood stay: that he might watch and know them,
What they had . . . whether they had . . . but that was insane:
One of the vile fancies men suffer
When they are too old for their wives. She in her grief?
He had not the faculty common to slighter minds
Of seeing his own baseness with a smile. When Hood had passed
The creaking hallway and gone down-stairs, and the other
Not moved an inch, watching her quiet dead,
Cawdor was cured of the indulgence jealousy,
He'd not be a spy again.

But Fera had heard
Hood pass; she knew Cawdor was watching; she thought
That likely enough Hood had risen before dawn
To leave the canyon forever. She sat like a stone
Turning over the pages of death in her mind,
Deep water, sharp steel, poisons they keep in the stable
To wash the wounds of horses . . .

VIII

Hood coming in to breakfast from the fragrant light
Before sunrise, had set his rifle in the corner by the door.
George Cawdor left the table and going out-doors
Stopped at the door and took the rifle in his hands
Out of mere idleness. Hood sharply: "Mine. Put it down!"
He, nettled, carried it with him to the next room,
There opened the outer door and lined the sights
With a red lichen-fleck on a dead cypress-twig.
Hood came behind him and angrily touched his shoulder,
Reaching across his arm for the rifle; then George
Who had meant to tease him and give it back in a moment,
Remembered a grudge and fired. The sharp noise rang
Through the open house like a hammer-blow on a barrel.
Hood, in the shock of his anger, standing too near
To strike, struck with his elbow in the notch of the ribs,
His hands to the rifle. George groaned, yet half in sport still
Wrestled with him in the doorway.

Hood, not his mind,
But his mind's eye, the moment of his elbow striking
The muscle over the heart, remembered his dream of the night.
A dream he had often before suffered. (This came to his mind later, not now; later, when he thought
There is something within us knows our fates from the first, our ends from the very fountain; and we in our nights
May overhear its knowledge by accident, all to no purpose, it never warns us enough, it never
Cares to be understood, it has no benevolence but only knowledge.) He struggled in his dream's twilight
High on the dreadful verge of a cliff with one who hated him

And was more powerful; the man had pale-flaming gray eyes, it was the wind blowing from the eyes,
As a wind blew from Fera's, that forced him to the fall
Screaming, for in a dream one has no courage nor self-command but only effeminate emotions,
He hung screaming by a brittle laurel-bush
That starved in a crack of the rock. From that he had waked in terror. He had lain and thought, if Fera should come
But yet once more pleading for love, he would yield, he would do what she wanted . . . but soon that sea-lion shrieking
From the hollow ocean thoroughly awaked him, his mind stepped over the weakness, even rubbed it from memory.
What came to him now was only the earlier dream
Mixed with its rage of fear, so that he used
No temperance in the strife with his brother but struck
The next blow with his fist shortened to the mouth,
Felt lips on teeth. They swayed in the gape of the door,
Hood the aggressor but George the heavier, entwined like serpents,
The gray steel rifle-barrel between their bodies
Appeared a lance on which both struggled impaled.
For still they held it heedfully the muzzle outward
Against the sky through the door.

Hood felt a hand
Close on his shoulder like the jaws of a horse
And force him apart from the other, he twisted himself
Without a mind and fought it without knowing whom
He fought with, then a power struck his loins and the hand
Snapped him over. He fell, yet with limbs gathered
Came up as he struck the floor, but even in the crouch
His mind returned. He saw his father, the old man
Still stronger than both his sons, darkening above him;

And George rigid against the wall, blue-faced
Beyond the light of the door; but in the light,
Behind Cawdor, Michal with pitiful eyes.
He said, "Give me the rifle." George, who still held it,
Sucked his cut lip and gave the rifle to Cawdor;
Then Hood rose and stood trembling.

But Fera on the stair behind them:
She had heard the shot and come down half way: "What have you killed," she said, "the mountain-lion? You snapping foxes
What meat will you take and be quiet a little? Better than you
Lies quiet up here." But why did her voice ring rather with joy than anger? "You deafen the ears of the dead.
Not one of you there is worthy to wash the dead man's body." She approached the foot of the stair; her face
Was white with joy. "Poor Hood, has he hurt you? I saw him pluck you off with two fingers a beetle from a bread-crumb.
It's lucky for them they'd taken your gun away from you." Cawdor said somberly, "What do you want here? The boys
Have played the fool, but you can be quiet." "And George," she answered, "his mouth is bleeding. What dreams have stirred you
To make you fight like weasels before the sun has got up? I am a woman by death left lonely
In a cage of weasels: but I'll have my will: quarrel your hearts out."
Then Cawdor turned to Hood and gave him the rifle,
And said to George: "I'm going to the hill with Hood
And mark a place for the grave. Get down some redwood
From the shop loft, the twelve-inch planks, when I come down
I'll scribe them for you. And sticks of two-by-four
To nail to at the chest corners." Fera cried "What a burial.
A weasel coffin-maker and another weasel

To dig the grave, a man buried by weasels."
Cawdor said heavily, "Come Hood." And Fera, "The gun too?
Be careful after the grave's dug, I wouldn't trust him."
He turned in the door: "By God I am very patient with you
For your trouble's sake, but the rope frays."

They had gone and Fera said "What would he do,
Beat me perhaps? He meant to threaten me, Michal?
The man is a little crazy do you think, Michal?"
She walked in the room undoing the dark braids of her hair.
"Why should he blame me for what I say? Blame God,
If there were any.
Your father is old enough to know that nobody
Since the world's birth ever said or did anything
Except from bitter need, except from bitter need. How old are you
   Michal?"
"Fifteen," she said. "Dear, please . . ." "Oh, you'll soon come to it.
I am better than you all, that is my sorrow.
What you think is not true." She returned up-stairs
To the still room where one window was blinded
But the other one ached with rose-white light from clouds,
And nothing breathed on the bed.

                                        But Michal hasted
And went up the hill to look to her caged eagle.
Hood and her father, she feared, would have to move
The cage, to make room for the grave.

                                        She returned and heard
A soft roaring in the kitchen of the house.
"Why have you got the stove roaring, Ilaria?"
"She want hot water," Ilaria Acanna answered,

"She put the boilers over and open the drafts,
I pile in wood." Fera came down. "Not boiling, not yet?
Put in more oak. Oh, are you there Michal?
Common water is fair enough to bathe in
At common times, but now. Let's look out-of-doors.
I want it hot, there are certain stains. Come on.
We'll be back when it's hot." In the wind out-doors
She trembled and said "The world changes so fast,
Where shall we go, to the shore?" Passing the work-shop
Beside the stable they heard a rhythmic noise
Of two harsh notes alternate on a stroke of silence.
Fera stopped dizzily still, and after a moment:
"Although it sounded like my father's breathing,
The days before he died, I'm not fooled Michal.
A weasel," she said, "gnawing wood. Don't be afraid."
She entered. George lifted his dark eyes
From the saw-cut in the wine-colored redwood planks,
And Fera: "Oh, have you planed them too? That's kind.
The shavings are very fragrant.
How long will these planks last in their dark place
Before they rot and the earth fills them, ten years?"
"These never will rot." "Oh, that's a story. Not redwood even.
There's nothing under the sun but crumbles at last,
That's known and proved. . . . Where's the other weasel?" He looked
Morosely into her face and saw that her eyes
Gazed past him toward the skin of the mountain-lion
That Hood had given her. It was nailed wide and flat
In the gable-end, to dry, the flesh side outward,
Smeared with alum and salt. "Your brother weasel,"
She said, "Hood, Hood. The one that nibbled your lip.
How it is swollen." Not George but Michal answered
That Hood was up on the hill; "they had to move

My eagle's cage." Fera looked up at the lion-skin:
"I'll take that, George, that's mine." "Hm, the raw skin?"
"No matter," she said, "get it down. It's for my father.
What else have we got to give him? I'll wrap him in it
To lie like a Roman among the pale people.
. . . On your fine planks!" "You're more of a child than Michal,"
He said compassionately. "When you said *child*,
Your face," she answered, "softened I thought.
It's not like Hood's." He climbed up by the work-bench and drew the tacks,
She stood under him to take the skin, Michal beside her. The scene in the
 dim workshop gable-end
Wakes a sunk chord in the mind . . . the scene is a descent from the cross.
 The man clambering and drawing
The tyrannous nails from the pierced paws; the sorrowful women standing
 below to receive the relic,
Heavy-hanging spoil of the lonely hunter whom hunters
Rejoice to kill: . . . that Image-maker, its drift of metaphors.
George freed the skin, Fera raised hands to take it.
Her small hard pale-brown hands astonished him, so pale and alive,
Folding the tawny rawhide into a bundle.
"Where's Cawdor," she said, "your father: on the hill with Hood?"
He had gone up to Box Canyon with Dante Vitello,
Michal answered. And Fera: "Oh, but how hard it is.
Perhaps it could be oiled? It is like a board.
I'll take it to him." But Michal remained with George,
Tired of her restlessness, and afraid of her eyes.

Fera went up carrying the skin in her arms
And took it into the house. Ilaria Acanna
Came out to meet her. "Your water's boiling." "Well, let it stand."
She laid, in the still room up-stairs, the hard gift
Over her father's body. "Oh, that looks horrible,"

She cried shuddering and twitched it off. To hide it from sight
She forced it into the wardrobe against the wall,
The one she had moved to block the broken window
In the wild time of storm. She stood and whispered to herself,
And eyed the bed; then she returned out-doors,
And up the hill to the grave, in the oak's earth-bench
Above the house. The pit was waist-deep already,
And Hood was in the pit lifting the pick-axe
Between the mounds of wet red earth and cut roots.
Acanna leaned on a shovel above the pit-mouth.
For lack of room they had dug west of the oak;
The two old graves lay east. The eagle's cage
Was moved a few feet farther west; Hood labored
Between the cage and the oak. Jesus Acanna
From under the low cloud of the oak-boughs, his opaque eyes
And Indian silence watched Fera come up the hill,
But the eagle from the cage watched Hood labor; the one
With dark indifference, the other
With dark distrust, it had watched all the grave-digging.

Fera stood among the cut roots and said,
Lifting her hand to her face: "I was worn out yesterday
With not sleeping; forgive me for foolish words.
I came up here to tell you: for I suppose
You'll go away to-night or to-morrow morning.
Well, I am taught.
I wish that when you go you'd take for a gift
One of my white ponies, they'll have to bear being parted.
Good-bye. Live freely but not recklessly. The unhappy old man
For whom you are digging the hole, lost by that.
He never could learn that we have to live like people in a web of knives, we mustn't reach out our hands

Or we get them gashed." Hood gazing up from the grave: "I'm sorry. Yes, early in the morning." He glanced at Acanna
And said, "One thing I know, I shan't find loveliness in another canyon, like yours and Michal's." She turned
Away, saying "That's no help," and seemed about to go down; but again turning: "I meant to gather
Some branches of mountain laurel. There are no flowers
This time of year. But I have no knife. It shouldn't be all like a dog's burial." "I'll cut some for you."
He climbed out of the grave and said to Acanna: "I'll soon be back. If you strike rock at this end,
Level off the floor." Fera pointed with her hand trembling: "The tree's in the gap behind the oak-trees.
It's farther but the leaves are much fresher. Indeed he deserves laurel, his mind had wings and magnificence
One dash of common cunning would have made famous. And died a cow's death. You and I, if we can bear
The knocks and abominations of fortune for fifty years yet, have as much to hope for. Don't come. I'm not
A cheerful companion. Lend me the knife."
He thought she had better not be trusted alone with it,
The mind she was in,
And went beside her, above the older graves,
He felt his knees trembling. Across the steep slope
To the far oaks. Dark aboriginal eyes,
The Indian's and the coast-range eagle's, like eyes
Of this dark earth watching our alien blood
Pass and perform its vanities, watched them to the far oaks.
But after the oaks had hidden them Acanna
Covetously examined the hunter's rifle
Left behind, leaning against the lichened fence

Of the older graves. It was very desirable. He sighed
And set it back in its place.

Fera in the lonely
Oak-shielded shadow under the polished laurel-leaves: "Before you came
I used to come here," she caught her quivering under lip with the teeth to keep it quiet, "for solitude.
Here I was sure no one would come, not even the deer, not a bird; safer than a locked room.
Those days I had no traitor in my own heart, and would gather my spirit here
To endure old men.

That I have to die
Is nothing important: though it's been pitied sometimes when people are young: but to die in hell. I've lived
Some days of it; it burns; how I'd have laughed
Last year to think of anyone taken captive by love. A girl imagines all sorts of things
When she lives lonely but this was never . . . Who knows what the dead feel, and it is frightful to think
That after I have gone down and stilled myself in the hissing ocean: roll, roll on the weed: this hunger
Might not be stilled, this fire nor this thirst . . .
For how can anyone be sure that death is a sleep? I've never found the little garden-flower temperance
In the forest of the acts of God . . . Oh no, all's forever there, all wild and monstrous
Outside the garden: long after the white body beats to bone on the rock-teeth the unfed spirit
Will go screaming with pain along the flash of the foam, gnawing for its famine a wrist of shadow,

Torture by the sea, screaming your name. I know these things. I am not one of the careful spirits
That trot a mile and then stand."

He had bared his knife-blade to cut the bough, enduring her voice, but Fera
Caught the raised wrist. "Let it be. We have no right. The trees are decent, but we! A redwood cut
To make the coffin, an oak's roots for the grave: some day the coast will lose patience and dip
And be clean. Ah. Is it men you love?
You are girl-hearted, that makes you ice to me? What do you love? What horror of emptiness
Is in you to make you love nothing? Or only the deer and the wild feet of the mountain and follow them
As men do women. Yet you could dip that little knife-blade in me for pleasure, I'd not cry out
More than a shot deer, but I will never leave you
Until you quiet me." She saw that his face was gray and strained as a spent runner's beaten at the goal.
"Will you kiss me, once, you are going away in a moment forever? What do you owe Cawdor, what price
Of kindness bought you? This morning it was: he struck you and flung you on the ground: you liked that?" He gathered his strength
And turned himself to be gone. She caught him and clung,
And fallen to her knees when he moved outward, "I swear by God," she said, "I will tell him that you have taken me
Against my will, if you go from here before I have spoken. You'll not be hurt, Hood, you'll be far off,
And what he can do to *me* is no matter." He said "You have gone mad. Stand up. I will listen." But she
Feeling at last for the first time some shadow of a power

To hold and move him would not speak nor stand up, but crouched at his feet to enjoy it. At length she lifted
Wide staring eyes and fever-stained face. "I am very happy. I don't know what has told me: some movement
Or quietness of yours." She embraced his thighs, kneeling before him, he felt her breasts against them, her head
Nuzzling his body, he felt with his hand the fire of her throat, "Nothing," he said
"Is worse nor more vile than what we are doing." "What? With a little . . . sin if you call it . . . kill a great misery?
No one," she thought, "ever tastes triumph
Until the mouth is rinsed with despair." She sobbed "I have found you." But when he had dropped the knife at the tree's root
To free his hand, and lay by her side on the drifted fall of the crisp oak-leaves and curled brown laurel-leaves,
Then she who had wooed began to resist him, to lengthen pleasure. "I have lighted the fire, let me warm my hands at it
Before we are burned." The face of her exultation was hateful to him. He thought of the knife in the leaves
And caught it toward him and struck the point of the blade into the muscle of his thigh. He felt no pain
A moment, and then a lightning of pain, and in the lit clearance: "I am not your dog yet," he said easily,
"I am not your thing." He felt her body shudder and turn stone above him. "What have you done?" "A half inch
Into the blood," he answered, "I am better." He stood up. "You will be grateful
To-morrow, for now we can live and not be ashamed. What sort of life would have been left us?" "No life
Is left us," she said from a loose throat.
"This mountain is dry." She stood and whispered "I won't do anything mean or troublesome. I pitied my father's

Failures from the heart, but then quietness came." Her teeth chattered
together, she said "I will now go down
If you will let me?" He followed, limping from the Attis-gesture,
Outside the oaks and watched her creep toward the house.
The blood gliding by his knee he rubbed a handful of earth
Against the stain in the cloth to embrown the color,
And went faintly to the work he had left.

IX

Michal
Came up after a time with meat for the eagle.
While she fed it they had sunk the grave though shallow
To the hard rock and ceased. "Have you seen Fera
Lately?" Hood asked, "she was here wanting some greens
Because there are no flowers, but seemed to be taken sick
With grief and went down." "No. I was into the house
But not up-stairs." "We'd better see how she is.
Bring down the axe and pick-axe," he said to Acanna,
"But leave the spades." He stepped short, to conceal
His lameness. Michal asked him "What's the long stain?"
"Sap from the oak-roots, they're full of water."

They looked for Fera
All over the house and found her lying on the floor
The far side of her father's bed. Hood watched in terror
While Michal touched; he thought she had killed herself.
He had held an obscure panic by force a prisoner
All day but now it was worse, it was a wish to be gone,
"There's nothing I wouldn't give to have gone yesterday.
Oh pitiful child." She moved; she was not self-slain. She rose
To Michal's tugging hands and was led to bed

In her own room, hanging back but in silence.
Toward evening she dressed herself with Concha helping
In the blue serge that was the darkest she had
And went with the others up the hill to the burial.

A man at each corner carried the oblong box,
Cawdor and his sons and Dante Vitello. But Hood was lame
And when his left foot slipped on a stone his right
Failed with the weight. The stiff unseasonable
Calla lilies that Michal had found by water
Fell down the tilted lid; she gathered them up,
And when the box was lowered into its place
Dropped them upon it. Jesus Acanna had brought
The cords to use for lowering. All was done awkwardly
By shame-faced people, and the eagle watched from the cage.
The coffin grounding like a shored boat, the daughter
Of the tired passenger sighed, she leaned in the blindness
Of sand-gray eyes behind Michal toward Hood.
Her hand touched his, he trembled and stepped aside
Beyond Concha Rosas. Then Fera pressed her knuckles to her mouth
And went down the hill; the others remained.

Because of the dug earth heaped at the oak's foot
They were all standing on the west side the grave
Or at either end, a curious group, Cawdor's gray head the tallest,
Nine, to count Concha's child,
Intent, ill at ease, like bewildered cattle nosing one fallen. Not one of them, now that Fera was gone,
Had any more than generic relation to the dead; they were merely man contemplating man's end,
Feeling some want of ceremony.

The sky had been overcast; between the
ocean and the cloud
Was an inch slit, through which the sun broke suddenly at setting, only a
fraction of his passing face,
But shone up the hill from the low sea's rim a reddening fire from a pit.
The shadows of the still people
Lay like a bundle of rods, over the shallow grave, up the red mound of
earth, and upward
The mass of the oak; beyond them another shadow,
Broad, startling and rectilinear, was laid from the eagle's cage; nine slender
human shadows and one
Of another nature.

Jesus Acanna
Saw something like a jewel gleam in the rays
On the heap of surface earth at his feet; he stooped
And picked it up; a knife-edged flake of wrought
Chalcedony, the smooth fracture was pleasant to feel.
He stood and fondled it with his fingers, not mindful
That his own people had chipped it out and used it
To scrape a hide in their dawn or meat from a shell.

Then Cawdor made a clearing noise in his throat
And said in heavy embarrassment: "We know nothing of God, but we in
our turn shall discover death.
It might be good to stand quietly a moment, before we fill in the dirt, and
so if anyone
Is used to praying"—he looked at Concha and Ilaria—"might say it in
their minds." They stood with their eyes lowered,
And Cawdor took up a shovel and said impatiently
"Let us fill in." The sun was gone under the wine-colored ocean, then the
deep west fountained

Unanticipated magnificences of soaring rose and heavy purple, atmospheres of flame-shot
Color played like a mountain surf, over the abrupt coast, up the austere hills,
On the women talking, on the men's bent forms filling the grave, on the oak, on the eagle's prison, one glory
Without significance pervaded the world.

Fera had gone down
To the emptied room in the vacant house to do
What she had imagined in the afternoon. In the pain of her mind
Nothing appeared fantastic; she had thought of a way
To trick death from the hands that refused life.
From Hood's own hands. She'd not be forgotten. She drew
The mountain-lion skin from where it was crumpled away,
And clothed herself in it, the narrow shoulders
Over her shoulders, the head over her head.
She bound it with bits of string and smoothed the wrinkles.
It would fool a hunter in the twilight; only her face
Must be turned from him. She fled from the house and hid
In the oaks against the hill, not far from the door.
The rosy light had waned from the cloud, wilderness-hearted
Twilight was here, embrowning the leaves and earth.
Concha and Ilaria and Concha's child came talking
And entered the house; kitchen windows were lighted.
The others delayed. Blue smoke began to veil out
And be fragrant among the leaves. She crouched in the oak-bush,
As every evening the wild lives of the mountain
Come down and lie watching by lonely houses.

Hood, when they took the redwood box to the house,
Had left his rifle in the stable, he came with Michal,

Having fetched it. They walked mournfully together,
For this was their last evening, he'd leave at dawn
For the free north. But nothing remained to say;
And through their silence, drawing near the house-door, Michal
Heard the stiff oak-leaves move, she looked and perceived
A life among them, laying her hand on his arm
She pointed with the other hand. The head and slant shoulder
And half the side unsheathed themselves from the oak,
The hindquarters were hidden. The long beast lifted
On straightened forelegs and stood quartering away,
The head raised, turned up the canyon. Hood held his fire,
Astonished at it, wasn't it one of the dogs?
Both dogs were splatched with white, the brindle was dead,
No white on this, and light enough yet remained
To show the autumn color and the hair's texture;
Here were the paws that killed the brindle and the calf;
In vain hunted; chance-met.

But Fera supposed
His weapon was in his room in the house, he'd slip
Into the house to fetch it and she'd have fled
When he returned; hunting alone up the twilight hill
Might he not even now discover a woman
In the beast's hide, pity that woman? Already in her mind
She wavered away from the necessity of death;
If Michal had not been present she might have stood up
And shown . . .
The stroke that ended her thought was aimed too low.
In the hunter's mind a more deep-chested victim
Stood in the dusk to be slain; what should have transpierced
The heart broke the left arm-bone against the shoulder
And spared the life.

He knew, as she fell. He seemed to himself
To have known even while he fired. That worm of terror
Strangled his mind so that he kept no memory
Of Cawdor and the others taking her into the house.
He was left in the dark with a bruised face, someone had struck him,
Oh very justly.

He rose and stood reeling
Like a boy whom bad companions have filled with sweetened
Liquor, to make him their evening sport. The yellow
Windows of the house wavered, he fought the sickness
And went in-doors. Someone stared at him passing
Up-stairs; he heard from the door her moaning breath.
Cawdor examined the wound, George held the lamp
Over the naked arm and breast, Concha
Was dipping a sponge: it was the dark clot
Stringing from the red sponge that overcame him.
Cawdor's face, like a rock to break on, turned
To say hoarsely "You bastard get out of this place,"
And turned back to the wound; terrible face in the lamp-shadow
Black as the blood-clot.

He stood outside the door
Half fainting against the wall. Wanted him to go?
Good God, did he want to stay? Michal came whispering:
"You can't do anything here; and I am afraid of father.
Please go. Please go. To-morrow I'll meet you somewhere.
Oh what can you do here?"

While he limped on the stairway
Fera's moan sharpened and became a voice.
He found himself out of doors; the blanket-roll

He had rolled ready to start to-morrow at dawn
Was in his hand. He looked for his rifle
On the ground between the shot and the mark, and stumbled over it
After he had failed to find it.

The sky had cleared
With its local suddenness, full of nail-sharp stars
And a frosty dust of shining; he went up the dim star-path
By the lone redwood into wide night. His usurped mind
Unheeding itself ran in its track of habit,
So that he went from the oaks as before, upward
The gravelly slope of spoiled granite to the Rock.
He soon gathered dead twigs and kindled a fire
On the dome of the Rock, wishing Michal might see it
And bring him word in the morning. The night had turned
Frostily cold with its cleared sky.

X

Fera's moan became vocal, she flapped the hurt arm, the hand
Lying still and hooked, the marbled flesh working between the shoulder and the elbow. Michal remembered
Her eagle in the fresh of its wound waving the broken flag: another one of Hood's rifle-shots. Cawdor
Gripped the shoulder quiet with his hand, and clinked in the basin
From his right hand the small red splinter of bone he had fished from the wound. Fera's eye-lids, that hung
Half open on arcs of opaque white, widened suddenly, and fluttered shut, and stood wide open,
The liquid pools of night in the rayed gray rings dilating and contracting like little hearts,

Each sparked with a minute image of the lamp above them. She tongued her lips and the dry teeth
And moved her head. "This must be life, this hot pain.
Oh, the bad hunter! I fail in everything, like my father." Cawdor looked sideways to place in his mind
The strips of a torn sheet laid ready, and smooth straight sticks of pinewood kindling fetched from the kitchen;
He pressed a ragful of pungent liquid to the wound's mouths. Fera lay quiet, but Michal trembled
To see her lips retract from the teeth, and hear the teeth creaking together. Then Fera whispered:
"Horse-liniment. Of course you would. It burns." But Cawdor answered: "Hold the lamp, Michal. George, hold her quiet."
He gripped with his hands the shoulder and the upper arm. Then Fera: "Oh God! Oh no! No . . . no . . .
I'll tell you anything . . ." The ends of the fracture were heard touching; but she writhing her body whipped over
In George's and Concha's hands; Cawdor held without failure but her movement baffled him, the ends of bone
Were heard slipping. He shifted his grasp and said to the others "Loose-handed fools. Hold firm." But Fera
Straining her chalky and diminished face, the earth-stain still unwashed on her cheek, clear of the pillow:
"Oh please. Dearest! I'll not hide anything. I'm not to blame." His mind was fixed on his work, yet even
While his muscles were setting themselves again her words entered his understanding. His grip relaxed;
He looked at her face, the eyes stared bright terror but the mouth
Attempting a fawning smile: "I'll tell you everything, dearest, but don't torture me. I thought I had tasted
Torture before. How little I knew." Her teeth chattered together and she said "He forced me. Hood forced me.

He threw me down under the laurel tree
And stopped my mouth with his hand. So that I couldn't be your wife any more, darling. But I
Never loved him. I only tried to be killed. Oh, Oh, his face
Is like a nigger's. George save me! Michal!" He sighed, "You lie. Be quiet." "Darling," she pleaded, "I feel
Pain so much more than you understand. I can't *bear* pain? *Bear* pain? I am not made like the people
You're used to." He wavered his head as if a fringe hung over the eyes, and bent to the wound, but she:
"I only tried to be killed." He muttered, "I don't kill women." And Fera: "You'd be so kind. Oh
But the darkness was sweet." And feeling his hands, "Oh Concha, she cried, I've told him everything and yet he'll hurt me.
Dear Concha pray to him for me, he used to love you. And I have never been mean to you because of that,
Concha." Then Cawdor suddenly turned to the Indian woman: "Is it true, what she says?" But Michal: "No, no,
Her mind," she stammered, "gone wrong. Ah you coward, Fera." "And what part," Cawdor said, "had *you* in the play?
By God, you all . . . When?" he said hoarsely to Fera. "Before he died," she answered, her breath hissing
In little pulses. He gathered his strength and said, "Out, Michal." And when she had gone: "Was it in this room,
Or his?" She answered "Under the laurel tree
He threw me down: I was not to blame not to blame more
Than a murdered man is." George said, "She is lying. Her madness is fear of pain. She is sick." "Though I've been played
For the fool of the world I know more than that. They make lies for pleasure but not
Get killed for pleasure. You sick whore does it hurt? Here is a different bed from the brown leaves

And the panting dog." Her face looking no bigger than a broken doll's on the pillow answered: "I knew
You'd kill me, I didn't think torture, why must I suffer alone? If I am to blame a little is he
Not rich with blame? He has got away I suppose. I swear by God I never consented to him.
It was all violence, violence . . . Have pity: no pity? Sweetheart: I never called you before: Sweetheart,
Have mercy on me." He stood as if to go out of the room; he was heard breathing, and slowly his hands
Crept to his throat. He turned and came back and said: "It is not to punish you.
I must set the bone. You can't stay here and be kept, you'll need both arms to live with. I will use all
Gentleness: but you lie still, it will be done in a moment. I'll send for the doctor, but when he comes
It will be too swollen perhaps for mending. Indeed I have other business. People take pain like bread
When their life needs it. After it is set the ache
Will quiet, you'll sleep."

Michal outside the door
Heard her screaming and went in; but then she had fainted
And Cawdor worked more easily. He bound the arm
And set the splints, and bound it again and passed
A leather belt about her body to fasten it
Against her side. He looked then at her face,
The dark lashes lying still, the parted white lips
Pencilled at the borders with fine blue lines,
Meek as a child's after the turn of fever
Folds its weakness in sleep. Concha prepared
To bathe the face but Cawdor: "Let her alone.

Let her have the poor mercy while it lasts.
Come George, I'll help you saddle. He'll come sooner
For you than another." He spoke quietly, but leaving
The room he walked against the wall by the door
And spread his hands both ways to feel the door-frame
Before he went out. He ran and found Hood's room
Empty, before he went with George to the stable.
"I think it has cleared," he said in the dark, "aren't the stars out?"
He saw the red star of Hood's fire on the Rock.
"Take your pick of the horses: I must go back
And warn the women: she will wake in delirium
And strain the bandages loose: I didn't speak of that,
That I remember? That I remember? Good-night,"
He said eagerly. He turned, then George went down
Alone, but Cawdor up the hill to the Rock
As one tortured with thirst toils up the sandhills
To the known rock spring. When he issued from the oaks
On the ridge of the steep neck of air-crumbled granite
The canyon redwoods were a stain of black shade
In the pit below, the gleam-powdered sky soared out of conception,
The starlight vastness and steepness were narrow to him
And no wind breathed. He was like one threading a tunnel
With anguished hunger of the air and light, all the arrows
Of desire strung to their heads on the pale spark
Of day at the end: so all the needs of his life
Hung on the speck of humanity by the red embers
On the rock dome. It heard him, and twitched and stood up.
He made in his mouth and waterless throat the words
"Come down," but no sound issued; he came nearer and said
"What did you steal? Come down." Hood screamed "Keep off,"
The same panic of brainless fear returning,
With a horror of his own cowardice, how could he bear

To run, but how could he bear to stand? He imagined
Fera had died. His very innocence of evil
Made the avenger unbearable, one of those hands
Could break his body, he snatched his rifle and stood
On the other side of the embers and sobbed "Stop there.
By God if you come nearer I'll fire. Keep off your hands.
I'm not hiding, I'll answer the law, not you.
I can't . . . Keep off. Oh! Oh!" For Cawdor blindly
Came through the fire; Hood with the rifle at his waist
Unshouldered, flung up the muzzle and shot in the air
Over his father's head: at the flash Cawdor
Felt a bright fear, not of death but of dying mocked,
Overreached and outraged as a fool dies,
Explode on his mind like light breaking on blindness
So that the body leaped and struck while the mind
Astonished with hatred stood still. There had been no choice,
Nor from the first any form of intention.
He saw Hood's body roll away from the fire
Like a thing with no hands; he felt in the knuckles
Of both his hands that both had been bruised on bone,
He saw Hood's body twist on the fall of the dome
Over the precipice and hands like weak flames
Scratch at the starlight rock: then one sharp moment's
Knife-edge a shadow of choice appeared: for all
Passed in a moment: he might have dived prone
And clutched after the hands with his hands: more likely
Gone down the granite slide into the gulf
With the other: but the choice had no consciousness
And in a moment no choice. There was no cry.
The curving hands scrabbled on the round of the rock
And slipped silently down, into so dreadful a depth
That no sound of the fall: nothing returned:

Mere silence, mere vanishing. Cawdor could hear the water
Whispering below, and saw the redwood forest
A long irregular stain in the starlit gorge-bottom,
But over the round of the rock it was not possible
To see the foot of the Rock. A little steady breeze
Blew curving up over the granite verge
From the night's drift in the chasm.

He turned and walked
Stealthily away, yet firmly, feeling no horror
But only a hollow unbearable sadness. But Hood had earned
The death he had got: not that he'd used violence
In adultery, that was incredible, the woman had lied:
But the crime however invited had no forgiveness,
Not even in death. Women are not responsible;
They are like children, little children grown lewd;
Men must acknowledge justice or their world falls
Piecemeal to dirty decay. Justice had been
Performed. He felt the sapping unbearable sadness
A little lightened, so muttered "Justice. Justice.
Justice": but the third time of saying it the word
Was pithed of meaning and became useless. He had come
Half way to the house and there remembered the things
Left on the Rock. He returned. Only his knowledge
Of what lay at the foot prevented him then
From casting himself down. Nor could he cast the rifle,
The silly rifle that Hood had loved,
For fear of its falling on the poor damned face.
He stood between the blanket-roll and the rifle
Beside a few burnt sticks and scattered red coals
On the bulge of the Rock. "Well, I have killed my son." Whether he continued living or quit living,

It would be a pity Michal should know. Quit, because it hurts? He thought he was not the make to do that.
His recent real temptation appeared a contemptible flourish of play-acting. "Well, I have killed my son.
He needed killing." The woman's story of the rape was now believed; it had become needful
To believe her story. "I will take these and bury them with him." When he'd again gone under the oaks
He heard one coming up the dark path. A moment of stupid horror he dreamed it was Hood coming
To claim the rifle. But Michal no doubt, Michal. He laid the things he carried into the darkness
Of the oaks by the path, and hardened his mind to meet Michal. Meet . . . whom? It brushed against the stiff leaves
Like something broken that crept and rested. With no terror but pity going down in the dark to meet it
He heard it snort and stamp hooves, a stray horse plunged from the path. "God damn you," he said and a voice answered
From down the path: "Hood, is that you?" She had been coming up to the Rock, and the strayed horse
Drifting ahead. She said "One of the horses: I guess it's gone. Oh Hood, Fera has said
Frightful . . . where are you?" She cried sharply "Who is that?" "The things were true," he answered, "all true." He heard her
Stop, and he seemed to feel her trembling. "Where's Hood," she said in a moment, trembling, "what have you done?"
"Nothing." He said in his heart "Well: I have killed him?" He possessed his voice in quietness and said, "I came
To ask him the truth, and he has confessed. It was all true." She sobbed and said "What have you done with him?"
"Nothing," he answered indifferently. "He ran when I came. A guilty conscience, Michal. He has done a thing

Never forgiven." He had reached her now; in the starless night of the oaks he saw the gleam of her face
Retreating, she moving slowly backward before him. He said "Like the scut of a deer." "What?" "When I came
He streaked up the hill into the starlight." "How did you make him confess?" "Oh Michal, a guilty conscience.
That does it. You know he wasn't a coward by nature, not a damned coward. I saw him run like a rabbit-scut
Between the hill and the stars. Come up to the Rock and call him." "I thought I heard a gun-shot," she faltered.
"I was in the house with . . . Then I went out." "A gun-shot? No. Come up and call him; perhaps he'll come down.
I promise you not to touch him. Come up and call to him, Michal. If you call loudly." They climbed to the Rock.
She saw it was vacant, the ends of a few sticks glowed on the stone, pale in their ash-crusts. "Hood. Hood,"
She called, and he said "Call louder. He has gone far." She answered,
"No, I won't call. I wish never to see him."

Who lay under the sheer below them, his broken shoulders
Bulging his coat in lumps the starlight regarded.
The bone vessel where all the nerves had met
For counsel while they were living, and the acts and thoughts
Been formed, was burst open, its gray and white jellies
Flung on the stones like liquor from a broken flask,
Mixed with some streamers of blood.

The vivid consciousness
That waking or dreaming, its twenty years, infallibly
Felt itself unitary, was now divided:
Like the dispersion of a broken hive: the brain-cells
And rent fragments of cells finding

After their communal festival of life particular deaths.
In their deaths they dreamed a moment, the unspent chemistry
Of life resolving its powers; some in the cold star-gleam,
Some in the cooling darkness in the crushed skull.
But shine and shade were indifferent to them, their dreams
Determined by temperatures, access of air,
Wetness or drying, as the work of the autolytic
Enzymes of the last hunger hasted or failed.

Yet there appeared, whether by chance or whether
From causes in their common origin and recent union,
A rhythmic sympathy among the particular dreams.
A wave of many minute delicious enjoyments
Would travel across the spilth; then a sad fading
Would follow it, a wave of infinitesimal pains,
And a pause, and the pleasures again. These waves both lessened
In power and slowed in time; the fragments of consciousness
Beginning to lapse out of the frailties of life
And enter another condition. The strained peace
Of the rock has no repose, it is wild and shuddering, it travels
In the teeth of locked strains unimaginable paths;
It is full of desire; but the brittle iniquities of pleasure
And pain are not there. These fragments now approached
What they would enter in a moment, the peace of the earth.

XI

When Cawdor had left the house, Concha
At once busied herself to recall to life
The milk-faced bandaged one on the bed, then Michal
Had intervened: "He said to let her alone.

He said to let her have peace." But Concha: "She stay
Fainting too long, she stop breathing, she die."
"I think that would be better." But the Indian woman
Trembling went on, then Michal held up the basin
While the other bathed the pale face, gray jewels of water
Ran down in the hair. There was no response; then Michal
Herself began to be frightened. She knew that her father
Had kept a bottle of whiskey somewhere in the room;
She set the basin on the blue chair and went
Searching on shelves.

Concha flung back the sheet
And blanket to bathe the breast. How the hard strap
That held the arm furrowed the flesh of the waist.
The fine-grained clear white skin was beautiful to her;
The coins of rose about the small nipples
Astonished her; hers were as black as the earth; she dipped her head
As if to a flower's fragrance and felt the quiet breasts
She had cooled with water move on her face: Fera
Moaned and then said faintly, "You are blind, father.
Both horses were white." She moved her head on her hair,
Her voice changed: "Do you love me Concha? You never were jealous,
I've wondered at you. Where's Cawdor?" Michal returned
And said sullenly: "I've found it, and there's no glass.
She'd better suck from the bottle." But Fera lay
Regardless of her, and dropping her right forearm
Across her breast explored the splints, and folds
On heavy folds of linen that shelled the shoulder
And the left arm; then with pain-dwindled lips,
"Well," she said, "give it to me. It's time for me now
To taste of my father's friend. Help me sit up, Concha."

She sipped and choked; it spilled on her chin, the burning fragrance
Filled all the room. Michal took back the bottle
And said, "Why did you lie? You lied. You lied.
Horrible things." Fera dull-eyed, with racked mouth,
The coughing had hurt her arm: "Not lies. Every word
Faithful as death. I lay between your father and your brother
Like a snake between the rock and the stone.
Give me the bottle, give it back to me Michal.
I have to hush this torment. Your father'll come back
And beat me with his fists like a wild beast,
He's like a beast in his rages." "Every word's lies.
But if it were true, why did you tell him?" "Because he tortured me."
Michal crossed the room to the corner and saw
In the east window high up in the dark pane
A little drop of red light. She pressed her face
Against the glass and cupped it with her two hands
To shut the lamplight away. Hood's waning fire,
Like a red star under the diamond stars.
"I'll go and ask him," she said turning. "He'll tell me
Every last word was a lie." "What did you see, Oh what did you see,
  Michal?"
Fera said shaking. "A fire on the Rock? It's only some vaquero from inland,
  Hood wouldn't build one,
Not to-night, not to-night." She answered "I saw nothing. I saw the sky
  and some stars. Concha,
Take care of her, will you. Get her to sleep." As Michal crossed to the door
  a dim noise like a gun-shot
Seemed to be heard, she said "Oh, what was that? Concha: you heard it?
  Listen." But Fera laughing
With an ashen face: "Lived here all her life long
And never has heard a wave slapping the sand at the creek-mouth."

When she'd
gone out, Fera said: "Concha,
My father's blindness was crystal to hers. How could she stay in the room and let Cawdor go out
To find his prey in the night? Did she know *nothing*? Give me the bottle, dear Concha. Dear Concha." She drank,
And said: "I'd no other way to keep him, he was going away. Poor hunter. I set a beast on his track
That he's no match for. The gun's no good boy hunter, you might as well toss acorns. Two bulls, Concha,
Fighting by starlight, the young one is gored. Ah: Concha:
One of my loves was locked in the hill by the oak, now the other's safe too. Listen: my birthday's to-night.
Has to be kept," she stammered, "I've told no one but you. And here's my father's friend to sit up with.
Go down and get two glasses, Concha, and a pitcher of water." She called her back from the door. "Concha!
The water in the house is all stale.
Go out to the spring among the calla lilies
And fill the pitcher. Don't hurry, Concha, I'm resting now."

As Concha
went out Fera stealthily
Undid the belt that locked her arm to her side; when the Indian was gone
She passed one-handed the strap through the buckle, the tongue thrown back
To let it slide free. She knotted the end of the strap
To the top of the carved bed-post, kneeling on the pillow,
Tightening the knot between her hand and her teeth.
She dropped the collar about her neck, and shuffled her knees
Until they slipped from the mattress. The right arm
Sustained the left one, to ease its pain in the fall.

She could have breathed by standing, but while her mind
Remained she would not, and then was unable.

Concha, down-stairs,
Had much to tell Ilaria. Acanna was there too
In the kitchen, and Concha's boy Romano, and Dante
Vitello, the Swiss. All questioned her. She'd forgotten
The water and found the glasses, when little Romano
In his child voice: "Escucha: un raton. – Listen mother,
A mouse in the ceiling." But no one looked up nor down
Until he fetched the gray cat from under the stove
And wanted to take her up-stairs. Concha forbade him,
But listened, and heard the noise in the ceiling change
From a soft stroking to a dull shudder in the wood.
The shudder was Fera's agony; the backs of her feet
Stroking the floor; she hung as if kneeling. But Concha said:
"A trade-rat maybe: no mouse. But I must go up."
The noise had ceased.

She screamed in the hallway above
And flung the glasses on the floor. The people below
Stared at each other. Her cries were timed, rhythmic,
Mechanical, like a ground-squirrel's when he sits up
Beside his burrow and watches a dog hunting
On the other side of the fence. At length Acanna
Ran to the stair, the others followed, and little Romano
With gray puss in his arms. They looked past Concha
Who stood in the door not daring to enter.

The girl
Appeared kneeling, only her knees were lifted
A little above the floor; her head devoutly
Drooped over. She was naked but the bandaged arm;

The coins about the small nipples were now
As black as Concha's; the lips dark, the fine skin
Mottled with lead-color. Ilaria pushed in and lifted
The body, Jesus Acanna then found his knife
And cut the strap. They stretched the slender body
On the bed and began to talk, but Dante Vitello
Remembered at length to pump the ribs with his hands.
They saw the lids of the eyes after a time
Flutter and close; the Swiss paused from his labor,
The breathing went on by itself.

Cawdor returned
From the Rock with Michal, but would not enter the house.
He seemed going toward the sea when she left him. He went
As far as the work-shop and fetched tools for digging,
A lantern, matches to light it. He chose the tools
With a clear mind; this work had to be done
Because of the coyotes. It proved more dreadful
Than he'd imagined; but when it was done the dreadfulness itself
Had purged his mind of emotion. He took no pains
To conceal the grave, for at this time discovery
Meant nothing to him, he desired nor feared nothing,
Not even to put back time and undo an act.
However, no person ever went up there.
He rolled stones on the grave against the coyotes,
And gathered the tools, but when he had carried them
Half way home, he threw them with the lantern too
Into the creek under the starless redwoods.
His mind ceased there, as if the tools had been strings
Between the world and his mind; these cut, it closed.

In the bright of dawn, before sunrise began,
The lank steers wheeled their line when he waved his arms.

He cursed them with obscene words . . . but why? . . . and there stood
Thirty in a row, all in a row like soldiers
Staring at him with strained-up heads. He was in the pasture
On the highest dome of the hill.
Wild fragrant wind blew from the burning east,
A handful of cloud high up in the air caught fire and vanished.
A point of more excessive light appeared
On the ridge by the lone oak and enlarged.
Without doubt, the sun. But if it were the horn of a flaming beast:
We'd have a horned beast to see by.
"What have I lost by doing through a blind accident
What I ought to have done in cold blood? Was Hood anything to me?
I have lost nothing." He'd have counted Fera
Lost, if he'd thought of Fera; she did not enter his mind.
"If I'd lost much: it's likely I'd not lie down
But gather again and go on." His flesh and bones were soaked
With aching weariness: but that was nothing either.
His eyes dazzled in the rivers of light
And the sea lay at his feet flat and lifeless
Far down but flecked with the steps of the wind. He went down to the
house
And heard that Fera had hanged herself and been saved,
But that was nothing either. No, something. Where were you?
He said to Concha. "She send me down. She send me.
She send me down for water. When I come back: Oh!"
"I'll not see her this morning," he answered.
"Bring my clothes to the little room on the north
And change the bed there. Hood's gone for good." He had done justly,
And could sleep very well there.

Two days passed
Before he remembered the blanket-roll and the rifle

Dropped in the oaks when Michal came. He went and sought
But never found them. But that was nothing either.

XII

Her voice was still roughened with an off whisper
In the bruised throat, and the white of one of her eyes
Grained with a drop of red, a little blood-vessel
Had broken there when the strap drew. When she was alone
She lay pointed on the bed, stiffened to the attitude
Of formal death, feeling the ache in her arm
But hardly conscious of it, the hours and scenes
And the form as a whole of all her life incessantly
Moving behind the blank wide open eyes.
She lay and contemplated it with little emotion
And hardly a thought. She thought of herself as dead,
Although she knew perfectly that she was living,
And had said to Concha: "You needn't watch me, you and Ilaria.
I'll never try death again, now I understand
That to fail is the very soul of my soul.
Failure is not so sweet that one who feels it
Beforehand will go running to meet it again.
Though death is sweet. That will come in its time
When I'm as old as my father, I fear not sooner;
Never for the asking."

She said to Concha another day:
"I wish you could get Michal to come and see me;
Or George even. Not one soul has come in,
Not since the doctor was here, and death is so lonesome.
I could get up, but when I begin to walk

Cawdor will send me away. You must never tell them
That I can get up." This was at noon; Concha
Painfully made a slow thought in her mind
All afternoon, and said to Cawdor in the evening,
Stammering, because her words were planned beforehand:
"She say that she is well enough to get up."
"Who says?" "Oh . . . she . . ." "You mean," he said frowning,
"My wife? Let her get up then." She turned sadly, and then said:
"When she get up you going to send her away?"
"What is that to you?" Then Concha recklessly: "You keep her
After she loving with Hood?" She curved her body
In fear of his hand; but he took hold of her wrist
And drove her up the stairway to Fera's room.

Who lay in the bed straightened to the shape of death
And looked at them with still eyes; the scarlet drop
In the white of the left one spoiled her eyes' peace. Cawdor
Put off the questions that had burned him to ask,
And stood still and then said: "You are well enough to get up,
Concha says, but you think I'd send you away."
She smiled at Concha. "I wondered whether you'd do it.
And then I thought you wouldn't, but it's no matter.
No: you won't send me," she said to Cawdor, "for I
Suffered my destruction in simple innocence.
Oh, certainly you'll not drink again from a mouthed cup,
But the cup's not blamed. You are much too just to punish the cup. There are more reasons." His face a moment
Was like her father's a scar; it formed itself to be dark metal again and he said: "No doubt
You were loving with him and so he went mad." She thought, and answered: "No. You did justice. I know what you did.
You'd better send out your brown tattle-tales

Before we say any more, she'd hear and go tell, wouldn't you Concha?
  Besides that her sour odor
Poisons the room. I've noticed lately, the living smell much worse than the
  dead. Oh never mourn them;
No one was ever sorry to have died." He shook his head, like the bull that
  has charged a man and found
Only the vacant flapping of a red blanket, and he said: "Be straight will you
  for once, I won't hurt you.
You hide in a smoke of words like lies. Perhaps"—his face hollowed with
  terror—"it was all a lie?
No, that can't be. You white poison you were in the boat with him and lied
To save your skin?" He turned on Concha: "Did you see her make love to
  him?" But the Indian woman feared to go on;
She shook her head, and looked aside at Fera, and shook her head. Cawdor
  made himself patient
And said, "Perhaps a kiss: or you saw her stroking his head: he had fine
  hair . . ." Fera lay faintly
Smiling and watched him; he looked, stooping his face to Concha's, like a
  tall old Jew bargaining, and said:
"Or you saw them . . . by God, you told me they kissed, you said that."
  She nodded her head, panting and shrinking backward,
Wiping her dark hands on her apron incessantly; and Fera: "She'll tell more
  lies if you make more faces,
And when that fails you could pinch her arm. How can you expect truth
  from such people, they're all afraid of you?"
He looked at Concha and said feebly: "If I could know.
I am stupid and things are hidden. What I have done. Was right, but the
  blood rushes me behind my eyes
And God sends chance. It all happened in the blindness of chance." Fera
  said quietly "Don't talk before her."
He looked at her eyes and said, "You have the secret, if I could trust you.
  That red drop comes from hanging

And will clear up. You seem quieter in mind
Than ever before. Do you know where I sleep now? Hood's room." "It was Concha's first." He groaned in his throat, feeling
That every thought in her mind was impure, how could he fish the truth from a dirty fountain? He said:
"And yet you'll tell me. It will make no difference to you but only to me. I will do nothing to punish you,
Whatever you say, nothing in your favor either." "I've told you already," she answered. "But whether you tempted him,
Invited him, you egged him on, you thought he was safe. A word: or only a damned smile: women
Can move hell with their eyes." She closed her eyes, and said keeping them closed: "What I said that night
Each word was true. You're right though, I've still a secret. Shoo tattle-tales out,
And then I'll tell you my secret." He said, "Concha: get out." She sighed and went out gladly, and Fera:
"Open the door; I won't have her at the door." However the hallway was empty, and Fera said:
"I was friendly with him, he was your son and Michal's brother. I never in act nor look nor thought
Stepped over that. Was he vicious when he was little? I never knew it. A beast lived in his blood,
But no one warned me and now he is gone." "That's the word: gone. You are safe to blacken him, he can't answer."
"If I should lie and whiten him," she said,
"And say he was innocent, some stitch of his nerves in him destroyed me but his heart was innocent: and you believed it:
How could you sleep? And after a night or two
That room you have taken might seem too little for you. You are very strong, you'd hold yourself quiet three nights,

Or four nights, and then wander on the hill scaring the cattle." He said gravely, " Does every one know?
Who told you this?" "No one," she answered. "And after a week of nights they'd find you with those big-boned
Fingers clenched in your throat quiet on the hill." "On the Rock," he said. "Oh, on the Rock. But since . . .
Or under the Rock. But since he was guilty you can sleep sound." The flesh of his face, that had sagged lately,
Was now become firm for danger, and he asked: "How do you know these things if no one watched me?" She answered
"I know you so well. I used to be near you, if you remember, before I was spoiled. And now, lying
Like this"—she lay pointed in the bed, her arms on her breast—"I mean alone and cut off from life,
I've had leisure and power to think of you plainly, so all your acts that night stand in my mind
Fixed and forever like pieces of stone. That's the way with us dead, we see things whole and never
Wonder at things." He said, "You lie here and dream and imagine. There's nothing in it." "So you won't send me,"
She answered, "to stay with strangers. I know too much and might tell: that's nothing to you: but as time darkens
You'll find me the only comforter you have. And I can teach you the way to blessedness: I've tasted life
And tasted death; the one's warm water, yellow with mud and wrigglers, sucked from a puddle in the road,
Or hot water that scalds you to screaming;
The other is bright and cool and quiet, drawn from the deep. You knocked the scummed cup from the boy's hand
And gave him the other: is that a thing to be sorry for? I know; I have both in my hands; life's on the broken

And splinted left so I never lift it. You did kindly, not terribly. If you were wise, you'd do
As much for yourself. If you were loving you'd do
As much for me." He stood and listened, and said "Is that all?"
She nodded. "Then it's not much.
I see there are two of us here twisting in hell,
Smile as you like." "Why yes," she answered, "by the left arm.
That's true. But I taste both." He was leaving the room
And she cried after him: "Oh my dear, dear, be merciful.
Life is so tough to cut, I never would have dreamed.
I fail. But nothing stops *you*."

He went out-doors
And felt a seeming-irresistible desire
To go to the foot of the Rock and lie with those stones
On the soft earth, his mouth whispering against it.
But now, he must never give in to any desire;
Strain the iron forever. Never do anything strange:
For even now their eyes followed him strangely.
No matter; they'd keep in subjection; they might have watched it
And not dare speak: but a pity if little Michal . . .
The stars in the sparse boughs, the skies are never
Darkened any more, a naughty glitter.
How does one commonly spend a winter evening:
Not letting the stars glitter through the split boughs.
He entered the house and sat down. Strain the iron forever:
He had strength for that.

Fera had little strength,
And the long hollow night coming looked unendurable.
Her right arm was flung free of the cover and lay
Bent on her eyes; after a while her teeth

Found the wrist: ugh, what was this? She raised it and saw
The yellow and brown scabs of the laceration
Where she had gnawed it before.

In the morning, when Concha
Came in to serve her, she said "Did you believe in heaven and hell
When you were little? (To-day I'll get up,
I've had enough of this bed, you'll help me dress.)
Because you know the dead rarely come back;
But I died and came back, and I can tell you
More than the priests know. Dying's not bad: Oh, bad enough,
But you can stand it, you have to. But afterwards . . . Ah, there's . . ."
She moaned, her tight small fist crept up to her cheek
And trembled there. She was playing a comedy, she played it so well
Her own flesh suffered and chilled. "Death is no sleep, Concha, death is eternal torment and terror
For all that die. Neither is there any heaven for anyone. I saw my father there crying blood
From the hollows of his blind eyes and tearing his beard with his hands. He said 'Oh my God have you come, Fera?
Who ever dreamed that death could be worse than life?' I said 'It is so,' and all the crowd of the dead
Began moaning 'It is so.' But then you managed to make me breathe with your hands and I could come back,
They said to me then, 'Never tell any living person what death is like, for if they imagined
What it's like, for they all must come, how could they live?
Who'd not go mad with fear to feel it approaching?'
Oh Concha, hug life with tooth and nail, for what
Comes after is the most horrible. And no end, no end.
(Come here and help me. We'll have to slit down the sleeve
And pin it over the shoulder.) I didn't tell you

To scare you, Concha. Don't think about it. Ah no,
Or we'd sit screaming.
I wasn't going to tell you but then I thought
That you can bear it as well as I can, after the trick
You played me last night, my rival!
Live. Live forever if you could. Oh it was frightful."

XIII

Though she was up, and began to live and go out,
She avoided Cawdor's presence, still fearing to be sent away
If seen too often. She kept her room at mealtimes,
And he was almost never about the house
The other hours of the day.

The first time she went out,
She only walked under the storm-broken cypresses
About the door and went in; but the next morning
She climbed the steep to the great oak by the graves.
Still weak and bloodless, dizzy with climbing, she lay
Face down on the dug earth, her mouth breathing against it
And whispering over her father's body below.
The grave retained its freshness, no rain had fallen
On the red earth. She heard after a time
A rustling and scraping noise and raised her head.
It was Michal's eagle hungrily astir in the cage;
She used to feed it about this time. Fera
Saw beak and eyes in the shadow, and the dark square
Of the box cage against the bright blue shining
Flat ocean and the arch of sky. She stood up, and walked
About the oak's bole; she seemed to be counting the graves,

But there were only three; the two ancient ones
Enclosed with pickets and the raw new one unfenced.

Michal came up with flesh and water for the eagle,
But Fera stood on the other side of the oak
Until she had come; then, coming forward from it:
"Why Michal, how strange to think that all these days,
No matter what's happened, you still go on steadily as sunrise.
My father dies of old age, I fish for death
And catch failure again, and Hood . . . but you and the sunrises
Go on as if our tears and our deaths were nothing.
He isn't glad to see you: I'd have been glad to see you
My lonely days in bed but you never came."
Michal had looked over her shoulder, her face
Growing white as it turned. She turned back to the cage.
"I didn't know you were here," she said, and poured out
The dirty water from the drinking-basin
Without turning again. "I see that you hate me,"
Fera said; "we'll not speak of that. I see that your father
Has thought *my* father's grave not worthy of a mark.
If the cold charity of the county had buried him
There'd be a stake with his name.
Yet he was here like a man among cattle,
The only mind in this ditch." Michal said nothing,
But rubbed the white slime from the basin and rinsed it,
And Fera said, "The oak's dying, they chopped its roots.
Or was it the storm that burned these baby leaves?
We ought to be friends, Michal." Michal set in
The filled basin and shut the door of the cage.
She opened her lips to speak, and then kept silence,
And Fera said "You'll listen, my dear, if you won't speak. Do you think I'll
swallow

These white and hating looks as if they were earned? What have I done? Tried to die? Yes; I tried twice;
And that was stupid, but people are pitied for that, not hated. You were quite kind my days of sunshine,
And now you peck the feathers from the sick bird." Michal said trembling, "Oh, no. Not that I'm spiteful,
Only, I can't understand." "That's true," she answered, "how could you?
Your life has been sweet and full of ignorance. But I, when my father was drunk in town, would hear my mother
Take lovers in the house. *There* was somebody to hate. Yet they were white men;
They weren't the color of Concha . . . no more of that. The second time I died I almost made it, you know.
They pumped me alive with their hands and I was born again
From the dark air: since then I can understand much that was dark before. So you, Michal,
Will understand . . . many things that are dark . . . when some wild night kills childhood in you. That's coming:
But don't pray for it, my dear.
Oh Michal that's the reason I so much want you to listen to me. The inflamed and dark season
And bitterness will come, and then I dread your saying to yourself: 'Fera she hated life; Fera
Preferred death; Fera was wise.' I wasn't; at least you mustn't think so. I welched on my fate,
(And failed of course, failure's my root in nature) but I am ashamed. So you must listen to me, Michal,
My praise of life, by my dead father, by the dying oak. What I've lived has not been lucky you know,
If I can praise it, who'd not? But how good it is, Michal, to live! Good for what? Ah, there's the question.

For the pleasure of it? Hardly for that. Take your own life, mine's marked, mine's worse than usual. Your mother
Lies yonder; you never knew her, you missed the *pleasure* of knowing her. You missed the pains too; you might have hated her.
More likely you'd have loved her deeply; you'd have been sad then to see her wasting with age and pain,
Those years would come; and you'd have felt the salt fountains of loneliness
Drain from your eyes when the day came and she died. There's not a pleasure in the world not paid for, Michal,
In pain with a penny or two for interest. But youth, they say, is a shining time, and no doubt for you
The pleasures outsun the pains. Then the hair grays, and the teeth blacken or drop, and the sky blackens.
You've swollen ankles and shrunk thighs, and horrible hanging breasts that flap like a hound's ears,
Or death comes first . . . Oh, but I'm wrong, it's life I was praising! And the pain to the pleasure is sun to candle.
Joy never kills, you know, the most violent joy
Never drove anyone mad. Pain kills, and pain drives mad; and extreme pain can feed for days
On the stretched flesh; the extremes of pleasure rot in two minutes.

Oh yes,
but, Michal,
Surely life's . . . good? My father—his thoughts were deep,
Patient and wise—believed it was good because it was growing.
At first it was a morsel of slime on the sea,
It grew to be worms and fishes, lizards and snakes,
You see the progress, then things with hair and hot blood,
It was coming up from the ocean and climbing mountains,
Subduing the earth, moulding its bundle of nerves

Into the magnificent mind of man, and passing
Beyond man, to more wonders. That helped my father!
He loved that. You and me of course it can't help,
Because we know nothing goes on forever.
What good is better and better if best draws blank?
Here's the oak was growing upward a hundred years
And now it withers. Sometime the world
Will change, only a little too hot or too cold
Or too dry, and then life will go like the oak.
Then what will all my father's magnificent thoughts,
Michal, and all the dreams of your children be worth?
Well, we must praise life for some other reason.
For surely it's . . . good? We know it must be. Here every morning
You bring food to this bird to keep it alive:
Because you love it: in its filth, in misery, in prison. What's wretcheder than a caged eagle? Guess. I'll not tell.
And you'd be bitter cruel to keep it alive: sick-feathered, abject, broken-armed: only, you know
Life is so *good*. It's true the creature seems ungrateful: but I am not grateful either: to Dante
Vitello who pumped the breath into my body."
She stopped and looked at Michal's white face, and said
"You haven't heard from Hood yet? He went so suddenly,
He ought to write you." Michal said "No," and Fera:
"You know nothing about him?" She cried trembling:
"Why do you ask about Hood? Why do you ask about Hood?
Let me alone." "Ah," Fera said, "do you think
That something has happened to him?" "He'll never come back.
It was your fault." "I'm sure he'll never come back,"
She said with a still face. "Now let's go down.
But I can't joke about your eagle Michal.

The hopeless cage of pain is a lamp
Shining rays that go right through the flesh
And etch the secrets of bone. Mine aches. Oh no, Michal,
I couldn't do it: but George would kill him for you:
Or ask your father: that's better: those are the hands."

Another morning Fera went up
Secretly under the redwoods to the Rock's foot,
Where the great ribbed and battering granite face
Came down and found earth. In spring the cliff-swallows nest
A third of the way up, and a pair of duckhawks
Two thirds of the way. High in air the gray dome
Seemed swaying from the sweep of the small fibrous clouds.
Fera crept back and forth at the foot with pale
Spying eyes: but this loose earth was only a squirrel's mound,
And that was a gopher's digging: for hours: and she found
Stones had been rolled together, their brown earth-bellies
Turned up to the sky, and the gray lichenous backs
Downward, there was fresh earth below, with grass-blades
Half buried and ferns trampled. One rain had fallen.
She stood and gazed and said to him there: "Did I not say beforehand
That after we were dead I should have no rest after all but run moaning
On the gray shore, gnawing for my hunger a wrist of shadow?" She found a
    brown scurf on the slope rocks
Above, and thought, "This is the blood that burst from your mouth when
    you fell"; caressing with hers the doubtful
Crust, that was really a brown lichen. "Oh why would you not listen to me?
    You chose, to die
Rather than live. Ah, you'd learned wisdom somewhere, you were too
    young to be wise, when with one beautiful
Act of delight, lovely to the giver as the taker, you might have made

A star for yourself and for me salvation." She rose and said to the grave: "It
was I that killed you. The old man
Who lives in hell for it was only my hands."

XIV

It was true; and it was Cawdor that paid the suffering.
The woman found ease in words and outcry; the man,
The more sensitive by sex and by his nature,
Had forbidden himself action because one act
Was grown his cancer; speech because speech betrays;
Even thought, in one regard, for if Hood's guilt
Were not monstrous the punishment became monstrous,
And if he had been solicited into adultery
His guilt was not monstrous but halved and natural;
There was evidence enough for that, and there
Thought was forbidden. Meanwhile his mind remained
Implacably clear for the rest, cloudless harsh light
On what he had done, memory not dimmed with time
But magnified and more real, not masked with any
Mysticism, that comes most often and stands
Between the criminal and his crime, a redeemer
Shifting the load onto fate; no failure toward unreason
Except the fantasy of his wife's innocence.

His loved canyon was grown hateful and terrible;
He longed to go away, go away, but that
Was cowardice, the set pride and code of his life
Prohibited that; he desired to kill himself,
But that was cowardice; to go and accuse himself,
But that was a kind of cowardice; all the outlets of action
Were locked and locked. But the most present desire,

And the most self-despised, was to ask advice
No matter of whom: of George, of Dante Vitello:
He yearned on them with his eyes: but that was cowardice
And ridiculous too. Day by day the tensions of his mind
Were screwed tighter in silence. He had some strength,
Though not the strength his vanity used to imagine,
And now in the deadlock of his powers endurance
Continued still. He felt the eyes of his house
That used to peer at him from behind now openly
Glitter before his face. He believed they all knew,
Save little Michal, and were kept quiet by fear,
They watched his face for weakness, as the blackbirds
In Carmel Valley watch the green fruit for softness.

After the flood in December the later rains
Fell scant, shrewd north wind heeling listless falls
Blew the hills dry; Cawdor discovered his mind
Building conjectural bridges between the drought
And the curse of his deed; he conquered the sick thought,
Another cowardice.

In March when the cows were calving
Came printed news of foot-and-mouth disease
Among the cattle in the north, it had come in
Through San Francisco from Asia. An infected herd
Had been destroyed. Cawdor read and feared nothing,
His herd in the isolation of the coast canyon
Would be the last. Yet he dreamed in the night
That he was slaughtering his herd. A bench was dug
To stand on, in the steep wall of a gully;
He stood there with the sledge-hammer and Jesus Acanna
All black on a black horse against the twilight

Drove in the cattle. One swing of the hammer for each
On the peak between the horns, but the white-faced heifer
Sidled her head and the blow crushed the horn.
Bawling and slopped with blood down the sleek shoulders,
Plunging among the carcasses . . . The dream returned
Too many times; the plague increasing in the north
He warned his men to guard the pasture and watch
For strays; then the dream ceased; but the hurt heifer
Still troubled his dreams.

His mind had relented toward Fera,
Innocent sufferer and as wretched as himself.
He saw now that both George and Michal hated her.
Her arm had knitted crooked, it pained always
In her pale eyes. He spoke to her kindly; she answered patiently.
He saw as in a vision that if he should choose
He might go back to his own room from Hood's
This very night, and all be as it was before.
To hell with the glittering eyes, they would keep quiet.
"No," he said and went out of the house. But she
Followed and overtook him under the cypresses
In the evening twilight.

Michal and George were left
In the lamplight in the room, and Michal said
"I want you . . ." she made more words but they were too mumbled
To understand; she stopped and drew breath and said
Astonishingly aloud, as if she were calling
Across a canyon: "I want you to kill my eagle.
I ought never to have kept it. Nothing but wretchedness.
George, will you kill it quickly and without pain
To-morrow morning?" He stared at her and said

"We've other troubles to think of." "Yes. If you won't
I'll do it myself." "I will. Don't cry, Michal."
She went up-stairs crying.

In the twilight under the trees
Fera touched Cawdor's arm and said timidly: "The best
Would be not to've been born at all; but if we are bound to live why should we hate each other?"
He turned in surprise, he had forgotten her. "You are not bound." "By failures of nature. I am like a sick beast . . .
Like Michal's eagle . . . I can't do for myself. I've tried. Think of *me* a little. You did the other
No evil but eternal good. Forget him now, and if I can't end: failure's my peg that I hang on:
Mayn't we go back and live as we were before? You loved me once, when I was a child and you
Were a man." He stood silent thinking of another matter, suddenly he barked with laughter and said
"What am I now?" "A living God: you could answer prayer if you pleased." "Don't be troubled," he said,
"About God. You talk about God
The day before you go mad." "I can't do that either. Are you afraid to live," she answered,
"Because they whisper? But they know nothing; they've not a thread of evidence. I've talked to them all, not one
But I, not one but I could betray you." She peered up at his face to see what it said in the twilight.
It said nothing; he was thinking of another matter, and walking the open way from the trees, slowly
Toward the sea's fading light. "Besides, they are all afraid of you. Oh listen!" she said. "We two alone

Have all the decision. Nobody but I can twitch the reins in your hands.
Look at me." She caught his arm.
"Am I changed?" He looked, and suddenly laughed with pleasure. "Why . . . like a blown-out candle. Perfectly changed.
The fragrance all gone, all the wind fallen." He failed to see the lightning pallor, he was so prisoned
In the surprise of his mind. "No more in my eyes than a dead stick. No more," he said in astonishment,
"Than Concha Rosas." He spoke with no intention of cruelty, his mind in the pain of its own bonds
Islanded alone, incapable of feeling another's. She clasped her throat with her hand and said shuddering:
"For this. No, not another time.
I went on my knees to Hood, I made myself a shameless beggar, I washed his feet with tears.
That's not done twice. To love me: and he would not.
Ah God how can I make you know it? I duped you too well. Ah dupe, Ah fool," she stammered, "Ah murderer.
Machine that one winds up and it goes and does it. I wound you, I was the one. Now the air's fire
To drink and the days and nights the teeth and throat of a dog: shall I hide your eyes with my hand always
From what you have done, to let you die in sweet ignorance?" He said "Go on. Strain it out, gasping, a heifer
With the first calf." "It's the only child I'll bear you. I hope you will like the child. You killed the other
Woman's but mine perhaps will spill *you*
From the same rock. For proofs: ask Michal, she heard me pray to him for love: ask Concha Rosas again,
The fat beast listened and saw, she heard me, she helped me fool you: ask Jesus Acanna,
Watched me lead Hood from my father's earth to the laurel to be my lover: *I* led him, *I* called him, *I* flung

Flowers and fire at his feet: he never at mine: and he refused me, he died
for that. Ask your eyes,
Heartless blue stones in their caves, wanted to be blind and they saw,
They saw me come down in the rain to call him, the rain steamed where it
struck, I was hot, I walked in a shameless
Burning heat; my father was dying but I ran down.
And again you saw me, Hood was naked in bed at dawn, you caught me in
his room. Had he received me
Gladly or kindly, had he raised his arms to receive me? I begged and he put
me by, I broke in to beg
And he was driving me out when you came. He remembered his father's
honor, he was a fool and faithful,
He's paid for it, he was faithful to you, you paid the wages. Ah, wait, I've
more.
It's precious to me to tell you these things, I've hardly desired honey-sweet
death a longer while."
"You lie too much," he answered, "I asked you before to tell me. Pour it
out."
He stood like a gray tree in the twilight, only a surface trembling, the axe
was blunted in the bark,
Fera thought; and she said: "I asked him to cut leaves from the laurel to lay
in my father's grave,
There are no flowers in this ditch,
And under the laurel I gave him my love. Are you glad that he had my love?
That saves you, that lets you live.
The old husband happy in his wife's pleasures.
Under the laurel it was, behind the concealing oaks, under the laurel it was.
Before,
I had only cried out and begged with tears, but there I gave him my body,
my arms about him, my breasts
Against him: be patient will you, this is not much, this is not the poison: I
gave him my flesh to eat,
As Michal takes up meat to the eagle, but he was wilder than the eagle.

He remembered his father's honor, he would not feed. My arms were his cage, I held the meat to his mouth,
He would not feed." Her face distorted itself and seemed to reflect flame, like the white smoke
Of a hidden fire of green wood shining at night, twisting as it rises. Gipsies crouch by the smoke's root
Watching strange flesh simmer in the pot between the forked sticks. When the wind varies their eyes prickle
And the shine of the smoke hides the gray stars. Her face writhed like the shining smoke and she cried and said:
"I wish the little rivers under the laughing kingfishers in every canyon were fire, and the ocean
Fire, and my heart not afraid to go down.
I broke my heart against his mouth like honeycomb, he would not take me, Oh the bitter honey, the black-blooded
Drops from the wax, no wonder he refused me. There was a lion-skin
I wore to my death, was it you stole it or Concha? He gave it to me, his one gift, but your house
Is a house of thieves. One boy was honest and so you killed him. The boy respected his father's possession.
He despised me, he spat me out. Then when I pressed him hard and set fire to his body: the heart and soul
I never could reach, they were both stones: he took his hunter's knife in his hand, he made the pain
Of the point in his flesh a servant against me. Into his thigh he drove it, he laughed and was lame, and triumphed,
And limped into the darkness of death."

She stood silent, and Cawdor remembered his son's lameness
Stumbling under the old man's coffin up the steep hill. He groaned aloud, then Fera's face

Gleaming spotted the darkness before his eyes. "I loved him," she said.
"Love is a trap that takes
The trapper and his game in the same teeth. The first to die has the luck.
They hang bleeding together.
But you were a mere dupe and a common murderer,
Not love but envy, dupe and fool, what will you do?"
He swayed against the dark hill, "You make the lies,"
He said hoarsely, "must I always believe them?
Time. Time. All my damnation draws
From having done in a haste. What do you want?"
"If I were you
And had your strength I'd kill the woman first,
Then cut out the eyes that couldn't tell my innocent
Boy's head from a calf's to butcher,
And smell my way to the Rock and take the jump."
"I asked you," he said, "because a known devil's
Word is a warning." She came and touched him. "The first's
Easiest," she said, "to kill the woman: the rest
Follows of its own accord." She stroked his face and said
"It is all easy." He took her throat in his hands,
She did not tremble nor flinch; he tightened his fingers
Slowly, as if he were dreaming the thing not doing it,
Then her mouth opened, but the ivory face
Kept its composure still; his fingers closed
A little harder and half checked the hot breath.
Suddenly she clawed at his hands with hers, she cried
"Have pity! I didn't mean it. Oh, Oh, I was lying.
Let me live!" He set her by and ran back to the house,
She heard him sob as he ran.

George was alone
In the lamplit room, Cawdor came in and said
"It's nothing," and went up-stairs, his eyes so sunken

That no gleam showed. He shut himself in the room
He used now, where Hood had slept before. George followed
Quietly and saw the crack under the door
Silent of light; he listened and heard no sound.
Then he returned down-stairs. Fera had come in;
She made a smile and passed him and went to her place.

XV

In the morning Cawdor failed to come down; Michal
At length knocked at his door. She listened, trembling,
And got no answer. She opened the door. He stood
Against the window and said "Is it you Michal?
I'm not well. Let me alone." She saw that the bed
Had not been slept in; she could not see his face
Against the shining light but his voice frightened her,
So gentle and forlorn. "Let me bring you some breakfast,
Father?" "No," he said, "no. But there's one thing
You could do for me." "What thing?" "To let me alone.
Nothing else. Nothing else." She saw that his face
Kept turning toward the bed, the eyes and features
Could hardly be seen against the morning light.
She thought he meant to lie down.

When Michal had gone
He locked the door, and leaning to the bed whispered:
"She didn't see you. How astonished she'd have been,
She thinks you're hunting in the north." He smiled fondly
And touched the pillow. "You always had fine hair
But now it has grown longer." A sad perplexity
Wrinkled his face; when he drew back his hand
His eyes were again serene. He went to the window

And stood with his back against the light. "From here
I see you the most clearly. Ah no, lie quiet.
You've had a fall," he said shaking, "don't speak.
This puts my eyes in heaven." He stood a long while
And his face darkened. "She keeps begging to die.
Plenty of others want that and make less noise.
It was only a sorrowful joke last night,
I'd not have done it. I made her beg off at least.
But when she squealed I hardly could let go,
My fingers cramped like the arms of breeding toads.
I've lived some months in pain."

He listened, and said:
"I know. Thank God. But if you had died, what then?
I had too much foolish pride to throw the game
Because it hurt." He paused and said "I thought
I needed punishment but death's no punishment.
I thought of telling the sheriff": he laughed. "I know him.
And a judge save me? I had to judge myself.
Run to a judge was only running away
From judgment: I thought I'd not do that; shame Michal
And do no good. Running away. I thought the same
Of killing myself. Oh, I've been thinking.
If I'd believed in hellfire I'd have done it
Most nights of the week." He listened, and shook his head.
"No value in needless pain? Oh yet if I lay
As damned with blood as I believed I was
I'd manage somehow. Tit for tat is good sense.
The debt was to myself as well as to you,
And mostly I've paid my debts. Well, I thank God.
This black's turned gray."

Michal had found her brother
Mending iron at the forge, the little shed
Behind the workshop; she'd heard the hammer and found him.
"Have you forgotten your promise?" "Why no," George answered,
"I'll do it for you. I thought you'd change your mind."
She was as pale as if a dear friend's death
Were being sealed in the plot. "Then do it quickly.
I think that father," she said, "is going to be sick.
Our lives perhaps will change, I'll not have time
For trapping squirrels to notch the dreary days
Of the cage with pitiful instants of pleasure." He frowned
And struck the iron, the red darkening, with scales
Of black, and white flecks.

While George went to the house
For his revolver, Michal climbed up the hill
Weeping; but when he came with death in his hand
She'd not go away, but watched. At the one shot
The great dark bird leaped at the roof of the cage
In silence and struck the wood; it fell, then suddenly
Looked small and soft, muffled in its folded wings.

The nerves of men after they die dream dimly
And dwindle into their peace; they are not very passionate,
And what they had was mostly spent while they lived.
They are sieves for leaking desire; they have many pleasures
And conversations; their dreams too are like that.
The unsocial birds are a greater race;
Cold-eyed, and their blood burns. What leaped up to death,
The extension of one storm-dark wing filling its world,
Was more than the soft garment that fell. Something had flown away. Oh
cage-hoarded desire,

Like the blade of a breaking wave reaped by the wind, or flame rising from fire, or cloud-coiled lightning
Suddenly unfurled in the cave of heaven: I that am stationed, and cold at heart, incapable of burning,
My blood like standing sea-water lapped in a stone pool, my desire to the rock, how can I speak of you?
Mine will go down to the deep rock.

This rose,
Possessing the air over its emptied prison,
The eager powers at its shoulders waving shadowless
Unwound the ever widened spirals of flight
As a star light, it spins the night-stabbing threads
From its own strength and substance: so the aquiline desire
Burned itself into meteor freedom and spired
Higher still, and saw the mountain-dividing
Canyon of its captivity (that was to Cawdor
Almost his world) like an old crack in a wall,
Violet-shadowed and gold-lighted; the little stain
Spilt on the floor of the crack was the strong forest;
The grain of sand was the Rock. A speck, an atomic
Center of power clouded in its own smoke
Ran and cried in the crack; it was Cawdor; the other
Points of humanity had neither weight nor shining
To prick the eyes of even an eagle's passion.

This burned and soared. The shining ocean below lay on the shore
Like the great shield of the moon come down, rolling bright rim to rim with the earth. Against it the multiform
And many-canyoned coast-range hills were gathered into one carven mountain, one modulated

Eagle's cry made stone, stopping the strength of the sea. The beaked and winged effluence
Felt the air foam under its throat and saw
The mountain sun-cup Tassajara, where fawns
Dance in the steam of the hot fountains at dawn,
Smoothed out, and the high strained ridges beyond Cachagua,
Where the rivers are born and the last condor is dead,
Flatten, and a hundred miles toward morning the Sierras
Dawn with their peaks of snow, and dwindle and smooth down
On the globed earth.

It saw from the height and desert space of unbreathable air
Where meteors make green fire and die, the ocean dropping westward to the girdle of the pearls of dawn
And the hinder edge of the night sliding toward Asia; it saw far under eastward the April-delighted
Continent; and time relaxing about it now abstracted from being, it saw the eagles destroyed,
Mean generations of gulls and crows taking their world: turn for turn in the air, as on earth
The white faces drove out the brown. It saw the white decayed and the brown from Asia returning;
It saw men learn to outfly the hawk's brood and forget it again; it saw men cover the earth and again
Devour each other and hide in caverns, be scarce as wolves. It neither wondered nor cared, and it saw
Growth and decay alternate forever and the tides returning.

It saw, according to the sight of its kind, the archetype
Body of life a beaked carnivorous desire
Self-upheld on storm-broad wings: but the eyes

Were spouts of blood; the eyes were gashed out; dark blood
Ran from the ruinous eye-pits to the hook of the beak
And rained on the waste spaces of empty heaven.
Yet the great Life continued; yet the great Life
Was beautiful, and she drank her defeat, and devoured
Her famine for food.

There the eagle's phantom perceived
Its prison and its wound were not its peculiar wretchedness,
All that lives was maimed and bleeding, caged or in blindness,
Lopped at the ends with death and conception, and shrewd
Cautery of pain on the stumps to stifle the blood, but not
Refrains for all that; life was more than its functions
And accidents, more important than its pains and pleasures,
A torch to burn in with pride, a necessary
Ecstasy in the run of the cold substance,
And scape-goat of the greater world. (But as for me,
I have heard the summer dust crying to be born
As much as ever flesh cried to be quiet.)
Pouring itself on fulfilment the eagle's passion
Left life behind and flew at the sun its father.
The great unreal talons took peace for prey
Exultantly, their death beyond death; stooped upward, and struck
Peace like a white fawn in a dell of fire.

XVI

Cawdor in the room in the house, his eyes fixed
On the empty bed: "Age tells. I've known the time . . .
But now from having fasted a night of sleep
After some bad ones, my eyes have a dazzle in them
So that I sometimes lose your face, then instantly

The trouble returns. I was cut deep:
But never half my deserving." He heard a listener
Lean at the door and the latch move a little;
His face blanked and was still. After long silence
A gentle tapping, and spoken through the shut door:
"I think you are not well: let me in a moment.
Your voice has been going on and on like fever
And now why has it stopped?" Cawdor stood shaking
Like a gray horse tethered short to the fence,
Unable to rear or step back, a serpent rattling
Its passionate sistrum in the lupin by the hooves.
He extended hands toward the bed, his eyes widened
To hold their vision, but as he feared it vanished,
Then he was not able to restrain his hands
From feeling the length of the bed, patting and stroking
Where there was nothing but the smooth coverlet.
He stood and hardened himself, the knocking renewed.
"I have been deceived. It began in the dark,"
He whispered, "and I've dreamed on after dawn.
Men go crazy this way . . . not I. All's black again,
But the dream was sweet. Black, black, black. Ah,"
He said to the door, "keep still!"

The knocking ceased
And steps retreated. Suddenly his black anguish
Compelled him to kneel by the bed. "What shall I do?
Kill that woman? I've promised not to kill
Fly nor stinking beetle. Nor myself: that
Would be a little too easy, I am a murderer
But not a coward yet. Nothing, is hardest to do.
Oh God show me a way. Nothing?" The prayer
And the attitude stiffened his nerves with self-contempt.

He ceased and stood up. "Nor this." Himself was responsible,
Himself must choose, himself must endure. He stood
And looked at the bed, remembering the sweet dream.

More steps came to the door and he drew it open
Before one knocked. Fera said "You are sick,
And I was afraid to come back alone. I brought
Concha Rosas." He looked from one to the other,
"Both my vomits," he said gently. "I'll never
Send you away. This is something." She whispered to him:
"You are in danger. Everyone here . . . knows.
Ask Concha. If you shut yourself up they'll tell; they've been asked;
Only the fear of your face stops them.
Jesus Acanna was asked in Monterey
When he drove in the steers." Cawdor said gently:
"Stay here. I'll keep you with me both days and nights
For a live spark between the eye-lid and the eye.
What ails you to bring good news?" "I knew he was going mad.
Good news? Why, they'll not hang you. I'll be your perfect
Witness to keep you alive. Buried alive
While all the strength you're proud of rots and drops off,
And all the stupid and deceived mind
Tears itself into red strips behind gray
Stones and black iron. Where is it, San Quentin? Oh, kill yourself Cawdor.
You have no better hope." "I am all you say,
Blind, blind, blind dupe," he answered, "but not a coward yet." " My God,
Watch the man cling, Concha. Who'd ever think
That *his* was sweet to live? But it's not love of life,
It's terror of death." He was not listening. He looked
With softened anxious eyes at the bed, his lips
Moved, though he did not speak. She, not in mockery:
"What do you see?" "A face that I know perfectly

Was crushed — what day of the month is it? — three months
And certain days ago, to a red lump
Of sudden destruction: but can you see? — he smiles at me.
I know there is nothing there." Fera laughed, "Concha
Has scuttled away. *I* see his angry eyes
And tumbled light brown hair and bare strong shoulders . . ."
"Yes: his hair." " . . . when I ran in here at dawn,
He lifted himself in the bed like a white sea-lion
Out of the running wave. His breast was bare.
And it was smooth, it was like smooth grooved stone.
You caught me here in the room." Cawdor looked down
And smiled and trembled. "Perhaps if I hadn't come.
Perhaps if I hadn't come." "You were pitiful enough,"
She said, "before. We'd both like to think that.
No, he was straight and true and faithful as light.
Hard as crystal, there was not a spot to hold by.
We two are damned." She watched him shaking
And thought that now he would make some end; but he
Looked downward sideways and said "It has faded now.
You needn't wait, I'll never again do anything
Until I have thought and thought. I'll find a way."
He said in the door, "I thought the woman was with you."
"Concha? She scuttled: I told you." "No, you said nothing."

She followed. When they were on the stair they heard
George's revolver-shot that killed the eagle,
And the quick echo. Cawdor stopped on the stair
And looked at Fera's face. "Why did you turn
So strangely," she said, "what do you see? I fear
You have waited too long already and now your mind
Is helpless among many voices and ghosts.